The Knowledge Plexus

A systemic view on the economic geography of technological knowledge

George Chorafakis

VERNON PRESS

www.vernonpress.com

In the Americas:
Vernon Press
1000 N West Street,
Suite 1200, Wilmington,
Delaware 19801
United States

In the rest of the world
Vernon Press
C/Sancti Espiritu 17,
Malaga, 29006
Spain

Library of Congress Control Number: 2014932227

ISBN 978-1-62273-006-3

Preface

Acknowledgements

This book is the product of several years of research on the economic geography of technological knowledge and on research, technological development and innovation (RTDI) policies which started in 2006, while I was working as a researcher at the Institute for Prospective Technological Studies (IPTS) of the European Commission's Joint Research Centre (JRC) in Seville. This undertaking was in many respects a solitary pursuit taking place far from the academic community, in a hybrid environment of 'soft' EU administration combined with policy research, which would not have been successful without the help and support of several people, among whom Professors Ron Martin and Bernard Fingleton from the University of Cambridge, as well as my former colleagues and collaborators from IPTS. The latter, and in particular Dr Dimitris Pontikakis, Professor Attila Varga, and Dr Patrice Laget, helped me clarify and, to a large extent, shape my current views on EU policies through fruitful and often heated discussions. Dimitris, besides being my co-author in several papers and a good friend, has always lent a critical ear to my theories, no matter how weird they are. Patrice, as the head of the IPTS Unit in which I was employed at that time, provided continuous support to my research, and shielded us, the junior research staff, from the hydra of euro-bureaucracy.

Data sources

The empirical chapters of this book involve the analysis of large amounts of data from the following sources: the CORDA database of the European Commission DG Research & Innovation, which contains data on projects funded by the EU Framework Programmes for RTD; the REGPAT database of the OECD, which contains regionalised data on patent applications and grants from the PATSTAT database of the European Patent Office; the Thomson Financial Securities Data - Joint

Ventures and Alliances (TFSD) database; and Eurostat's GISCO and New Cronos databases.

Software

Open source software, which in many respects is superior to similar proprietary software, has been extensively used in the production of this book as a matter of principle. This includes the office suite *LibreOffice*, the reference management application *Zotero*, the database management system *PostgreSQL*, the programming languages *Python* and *R*, the Python package for network analysis *NetworkX*, as well as numerous other Python packages for various specific uses, a large number of R packages for statistical and network analysis (among which *igraph*, *statnet*, *lme4*, *nlme*, *plm*, *splm*), the GIS application *QuantumGIS*, the integrated development environments *Eclipse* and *RStudio*, and the network visualisation package *Gephi*.

Contents

Introduction

Topic

This monograph is a collection of 5 essays on the economic geography of knowledge. The essays were initially conceived as self-standing articles, but also tightly interconnected in terms of their subject-matter as well as of their fundamental theoretical and methodological underpinnings. Earlier versions of some (or parts) of these essays have been published in peer-reviewed journals, in edited books or as working papers, but subsequently reworked and extended substantially for the purposes of this book. Their common threads are the quest for a coherent theoretical framework in economic geography, which I call the *systemic paradigm*, based on the epistemological premise of *emergence* and the theories of *evolution* and *complexity* from a critical realist perspective, and the exploration of the technological knowledge production process in an 'extended', physical and relational, geographical space within this proposed systemic framework.

Common threads

The systemic paradigm in economic geography

Economic geography as a subdiscipline of economic science is highly susceptible to new epistemic trends in economics and, indeed, more receptive to them than mainstream economic theory itself. The latter has been dominated almost since the late nineteenth century by Marshallian and Austrian marginalism, later coined 'neoclassical' and consolidated in the second half of the twentieth century into an epistemic paradigm, which dominated over and even displaced all other trends from mainstream academia, and has managed to stay afloat until today in defiance of its numerous critics and its evident state of paradigmatic crisis. By contrast, economic geography does not have a closed epistemological corpus, as it has always been eclectic, hybridist and cross-disciplinary [HODDER & LEE, 1974: 22; BOSCHMA & MARTIN, 2010: 31]. This has been both a strength and a weakness: The very fact that it has retained its epistemological and methodological openness, pluralism and cross-disciplinarity has helped it escape the epistemic closure, the dogmatic rigidities and many of the theoretical shortcomings of orthodox economic theory, and become more malleable and responsive to empirical reality. On the other hand, the lack of a dominant epistemological paradigm in the subdiscipline has meant that there is no single economic geography as 'normal science' (in the Kuhnian sense),[1] but several concurrent and largely disparate strands of theory, most of them epistemologically dependent on their counterparts in economics or political economy. Isard's regional science and Krugman's New Economic Geography, for instance, have little to do with the evolutionary, institutional, relational, or radical economic geographies, while in turn they are almost epistemologically indistinguishable from the corresponding, and in most cases homonymous, strands in economics and political economy.

In economic science, and by extension in economic geography, there are two broad traditions, which can be seen as a modern projection of the late-nineteenth century historicist-marginalist 'Methodenstreit', the *arithmomorphic* and the *dialectical* – to use the terms coined by GEORGESCU-ROEGEN, 1971.[2] The former lays emphasis on formal modelling and on the (reduced) mathematical representation of economic phenomena, whereas the latter on their contextual, historical and case-specific explanation. The neoclassical strand falls wholeheartedly in, and actually is an extreme expression of, the former tradition, whereas 'old' institutionalism and some critical realist approaches belong to the latter.[3] Some of the most fertile 'post-neoclassical' trends in the arithmomorphic tradition address several of the serious epistemological and methodological shortcomings of neoclassical theory, for instance the exclusion of direct interactions among economic agents, its indifference for out-of-equilibrium dynamics, its failure to explain novelty and structural change in economic systems which are the foundations of technological progress, and also add their distinctive epistemological and methodological perspectives. Evolutionary economics introduces a plethora of insightful biological and ecological metaphors to the study of socio-economic phenomena, and most importantly the Darwinian processes of selection, mutation and retention. The still young 'complexity economics' introduces a macro-systemic view of economic phenomena inspired by statistical mechanics and condensed matter physics, nonlinear dynamics emerging from direct and out-of-equilibrium interactions of adaptive heterogeneous agents, as well as a novel *generative* agent-based simulation methodology. Network analysis, a well-established methodological trend in mathematical sociology, contributes to the relational-structural conceptualisation of economic systems.

This book proposes a unifying 'systemic' framework that brings together the above strands of theory, connects them under the anti-reductionist premise of *emergence* which is assumed to cohere a 'layered model' of the economy,[4] and integrates the particular spatial perspective of economic geography by reinstating the *relational space* as a par excellence geographical space. In addition to this, the proposed framework helps explain the articulation of the micro and macro levels of economic systems with the mediation of an ontologically necessitated *meso level,* all connected through multi-domain emergence, and proposes a new concept, the *mesoeconomic plexus,* as the fundamental ontological category of this level which describes a complete external division of labour in a specific production process. This concept is intended to integrate various aspects of organisation theory under the overarching systemic framework, and in particular the notion of *quasi-integration,* ideas drawn from the neo-institutionalist 'economics of governance' [WILLIAMSON, 1979; 1985; 2005] – albeit in a significantly different epistemological context, the notion of *untraded interdependences* [DOSI, 1984; STORPER, 1997], and the Marshallian idea of *external economies of scale* commonly considered as the raison d'être of industrial districts. The book also postulates the existence of a new fundamental type of increasing returns termed *economies of complexity,* which emanates from increasing connectivity among the micro-units of a system. This type of increasing returns is assumed to occur in the relational space, and indeed in the mesoeconomic plexus, and to dominate in the production of technological knowledge.

The economic geography of technological knowledge production

Technological knowledge, by which here is meant 'knowledge capable of affecting the production process', and hence knowledge as a factor of production, is an intangible economic asset estimated to account for more than half of post-war growth in OECD countries [BOSKIN & LAU, 2000].[5] Technological knowledge is therefore not only the most valuable factor of production but also the principal generator of macroeconomic growth, the main driver of productivity, and the ultimate source of absolute advantage for advanced industrial economies. Its importance as a factor of production is reflected in the dramatic rise in R&D investment and human resources over the past 60 years in both industrial and industrialising economies followed by the rapid expansion of the technological frontier of the world economy and the radical restructuring of national production systems. The participation in the global knowledge-based economy has become a policy priority in most OECD and newly industrialising countries. Nevertheless, the conceptual and analytical tools for understanding how economically-relevant knowledge is generated, diffused and employed in the production process and how it affects economic processes and systems are not yet fully developed.

Opening the black box of technological knowledge requires the incorporation of two elements missing from mainstream economic theory, which has been hitherto dominated by the rational choice model of economic behaviour. The first is a formal but realistic theory of cognition by economic agents. Economically relevant knowledge is generated by interacting groups of heterogeneous human agents with bounded, procedural rationality, satisficing behaviour, limited and asymmetric information and often interdependent (synergetic or antagonistic) strategies. The second is a model of the continuum in which knowledge is generated and transmitted. Due to its immaterial nature, knowledge is conditioned by its physical embodiment as well as the relational space in which it is created and diffused. Information is the principal 'raw material' in the knowledge production process, which is transmitted in structured social networks with non-trivial topologies, instead of the isotropic neoclassical space. Since the creation of knowledge involves intensive exchange of information, it can be said that knowledge is also created in and diffused through social networks with particular topologies, structural characteristics and modi operandi, and varying degrees of complexity and local embeddedness.

The first element is introduced naturally in the systemic framework proposed by this book. In this context, knowledge is conceived as the outcome of a co-adaptation process of economic agents, which involves both mutualistic and antagonistic co-evolutionary dynamics. An alternative approach to this 'constructivist' conception of technological knowledge as a systemic process, is its 'objectivist' conception as *cognitive capital*. The book discusses the construal of technological knowledge as a specific form of social capital, which is also consistent with the systemic paradigm.

The second element requires the reinstatement of the spatial dimension of economic activity and, therefore, makes the case for an enhanced role of economic geography within the discipline of economics. However, modelling the continuum in which technological knowledge is moulded can only be handled by an economic geography which is capable of construing geographical space as a relational space conditioned by networks and structural dependence, in addition to or beyond its traditional conception as a physical space conditioned by distance and spatial dependence. This continuum, henceforth referred to as the *knowledge plexus*, is conceived as a particular type of mesoeconomic plexus describing the division of labour in the production of technological knowledge, which can be visualised as a super-structure of intertwined and often interdependent knowledge networks. The book postulates that the knowledge plexus behaves as a *complex adaptive system* and generates *economies of complexity.*

Research aims

The purpose of this book is threefold: The first aim is to sketch the outline of and to contribute with new theory to the construction of a unifying epistemological framework for economic sciences based on the principle of emergence and the theories of complexity and evolution, which may function as a non-reductionist paradigm for the 'post-neoclassical' economic science, and to explore its applicability to economic geography, and in particular to the economic geography of technological knowledge production. This framework will be partially constructed in dialectical opposition to the dominant paradigm in orthodox economic theory, which is deemed inadequate for the analysis of the technological knowledge production process or, indeed, of the knowledge economy at large. The aim is to avoid the reductionisms, inconsistencies, shortcomings and epistemic closure of the dominant paradigm, and to integrate some particularly promising 'heterodox' strands of economic theory in a more 'holistic' approach to the economic geography of technological knowledge production.

The second aim is to examine some empirical aspects of the European knowledge plexus. In this context the book aims to analyse the structure of interregional knowledge networks, and more specifically of networks of research collaboration in the production of two different types of technological knowledge, namely the *universal* and the *instrumental* type; to investigate the factors that affect their formation; to examine their role in knowledge production as the locus of accumulation of *relational cognitive capital*; to probe the role of the dual (physical and relational) geographical space in this process as a source of spatial and structural dependence; and last but not least, to analyse some of the economic effects of the knowledge plexus on knowledge productivity – notably economies of complexity.

Building on these tasks, the third aim is to examine the normative implications of the proposed systemic paradigm for technological knowledge-related policies in the EU. In this light the book aims to identify and scrutinise the theoretical underpinnings and the actual direction and instrumentalities of EU research, technological development and innovation policies in conjunction with regional, cohesion and industrial policies. More specifically it aims to explore to what extent these policies (should) promote techno-economic cohesion or, instead, the regional concentration of cognitive resources, and whether moving in any of these two directions would affect the dynamic efficiency of the European knowledge plexus. It also aims to examine the potential developmental implications of these policies for the European techno-economic periphery.

Outline

The book is divided in three parts. The first part consists of Chapters 1 and 2, and is dedicated to the investigation of the epistemological underpinnings of the proposed systemic paradigm in economic science, and its relevance to the economic geography of technological knowledge production. Chapter 1 identifies the basic components and sketches a general outline of the systemic paradigm in economic theory. More specifically, it explores the applications of the theories of evolution and complexity in the study of economic phenomena and the meaning and implications of the premise of emergence in economic systems as a potential remedy to the neoclassical reductionisms. Chapter 2 examines the relevance of the systemic paradigm for economic geography, arguing that economic geography should expand its boundaries by embracing the relational space perspective. It introduces the concept of *mesoeconomic plexus* and presents the idea that this entity exhibits the macroscopic features of a complex adaptive system. It also introduces the novel concept of *economies of complexity* from a theoretical perspective, which is further discussed from an empirical perspective in chapter 4. Last but not least, it proposes an outline for a systemic theory of cognition by economic agents based on the perception of cognition as a co-evolutionary process, and the idea that technological knowledge is an emergent phenomenon in a particular type of mesoeconomic plexus, the *knowledge plexus.* The second part consists of Chapters 3 and 4, which present empirical aspects of the European knowledge plexus. Using network-analytical methods Chapter 3 measures the topological structure of three different types of knowledge networks, notably interregional networks of research collaboration under the EU Framework Programme for RTD, of patent co-invention, and of joint ventures and strategic alliances in R&D, compares them, and examines the positions of the regions in them. With the use of econometric methods Chapter 4 examines the effect of relational cognitive capital and of structural and spatial proximity and dependence on factor productivity in the knowledge production process. The third part consists of Chapter 5, which investigates some normative implications of the theory and of the empirical analyses developed in the previous chapters. It poses and attempts to answer a set of questions concerning the right direction of

European research, technological development and innovation policies, notably whether they should promote the concentration of cognitive resources and regional specialisation instead of cohesion. The conclusion of this book wraps up the findings of the previous chapters and indicates some new directions for research.

References

BOSCHMA, R.A., & R.L. MARTIN (2010): *The handbook of evolutionary economic geography.* Cheltenham: Edward Elgar Publishing.

BOSKIN, M.J., & L.J. LAU (2000): Generalized Solow-neutral technical progress and postwar economic growth. *NBER Working Paper Series,* no. 8023.

DOSI, G. (1984): *Technical Change and Industrial Transformation. The Theory and an Application to the Semiconductor Industry.* Basingstoke: Palgrave Macmillan.

GEORGESCU-ROEGEN, N. (1971): *The Entropy Law and the Economic Process.* Cambridge, MA: Harvard University Press.

HODDER, B.W., & R. LEE (1974): *Economic geography.* New York, NY: St. Martin's Press.

KIM, J. (1999): Making sense of emergence. *Philosophical studies 95* (1): 3–36.

LAWSON, T. (1997): *Economics and Reality.* London: Routledge.

STORPER, M. (1997): *The Regional World. Territorial Development in a Global Economy.* New York, NY: Guilford Press

VEBLEN, T. (1898): Why is economics not an evolutionary science? *Quarterly Journal of Economics 12* (4): 373–397.

WILLIAMSON, O.E. (1979): Transaction costs economics: The governance of contractual relations. *Journal of Law and Economics 12* (2): 233–261.

WILLIAMSON, O.E. (1985): *The Economic Institutions of Capitalism. Firms, Markets, Relational Contracting.* New York: Free Press.

WILLIAMSON, O.E. (2005): The economics of governance. *American Economic Review 95* (2): 1–18.

Notes

[1] The same, of course, applies to the social sciences in general.
[2] Here the term 'dialectical' characterises concepts which are discursive, contextual, and non-reductionist, and which are better understood in their historical context.
[3] e.g. VEBLEN,1898; LAWSON, 1997.
[4] The 'layered model of the world' is a necessary condition for emergence [KIM, 1999].
[5] Tangible capital is found in the same study to account for only a quarter of growth.

Chapter 1

Neoclassical anomalies, evolution, complexity and emergence

Introduction

KUHN, 1962, asserts that the appearance of epistemic 'anomalies' in the natural sciences normally causes paradigmatic crises and, eventually, change. This has not been the case in economics. Despite a plethora of well-identified epistemic anomalies, the discipline has demonstrated a degree of paradigmatic resilience unparalleled in the history of science. The neoclassical core of the discipline has been identified as the main culprit for the anomalies, battered from all sides and even pronounced 'dead' [ACKERMAN, 2002]. In the face of these attacks neoclassical theory has shown a remarkable ability to maintain its dominance both in the academic curricula and in policy discourse. This has been largely a result of the theory's capacity to transform itself and extend its scope either by absorbing the anomalies in an ad hoc way, or by simply bypassing them. Today it is still unclear whether the discipline is undergoing a very slow Kuhnian-style paradigmatic shift or whether it evolves dichotomously in a way that the neoclassical construct and its ramifications retain their dominant position as 'normal (quasi-) science', while 'heterodox' theories coexist with it at the margin. It is, however, certain that the heterodox camp is becoming more populous and vociferous as the shortcomings of orthodox theory and the failures of its normative implications in policy-making become more and more exposed to common view.

But how is the epistemological crisis of neoclassical economics relevant to economic geography? Economic geography is heavily influenced by concurrent epistemological and methodological trends in economics due to its genealogical descent from it, as well as due to the partial overlap of their subject-matters and methods. This epistemic 'crossover' becomes particularly evident whenever economic geography focuses on quantifiable economic phenomena. Seen as an 'economic science', an influential strand of economic geography (also dubbed 'geographical economics') shares the same epistemological roots and methodological tools as modern economics and, inevitably, is more susceptible to epistemological and methodological 'contamination' from economic 'orthodoxy'. This is particularly evident in the comeback of economic geography to the mainstream as a 'New Economic Geography' scrutinised in Chapter 2.

The construction of a new, coherent epistemological paradigm for economic geography necessarily passes through the dialectical confrontation of the neoclassical paradigm with alternative approaches to economic theory and method and its demise. In this chapter I sketch some of the characteristics which a suitable candidate for the vacuum that will be left by the eventual demise of the neoclassical paradigm should have: At an abstract epistemological level, it should be a coherent corpus of theories and methods which overcomes reductionism and methodological individualism, thus allowing economics to become a real social science. It should abandon the mechanistic model of Newtonian physics on which Walrasian economics is built in favour of an evolutionary theory inspired by life itself; that will give post-neoclassical economics the capacity to accommodate the dynamical aspects of economic phenomena such as growth, learning, etc. It should divorce itself from its deeply entrenched positivist tradition in favour of a third way between Humean empiricism and Kantian idealism, that of critical realism [BHASKAR, 1975; 1979]. It should bypass 'deductivism' [LAWSON, 1997], and embrace the 'generative method' [EPSTEIN, 2007]. From a more applied perspective, it should acquire a convincing theory of cognition by economic agents, which completely replaces rational choice theory. This theory should be coupled and be consistent with a theory of knowledge creation able to explain how the most important factor of production, technological knowledge, comes about as a result of collective action. It should be able to resolve the conundrum of micro-macro articulation, first by formally recognising the existence and the analytical importance of the 'meso' level [DOPFER *et al.*, 2004]; precisely here emergence can play a crucial role as the epistemological principle which connects the micro, meso and macro levels. It should acknowledge the complex and systemic nature of the economy by treating it as a self-organising complex adaptive system [ARTHUR, 1999], which co-evolves with socio-political institutions; here the theories of complexity would play a key role. Finally, it should replace the structureless space of the neoclassical market with the relational space where real economic transactions and economically relevant information diffusion take place and technological knowledge is generated.

I call this emerging paradigm 'systemic' due to the fact that its three epistemic pillars, emergence, evolution and complexity, are all premises or theories referring to systems rather than individuals. Many of the elements of the systemic paradigm outlined here already exist as disconnected theories: Some of them originate from an epistemology akin to that of general systems theory and cybernetics; others are found as dispersed ideas in various theories of national or regional systems of innovation, the 'triple helix', 'mode 2', etc.;[1] and finally, others exist in the diverse strands of 'heterodox' economics, including Schumpeter's conception of the process of capitalist development [SCHUMPETER, 1934; 1942], and neo-Schumpeterian or other varieties of evolutionary economics,[2] the Veblenian strand of institutional economics [VEBLEN, 1898; 1904; HODGSON, 1998], or the still developing field of 'complexity economics'.[3] The common meta-theoretical thread in this otherwise heterogeneous group of theories is the implicit or explicit rejection of the epistemological reductionisms of the neoclassical paradigm in favour of structurality, contextuality and systemicity.

The rest of this chapter is structured as follows: The second section begins with a brief identification of three meta-axioms which constitute the core of the neoclassical epistemology, and then examines their limitations and failures as results of the influence of reductionism and positivism, which are deemed to be ultimately responsible for the paradigmatic crisis of the theory. The critical realist position and other related critiques against orthodox economics are also reviewed in this section. The third section reviews some landmarks in the development of evolutionary economics and then examines in detail the evolutionary concepts which are essential for the construction of the systemic paradigm. The fourth section is dedicated to the theories of complexity whose assimilation in economic theory is still at its infancy despite the fact that relevant computational models are already relatively well-developed. This section provides an account of the generic properties of complex adaptive systems and their network representation. The last section is dedicated to the foundational principle of emergence, which, it is argued here, is a potential remedy to the ills of neoclassical reductionisms. This section begins by synthesising a formal definition of the concept of emergence from existing work in analytical philosophy. So far emergence has been known to social scientists mostly through the lens of popular science, if at all. A rigorous approach of this kind is, therefore, much needed in order to disperse misconceptions and help establish a robust use of the premise in social and economic sciences.

This chapter identifies the shortcomings of the neoclassical theory and a set of potential remedies; it does not propose how the potential remedies can be used to overcome the identified problems. This task is left for Chapter 2.

Epistemic anomalies of the neoclassical paradigm

Neoclassical meta-axioms

During its long period of academic dominance the neoclassical paradigm has managed to survive despite the accumulation of epistemic anomalies by incrementally adapting its framework and expanding its scope. This stepwise expansion has stretched the boundaries of the theory to such an extent that today it is difficult to identify a single coherent paradigm other than a group of models connected through a set of overarching, strongly reductionist 'meta-axioms', which is indispensable for neoclassical economics and distinguish it from all other social sciences. ARNSPERGER & VAROUFAKIS, 2006, observe that the neoclassical meta-axioms involve three axiomatic reductionisms: methodological individualism, methodological instrumentalism, and methodological equilibration. In a similar vein, I identify three sine-qua-non conditions of neoclassical theory, the first two of which are methodological, while the third is essentially epistemological:

1. Ex ante equilibration
2. Reductionist aggregation
3. Individualistic-instrumental rationality

Neoclassical economics is principally concerned with how economic agents make consistent choices, how these choices become compatible in a predetermined institutional framework, and how agents' individual plans are aggregated in collective outcomes. The first concern is addressed in the context of *rational choice theory*. In the core of this theory lies individualistic-instrumental rationality – a premise of utilitarianist origins, which entails that self-interested economic agents always make choices among available options in a way fully consistent with their preferences. In other words, economic agents optimise their objective functions consistently, globally and independently from other economic agents subject to feasibility constraints. Nelson & Winter, 1982, consider the optimisation principle as the first pillar of neoclassical economics. The second concern is addressed by the concept of *ex ante equilibrium*: In Walrasian general equilibrium theory the plans of all economic agents become compatible in a way that permits market clearing before any marketplace interaction through an implicitly instantaneous (or at least atemporal) *tâtonnement process* with the hypothetical mediation of a fictitious *Walrasian auctioneer*. The behavioural adjustment of economic agents to exogenous shocks is frictionless, and, under the assumption of perfect foresight, even future shocks are fully anticipated. In this context, the adjustment of economic systems, which is essentially a dynamic phenomenon, occurs in the transitional phases between equilibria and is considered of limited importance to the theory. Equilibrium has become the most indispensable methodological premise of neoclassical theory, as its models tend to focus almost exclusively on the equilibrium state of economic systems, partly because systems in equilibrium are more analytically tractable and deterministic. Nelson & Winter, 1982, again, consider it as the second pillar of neoclassical economics. The third concern is addressed through the construct of *representative agent*. This concept follows from the Weberian premise of *methodological individualism*, according to which all social phenomena can be ultimately explained as aggregations of individual actions. In turn, methodological individualism is an expression of a broader epistemological tendency in science, that of *reductionism*, explained in a following section.

One by one the neoclassical meta-axioms have failed. Their failures and shortcomings are of three types: logical inconsistencies, nomological impossibilities, and epistemological limitations as seen from alternative epistemological standpoints.

The impasse of equilibrium theory

In the context of the first type of neoclassical shortcomings a strand of critiques focuses on specific internal inconsistencies of the cornerstone of neoclassical economics, the theory of general equilibrium. The coup de grâce to the theory of general equilibrium ironically came from three neoclassical economists, SONNENSCHEIN, 1973; MANTEL, 1974; and DEBREU, 1974, in the form of the famous among the critics of neoclassical theory Sonnenschein-Mantel-Debreu (SMD) theoremwhich states that for any function which is continuous, homogeneous of degree zero and complying with Walras's law, there is at least one price vector corresponding to an economy whose aggregate demand function is the function in question. This implies that while the properties of the aggregate excess demand function inherited from individual excess demand functions guarantee the *existence* of an equilibrium, they are not sufficient to guarantee its *uniqueness*, and as it has been additionally shown, its *stability* [SONNENSCHEIN, 1973]. In order for a unique price vector (a unique equilibrium) to exist, additional artificial and arguably unnatural assumptions have to be imposed on individual preferences, beyond those ensuing from the Weak Axiom of Revealed Preference (WARP). Moreover, most attempts to support the uniqueness of equilibrium by imposing additional micro-behavioural assumptions (e.g. homothetic preferences, collinear initial endowment vectors, etc.) have eventually proven to be futile [MANTEL, 1976; KIRMAN & KOCH, 1986]. The failure to prove the stability and uniqueness of equilibrium leads to the conclusion that the theory is, in Popperian terms, 'unfalsifiable' and for this reason the SMD theorem has become to be colloquially known as the 'anything-goes' theorem.

The implications of the SMD theorem are devastating for the theory of general equilibrium [RIZVI, 2006]: KEHOE, 1985, shows that comparative statics analysis fails unless either the demand side of an economy behaves like a single consumer or the supply side is an input-output system. ROBERTS & SONNENSCHEIN, 1977, extend the implications of the SMD theorem in the case of the imperfectly competitive general equilibrium. KEMP & SHIMOMURA, 2002, show that under less restrictive (and more realistic) assumptions, the stylised Heckscher-Ohlin model of international trade fails to fulfil the comparative statics propositions of general-equilibrium trade theory, even 'without appealing to increasing returns to scale, the multiplicity of equilibrium or the non-competitiveness of markets". STOKER, 1984, shows that econometric identification when analysing relationships between averaged economic variables may fail due to the lack of correspondence between microeconomic behaviour and the estimated relations between averaged data. The list of articles underlying the negative implications of the SMD theorem for the consistency of the general equilibrium theory and, by extension, for the neoclassical paradigm is endless.

Ultimately, the SMD theorem demonstrates the non-aggregativity of individual economic behaviours, even if the fundamental axiomatic assumptions about individual economic behaviour which make up rational choice theory are taken to be correct. Of course, even those axiomatic assumptions have been challenged and criticised extensively, as we see in following paragraphs.

Beyond the issues of internal consistency of the general equilibrium theory, more problems emerge when the process of equilibrium adjustment per se is considered: Walras assumed that the attainment of equilibrium prices occurs through a 'tâtonnement' process, whose dynamic convergence is, nevertheless, by no means guaranteed unless additional unrealistic assumptions about the convergence process itself are made [ACKERMAN, 2002]. The unresolved issue of tâtonnement convergence is simply shrugged off by assuming that economic agents do not transact with each other in a decentralised way or out of equilibrium, but only through a centrally coordinated price mechanism (by the Walrasian auctioneer) and only when the system has already attained equilibrium. This seemingly innocuous assumption has very serious implications: As TESFATSION, 2006: 176, observes, this centrally coordinated price mechanism aims to eliminate the possibility of strategic behaviour and to replace decentralised agent interactions by an orderly payment system, whereby both households and firms "take prices and dividend payments as given aspects of their decision problems outside of their control [...] with no perceived dependence on the actions of other agents". In the absence of this fictitious centrally coordinated price mechanism the model becomes analytically intractable. In Tesfatsion's words, "the modeller must now come to grips with challenging issues such as asymmetric information, strategic interaction, expectation formation on the basis of limited information, mutual learning, social norms, transaction costs, externalities, market power, predation, collusion, and the possibility of coordination failure (convergence to a Pareto-dominated equilibrium). The prevalence of market protocols, rationing rules, antitrust legislation, and other types of institutions in real-world macroeconomies is now better understood as a potentially critical scaffolding needed to ensure orderly economic process." [TESFATSION, 2006: 176-177].

Reductionism(s) and the limitations of reductionist aggregation

Several epistemic anomalies of the neoclassical theory ultimately have their roots in the theory's wholehearted espousal of epistemological reductionism coupled with positivism and a strong version of nomological determinism. A closer look into neoclassical theory from this perspective reveals the failure of the second neoclassical meta-axiom, that of reductionist aggregation, as well as other aspects of the failure of ex ante equilibration.

Reductionism and the positivist Homo Œconomicus

The classic model of epistemological reduction by NAGEL, 1961, is a model of 'inter-theoretic' reduction, which essentially consists in a Hempelian-style deductive-nomological explanation of the reduced theory by the reducing one [SARKAR, 1992: 172]. Reduction works out under two necessary conditions, 'connectability' and 'derivability'. The first condition necessitates the existence of 'bridge laws',[4] which essentially 'translate' the predicates of the reduced theory into those of the reducing one. This is considered as the most standard model of epistemological reduction, and as SILBERSTEIN, 2002: 85, observes the ones that followed are in one way or another either modifications or refutations thereof.[5]

In its ontological formulation reductionism entails that higher-level entities *Y* are fully reducible to their constituent lower-level entities *X*. As SILBERSTEIN & MCGEEVER, 1999: 182-183, explain, there are two interpretations of this type of reduction, one proposed by SCHARF, 1989, according to which *Y*-entities are *nothing but* sums of *X*-entities, and the properties of *Y*-entities are explainable in terms of *X*-entities and their inter-relations, and one proposed by KIM, 1978, according to which *Y*-entities are causally and ontologically fully determined by *X*-entities. In its first, strong version, ontological reduction is *mereological fusion*, i.e. the precept that "the whole is exactly the sum of its parts", whereas in its second, weak version, ontological reduction is *micro-determination*, which KIM, 1978, calls *mereological supervenience*. The latter merely implies a dependence relationship between a higher (supervenient) and a lower (subvenient) level, which ultimately preserves the stratification of the relata, whereas the former implies a fusion of ontological levels, and thus the elimination of the stratification of the relata.

Epistemological reductionism is at the heart of the project for the '*Unity of Science*': this refers to the positivist quest for a universal scientific 'language' that will ultimately unify all scientific disciplines corresponding to the different stratified levels of perceivable reality, the 'special' ones (e.g. the social sciences) included, in terms of the vocabulary of the most fundamental level, usually considered to be that of fundamental particle physics.[6]

In the social sciences this quest is reflected in the Comtean perception of sociology as 'social physics'. More than any other social science, modern economics adheres to the positivist quest for universal behavioural laws, which are supposed to govern the life of *Homo Œconomicus* similarly to the way Newtonian 'laws of motion' govern celestial bodies. These fundamental laws are assumed to fully explain observed reality, even in systems as complex as human societies. Newtonian-Laplacian mechanical systems are structurally invariable and symmetry-preserving, in that their dynamic evolution over time does not alter their qualitative characteristics and their internal structure and symmetry. As a result of this, they are also time-symmetric, they exhibit deterministic, path-independent dynamics, and novelties are completely exogenous to them. Such systems possess no endogenous ability to generate innovations and their attained equilibrium depends exclusively on their initial conditions and their laws of motion. The neoclassical paradigm introduces this type of Newtonian-Laplacian determinism in the study of economic phenomena. All these attributes of mechanical dynamical systems are also present in the perceived 'dynamics' of equilibrium models. Another manifestation of the influence of logical positivism on neoclassical theory is 'arithmomorphism' [GEORGESCU-ROEGEN, 1971], i.e. the entrenched belief that in order for a discipline to be considered as a science it must be formulated in the language of mathematics.[7]

Laplacian determinism and hyper-computational demons

Epistemological reductionism also has close ties with *nomological determinism*, the precept that all phenomena are completely nomologically necessitated by – and hence fully explainable in terms of – fundamental laws and their set of initial conditions. The strongest forward-looking expression of this precept, which I shall call 'Laplacian determinism', asserts that the future state of a (closed) system can be fully predicted on the basis of fundamental laws and a full knowledge of the sets of initial conditions of its constituent entities.[8] The Laplacian conjecture of a fictitious intelligence that can conduct the necessary calculations for such a prediction at a universal scale has been termed *Laplace's demon*, and bears considerable similarities to *Maxwell's demon* in thermodynamics. Both fictional entities are of interest in this study because of their similarities to the *Walrasian auctioneer* in economics – a hyper-computational 'demon' who drives the general equilibrium adjustment process by matching supply and demand in all markets before any real transaction takes place and without transaction costs, and then announces equilibrium prices.[9]

Today it is widely understood that Laplace's conjecture is computationally intractable as the computational requirements of his demon would exceed the information capacities of the observed universe, and that, by extension, his as well as Maxwell's demons are nomologically impossible. In the case of the Walrasian demon, a number of ad hoc assumptions about the behaviour of the 'atomic particles', i.e. the economic agents, and about the way the equilibrium adjustment process occurs ensure that in principle the demon is not nomologically impossible: The theory assumes that individual economic agents do not transact out-of-equilibrium or in a decentralised manner, and that their behaviour is governed by the axioms of rational choice. These restrictions permit the existence of equilibrium and make the work of the auctioneer easier. But even then, the computability of general equilibrium is not always guaranteed [RICHTER & WONG, 1999], while the informational requirements to ensure convergence are discouragingly large [SAARI, 1985]. More importantly, it seems that in the absence of this centralised control of the adjustment process, i.e. in the absence of an actual Walrasian auctioneer, there is no unique 'natural' convergence path to equilibrium.

Methodological individualism and the representative agent

The most prominent expression of the premise of reduction in the social sciences is the Weberian doctrine of *methodological individualism.*[10] According to this principle social and, by extension, economic phenomena can be *fully explained* on the basis of individuals' actions. Methodological individualism is a form of *epistemological* reductionism: Higher level (supervenient) phenomena are epistemologically fully reducible to the (subvenient) properties of lower-level entities in the sense of micro-determination, not elimination.[11]

Neoclassical economics goes a step further, to assume the existence of a representative agent as the embodiment of economic collectivities and as a bridge between the macro-economy and the assumed micro-behaviour of individual rational optimisers. A strident critique of this concept comes from KIRMAN, 1992, who argues that the premise of the 'representative agent' has been devised to save the general equilibrium theory vis-à-vis its failure to provide micro-foundations to collective economic behaviour. He claims that "whatever the objective of the modeller, there is no plausible formal justification for the assumption that the aggregate of individuals, even maximisers, acts itself like an individual maximiser. Individual maximisation does not engender collective rationality, nor does the fact that the collectivity exhibits a certain rationality necessarily imply that individuals act rationally. There is simply no direct relation between individual and collective behaviour", and he concludes that "it is clear that the 'representative' agent deserves a decent burial, as an approach to economic analysis that is not only primitive, but fundamentally erroneous" [KIRMAN, 1992: 118]. Elsewhere, he demonstrates why this premise is fundamentally fallacious. His arguments are that "well-behaved individuals need not produce a well-behaved representative agent; that the reaction of a representative agent to change need not reflect how the individuals of the economy would respond to change; that the preferences of a representative agent over choices may be diametrically opposed to those of society as a whole – it is clear that the representative agent should have no future. Indeed contrary to what current macroeconomic practice would seem to suggest, requiring heterogeneity of agents within the competitive general equilibrium model may help to recover aggregate properties which may be useful for macroeconomic analysis." [KIRMAN, 1992: 134].

The concept of the representative agent goes beyond the epistemological reductionism of the Weberian doctrine: it is a fundamentally *eliminativist* premise in that it replaces socio-economic structure with a hypothetical representative agent, and thus a whole ontological level – that of society and/or of the macro-economy – collapses into the subvenient level of individual agents; in that sense society becomes *nothing but* an (essentially structureless) fusion of homogeneous individuals. By this approach whole economic systems with internal structure and interactions are replaced by a single hypothetical entity, whose properties are deduced from axiomatically determined behavioural rules of individual entities.

Even if the representative agent receives a 'decent burial' as Kirman suggests, the problem of reductionist aggregation remains: As we already saw, the centrally coordinated (by the fictitious Walrasian auctioneer) frictionless and a-temporal tâtonnement process is a conceptual device invented to exclude decentralised agent interactions, which in the opposite case would generate feedback loops and complex nonlinear dynamics. In other words, it is a device essentially used to 'linearise' agents' actions before aggregating them, thus generating a macro system which is functionally decomposable, in accordance with the doctrine of methodological individualism.

The irreconcilable micro-macro divide in the quest for micro-foundations

Economic theory has for a good part of the twentieth century been seeking to reconcile the macroeconomic Keynesian edifice with the microeconomic Walrasian construct of general equilibrium. However, the attempts to establish 'micro-foundations' in macroeconomic theory in the spirit of the 'neoclassical synthesis' have yielded poor results. From their initial conception the two theoretical constructs seem to have very few common points of reference. As a matter of fact, the implicit epistemological foundations on which they lay are quite distinctive: While, as we saw, Walrasian microeconomics is built on the pillars of rational choice theory and general equilibrium, Keynesian macroeconomics is an essentially non-equilibrium theory, in which economic agents implicitly have adaptive expectations without any intrinsic hyper-rationality assumptions. WEINTRAUB, 1977: 5, observes that "since Keynes's analysis seemed to require a disequilibrium theory, or a time-intrinsic general equilibrium structure, and since even static general equilibrium analysis was immensely difficult, there was no sound microeconomic system that, when aggregated, yielded Keynesian insights. There was only the negative but useful result that neoclassical value theory was inconsistent with Keynes's *General Theory*".

The divide between the two theoretical constructs extends to their meta-theoretical bases: Walrasian microeconomics is a *deductive-nomological* theory in Hempelian terms:[12] It starts with the formulation of nomological axioms that are supposed to globally govern human economic behaviour and it proceeds with the deduction of the properties of the whole economy by linearly aggregating individuals' actions. Keynesian macroeconomics, on the contrary, is an *inferential* theory or, to the extent that it identifies underlying causal mechanisms, it can even be argued that it is *retroductive*: It observes an empirical reality and it attempts to identify relations between real aggregate variables (and also the potential causal mechanisms thereof) without any explicit a priori assumptions on the attributes of the lower-level units, i.e. the economic behaviour of individuals. Keynesian economies are thus 'irreducible to their basal conditions'. It is no wonder that the reconciliation of these two non-tangential worlds has proven to be a titanic task, and all attempts have only managed to extend the dysfunctions of the neoclassical paradigm in the Keynesian realm. This impasse ultimately also reflects the failure of the reductionist-positivist project in economic theory.

Critical realist critique

A different line of critique to the epistemological 'deficiencies' of the neoclassical paradigm comes from the strand in the philosophy of science known as 'critical realism' founded on *transcendental realism* and *critical naturalism* [BHASKAR, 1975; 1979]. Transcendental realism rejects Humean empirical realism without embracing neo-Kantian transcendental idealism – actually it constitutes a 'third way' between the two, as implied by its name. Bhaskar contests the Humean interpretation of 'constant conjunctions of events', i.e. empirical regularities, as 'laws'. He contends that "[t]he weakness of the Humean concept of laws is that it ties laws to closed systems, viz. systems where a constant conjunction of events occurs" [BHASKAR, 1975:14]; these 'laws', however, are inadequate for the explanation of phenomena in open systems without constant conjunctions. He claims that empirical regularities are neither sufficient nor necessary conditions for a scientific law, and he calls for the ontological distinction between 'scientific laws' and 'patterns of events' by underlining the need for a separation of the ontological and the epistemological dimensions of reality. Causal laws are independent from the events they generate: "Real structures exist independently of and are often out of phase with the actual patterns of events" [BHASKAR, 1975:13]. Transcendental realist 'laws' are *transfactual conditionals*, i.e. conditionals "designating the activity of generative mechanisms and structures independently of any particular sequence or pattern of events" [BHASKAR, 1975:14]. Bhaskar concludes that "the domains of the real, the actual and the empirical are distinct" [Ibid.]. Ultimately, Bhaskar's theory of science is fundamentally anti-reductionist, and fully consistent with emergence.

In line with Bhaskar's theory of science, critical realist economists believe that a realist science of economics should focus on the latent generative structures of socio-economic reality, instead of its empirically observed regularities. LAWSON, 1997, argues that mainstream economics is plagued by *deductivism*, which he defines as the premise that science is based on the elaboration of regularities of the 'whenever event *x* then event *y*' type – essentially Bhaskar's 'constant conjunction of events'. Deductivism coupled with mathematical formalism resulting from an instrumentalism devoid of any concern for truth leads to 'epistemic closure' [LAWSON, 1996; 2001].

Moreover, it encourages social atomism (in the form of methodological individualism combined with instrumental rationality) for the reason that social atomism construes the entities of analysis as being subject to deductivist regularities [LAWSON, 1996]. He proposes *retroduction* as a method of explaining social structure alternative to induction or deduction, i.e. the move from the level of the phenomenon under examination to the deeper level of the causal mechanisms responsible for it.

The limits to individualistic-instrumental rationality

Informational requirements of equilibrium adjustment

Cognition, information processing and knowledge generation are the most fundamental functions of individual economic agents and economic systems. The rudimentary theory of cognition that is implicit in neoclassical economics, however, does not actually tell us much about the way economic cognition and techno-economic knowledge come about. The neoclassical market is conceived as an information-processing apparatus whose main purpose is to make compatible the plans of economic agents by generating price signals *when general equilibrium is attained.* This adjustment process is assumed to take place at a pre-equilibrium stage instantaneously and without incurring transaction costs.[13] However, any simulation of the tâtonnement process is computationally intensive (and, needless to add, cost-incurring), and its convergence is by no means guaranteed even in the case of artificial markets with relatively few and 'well-behaved' households and firms [SAARI, 1985]. In reality, the information-intensive and time-and-resource-consuming process of equilibrium adjustment depends entirely on the real information-processing capacities of the market apparatus. Nevertheless, despite the importance of this process for the coherence and tenability of the theory, it is treated as exogenous and implicitly not particularly relevant.

Rational choice and cognitive capacities of economic agents

At the level of the individual economic agent, the axiomatic assumptions of hyper-rationality and of perfect information,[14] which underlie the behavioural model of *Homo Œconomicus*, also attribute to microeconomic agents infinite cognitive and information-processing capacities permitting global optimisation. More specifically, the rational choice model assumes that the economic agent has [RUBINSTEIN, 1997: 8-9]:

1. a complete knowledge of the choice problem, i.e. of the set of alternatives from which (s)he can choose;
2. consistent preferences, i.e. a complete ordering of the entire set of alternatives;
3. unlimited ability to optimise, without making mistakes;
4. indifference between equivalent choice sets.

Again here, the assumptions on the cognitive capacities of economic agents do not originate from a consistent theory of economic cognition: Information processing and cognition are implicitly assumed as instantaneous and automatic processes which do not reside within the sphere of the economic system under study. A direct consequence of these assumptions is the exclusion of two fundamental dynamic processes of real socio-economic systems, learning and adaptation. As HODGSON, 1993a: 4, queries, "how can agents be said to be rational at a given point in time when they are in the process of learning and acquiring relevant information? The very act of learning means that not all information is possessed and global rationality is ruled out".

In the real world, the natural computational and informational limitations of economic agents, but also of economic systems, permit only local, not global, optimisation. Moreover, the optimisation process takes place, if at all, in real time through decentralised, potentially strategic, interactions of economic agents – it is therefore a nonlinear dynamic, not static, procedure, which involves learning and adaptation. To complicate things even further, real economic experiments have shown that preferences, depending on various circumstances, may be inconsistent, intransitive, or even incommensurable (in the sense that the choice set is not fully ordered), and eventually incompatible with the instrumental type of rationality postulated by rational choice theory. For instance, 'framing effects' (i.e. the effect on choice of the way the decision problem is framed), the tendency to simplify decision problems, and case-dependent preferences have been found to affect economic agents in a way inconsistent with the rational choice paradigm [RUBINSTEIN, 1997: 20], but consistent with the premise of *procedural rationality*, i.e. behaviour that is "the outcome of appropriate deliberation", as opposed to *substantive rationality*, i.e. instrumental behaviour that is "appropriate to the achievement of given goals within the limits imposed by given conditions and constraints" [SIMON, 1976: 130-131].

These facts point to the need for a drastic change in the cognitive assumptions about economic agents. SIMON, 1991, proposes the alternative concept of *bounded rationality*, a type of rational choice constrained by incomplete, localised information, the real-world computational capacities of the agents, and time. A behavioural assumption which often (but not necessarily) complements the bounded rationality model and has been proposed as an alternative to the utility maximisation principle is the principle of *satisficing*, whereby it is assumed that the economic agent conducts search until an aspiration level of utility, i.e. a pay-off threshold, is reached, beyond which the search process is over [SIMON, 1956]. A satisficing strategy is obviously suboptimal within the complete set of alternatives, but its suboptimality is mitigated when the real costs of obtaining and processing complete information are taken into consideration.

Evolution

Developments in evolutionary economics

More than a century ago, when economics was still at its infancy, VEBLEN 1898, observed the affinity of its subject-matter to that of evolutionary biology. In his above cited article he contends that "economics is helplessly behind the times, and unable to handle its subject-matter in a way to entitle it to standing as a modern science", criticises the deductivism and nomological determinism of contemporary economics, which resembles that of natural sciences, and the discipline's quest for 'normality' and 'natural law', and observes that path dependence and adaptation are guiding forces of human economic behaviour. Despite the fact that the evolutionary analogy has been central in Veblen's economic thought, especially with regard to the process of capitalist technological development and his renunciation of the static notion of equilibrium as a relic from the natural sciences, he never attempted to develop a formal evolutionary economic theory [HODGSON, 1992].

MARSHALL, 1920, in the preface to the 5th edition of his 'Principles' expresses his ambivalence towards the mechanistic foundations of modern equilibrium-dominated economics, which however seems to him inevitable given the complexity of a potential evolutionary approach based on biological analogies.[15] His plan to dedicate the second volume of his magnum opus to economic dynamics remained unfulfilled, and as HODGSON, 1993b, observes, with his death any reference to biology was virtually purged from mainstream economic theory until the rediscovery of the evolutionary analogy by ALCHIAN, 1950. Alchian challenges the neoclassical perception of economic agents as rational optimisers in view of incomplete information and uncertainty arising from imperfect foresight and the computational limits to the knowledge of the individual. He proposes the incorporation of imperfect foresight and incomplete information as axiomatic principles in an economic theory inspired by biological evolution and natural selection. Instead of profit maximisation, which he sees as irrelevant, he argues that economic action is characterised by "adaptive, imitative, and trial-and-error behaviour in the pursuit of 'positive profits'". He goes on to suggest that the outcome of economic actions is determined by the economic system itself, not by individual decisions, "by interpreting the economic system as an adoptive mechanism which chooses among exploratory actions generated by the adaptive pursuit of 'success' or 'profits'" [ALCHIAN, 1950].

The next turning point in the development of evolutionary economic theory is the model of technical change by NELSON *et al.*, 1976, and a few years later the influential book by NELSON & WINTER, 1982. The main characteristics of this family of 'Schumpeterian' models are the following assumptions: (i) At the micro-level firm behaviour is governed by a limited number of decision rules or 'routines' linked to environmental stimuli instead of global optimisation; rules are strongly path-dependent but may change in the longer run through search, i.e. deliberate problem-solving (e.g. R&D), imitation or learning-by-doing. (ii) At the macro-level economic growth is an open-ended disequilibrium process driven by technological change, which comes through (evolutionary) selection. The latter diffuses 'fit' routines and extinguishes ineffective ones, while, in the Schumpeterian spirit, firm competition is driven by technological innovation instead of cost minimisation [BOSCHMA & FRENKEN, 2006].

The main direction of theoretical and empirical investigation in contemporary evolutionary economics is on micro-level firm dynamics in the neo-Schumpeterian tradition. Evolutionary game theory, an almost independently-developing line of theoretical investigation, has more limited empirical applicability and exhibits a certain affinity for equilibria.[16] On the other hand, evolutionary studies in macroeconomics, international trade and development are much less common.[17] This shortage shows a certain indisposition of this corpus of theory to make the transition from modelling technological change at the level of firm micro-dynamics to analysing systemic, economy-wide macro-dynamics, thus bridging the micro and the macro domains of economic reality. This is not, however, an inherent limitation of the evolutionary approach; it just reflects the fact that this corpus of theory is not yet sufficiently developed. As DOPFER & POTTS, 2004, argue (and this view is fully shared by the author of this book), the proliferation of ad hoc evolutionary models and the excessive hybridisation of theory has taken place on an ontological vacuum, an absence of a 'deep theory' able to fit all the disjoint pieces together. In my view, the neo-Schumpeterian 'paradigm' in evolutionary economics has not managed to explore the whole breadth and depth of the Darwinian analogy. Among other things, a better focus on co-evolutionary processes driving the macro-dynamics of ecosystems is needed. These processes are rich in intuition and can prove useful for understanding macroscopic socio-economic processes, and in particular macro-economic dynamics and technological development.

Evolutionary principles

Fundamental evolutionary processes

A dynamical system can be considered to be evolutionary when its dynamics can be explained in terms of the fundamental evolutionary processes of *selection, variation* and *retention* [VEGA-REDONDO, 1996]. Selection is the process that favours some explicit behavioural patterns (or 'phenotypes' in a biological context) over others. Selection determines the chances of survival and reproductive success of an individual endowed with a particular behavioural pattern, but it is a systemic process that operates at the level of whole populations rather than individuals. Variation is the force that infuses evolutionary dynamics with new behavioural patterns and enables adaptation to changing external conditions. Mutation is considered as the ultimate source of variation in biological systems and is a random process; however, it is neither the only nor the most frequent source of variation (at least in the biological context): recombination (or 'crossover'), the reciprocal exchange of genetic material between chromosomes that occurs during the process of meiosis, is the most common biochemical way of re-arranging chromosomal material and generating variation. Retention (or inheritance) is the process of transmission of genetic material from individuals to their offsprings. Through this process mutations occurred to individuals accumulate and cause macroevolution and speciation.

In terms of modelling, selection dynamics are represented by dynamical systems which describe the underlying model of the selection process. Deterministic models of selection dynamics lay particular emphasis on the continuity and the reproduction of existing strategies. The process of mutation is introduced negatively, through the study by means of stability analysis of the *robustness against mutations.* Mutations in such models are assumed to be isolated, infrequent and small perturbations of the population state. A simple deterministic model of selection dynamics is the well-known *replicator dynamics.* However, stability analysis has little to say about robustness against sequential or simultaneous cascades of shocks that cause large perturbations of the population state [WEIBULL, 1997]. In general, modelling mutation, which is an intrinsically stochastic phenomenon, requires a fully stochastic model [VEGA-REDONDO, 1996].

Co-evolution, symbiosis and dynamic fitness landscapes

Individual fitness is the measure of the outcome, in terms of survival and reproductive success, of adopting (or of being endowed with) a particular behavioural pattern that undergoes the selection process. A payoff function assigning fitness values to different evolutionary strategies is called a 'fitness function', while *fitness landscape* is nothing more than the graph of a function of this kind. Simple models of selection dynamics focus on the way individual fitness is determined by selection in static fitness landscapes. It has been argued, however, that inter- and intra-species interactions may result in the fitnesses of interacting individuals being jointly determined in dynamic fitness landscapes, and in systemic fitness being determined endogenously. This process of reciprocal evolution that occurs to species as a result of their ecological interaction is known as *co-evolution.*

MAYNARD SMITH, 1989, distinguishes three types of co-evolutionary interactions in biological ecosystems: *Competitive* (or *antagonistic*), *mutualistic,* and *exploitative.* Competitive co-evolution occurs between different species competing for the same resource. Mutualism is a reciprocally beneficial form of symbiosis.[18] Exploitative co-evolution occurs when a species itself is the resource of another, and ranges from *predation,* in which individuals from the exploited species are totally annihilated, to *parasitism.* In a similar vein, LEWONTIN, 1983, criticises the metaphor of unidirectional adaptation of organisms to their environment and proposes instead the alternative metaphor of *niche construction.* This concept refers to the process by which biological systems in the evolutionary process affect and shape their microenvironment by creating their own niches of existence.

Evolutionary dynamics in socio-economic systems

Analogies between biological and socio-economic systems

All the above mentioned concepts which are primarily drawn from biological systems have ample applicability to socio-economic systems.

Evolutionary economics focus on the adjustment dynamics instead of the equilibrium outcome of agents' economic interaction. Evolutionary selection in a socio-economic context drives macroeconomic adjustment dynamics, and similarly to biological selection, is a systemic principle operating at the level of entire populations of economic agents rather than that of individuals. Selection in socio-economic environments is the driving force of Schumpeterian *creative destruction* that leads uncompetitive firms to extinction. In this context, firm competitiveness is the equivalent of the Darwinian concept of individual fitness.

In evolutionary economics both individual and systemic adjustment is neither instantaneous nor cost-free, and additionally, it is a *path-dependent* process. Agents are assumed to possess bounded rationality and imperfect information about market conditions, and of course no perfect foresight. As a result, their response to changes in market conditions, which are often unanticipated, are at best locally optimal – even more so since behavioural adjustments are time-consuming and incur transaction costs. In evolutionary models adaptive behaviour is recognised as more realistic than globally optimising behaviour given the agents' mental, cognitive and informational limitations, and therefore, adaptive procedural routines become the basic behavioural patterns that replace the global optimisation principle. Organisational routines should be seen as the socio-economic equivalent to biological phenotypes.

An underlying assumption in evolutionary models is that agents are usually heterogeneous. As a matter of fact, as NELSON & WINTER, 1982 argue, heterogeneity in firms in terms of strategy, structure and core competences is the necessary micro-foundation for understanding macroeconomic change as an evolutionary process and vice versa. This heterogeneity introduces nonlinearities in the economic systems and can be the source of innovation.

Innovation in socio-economic environments can be seen as the equivalent of variation by mutation or crossover (i.e. genetic recombination) in biological environments. Organisational innovation is the result of the introduction of new procedural routines or the recombination of existing ones in analogy to the way mutation and crossover cause the appearance of new phenotypes in biological populations. Innovation comes about as a result of either search by incumbent firms or entry of new firms with novel procedural routines [Nelson & Winter, 1982]; in that respect it is often an intentional or even 'designed' variation consciously introduced in the selection dynamics with the aim to increase individual fitness, i.e. competitiveness. By contrast, biological mutation is not considered to involve intentionality or determinism: It is usually stochastic.

Incremental technological innovation, which is the most common and persistent form of innovation in technological dynamics, results from the recombination of existing elements of technological knowledge in analogy to crossover, the most common form of variation in biological systems. On the contrary, *radical technological innovation* occurs much less frequently and, when successful, it has the power to cause major shifts in the trajectories of technological dynamics, and by extension to the techno-economic paradigm, in analogy to the extremely rare phenomenon of (successful) mutation in biological systems, which has the power to cause speciation.

The biological concepts of co-evolution and niche construction can find interesting analogies in economics: Niche construction resembles the way oligopolists create market niches for their products, thus shaping consumer preferences instead of adapting their products to existing preferences. Similarly, new technologies open up new market niches instead of merely improving market efficiency and adapting to existing market demand. An example of this process is the way personal computers, and more recently smartphones and tablets, created a market that did not exist before and became a 'necessity' by shaping demand. When the personal computer market matured, demand and consumer preferences shaped it further. In this case, as in many others, consumer preferences and oligopolistic production trends seem to co-evolve. Further along this line of reasoning, competitively successful firms are not necessarily those that adapt better to existing market demand but those that are able to shape new market trends. A similar approach can be followed in the study of the way multinational corporations are shaped by capitalist competition and in turn shape the global economy, or in the study of productive agglomerations, such as 'industrial districts' (more extensively discussed in the next chapter). The latter can be seen as niches shaped by the co-evolution of particular types of firms with own behavioural rules and local operational regimes. These niches, depending on their size and importance in the global economy, may affect the macroscopic dynamics of capitalist growth and be simultaneously affected by it.

The *Red Queen effect*, a term coined by the evolutionary biologist L. van Valen, refers to the fact that "for an evolutionary system, continuing development is needed just in order to maintain its fitness relative to the systems it is co-evolving with" [VAN VALEN, 1973]. BAUMOL, 2004, MARKOSE, 2005, and others use this notion in an economic context to characterise the dynamics generated by innovation-based competition aiming at preserving firms' market shares that are being eroded by entrants and imitators. The result of this 'arms race' is a zero-sum game that maintains constant the relative fitness of competitors.

Finally, the concept of co-evolution can be applied in the study of social institutions: These not only determine the framework of agents' interactions in a top-down fashion, but also emerge in a bottom-up way as a result of these interactions, which clearly implies that social institutions co-evolve with the structure of socio-economic relationships.

... and disanalogies

However, there are some fundamental differences between biological and socio-economic systems. In the former, the adaptation of an organism increases its survival prospects and its fitness, i.e. its probability of creating a higher number of offsprings. These offsprings inherit the parents' genetic material recombined through *crossover* and, less frequently, modified through *mutation*. In terms of time-scale, individual adaptation is a process distinct from evolution: The former is essentially an intra- or inter-generational, short-run process of behavioural adjustment of individuals to environmental stimuli; the latter, on the other hand, concerns the adaptation of whole populations of individuals and it involves the inter-generational, long-run adjustment through selection, mutation and inheritance. In this process, evolutionary robust genetic building blocks are passed over from one generation to another. HOLLAND, 1996: 79, observes that "evolution 'remembers' combinations of building blocks that increase fitness. The building blocks that recur generation after generation are those that have survived in the contexts in which they have been tested. These contexts are provided by (1) other building blocks, and (2) the environmental niche(s) the species inhabits" In biological systems evolution, as opposed to adaptation, assumes no intentionality or consciousness.

In socio-economic systems, the limits between adaptation and evolution are blurred: Individual agents adjust not only their behavioural patterns but also their internal organisational schemes and technology without the mediation of inter-generational inheritance. The transmission of behavioural patterns among individuals, and thus also of 'acquired traits', usually occurs through imitation or learning and 'evolution' may take place *within* the lifespan of the individual. Not only adaptation but also evolution in socio-economic systems is often intentional: Agents are considered to be conscious and intelligent and mutations in the form of innovations are introduced purposively. These attributes make the selection process in economics more Lamarckian than Weismannian. Intentionality is, therefore one of the main factors that differentiate socio-economic from biological systems.

Complexity

Origins and development of complexity theory

'Complexity science', which is essentially indistinguishable from the theory of complex adaptive systems (CAS), is an interdisciplinary field whose aim is the investigation of the generic properties of complex dynamical systems. Complex systems are multiagent systems exhibiting the specific properties examined in the following paragraphs. CAS is a particular class of multiagent systems, whose constituent elements are adaptive agents.

The modern field of complexity is the natural extension of von Neumann's work on cellular automata, Wiener's cybernetics and von Bertalanffy's general systems theory in that it is a theory (or group of theories) of multidisciplinary applicability and with a 'systemic perspective'. Similarly to its predecessors the theory has a wide range of applications in physical, chemical, biological and socio-economic systems.

Even though complexity theory has been initially applied in the fields of natural and life sciences, it finds an increasing range of applications in the social sciences and economics. This modern extension of systems theory has drawn inspiration from, and actually incorporated many notions of, the evolutionary epistemology. As a result of this, at least in the context of the social sciences the complexity paradigm is perfectly compatible and exhibits strong cross-semination with the evolutionary paradigm in economics. Nevertheless, 'complexity economics', much more than evolutionary economics, is a field in the making, and as such, it does not have a consistent epistemic corpus with well-defined epistemological principles and methodology, but it is rather a collection of disparate models and theories, many of which originate in or are inspired from the multidisciplinary work produced at the Santa Fe Institute [e.g. ANDERSON *et al.*, 1988; ARTHUR *et al.*, 1997]. These models employ a wide range of quantitative methods including methods from statistical mechanics, nonlinear dynamical systems and topology, theory of computation (e.g. cellular automata and computational complexity), evolutionary game theory, artificial intelligence (e.g.

genetic algorithms), graph theory and network analysis, and last but not least, agent-based simulation, which is becoming a standard modelling approach to complex systems.

Generic properties of complex adaptive systems

In complexity literature there is no commonly agreed, rigorous definition of a CAS nor a minimum set of sufficient formal conditions for a system to be a CAS.[19] On the contrary, what is frequently found in this body of literature are colourful and sui generis descriptions of phenomena indicating CAS properties. Things become even more obfuscated by the fact that there is not even a commonly agreed nomenclature for the identified properties of the CAS, probably because of the extremely broad scope and the trans-disciplinary applicability of this generic concept (or more accurately, set of concepts), and the still low degree of maturity of the theory.

In this subsection I isolate some characteristics of CAS from the existing literature, which are most relevant to the modelling of socio-economic systems, and, as it will be shown in the next chapter, also to the study of technological knowledge production from a systemic perspective.

Complex systems is a particular class of nonlinear dynamical systems. 'Complex' has two potential interpretations: it either refers to systems which consist of a large number of interacting *heterogeneous* micro-components, i.e. *multiagent* systems, or to systems that exhibit *complex dynamics* (see below). Of course these two interpretations are related, even though they are not formally equivalent. CAS are a particular class of multiagent systems, whose constituent elements are *adaptive agents.* Systems in this very particular class are open, dissipative, nonergodic, self-organised, adaptive (at the macro-scale), heterarchic, and capable of generating novelty. These properties are explained in the following paragraphs.

Time-irreversibility, anisotropy, nonergodicity and dissipation

The deterministic systems of Newtonian mechanics exhibit in their steady state the same structural properties and symmetry as in their initial state and, therefore, their qualitative characteristics are *time-invariable.* As ALLEN, 1997: 22, observes, deterministic models "do not anticipate structural change or symmetry-breaking, and even when their stationary solution is not unique, as in the case of multiple equilibria, the analysis will be biased towards selecting equilibria with the same symmetry as in the initial conditions".

The second law of thermodynamics introduced the notion of *time-irreversibility* in the natural sciences, which is in sharp contrast to the implicit time-symmetry of Newtonian mechanics. A corollary of this universal law is that at (thermodynamic) equilibrium, and under the condition that the system is closed, the optimisation principle entails entropy maximisation in the system: As a general rule, closed dynamical systems move irreversibly towards a state of increased entropy (the thermodynamic equilibrium), at which the internal structure of the system is eroded [ALLEN, 1997: 10]. The attainment of a steady state is thus equivalent to entropy maximisation [WILSON, 1974]. Systems of this type are called *conservative.*

Time-irreversibility is related to *nonergodicity.* In nonergodic systems exogenous shocks have permanent effects on the long-run state of the system. This property is equivalent to *path dependence,* whereby the steady state of a dynamical system depends not only on the initial conditions but also on the adjustment path [DURLAUF, 2001].

Some types of open dynamical systems under certain conditions may exhibit an internal decrease in their entropy related to anisotropy, i.e. symmetry-breaking, and the emergence of new structure and new qualitative characteristics. These systems receive energy from and dissipate entropy to their environment, i.e. they decrease their entropy locally. This class of dynamical systems is called *dissipative.* Biological systems typically belong to this class.

The near-equivalence of thermodynamic and informational entropy means that in information-theoretic terms dissipative systems can be considered as absorbing information to increase their internal structure ('negentropy'),[20] and by extension their *systemic complexity,* or equivalently, to decrease their *informational* (*Shannon's*) *entropy.*

Self-organisation, nonlinearities and phase transitions

The emergence of new structure sometimes observed in open dissipative systems is an indication of the presence of an attractive systemic property, *self-organisation.* This is the spontaneous process by which the internal structure of a system increases in complexity without this increase being controlled by an external system. Self-organising systems are, therefore, complex dissipative structures capable of reducing their internal entropy.

In the socio-economic context, as LANSING, 2002, observes, systems of (cognitive) heterogeneous agents with limited knowledge of their environment and bounded rationality may exhibit emergent properties of self-organisation and order.

Two necessary, but not sufficient, conditions for self-organisation are, first, that the system is in *far-from-equilibrium* state, and second, that *nonlinearities* in the interactions between the lower-order elements of the system are in place. This is related to the fact that, while a linear system can be fully analysed by being decomposed to its elements due to the additivity of the elements' functional forms, in a nonlinear system the interaction between the constituent elements generate results that do not allow the decomposition of the system. Bifurcations, for instance, which is a usual phenomenon in nonlinear systems, may result in that a marginal change in the parameters of the system cause qualitative change in the system's aggregate properties. This may lead to chaotic behaviour or, alternatively, to *life-at-the-edge-of-chaos.* This term, coined by LANGTON, 1992, refers to the *phase transition* between 'order' and chaos, in which novelties emerge. A *self-organised criticality* occurs when a dynamical system has a critical point as its attractor,[21] and is similar to the notion of life-at-the-edge-of-chaos.[22]

Complex dynamics and endogenous novelty

WOLFRAM, 1984, in his study of the evolutionary dynamics of *cellular automata* demonstrates that systems dynamics fall under four 'universal classes' according to the qualitative nature of the *attractors* of the dynamical systems in which they emerge; these classes are believed to characterise the behaviour of a much broader range of complex physical, biological and even socio-economic systems beyond the basic one-dimensional automaton model. The first class includes *finite automata* with *point attractors*; the second class *push-down automata* with *periodical* or *quasi-periodical attractors*; the third class *linear-bounded automata* with *strange attractors* and chaotic behaviour. The fourth class consists of automata described as *Turing machines* exhibiting *undecidable* or *complex dynamics*, whose particularity is that they are algorithmically incomputable despite the fact that they are generated by algorithmic agents, often as simple as cellular automata. Life-at-the-edge-of-chaos occurs in the domain of complex dynamics (class 4) between computable order (classes 1 and 2) and chaos (class 3).

ROSEN, 1999, considers *Turing-incomputability* as a definition of *systemic complexity*.[23] According to him, "[a] system is simple if all its models are simulable. A system that is not simple, and that accordingly must have a non-simulable model, is complex" [ROSEN, 1999: 292]. Complex systems of this type, according to MARKOSE, 2005, exhibit "irregular innovation-based structure-changing dynamics associated with evolutionary biology and capitalist growth". These systems develop complex behavioural patterns along their evolutionary trajectories which are considered as indications of spontaneous emergence of *novelty*.

Adaptation and resilience

Adaptation is the ability of a system to detect environmental variation and to adjust without losing its cohesion and its systemic properties. By doing so the system increases its fitness and its survival probability. *Resilience* is a related notion that refers to the ability of an open system to restore internal stability, or more precisely to remain within its current attractor basin, after an exogenous perturbation. The resilience of a system vis-à-vis dynamic exchanges of matter and energy between the system and its environment, achieved by means of internal self-regulatory apparatuses is more specifically called 'homeostasis'.

Emergence and universality

A notion related to resilience is that of *universality*, proposed by DURLAUF, 2001, i.e. the robustness of the aggregate behaviour of the system to alternative specifications of its microstructure. Universality is directly related to the notion of *emergence* in a way that will become apparent in the next section.

Last but not least, *emergence* is probably the most salient property of CAS. Besides being an *ontological* principle responsible for 'ontogenesis' (although this view is strongly contested by many philosophers of science), it is also an epistemological premise able to explain a broad range of systemic phenomena, and in particular their relationship to the properties of the constituent elements of the system. For this reason it is extensively treated in a separate section of this chapter.

The macro-properties of complex adaptive systems are summarised in Table 1.1 below.

Table 1.1: Macro-properties of complex adaptive systems

Emergence	Spontaneous generation of mereologically irreducible macro-properties of a system from the interaction of its micro-elements with downwardly determinative influence.
Universality	Robustness of macro-properties of a system to alternative specifications of its micro-structure.
Phase transition	Qualitative change in the macro-properties of a system caused by small perturbations in its parameters.
Self-organised criticality	Emergence of a critical point as attractor in a dynamical system (similar to life-at-the-edge-of-chaos).
Nonergodicity	Dependence of the long-run state of a dynamical system on its adjustment path.
Anisotropy	Directional dependence due to symmetry-breaking emergence of new structure.
Dissipation	Ability of an open system to absorb information from its environment in order to increase its internal structure, or equivalently, to decrease its informational entropy.
Self-organisation	Spontaneous increase in (the complexity of) the internal structure of a dissipative system in far-from-equilibrium state without this increase being controlled by an external system.
Novelty	Emergence of irregular new structure in dynamical systems characterised by complex dynamics.
Complex dynamics	'Undecidable' dynamics capable of generating endogenous novelty characterised by systemic complexity (or Turing incomputability, or non-simulability).
Adaptation	Ability of a system to increase its fitness and survival probability by detecting environmental variation and adjusting without losing its cohesion and systemic properties.
Resilience	Ability of an open system to remain within its current attractor basin after an exogenous perturbation.

Complex networks

The network perspective of complex systems

The generic properties listed above refer to the macroscopic dynamical behaviour of CAS. The main sources of scientific metaphor in this approach are the fields of (soft) condensed-matter physics and thermodynamics.[24] When it comes to its socio-economic applications, a limitation of this approach, which is largely formulated in the language of statistical mechanics,[25] is its inability to represent economic agents as individuals – agents can be nothing more than attribute-less atomic particles. An alternative approach to the study of complex systems, which is increasingly becoming part of the 'complexity methodology' and has more direct applicability to discrete socio-economic systems of intelligent agents, in particular the type of systems examined in the following chapters of this book, is the analysis of the structure of interactions and interdependencies between the micro-components of the systems, i.e. between the adaptive agents. The network representation of CAS shifts the focus from aggregate systemic macro-dynamics to the topological structure of the micro-interactions.

In this spirit, FRENKEN, 2006, defines complex systems as networks with a nontrivial topology,[26] and with both strong and weak interactions (by which he means essentially graphs with varying tie strengths). A more complete definition found in VEGA-REDONDO, 2007, requires complex networks to be large and heterogeneous, to have an 'intricate architecture', by which he means 'many degrees of freedom and no recurrent patterns', and to exhibit complex patterns of diffusion and phase transitions. Still, this definition is not sufficiently rigorous or complete. In the following paragraph I examine a broader range of properties which are deemed necessary (although not sufficient) for a network to be complex.

Properties of complex networks

A complex network has a *nontrivial topology*. There is no formal definition of what constitutes a nontrivial graph topology; my interpretation is that it is a *non-simulable topological structure*, i.e. one that does not have a simple algorithmic representation. This obviously excludes networks that are null and complete (i.e. fully connected) as already noted, but it also excludes all types of topological regularity or perfect randomness, notably lattices, star graphs corresponding to a fully hierarchical structure, and equiprobable random graphs, (i.e. graphs whose vertices have an equal probability to form a tie). In the extreme cases of perfect regularity (e.g. a regular lattice) and perfect randomness (e.g. an Erd s-Rényi graph) the informational content ('negentropy') and hence the systemic complexity of the network are minimised.

Other features of complex networks are the following:

- *Assortativity,* i.e. selective interaction or *preferential attachment*;
- *Modularity,* i.e. community structure;
- High degree of *clustering* (or *cliquishness*);
- *Scale invariance,* related to a power-law distribution of connectivity;
- Node heterogeneity;
- Tie-strength variation;
- Increasing graph complexity from a diachronic perspective;
- Global *heterarchy,* which may embed local hierarchical structures.

The concept of *heterarchy* deserves some clarification: I define a heterarchy to be a form of organisational (network) structure, whose micro-elements interact and their interactions are coordinated endogenously and locally without the mediation of centralised control. In a heterarchy, as opposed to a hierarchy, dependence relations between the micro-elements are horizontal (i.e. interdependence) instead of vertical (i.e. authority). A heterarchy may coexist with a hierarchy, be a local substructure of a global hierarchy, or contain local hierarchies. Heterarchies introduce feedback loops and nonlinearities in the system, which need not be present in a pure hierarchy; they are therefore a source of complex dynamics. Complex systems are in principle globally heterarchical, possibly with locally embedded hierarchies.

The applications of the network-analytical approach to socio-economic systems, and in particular to the study of collective knowledge production, such as in research collaboration networks, are numerous and presented in detail in Chapters 3 and 4 of this book.

Emergence

Context and definitions of emergence

Emergence is a notion largely misunderstood: Although traces of the concept of 'emergence' are found throughout the history of philosophy, emergentism, as such, made a comeback in the late 19th century as an ontological theory primarily intended to explain the relationship between the 'mind' and intangible mental processes such as consciousness, on the one hand, and the biological and physical constitution of the 'body' on the other.[27] The metaphysical and epistemological foundations of emergence have been challenged by mainstream philosophy of science, especially in the analytical-positivist tradition [NAGEL, 1961; HEMPEL, 1965]; this led to the discrediting of emergentism in favour of reductionism for a good part of the twentieth century. In more recent times, however, an opposite tendency is observed: the failure of the epistemological programme of reductionism leading to the resurgence of emergence as a mainstream epistemic principle [KIM, 1999]. Modern analytical philosophy has begun to take emergence more seriously than ever before and the related literature is proliferating [HUMPHREYS, 1997; SILBERSTEIN & MCGEEVER, 1999; KIM, 1999, 2006; MOULINES, 2006; *et al.*]. In the last two decades, in particular, this tendency has been reinforced by the rise of the 'science(s) of complexity' and the theory of complex adaptive systems, whereof emergence is often considered a foundational concept. In this context emergence is an essential epistemic principle applicable to a wide range of physico-chemical, biological, cognitive and socio-economic phenomena. On the other hand, in the attempt to avoid mainstream methodological reductionism a tendency in certain strands of social science in recent years is to resort to vernacular uses of the concept as a sort of anti-reductionist panacea, mostly borrowed from popular science literature. One way or another, emergence has yet to find its place in the social sciences, and even more so in strongly reductionist mainstream economic theory. For this reason a systematic clarification of the concept and of its implications for economic theory is much needed.

Mereology and the layered model of the world

The common understanding of the concept of emergence is summarized in the motto "the whole is more than the sum of its parts" inaccurately attributed to Aristotle.[28] Emergence as a philosophical concept has more subtle ontological and epistemological ramifications than this aphorism implies, yet this resonates an important aspect of the concept, namely that it is primarily a principle governing mereological (i.e. 'parthood') relationships, which in philosophy are considered as fundamental ontological issues in their own right.[29]

That "the whole is more than the sum of its parts" is a simplified interpretation of the principle of *non-mereological composition*; this principle refers to the "composition of elements which results in a whole that is different from the mereological fusion of these elements" and is indeed discussed in Aristotle's *Μετὰ τὰ Φυσικά* [SCALTSAS, 1990: 583]. Non-mereological composition is one of the widely recognised necessary conditions for emergence,[30] and is equivalent to the condition of *non-aggregativity* [WIMSATT, 2000].

An essential framework for the emergentist/ reductionist debate is the 'layered model' of the world [KIM, 1999]. The layered model assumes that perceivable reality is organised in an ordered hierarchy of domains according to the degree of complexity of the entities that belong to each domain, or in other words, "it takes the natural world as stratified into levels, from lower to higher, from the basic to the constructed and evolved, from the simple to the more complex" [KIM, 1999: 19]. The layered model of the world implicitly assumes a mereological relationship among different hierarchical levels, with lower-level entities being constituent parts of higher-level entities; this generates a 'nested hierarchy' of levels with an upwardly increasing degree of complexity. The layered model also implicitly assumes ontological monism – a common feature of both reductionist and emergentist theories.[31] The fundamental difference between the two theories, however, is that in the case of reductionism, as SILBERSTEIN, 2002: 81, explains, the most fundamental physical level is assumed to be the 'real' ontology of the world, while all other levels must be able to be 'mapped onto' or 'built out of' its elements, and as a result, 'fundamental theory' is perceived as having greater predictive and explanatory power, and providing a deeper understanding of the world. On the contrary, emergentism "[rejects] the idea that there is any fundamental level of ontology. It holds that the best understanding of complex systems must be sought at the level of the structure, behaviour and laws of the whole system and that science may require a plurality of theories" [Ibid.]. In other words, emergentism unlike reductionism considers that higher level ontologies are irreducible to lower level ones. The implications of this irreducibility for economic theory, if we are to accept emergence as an epistemological principle governing the analysis of economic phenomena, are very serious, and are examined below.

Emergence defined

It has been notoriously difficult to define emergence in a robust, non-trivial and theoretically useful way.[32] In recent work in complexity theory and analytical philosophy there is a growing consensus as to the minimal conditions for an entity, a property, a law or a phenomenon to qualify as 'emergent'. Much of this common basis for a definition of emergent ontologies can be found by looking back to the source: One of the most prominent British emergentists of that time, BROAD, 1925, comparing the two competing construals, 'Mechanism' – which roughly corresponds to reductionism – and 'Emergence', gives the following description of the latter: "On the emergent theory we have to reconcile ourselves to much less unity in the external world and a much less intimate connexion between the various sciences. At best the external world and the various sciences that deal with it will form a kind of hierarchy. We might, if we liked, keep the view that there is only one fundamental kind of stuff. But we should have to recognise aggregates of various orders. And there would be two fundamentally different types of law, which might be called "intra-ordinal" and "trans-ordinal" respectively. A trans-ordinal law would be one which connects the properties of aggregates of adjacent orders. A and B would be adjacent, and in ascending order, if every aggregate of order B is composed of aggregates of order A, and if it has certain properties which no aggregate of order A possesses and which cannot be deduced from the A-properties and the structure of the B-complex by any law of composition which has manifested itself at lower levels. An intra-ordinal law would be one which connects the properties of aggregates of the same order. A trans-ordinal law would be a statement of the irreducible fact that an aggregate composed of aggregates of the next lower order in such and such proportions and arrangements has such and such characteristic and non-deducible properties." [BROAD, 1925: 77]

What is stated about emergence in this passage is that first, it assumes a layered model of the world and a nested hierarchy of levels or, as Broad calls them, 'orders'. Second, emergence is consistent with ontological (materialist) monism ("there is only one fundamental kind of stuff"); however, emergence is a form of non-reductionist monism – an ontological monism coupled with property pluralism. This means that the *emergent* shares the same substance as the *emergens* but possesses new properties that are novel and mechanistically irreducible to their 'basal conditions', i.e. the properties of their lower level bases.[33] A commonly agreed additional condition not included in Broad's account is that emergent properties should be downward causal in the sense that "they have powers to influence and control the direction of the lower-level processes from which they emerge" [KIM, 1999: 6].

The most interesting assumption of the theory of emergence is that the nested ontological levels of the world are not simply irreducible but that they are dependent in very specific ways. Contemporary definitions of emergence use the concept of *supervenience* to denote this type of inter-level dependence. A generic definition of the concept is that "a set of properties *Y* supervenes upon another set *X* only when no two objects can differ with respect to their *Y*-properties without also differing with respect to their *X*-properties" [MCLAUGHLIN & BENNETT, 2005]. A stronger version of supervenience, which is also known as 'upward necessitation' or 'micro-determinism', says that "wholes are completely determined, causally and ontologically, by their parts" [KIM, 1978: 154]. An equivalent statement would be that two (mereologically composite) entities identical with regard to their micro-specification, i.e. identical at the ontological level of their constituent entities, cannot differ at their own ontological level; or in other words, that a higher-level difference between two composite entities requires a lower-level difference between their constituent parts.[34] Supervenience is a reflexive, transitive but non-symmetric relation which can hold with nomological and/ or metaphysical necessity, and does not require ontological dependence or entailment [McLaughlin & Bennett, 2005]. Paradoxically, supervenience is a necessary condition for both reduction and emergence, but sufficient for neither.

A formal definition of an *emergent property* by O'Connor, 1994: 97-98, is the following: "Property *P* is an emergent property of a (mereologically-complex) object *O* if:

1. *P* supervenes on properties of the parts of *O*;
2. *P* is not had by any of the object's parts;
3. *P* is distinct from any structural property of *O*;[35]
4. *P* has direct ('downward') determinative influence on the pattern of behaviour involving *O*'s parts."

Condition (1) is the standard supervenience assumption, which, when applied to causal properties, is also known as 'micro-determinism' or 'upward necessitation'. Condition (3) distinguishes emergent from resultant properties and is what O'Connor calls elsewhere the condition of 'non-structurality'. This condition jointly with (2), which I call the condition of '(mereological) non-inheritance', make up the condition of mereological irreducibility. Condition (4) is the widely debated premise of 'downward causation' or 'macro-determinism'. Less formally, Humphreys, 1997: S341-342, identifies the following criteria for emergent properties: They are characterised by novelty, by which is meant that "a previously uninstantiated property comes to have an instance", and they are qualitatively different from the properties from which they emerge; it is logically or nomologically impossible to be possessed at a lower level; different laws apply to their features than to the features from which they emerge; it is nomologically necessary for their existence that there is an essential interaction between their constituent properties; and they are holistic properties of the entire system rather than local properties of its constituents. Van Cleve, 1990: 222, defines emergent properties as properties *determined by* and *dependent upon* the properties of the parts of *wholes* but not *deducible from* them (i.e. epistemically irreducible). Equivalently, Teller, 1992: 140-141, says that "a property is emergent if and only if it is not explicitly definable in terms of the non-relational properties of any of the object's proper parts".

To sum up, emergence has the following conditions:

C1. Ontological (materialist) monism
C2. Non-mereological composition (non-aggregativity)
C3. Mereological irreducibility of properties consisting in:
 C3A. Non-inheritance
 C3B. Non-structurality
C4. Multiple-domain supervenience with nomological necessity (upward necessitation, micro-determinism)
C5. Downward causation (macro-determinism)

The first condition essentially says that the 'world' where emergence is observed is composed by a single 'substance'; the second and third conditions describe part-whole relationships in terms of the constitution of entities and of properties; and the fourth and fifth conditions talk about inter-domain dependence, determination and causal powers.

Varieties of emergence

BEDAU, 1997; 2002, proposes a *weak* version of emergence (as defined above), which relaxes the disputed assumption of downward causation as well as the condition of non-structurality, and which, according to him, is "metaphysically innocent, consistent with materialism, and scientifically useful, especially in the sciences of complexity" [BEDAU, 1997: 376]. He defines a macrostate of a system (i.e. a structural property of a system constituted wholly out of its microstates) to be *weakly emergent* if it can be derived from the system's external conditions and its microdynamic (i.e. the dynamic which governs the time evolution of the system's microstates – the states of its parts) only by simulation [BEDAU, 1997: 378].

A distinction between *ontological* and *epistemological* emergence, similar to that between ontological and epistemological reduction, is drawn in SILBERSTEIN & MCGEEVER, 1999. They define the former, rather loosely, as the failure of both strong and weak forms of reductionism (corresponding to mereological fusion and mereological supervenience respectively). Their perception of epistemological emergence, on the other hand, is that it occurs whenever a property is reducible to or determined by the intrinsic properties of its lower-level units, while at the same time it is very difficult to be explained, predicted or derived on the basis of the properties of the lower-level units. They conclude that "epistemologically emergent properties are novel only at a level of description" [SILBERSTEIN & MCGEEVER, 1999: 186]. This definition of epistemological emergence is almost equivalent to that of weak emergence proposed by BEDAU, 1997. More succinctly, ontological emergence should be perceived as the formation of new autonomous supervenient entities which are also downwardly causal. Epistemological emergence is the formation of new patterns, analytical classes, forms of organisation, etc. at the supervenient level, whose (exact) explanation on the basis of the subvenient properties is computationally intractable (although the possibility of explanation by simulation is not excluded). A fundamental condition of epistemological emergence is, therefore, *analytical irreducibility*. Ontological emergence entails epistemological emergence, but of course the converse does not hold.

A further distinction is drawn between *synchronic* and *diachronic* emergence by RUEGER, 2000, who, nevertheless, refers in both cases to a weak version of emergence. Diachronic emergence is an 'evolutionary' phenomenon observed in the structural properties of dynamical systems strongly associated with endogenous novelty. CRUTCHFIELD, 1994: 12, defines diachronic emergence as "a process that leads to the appearance of structure not directly described by the defining constraints and instantaneous forces that control a system". In a similar vein, DURLAUF, 2001, considers (diachronic) emergence to be the spontaneous generation of new higher-order properties that are not present at the level of the constituent lower-order elements of a system; as a result, the examination of individual parts of the system in isolation does not reveal its aggregate dynamics, despite the fact that its initial conditions and its evolutionary trajectory (its 'history') are still relevant in understanding its present condition.

Emergence and the generative method

From the methodological perspective, the weak version of emergence is compatible with a new approach to scientific method different from the Hempelian deductive-nomological and the inductive-statistical methods, which has been termed *generative* (or *constructive*) [EPSTEIN, 2005; 2007; TESFATSION, 2005].[36] This approach is concerned with the way the explanans – the behavioural traits of the micro-elements of a system (i.e. individual agents) – generates the explanandum – observable macroscopic patterns of systemic behaviour. The method consists in simulating in a bottom-up, iterative fashion the interactions of the micro-elements in an artificial environment with the objective to derive the macroscopic properties of the complex system from its simple basal conditions, i.e. the subvenient properties of the micro-elements. This is the opposite to the top-down approach of both the deductive and the inductive methods, which consist in subsuming the explanandum under 'general' (deterministic) or 'statistical' laws respectively.

The exponential increase of the computational capacities of modern micro-processors and the advancements in object-oriented programming have made possible the proliferation of agent-based simulation techniques and the rapid development of the field of agent-based computational economics. Agent-based modelling (ABM) has become the main instrument of the generative method. As EPSTEIN, 2007: 42-43, observes, ABM aims at providing "computational demonstrations that a given microspecification is in fact *sufficient to generate* a macrostructure of interest", adding that the motto of generative social science is "if you didn't grow it, you didn't explain its emergence". The generative approach to economic phenomena is only weakly reductionist,[37] in that ABM allows for a more realistic representation of individual diversity, the bounded cognitive and learning capacities of economic agents, and their ability to engage in face-to-face interactions within systems potentially exhibiting complex dynamics. The epistemic adequacy of the empirical validation of ABM has been challenged on the grounds of the *under-determination problem* [FAGIOLO *et al.*, 2005].[38]

Emergence in the economy

The premise of emergence has two types of potential applications in the social and more specifically in the economic sciences: It can be used as an 'epistemic theory of explanation' to replace traditional reductionism, i.e. as an epistemological frame for developing new non-reductionist analytical methodologies and models, or it can be directly applied to the study of economic phenomena as an 'ontic theory of explanation', providing an ontological justification of observed regularities which remain inexplicable in the positivist frame. To the present none of these potential applications of emergence has been sufficiently explored in the context of the social sciences, and particularly in economics: Emergence remains a premise largely misunderstood, misused and, more often, totally neglected.

Emergence and micro-meso-macro articulation

The structure-agency problem and the micro-foundations of the macro-economy

Emergence is a potential unifying epistemological solution to the long-standing structure-agency duality problem in the social sciences: In hierarchically stratified socio-economic systems where emergence occurs, the properties of the macro-structure supervene on those of the micro-parts, i.e. individual agents; individual agents determine social structure with upward necessitation, while structure affects individual agents with downward causation; and finally, the macro-structure has properties which are not inherited from the micro-parts. In the end, despite the fact that 'structure' is not reducible to 'agency', the two perspectives are reconciled in a unified epistemological framework, in which simply structure emerges from agency without compromising the 'ontological' autonomy of the agents.

Emergence can similarly reconcile another duality specific to the economic sciences: the micro-macro divide. A first step in this direction is the recognition that the positivist quest for micro-foundations of the macro-economy is per se misplaced. It is not uncommon in economic systems that all formal conditions for weak emergence of their properties from those of the underlying economic agents be in place, namely supervenience, non-aggregativity, non-inheritance, and non-structurality. There is also often downward causation, when a particular property of economic systems affects individual agents, in which case emergence is strong. The macro-systems emerge from their micro-elements, which entails that there can be no mereological decomposition of the macro-systems to the functions and properties of their micro-elements. This plainly means that there cannot be found any micro-foundations of the macro-economy in the frame of methodological individualism, whereby the economic behaviour of individual agents is considered to be sufficient for explaining aggregate social phenomena. In the specific context of general equilibrium theory, this conclusion is fully consistent with the SMD theorem. Therefore, applied to the economic sciences as an epistemic theory of explanation, the premise of emergence directly challenges the Weberian doctrine of methodological individualism.

A second step in the direction of bridging the micro-macro divide is to see emergence as an ontological principle which pervades and coheres the levels of economic reality. The following two subsections propose a framework in which this can be achieved.

Ontological domains

The economy is structured in hierarchically nested levels of increasing complexity from the individual agent, through multiagent organisations and groups of organisations to the macro-economy, which in turn is also organised at various levels from the regional to the global. One may distinguish almost as many descriptive layers of economic activity as one needs for specific analytical purposes – for instance, the subnational level of regional economies, the supranational level of trading blocks, etc. However, when it comes to determining levels that correspond to distinct, meaningful economic ontologies instead of being merely *resultant*, their number is much more limited and fixed. I call these levels 'ontological domains'. Mainstream economics usually considers only two; I assert that there are three, the *micro*, the *meso* and the *macro*. A conventional perception of these levels is that they literally denote differences in terms of the size of their units – it has even been naïvely suggested that a 'mini' and a 'mega' level should be added to the range of levels of economic analysis. My approach is different and in line with the 'layered model of the world': the levels are not defined in terms of the scale of their constituent units but in terms of their relative complexity, their hierarchical relationship and the focus of the analysis. The micro domain is simply the level of the atomic ontologies, the 'individuals'. The macro is always the level of the compound (or 'aggregate') ontologies, the systems. The meso is the transitional space in-between, the space of interactions of the atomic ontologies, the space of the dyads, triads, etc., and the generative space of the level above.

Any entity seen as unitary and with properties subvenient to those of a system belongs to the micro level, even if this entity is itself compound from a different point of view, as in the case of a corporate organisation. Any compound entity seen as a system with properties supervenient to those of its constituent micro-units belongs to the macro level. Any set of interactions among micro-units belongs to the meso level. Individuals, households, and firms considered as unitary agents predictably reside in the micro domain; regional, national and supranational economies considered as systems reside in the macro domain; networks of interacting micro-agents reside in the meso domain. The fundamental ontology of the meso domain is defined and examined in Chapter 2.The meso domain as the missing link

Assuming, as the neoclassical theory does, that there exist no meaningful direct interactions between economic agents capable of influencing their choices and, by extension, their consumption and production patterns, how would a hypothetical neoclassical 'space of transactions' look like? This hypothetical space would be an isotropic continuum of infinitely many agents (hence a 'continuum'), representable as a random network in which any node can connect with any other with equal probability, given that prices are ex ante determined, information is symmetric and complete and the cost of transactions is zero. This equiprobable network would have a trivial topology.[39]

Contrary to the neoclassical assumptions, real economic systems consist of heterogeneous, boundedly rational agents with interdependent, adaptive and only locally optimal responses to limited informational stimuli, strategic interactions that condition their economic decisions, nonlinear complex adjustment dynamics and long out-of-equilibrium transitions. How does the hypothetical space of transactions in this case look like? This will be an anisotropic, discrete space of a finite number of agents who transact very selectively given all the above limitations. This space corresponds to a complex network with nontrivial topology, in which the probability of connection between pairs of nodes is highly unequally distributed, depending on a number of diverse factors. Among the structurally determined factors are the asymmetric positional power of some nodes, asymmetric information flows, and transaction costs; among the agent-specific factors are the cognitive and computational limitations of the agents, and path-dependent and assortative preferences. As a result of all these, only a small segment of economic interactions is purely random.

The meso domain of the economy conceived as the locus where the interactions of all sorts of micro-economic agents occur, where productive relations are articulated, where the division of labour unfolds, where 'social capital' is accumulated, and where technological knowledge is generated, has the shape of the latter hypothetical 'transaction space'. It is evident then that in the context of the neoclassical model a meso domain would have a trivial topology and hence would be largely obsolete. On the contrary, in the case of a 'realist' model of the economy this domain is not only useful and meaningful but also highly fascinating as some of the most interesting economic phenomena happen there. It is also the first stage of multi-level emergence leading to the formation of the macro-economies: The systemic integration of individual economic agents becomes possible in the meso domain. Moreover, many aggregate phenomena which cannot be fully imputed to individual economic agents (and therefore whose 'micro-foundations' cannot be found), such as externalities and increasing returns, originate at the meso level, not at the micro level.

The meso domain is the hitherto missing link which coheres and articulates the layers of the economy. The meso domain is the par excellence locus of a systemic economic geography.

Emergent and resultant economic entities

The corporate organisation as an emergent ontology

Several empirical and theoretical studies postulate that the corporate organisation is itself a multiagent system of reflective agents, its employees and stakeholders (which collectively will be referred to as 'members'), and more specifically a complex adaptive system [Dooley, 1997; Fuller & Moran, 2000; 2001]. As such, this entity embodies a structure or hierarchically nested levels articulated, as argued here, through ontological emergence:[40] While higher-order properties of the firm supervene on the lower-order properties of its members, its objective function and optimisation scheme is normally quite different and cannot be deduced from those of its members. Small changes in its workforce do not normally affect its macro-behaviour, and hence it can be postulated that the firm as a system is 'robust to alternative specifications of its microstructure' – in other words, that it exhibits the property of universality. The firm, more specifically the corporation, is an autonomous entity with a separate legal personality, which exists independently of its members. Finally, the firm clearly has downward causal powers on its members. The firm is therefore a clear-cut case of ontological emergence.

Despite being compound, multiagent entities, corporate organisations are considered to reside in the micro domain of the economy because they behave (or at least they can be realistically be modelled to behave) as unitary entities or 'meta-agents'. As explained in Chapter 2, corporate organisations are hierarchical networks with centralised 'schemata', i.e. internal information processing and administrative control mechanisms.

Are regional economies resultant or emergent entities?

The notion of 'region' occupies an exceptionally central position in economic geography, often being considered as the defining ontology of the discipline together with the notion of 'space'. But is the region really a fundamental ontology in the emergentist framework set in this section?

In trying to answer this question the first problem that arises is the elusiveness of the term 'region' itself. The term has been used in a flexible manner to denote various forms of agglomeration, such as industrial districts and territorial clusters, subnational administrative divisions, statistical territorial units, various types of sub-, supra- or trans-national historical territories, country blocs, etc. Almost any type of geographical or geo-political formation can be termed a 'region'. For this reason almost any statement about the 'region' can hold. The region, in the most common use of the term in the European context, as a subnational statistical or administrative territorial unit, may or may not have historical origins and continuity, administrative autonomy, self-governed economy and own resources, etc. It is, therefore, very difficult to generalise even among relatively well-defined regional entities of comparable geographical scale and governance level, such as the NUTS-regions.[41]

In most cases regional economies cannot be considered as emergent entities, but merely resultant. While the supervenience assumption commonly holds, no other emergence condition seems tenable in these cases: Regional economies are aggregations of economic agents at various levels, whose characteristics are entirely inherited from their constituent entities, while often they do not possess downwardly causal powers outside the limited administrative powers devolved to the regional administrations by the national states. The formal institutional frameworks in which regional economies of this type operate are usually indistinct from those of the countries to which they belong. More than anything else, these cases are statistical disaggregations of national economies. In some exceptional cases, where regional identities are strong, region-specific formal or informal institutions are in place, and the degree of administrative autonomy and of economic self-governance is high, regional economies could qualify as emergent entities. Whether the characteristics of the entities it refers to are resultant or emergent, the concept of the region, nevertheless, remains useful as an analytical tool in economic geography.

Conclusion

The neoclassical paradigm in economic theory has been repeatedly pronounced dead but is still alive. Nevertheless, its chronic illness appears now, more than ever before, to be terminal. One by one its foundational pillars, the concept of ex ante equilibrium, methodological individualism and the representative agent, and individualistic-instrumental rationality, are collapsing in three respects: they exhibit very serious symptoms of internal inconsistency; they are based on assumptions which constitute nomological impossibilities; and they fail to define a theory able to propose a realist explanation of economic phenomena.

Mainstream economic theory essentially leaves no space for decentralised interactions among economic agents, is indifferent to economic dynamics, and rules out the possibility of novelty and structural change to emerge in economic systems. The economic system of general equilibrium is intended to be a closed, time-invariable, conservative, ergodic, deterministic system similar to those of Newtonian celestial mechanics. Moreover, it is assumed to be a system fully reducible to the behavioural properties of its constituent elements, the hyper-rational homines œconomici (even though this assumption has been shown to fail). Novelty and structural change are, however, the foundations of technological progress; these cannot be explained in the context of neoclassical economics.

On the contrary, emergence on the one hand and evolutionary dynamics characterised by selection, retention, recombination and mutation on the other, are powerful explanatory tools for constructing a theory about the origins of technological knowledge. This is generated and diffused in complex systems consisting of heterogeneous adaptive agents with bounded rationality and limited and asymmetric information on their economic environment. Economic activity is embedded in a structured, network-like space that bears little similarity to the 'isotropic' neoclassical market. Populations of economic agents as well as norms, institutions, and technologies undergo a co-evolutionary process that involves selection, variation and retention. At the same time individual agents co-adapt through competitive, mutualist and exploitative interactions; competitive co-adaptation is responsible for 'Red Queen' type of technological dynamics.

More generally, real economies are complex multiagent systems organised in hierarchically nested levels imbued by multiple-domain emergence. These systems are open, dissipative, far-from-equilibrium, with complex dynamics and phase transitions, and inherently capable of generating novelty.

In this chapter the epistemological underpinnings of the dominant neoclassical paradigm and some of its epistemic anomalies were investigated, and the systemic premises and theories of emergence, evolution and complexity were proposed as potential building materials for a successor paradigm in the economic sciences. These building materials include the following:

- a critical realist view on economic phenomena which allows the theory to look into their generative structures behind empirical regularities;
- an antireductionist approach to socio-economic structure and agency which refutes the doctrine of methodological individualism and the concept of the representative agent;
- an emergentist explanation of the micro-meso-macro articulation of the economy;
- an evolutionary and complex adaptive systems perspective on economic agents and systems.

The differences between the dominant and the proposed systemic paradigms are summarised in Table 1.2 below.

So far some of the above principles have been presented in their broadest context and mostly with reference to the natural and biological sciences. The applicability of this theory to economics and economic geography will be explored extensively in the following chapter through the prism of the novel concept of 'mesoeconomic plexus' introduced there.

Table 1.2: Comparison of paradigms

	DOMINANT PARADIGM	SYSTEMIC PARADIGM
Ontological domains	Micro-macro	Micro-meso-macro
Inter-domain articulation	Inconsistent; lack of real micro-foundations of the macro-economy	Hierarchically nested domains; supervenience with upward determination and possibly downward causation
Domain reducibility	(Assumed) complete reducibility of the macro to the micro	Semi- or non-reducibility
Mereological relationship	Economic systems are just aggregations of individuals; each analytical level is just a product of the level below, hence ontologically dependent on the one below	Economic systems are nearly irreducible and embedded in nested hierarchies; levels are ontologically independent
Epistemological	Reductionism;	Emergence (weak or strong)

principle	eliminativism	
Philosophical theory	Empirical realism	Transcendental realism
Source of metaphor	Newtonian/Laplacian mechanics	Evolutionary biology; condensed-matter physics; statistical mechanics; cybernetics
Method of explanation	Deductive-nomological	Generative
Agency-structure premise	Methodological individualism; prominence of agency	Structuralism; systemicity; agency-structure co-determination
Agency	Representative agent	Heterogeneous agents
Rationality	Hyper-rationality (rational choice theory)	Bounded rationality; procedural rationality; satisficing
Optimisation	Global	Local; aspiration level
Micro-interactions	None	Casual or strategic
Adjustment coordination	Centralised; Walrasian auctioneer; tâtonnement	Decentralised; iterative
Relational space	Isotropic; lattice; trivial topology	Anisotropic; network; non-trivial topology
Physical space	Geometric; abstract; flat	Material; real; rugged
Type of system	Closed; conservative; ergodic	Open; dissipative; nonergodic
System dynamics	Deterministic	Undecidable
Attractor	Fixed point; equilibrium	Manifold, strange attractors, etc.; multiple, local, punctuated equilibria; self-organised criticality
Origins of novelty	Exogenous	Endogenous

References

ACKERMAN, F. (2002): Still dead after all these years: interpreting the failure of general equilibrium theory. *Journal of Economic Methodology 9* (2): 119–139.

ALCHIAN, A. (1950): Uncertainty, evolution, and economic theory. *Journal of Political Economy 58* (2): 211–222.

ALEXANDER, S. (1920): *Space, Time and Deity. The Gifford Lectures at Glasgow, 1916-1918.* London: Macmillan.

ALLEN, P.M. (1997): *Cities and Regions as Self-Organizing Systems. Models of Complexity.* London: Gordon & Breach Science Publishers.

ANDERSON, P.W., ARROW, K.J. & PINES, D. (1988): *The Economy as an Evolving Complex System.* Santa Fe Institute studies in the sciences of complexity.

ARNSPERGER, C. & VAROUFAKIS, Y. (2006): What is neoclassical economics? *Post-autistic Economics Review no. 38.*

ARTHUR, W.B. (1999): Complexity and the economy. *Science 284* (5411): 107–109.

ARTHUR, W.B., DURLAUF, S.N. & LANE, D.A. (1997): *The economy as an evolving complex system II.* Reading, MA: Addison-Wesley.

BAUMOL, W.J. (2004): Red-Queen games: arms races, rule of law and market economies. *Journal of Evolutionary Economics 14* (2): 237–247.

BEDAU, M.A. (2002): Downward causation and the autonomy of weak emergence. *Principia 6* (1): 5–50.

BEDAU, M.A. (1997): Weak emergence. *Noûs 31* (Suppl. 11): 375–399.

BEINHOCKER, E.D. (2007): *The Origin Of Wealth: Evolution, Complexity, and the Radical Remaking of Economics.* London: Random House.

BHASKAR, R. (1975): *A Realist Theory of Science.* 3rd edition. London: Verso.

BHASKAR, R. (1979): *The Possibility of Naturalism. A Philosophical Critique of the Contemporary Human Sciences.* 3rd edition. London: Routledge.

BOSCHMA, R.A. & FRENKEN, K. (2006): Why is economic geography not an evolutionary science? Towards an evolutionary economic geography. *Journal of Economic Geography* 6 (3): 273–302.

BROAD, C.D. (1925): *The Mind and Its Place in Nature.* London: Routledge & Kegan Paul.

COOKE, P. (1992): Regional innovation systems: Competitive regulation in the new Europe. *Geoforum 23*: 365-382.

CRUTCHFIELD, J.P. (1994): The calculi of emergence: computation, dynamics and induction. *Physica D: Nonlinear Phenomena 75* (1-3): 11–54.

DEBREU, G. (1974): Excess demand functions. *Journal of Mathematical Economics 1* (1): 15–21.

DOOLEY, K.J. (1997): A complex adaptive systems model of organization change. *Nonlinear Dynamics, Psychology, and Life Sciences 1* (1): 69–97.

DOPFER, K. (2001): *Evolutionary Economics: Program and Scope.* Dordrecht: Kluwer Academic Publishers.

DOPFER, K., FOSTER, J. & POTTS, J. (2004): Micro-meso-macro. *Journal of Evolutionary Economics 14* (3): 263–279.

DOPFER, K. & POTTS, J. (2004): Evolutionary realism: a new ontology for economics. *Journal of Economic Methodology 11* (2): 195–212.

DURLAUF, S. (2001): A framework for the study of individual behavior and social interactions. *Sociological Methodology 31* (1): 47-87.

EDQUIST, C., ed. (1997): *Systems of Innovation. Technologies, Institutions and Organizations.* London: Pinter.

EPSTEIN, J.M. (2007): Agent-based computational models and generative social science. In: EPSTEIN, J.M., ed.: *Generative Social Science: Studies in Agent-Based Computational Modeling,* pp. 4–46. Princeton, NJ: Princeton University Press.

EPSTEIN, J.M., ed. (2007): *Generative Social Science: Studies in Agent-Based Computational Modeling.* Princeton, NJ: Princeton University Press.

EPSTEIN, J.M. (2005): Remarks on the foundations of agent-based generative social science. In: TESFATSION, L. & JUDD, K.L., eds: *Handbook of Computational Economics, Vol. 2: Agent-based Computational Economics*, pp. 1585–1604. Amsterdam: North-Holland.

ETZKOWITZ, H., & L. LEYDESDORFF, eds (1997): *Universities in the global knowledge economy: A triple helix of university-industry-government relations.* London: Cassell.

FAGIOLO, G., WINDRUM, P. & MONETA, A. (2005): *Empirical validation of agent-based models: A critical survey.*

FRENKEN, K. (2006): Technological innovation and complexity theory. *Economics of Innovation and New Technology 15* (2): 137–155.

FULLER, T. & MORAN, P. (2000): Moving beyond metaphor: towards a methodology for grounding complexity in small business and entrepreneurship research. *Emergence 2*: 50–71.

FULLER, T. & MORAN, P. (2001): Small enterprises as complex adaptive systems: A methodological question? *Entrepreneurship and Regional Development 13*: 47–63.

GEORGESCU-ROEGEN, N. (1971): *The Entropy Law and the Economic Process.* Cambridge, MA: Harvard University Press.

GIBBONS, M., C. LIMOGES, H. NOWOTNY, S. SCHWARTZMAN, P. SCOTT, & M. TROW (1994): *The New Production of Knowledge: The Dynamics of Science and Research in Contemporary Societies.* London: Sage Publications.

HARTMANN, N. (1940): *Ontologie Vol. III: Der Aufbau der realen Welt : Grundriß der allgemeinen Kategorienlehre.* Berlin: Walter de Gruyter.

HEMPEL, C. G. (1965): *Aspects of Scientific Explanation and Other Essays in the Philosophy of Science.* New York, NY: Free Press.

HODGSON, G.M. (1992): Thorstein Veblen and post-Darwinian economics. *Cambridge Journal of Economics 16* (3): 285–301.

HODGSON, G.M. (1993a): *Economics and Evolution. Bringing Life back into Economics.* Ann Arbor, MI: University of Michigan Press.

HODGSON, G.M. (1993b): The Mecca of Alfred Marshall. *Economic Journal 103* (417): 406–415.

HODGSON, G.M. (1998): The approach of institutional economics. *Journal of Economic Literature 36* (1): 166–192.

HOLLAND, J.H. (1996): *Hidden Order. How Adaptation Builds Complexity.* New York, NY: Basic Books.

HUMPHREYS, P. (1997): Emergence, not supervenience. *Philosophy of Science 64*: S337–S345.

HUSSERL, E. (1901): *Logische Untersuchungen. Zweite Teil: Untersuchungen zur Phänomenologie und Theorie der Erkenntnis. Vol. II1*. Tübingen: Niemeyer.

KEHOE, T.J. (1985): Multiplicity of equilibria and comparative statics. *Quarterly Journal of Economics 100* (1): 119–147.

KEMENY, J., & P. OPPENHEIM (1956): On reduction. *Philosophical Studies 7* (1): 6-19.

KEMP, M.C. & SHIMOMURA, K. (2002): The Sonnenschein–Debreu–Mantel proposition and the theory of international trade. *Review of International Economics 10* (4): 671–679.

KIM, J. (1978): Supervenience and nomological incommensurables. *American Philosophical Quarterly 15*: 149–156.

KIM, J. (1999): Making sense of emergence. *Philosophical studies 95* (1): 3–36.

KIM, J. (2006): Emergence: Core ideas and issues. *Synthese 151* (3): 547–559.

KIRMAN, A.P. (1992): Whom or what does the representative individual represent? *Journal of Economic Perspectives 6* (2): 117–136.

KIRMAN, A.P. & KOCH, K.J. (1986): Market excess demand in exchange economies with identical preferences and collinear endowments. *Review of Economic Studies 53* (3): 457–463.

KUHN, T.S. (1962): *The Structure of Scientific Revolutions.* Chicago: University of Chicago Press.

LANGTON, C. (1992): Life at the edge of chaos. In: C. Langton, *et al.*: *Artificial Life II.* Reading, MA: Addison-Wesley.

LANSING, J.S. (2002): 'Artificial societies' and the social sciences. *Artificial Life 8* (3): 279–292.

LAPLACE, P.-S. (1825): *Essai Philosophique sur les Probabilités.* Paris: Bachelier.

LAWSON, T. (1996): Developments in economics as realist social theory. *Review of Social Economy 54* (4): 405 – 422.

LAWSON, T. (1997): *Economics and Reality.* London: Routledge.

LAWSON, T. (2001): Two responses to the failings of modern economics: the instrumentalist and the realist. *Review of Population and Social Policy 10*: 155–181.

LEWES, G. H. (1875): *Problems of Life and Mind.* London: Kegan Paul.

LEWONTIN, R.C. (1983): Gene, organism, and environment. In: D.S. BENDALL: *Evolution from Molecules to Men,* pp. 273–285. Cambridge: Cambridge University Press.

LLERENA, P. & LORENTZ, A. (2003): Alternative theories on economic growth and the co–evolution of macro–dynamics and technological change: A Survey. *Laboratory of Economics and Management Working Paper Series,* no. 2003-27. Pisa, Italy.

LUNDVALL, B.-Å., ed. (1992): *National Systems of Innovation: Towards a Theory of Innovation and Interactive Learning.* London: Pinter.

MANTEL, R.R. (1976): Homothetic preferences and community excess demand functions. *Journal of Economic Theory 12* (2): 197–201.

MANTEL, R.R. (1974): On the characterization of aggregate excess demand. *Journal of Economic Theory 7* (3): 348–353.

MARKOSE, S.M. (2005): Computability and evolutionary complexity: Markets as complex adaptive systems (CAS). *Economic Journal 115* (504): F159–F192.

MARSHALL, A. (1920): *Principles of Economics.* 8th edition. London: Macmillan.

MAYNARD SMITH, J. (1989): *Evolutionary Genetics.* Oxford: Oxford University Press.

MCLAUGHLIN, B. P., & K. BENNETT (2005): Supervenience. In: EDWARD N. ZALTA, ed.: *The Stanford Encyclopedia of Philosophy* (Winter 2011 Edition). http://plato.stanford.edu

MILL, J. S. (1843): *System of Logic. Ratiocinative and Inductive.* London: Longmans, Green, Reader, and Dyer.

MORGAN, C. L. (1931): *Emergent Evolution. The Gifford Lectures, 1922.* New York, NY: Henry Holt.

MOULINES, C.U. (2006): Ontology, reduction, emergence: A general frame. *Synthese 151* (3): 313–323.

NAGEL, E. (1961): *The Structure of Science.* London: Routledge and Kegan Paul.

NELSON, R.R. & WINTER, S.G. (1982): *An Evolutionary Theory of Economic Change.* Cambridge, MA: Belknap Press.

NELSON, R.R., WINTER, S.G. & SCHUETTE, H.L. (1976): Technical change in an evolutionary model. *Quarterly Journal of Economics 90* (1): 90–118.

NICKLES, T. (1973): Two concepts of inter-theoretic reduction. *Journal of Philosophy 70* (7): 181-201.

O'CONNOR, T. (1994): Emergent properties. *American Philosophical Quarterly 31*: 97–98.

O'CONNOR, T. & WONG, H.-Y. (2005): The metaphysics of emergence. *Noûs 39* (4): 658-678.

RICHTER, M.K. & WONG, K.-C. (1999): Non-computability of competitive equilibrium. *Economic Theory 14* (1): 1–27.

RIZVI, S.A.T. (2006): The Sonnenschein-Mantel-Debreu results after thirty years. *History of political economy 38* (Suppl.1): 228–245.

ROBERTS, J. & SONNENSCHEIN, H. (1977): On the foundations of the theory of monopolistic competition. *Econometrica 45* (1): 101.

ROSEN, R. (1999): *Essays on Life Itself.* New York, NY: Columbia University Press.

RUBINSTEIN, A. (1997): *Modeling Bounded Rationality.* Cambridge, MA: MIT Press.

RUEGER, A. (2000): Physical emergence, diachronic and synchronic. *Synthese 124* (3): 297–322.

SAARI, D.G. (1985): Iterative price mechanisms. *Econometrica 53* (5): 1117–1131.

SAMUELSON, L. (1998): *Evolutionary Games and Equilibrium Selection.* Cambridge, MA: MIT Press.

SARKAR, S. (1992): Models of reduction and categories of reductionism. *Synthese 91* (3): 167-194.

SCALTSAS, T. (1990): Is a whole identical to its parts? *Mind 99* (396): 583-598.

SCHAFFNER, K. F. (1967): Approaches to reduction. *Philosophy of Science 34* (2): 137-147.

SCHARF, D. C. (1989): Quantum measurement and the program for the unity of science. *Philosophy of Science 56* (4): 601-623.

SCHUMPETER, J.A. (1908): *Das Wesen und der Hauptinhalt der theoretischen Nationalökonomie.* Leipzig: Duncker & Humblot.

SCHUMPETER, J.A. (1934): *The Theory of Economic Development. An Inquiry into Profits, Capital, Credit, Interest and the Business Cycle.* Cambridge, MA: Harvard University Press.

SCHUMPETER, J.A. (1942): *Capitalism, Socialism and Democracy.* London: Harper & Bros.

SILBERSTEIN, M. (2002): Reduction, emergence and explanation. In: MACHAMER, P. & SILBERSTEIN, M., eds: *The Blackwell Guide to the Philosophy of Science,* pp. 80–127. Oxford: Blackwell.

SILBERSTEIN, M. & MCGEEVER, J. (1999): The search for ontological emergence. *Philosophical Quarterly 49* (195): 182–200.

SIMON, H.A. (1991): Bounded rationality and organizational learning. *Organization Science 2* (1): 125–134.

SIMON, H.A. (1976): From substantive to procedural rationality. In: LATSIS, S., ed.: *Method and Appraisal in Economics.* Cambridge: Cambridge University Press.

SIMON, H.A. (1956): Rational choice and the structure of the environment. *Psychological Review 63* (2): 129–138.

SONNENSCHEIN, H. (1973): Do Walras' identity and continuity characterize the class of community excess demand functions? *Journal of Economic Theory 6* (4): 345–354.

STOKER, T.M. (1984): Completeness, distribution restrictions, and the form of aggregate functions. *Econometrica 52* (4): 887–907.

TELLER, P. (1992): A contemporary look at emergence. In: BECKERMANN, A., FLOHR, H. & KIM, J., eds: *Emergence or Reduction?*, pp. 139–153. Berlin: Walter de Gruyter.

TESFATSION, L. (2005): Agent-based computational economics: A constructive approach to economic theory. In: TESFATSION, L. & JUDD, K.L., eds: *Handbook of Computational Economics, Vol. 2: Agent-based Computational Economics*, pp. 831–880. Amsterdam: North-Holland.

TESFATSION, L. (2006): Agent-based computational modeling and macroeconomics. In: COLANDER, D., ed.: *Post Walrasian Macroeconomics: Beyond the Dynamic Stochastic General Equilibrium Model*, pp. 175–202. Cambridge: Cambridge University Press.

VAN CLEVE, J. (1990): Mind-dust or magic? Panpsychism versus emergence. *Philosophical Perspectives 4*: 215–226.

VAN VALEN, L. (1973): A new evolutionary law. *Evolutionary Theory 1* (1): 1–30.

VEBLEN, T. (1904): *The Theory of Business Enterprise.* New York, NY: Charles Scribner's sons.

VEBLEN, T. (1898): Why is economics not an evolutionary science? *Quarterly Journal of Economics 12* (4): 373–397.

VEGA-REDONDO, F. (2007): *Complex Social Networks.* Cambridge: Cambridge University Press.

VEGA-REDONDO, F. (1996): *Evolution, Games, and Economic Behaviour.* Oxford: Oxford University Press.

WEBER, M. (1921): *Wirtschaft und Gesellschaft: Grundriß der Verstehenden Soziologie.* Tübingen: Mohr.

WEIBULL, J.W. (1997): *Evolutionary Game Theory.* Cambridge, MA: MIT press.

WEINTRAUB, E.R. (1977): The microfoundations of macroeconomics: A critical survey. *Journal of Economic Literature 15* (1): 1–23.

WILSON, A.G. (1974): *Urban and Regional Models in Geography and Planning.* London: Wiley.

WIMSATT, W.C. (1976): Reductionism, levels of organization, and the mind-body problem. In: GLOBUS, G.G, MAXWELL, G. & SAVODNIK, I. eds: *Consciousness and the Brain,* pp. 205-267. New York, NY: Plenum.

WIMSATT, W.C. (2000): Emergence as non-aggregativity and the biases of reductionisms. *Foundations of Science 5* (3): 269–297.

WOLFRAM, S. (1984): Universality and complexity in cellular automata. *Physica D: Nonlinear Phenomena 10* (1-2): 1–35.

Notes

[1] These include LUNDVALL, 1992; EDQUIST, 1997; COOKE, 1992; ETZKOWITZ & LEYDESDORFF, 1997; GIBBONS *et al.*, 1994.
[2] See, among others, ALCHIAN, 1950; NELSON & WINTER, 1982; HODGSON, 1993a; DOPFER, 2001.
[3] This includes ANDERSON *et al.*, 1988; ARTHUR *et al.*, 1997; BEINHOCKER, 2007.
[4] *Bridge law* is a well-defined biconditional between nomically coextensive predicates of the reduced and reducing theories.
[5] Models along these lines include KEMENY & OPPENHEIM, 1956; SCHAFFNER, 1967; NICKLES, 1973; WIMSATT, 1976, et al.
[6] The origins of the epistemological reductionism found in NAGEL, 1961, but also of the deductive-nomological method of explanation by HEMPEL, 1965, and their successors should be sought in the logical positivism of the 'Wiener Kreis' of Carnap, Neurath, Feigl and others.
[7] DOPFER *et al.*, 2004, call this 'algebraicism'.
[8] This precept has been most explicitly advocated by LAPLACE, 1825.
[9] The concept of *Walrasian auctioneer* was invented, not without a hint of irony, by the post-Keynesian economist Axel Leijonhufvud.
[10] The term *methodische Individualismus* was coined by SCHUMPETER, 1908, but it is considered to have been introduced in modern economics by the work of Carl Menger.
[11] An *eliminativist statement*, i.e. strongly reductionist in the sense of mereological fusion, would be, for instance, that the society is *nothing but* an aggregation of individuals.
[12] HEMPEL, 1965.
[13] There are alternative approaches to Walrasian tâtonnement which model it as a centralised real-time auction; this does not, however, increase the tenability of the theory.
[14] The latter assumption is relaxed in equilibrium models of imperfect and asymmetric information, it is therefore not essential for the neoclassical theory.
[15] There he famously stated that: "[the] Mecca of the economist lies in economic biology rather than in economic dynamics. But biological conceptions are more complex than those of mechanics…".
[16] See VEGA-REDONDO, 1996; WEIBULL, 1997; SAMUELSON, 1998.
[17] See, for instance, LLERENA & LORENTZ, 2003, for a survey on evolutionary theories of economic growth and an interesting proposal on how to bridge the gap between macro-evolution and micro-dynamics of technological change by integrating the New Growth Theory and Kaldorian cumulative causation in an evolutionary context.
[18] Other forms of symbiosis are *parasitism* (beneficial to one agent and detrimental to the other), *commensalism* (beneficial to one agent and neutral to the other), and *amensalism* (detrimental to one agent and neutral to the other).
[19] A set of conditions identified by HOLLAND, 1996, which are often considered as a standard definition of a CAS, are four properties, namely 'aggregation', 'nonlinearity', 'flows' and 'diversity', and three mechanisms, namely 'tagging', 'internal models' and 'building blocks'. These by no means constitute a rigorous definition, but just a description of certain aspects of a CAS. 'Aggregation'

corresponds to *multilevel emergence*, 'flows' refers to the structured exchange of information, energy or matter through networks, 'tagging' to *assortativity*, 'building blocks' to *modularity*, and 'internal models' to *schema-based cognition* (explained in Chapter 2).

[20] *Negentropy*, a term coined by L. Brillouin, is similar to E. Schrödinger's *negative entropy*, and a near-equivalent to information, often seen as a measure of *systemic complexity*.

[21] *Attractor* or *attracting set* is an invariant subset of the phase space of a dynamical system, towards which the trajectories of the system within a given *attraction basin* converge in the course of time, irrespective of the initial conditions. A system may have multiple attractors. Unlike dissipative systems, conservative systems do not have attractors, as they settle in a stable state determined by their initial conditions. An attractor can be a fixed point corresponding to a steady state in the simplest of the cases (*point attractor*), a limit cycle that corresponds to stable oscillations (*periodic attractor*), a n-dimensional manifold, such as a hypertorus, that corresponds to compound oscillations (*quasi-periodic attractor*) or of fractal dimension corresponding to deterministic chaos (*strange attractor*). As WOLFRAM, 1984, observes, "evolution to attractors from arbitrary initial states allows for 'self-organising' behaviour, in which structure may evolve at large times from structureless initial states".

[22] *Critical point* is the point at which a dynamical system undergoes a *phase transition*, i.e. the phenomenon that occurs when small changes in the parameters of the system cause a qualitative change in its aggregate properties [DURLAUF, 2001]. An *ordinary criticality*, such as the point of phase transition from water to ice, is obtained by exogenously varying a control parameter – in this case temperature. On the contrary, a self-organised criticality results from endogenous dynamics of certain classes of systems independently of the value of any control parameter.

[23] *Turing incomputability* is equivalent to *non-simulability*, which relates to the insolvability of Hilbert's *Entscheidungsproblem*, independently proven by Church and Turing, and Gödel's famous *Incompleteness Theorems*.

[24] Condensed-matter physics (CMP) is the branch of physical sciences which explores the macro- and microscopic properties of matter, how the latter emerges from interacting atoms and subatomic particles, and what physical properties it exhibits as a result of these interactions. 'Hard' CMP is concerned with the quantum field aspect of matter, while 'soft' CMP studies the non-quantic properties of condensed matter, uses statistical mechanics, and is the main source of inspiration for complex systems theory.

[25] The statistical mechanics approach and the thermodynamical metaphor have inspired a young branch of 'complexity economics' known as 'thermoeconomics' or 'biophysical economics'.

[26] By 'nontrivial typology' FRENKEN, 2006, refers to graphs which are not null or complete. However, a nontrivial topology should also exclude regular lattices.

[27] The revival of emergentism in the modern era is connected with the work of LEWES, 1875, preceded by MILL, 1843, and followed by a generation of 'British emergentists' such as ALEXANDER, 1920; BROAD, 1925; MORGAN, 1931, et al.; or in the Continental post-Kantian tradition with the idiosyncratic work of HARTMANN, 1940.

[28] The Aristotelian theory of mereology which unfolds in *Metaphysica* does not contain this phrase as such.
[29] The study of parthood relationships is the subject-matter of the domain of philosophy known as 'mereology', whose origins and systematic foundations can be traced as far back as Aristotle's *Metaphysica*. In more recent times mereology is established as a formal branch of philosophy in Edmund Husserl's third Logical Investigation "On the Theory of Parts and Wholes" [HUSSERL, 1901], and it receives its name and a highly formalist formulation by Stanisław Leśniewski, one of the founding members of the so-called 'Polish School of Analytical Philosophy' or the 'Lwów-Warsaw School of Logic'.
[30] One of the first modern-age emergentists, MILL, 1843: III.6§1, alludes to the same principle as follows: "All organised bodies are composed of parts, similar to those composing inorganic nature, and which have even themselves existed in an inorganic state; but the phenomena of life, which result from the juxtaposition of those parts in a certain manner, bear no analogy to any of the effects which would be produced by the action of the component substances considered as mere physical agents. To whatever degree we might imagine our knowledge of the properties of the several ingredients of a living body to be extended and perfected, it is certain that no mere summing up of the separate actions of those elements will ever amount to the action of the living body itself."
[31] Monism is the philosophical premise that the natural world is constituted by a single 'substance', contrary – for instance – to Cartesian 'substance dualism' which assumes that there are two types of substance, a 'mental' and a 'material' one. Most ontological monisms of relevance to the philosophy of science are essentially materialist or 'neutral', but there are, of course, idealist monisms of the transcendental kind.
[32] As KIM, 2006: 548, observes in a critical tone, "the intuitive associations this word evokes in us do not add up to a concept robust enough to do any useful work, or even to serve as helpful constraints on a theoretical account or construction of the concept. 'Emergence' is very much a term of philosophical trade".
[33] These conditions combined distinguish emergence from ontological reductionism – which is also monist but claims that higher-level properties are fully reducible to lower-level, 'basal' ones, from epiphenomenalism – which is monist, allows for novel irreducible properties, but claims that they are not downward causal, and finally, from all forms of ontological dualism, which accept the existence of more than one 'substances'.
[34] The relationship between supervenience and reduction is a source of confusion in analytical philosophy, as it leads many to believe that (mereological) supervenience is a form of ontological reduction: SARKAR, 1992, for instance, calls ontological reduction 'constitutive' and subsumes under this term mereological supervenience; SILBERSTEIN, 2002: 83, also considers mereological supervenience as a form of ontological reduction. In this chapter, following MCLAUGHLIN & BENNETT, 2005: §3.3, I treat supervenience and reduction as distinct concepts.
[35] *Structural properties* are *resultant* macro-properties. O'CONNOR & WONG, 2005: 663, define a *structural property* as follows: "A property *S* is structural if and only

if proper parts of particulars having *S* have properties not identical with *S* and jointly stand in relation *R*, and this state of affairs is the particular's having *S*."

[36] Confusingly, EPSTEIN, 2007, claims that the main instrument of the generative method, agent-based modelling, is incompatible with classical emergentism. The version of emergence advocated by classical emergentists is, however, the strong, ontological version, which is also widely contested by many epistemologists.

[37] Again here, EPSTEIN, 2007, in his narrow interpretation of the reductionism-emergentism divide claims the opposite, namely that ABM are reductionist.

[38] In brief, the fact that there are many different microspecifications from which the same macrostructure of interest can be 'grown'.

[39] Even this rudimentary hypothetical space of transactions is eliminated by two different devices of neoclassical theory: the Walrasian auctioneer eliminates the need for transactions *before* the attainment of a general equilibrium; the representative agent does the same *after* the attainment of a general equilibrium.

[40] 'Hierarchically' in this sentence does not refer to organisational but to ontological hierarchy.

[41] 'NUTS' stands for 'Nomenclature d'Unités Territoriales Statistiques'. It is the standard classification system of subnational administrative divisions used by Eurostat for statistical purposes. It currently comprises three levels mainly determined by population size, complemented with two more levels of 'Local Administrative Units' (LAU) below.

Chapter 2

The emergence of technological knowledge in the mesoeconomic plexus

Introduction

This chapter brings together the previously identified elements of the 'systemic paradigm' in the context of economic geography by connecting the theoretical premises with economic phenomena circumscribed in an *extended geographical space*, i.e. a geographical space with a *relational* dimension. Geographical space had hitherto been purged from mainstream economic theory, and even when it was re-introduced in certain 'peripheral' subfields of the discipline (e.g. urban, regional and geographical economics), it was in the form of an abstract, immaterial, Euclidean space – a space which was more geometrical than geographical. Moreover, economic geography (with few exceptions reviewed here) has traditionally limited itself in the study of socio-economic phenomena related to the physical dimension of space, leaving outside its scope the most rich in economic intuition aspect of space, the relational aspect. The proposed systemic paradigm is intended to reinstate not only the geographical space in economic theory but also the relational dimension of the geographical space in economic geography. By this approach the 'extended' space mediates the interactions of economic agents, and by extension, the formation of economic relationships and of the division of labour.

This chapter also synthesises in the above context a theory of techo-economic cognition aiming to explain how technological knowledge comes about in relational space. The neoclassical paradigm is inherently ill-equipped when it comes to explaining and modelling processes like technological knowledge creation, which is governed by out-of-equilibrium complex dynamics characterised by novelty and structural change. As a result, technological knowledge remains a black box for mainstream economic theory. Neoclassical growth models, for instance, treat technological change as exogenous: In the neoclassical Solow-Swan model, technological progress is the only determinant of the long-run (steady-state) growth rate, but the rate of technological progress itself is exogenously determined, and therefore out of the scope of the model.[1] More recently, endogenous growth models 'endogenise' technological change by incorporating in the production function important determinants of economic growth relevant to knowledge creation and diffusion, such as human capital and R&D investment, thus allowing for increasing returns and technological knowledge spillovers.[2] Despite the rhetoric about that being the third wave of an 'increasing returns/ imperfect competition revolution' [KRUGMAN, 1998], endogenous growth models are improved extensions of the neoclassical growth model, and still fail to explain why and how economic cognition and technological knowledge emerge in economic systems – these are just taken as given. The 'endogenisation' therefore of technological change in these models is only stylised, not substantial. This limitation results from the fact that they are founded on the same reductionist and equilibrium-centred epistemology as the neoclassical model.

In this chapter it is argued that the emergence of technological knowledge can only be explained when examined at the *meso domain* of the economy – the locus of interactions of economic agents and of articulation of economic relationships. This chapter introduces the concept of *mesoeconomic plexus* as the fundamental ontology of this domain, whose instantiations behave as complex adaptive systems and exhibit a network-like, nontrivial topology. Individual techno-economic cognition is seen in this context as the outcome of a co-adaptation process which takes place inside the mesoeconomic plexus, while collective knowledge creation is treated as a systemic phenomenon of a particular type of mesoeconomic plexus, the *knowledge plexus*. This emergent phenomenon is characterised by co-evolutionary dynamics and *economies of complexity* rather than by traditional economies of scale.

The rest of this chapter is organised as follows: The second section reviews the conceptions of space in different strands of economic geography from traditional location theories and the neoclassical legacy of Isard's 'regional science', through the 'New Economic Geography', to heterodox approaches, including the neo-Schumpeterian evolutionary approach, and the relational approach which lays emphasis on the relational space. The third section re-defines the relational space as the generative structure where the interactions of economic agents take place and proposes the enhancement of the scope of economic geography with its inclusion in the picture. This section then presents the relational space as a nexus of interdependencies where not only production externalities but, most importantly, an *external division of labour* is realised. It then presents the meso domain of the economy as the par excellence relational space, whose fundamental ontological category is the *mesoeconomic plexus*. The rest of the section develops the notion of mesoeconomic plexus, the hypothesis that it behaves as a complex adaptive system, and the premise of *economies of complexity* as a distinct form of increasing returns in certain types of organisational structures from that of increasing returns to scale. The last section of this chapter begins by presenting a typology of economically relevant knowledge. It then examines the relationship between knowledge management and the organisation of production starting from the 'objectivist' knowledge-based theory of the firm and continuing with the modes of industrial organisation. The chapter concludes by sketching a systemic theory of synergetic, *distributed* knowledge production in economic systems, starting from a 'constructivist' theory of individual cognition by economic agents on the basis of co-adaptation. Here distributed technological knowledge is presented as an emergent phenomenon of the knowledge plexus.

Economic geographies and the conception of space

Mainstream economics has always neglected space. KRUGMAN, 1998, attributes this neglect to the lack, up until the 1990s, of an analytical apparatus for modelling economies of scale, which he identifies as the fundamental mechanism behind the geographic concentration of economic activity. He also claims that all past theories of location entailed implicitly or explicitly the existence of economies of scale, which inevitably undermine perfect competition. In the 1950s and 60s, when location theory was becoming popular in US academia mainly through the work of Isard – the argument goes – no workable model of imperfect competition was known to the economists and, as a result, they simply chose to ignore space, increasing returns and agglomeration economies altogether.

Krugman's justification is rather lame. The real reasons for the a-spatiality of mainstream economic theory are not conjunctural and practical, or even methodological, but substantial and epistemological: In the neoclassical world there is no need for space, since there is no real interpersonal interaction between economic agents; moreover, the economic subject is not an entity bound by physical laws, but rather by the behavioural determinism ensuing from the axioms of the theory. The problem of space in that world enters only tangentially through the issue of land, as a factor of production, and land use, and for this reason spatial economics remains a peripheral sub-discipline of 'orthodox' economic science.

The a-spatiality of neoclassical economics is one more on the long list of its epistemological reductionisms, which ensue from its axioms. This is a substantial reason for a permanent divorce with economic geography, whose subject-matter is precisely the spatiality of economic phenomena and agents. But the question which naturally emerges is, what type of spatiality? HARVEY, 1973; 2006, distinguishes three construals of space, the *absolute*, the *relative* and the *relational*, which he connects to Descartes, Einstein and Leibniz respectively. This classification is not, however, completely unproblematic: To start with, the concept of 'relative space' lacks theoretical clarity, and is difficult to justify as a distinct category from that of 'relational space', especially in the context of economic geography, as their perceived attributes are almost identical. Moreover, the association of the former with the relativistic space-time is rather crude and seems to have been inspired by popular science.[3] As a result, the distinction between relative and relational, but also between absolute and relative spaces is blurred. I propose a different categorisation of the conceptions of space relevant to economic geography, which distinguishes between the *geometrical* space, i.e. a space conceived as an immaterial, abstract mathematical entity (which can be Euclidean, Minkowskian, Riemannian, etc.); the *physical* or 'cartographical' space, i.e. the reified, material space conceived as a thing-in-itself, and whose properties emanate from physical laws; and the *relational* space – a space shaped by socio-economic relationships, with properties emanating from them.

As we see in the following paragraph, the neoclassical space, whenever it emerges in theory, is predominantly a geometrical space. Physical space is traditionally the subject-matter of physical geography, but very often it is treated as pertaining to the disciplinary domain of economic geography as well. This constitutes what I call a 'physicalist' fallacy – the misconception of economic-geographical space as an ontological category in itself with a priori properties beyond those conferred to it by socio-economic relationships. The approach of this book is that the space of economic geography should be construed as a *relational space,* which may or may not overlap with physical space, depending on the extent to which the generative relationships of the former are conditioned by physical proximity.

The neoclassical space

Regional science and location theories

Isard's 'Location and Space-Economy' is widely acknowledged as the point of departure for a new field in economics known as 'regional science' [ISARD, 1956]. This book aspires to lay the foundations of a general theory for the location of economic activity incorporating the Walrasian general equilibrium and the Ricardian international trade theories; it is therefore vehemently neoclassical. The strand of theory Isard introduced in Anglosaxon academia, as a matter of fact, follows the long tradition of the continental (predominantly German) 'Raumwirtschaft' School of spatial economic theory established more than a century earlier by von Thünen and his successors, Launhardt, A. Weber, Christaller and Lösch. The central problem of this earlier tradition is almost exclusively the optimal location problem vis-à-vis transport costs, mainly for agriculture and industry. All treatments of the location problem in this tradition are predominantly of a mathematical, specifically geometrical, nature. In the still largely agricultural state of Mecklenburg of the early 19th century, VON THÜNEN, 1826, is principally concerned with the optimal use of agricultural land, assuming profit-maximising behaviour of rationally optimising farmers, and a unipolar and totally isotropic in geomorphological terms space resembling an abstract Euclidean space, within an 'isolated state', i.e. a state completely cut-off from external influences. As a result of the farmers' optimising behaviour and the diminishing with distance 'locational rent' of the land, this unipolar space will be organised in concentric rings surrounding a perfectly centrally located city-market, with different land uses determined by the opportunity cost of the corresponding agricultural activities and types of crop.

Later theorists from the same School of thought, having experienced the rapid industrialisation of the Prussian and other German states' economies in the late 19th century, are concerned almost exclusively with the optimal location of industry. WEBER, 1909, drawing considerably on previous work by LAUNHARDT, 1872; 1885,[4] develops a theory of industrial location on the basis of cost minimisation, determined by the material index of the product and the related transport costs,[5] labour costs, and agglomeration economies. He is one of the first to explicitly recognise that "an agglomerative factor [...] is an advantage or a cheapening of production or marketing which results from the fact that production is carried on to some considerable extent at one place, while a deglomerative factor is a cheapening of production which results from the decentralisation of production" [WEBER, 1909 (1929: 126, English translation)]. In addition to that, he distinguishes between two types of scale economies, those accruing from the simple enlargement of a productive unit, i.e. a plant, and those from the "close local association of several plants". Weber's space is almost identical to that of von Thünen's, namely isolated and isotropic, the only difference being that the model does not explicitly assume a unipolar configuration, but allows a limitedly polycentric spatial structure in which, however, the location of production factors remains fixed. He additionally assumes explicitly a perfectly competitive market, ubiquity of and unrestricted access to certain natural resources, and the local specificity of labour and other production inputs.

Later in the century CHRISTALLER, 1933, lays the foundations of modern regional planning with his influential 'central place theory',[6] which conceives the spatial configuration of (urban) settlements in a region as a hierarchically nested system of interconnected entities dominated by a few 'central places', i.e. cities whose centrality is determined by their unique ability to supply goods and services not available in their surrounding settlements. Lösch, who is considered, jointly with Isard, as the founder of 'Regional Science', extends in a formal and mathematically rigorous manner Christaller's ideas of central places, albeit from a totally different perspective: his magnum opus develops a spatially distributed general equilibrium model which assumes the existence of self-sufficient farms located on a spatial lattice, and proves that the optimal configuration of this lattice would be hexagonal [LÖSCH, 1940]. In line with the aforementioned spatial theorists, both Christaller's and Lösch's models assume (the former implicitly and the latter explicitly) a competitive market, distance-dependent exchange and transaction costs, and an abstract and isotropic, despite its polycentricity, geometrical space. As KRUGMAN, 1998, remarks, both models imply the existence of agglomeration economies but, given the lack of analytical tools for economies of scale, "both seem to be describing planning solutions rather than market outcomes".

The New Economic Geography

In more recent times, a response to the absence of space from mainstream economic theory has taken the form of a 'geographical turn' in economics [MARTIN, 1999], most prominently expressed in Krugman's 'New Economic Geography' (henceforth NEG). The subject matter of the NEG is the concentration of economic activity in geographical space, notably the phenomenon of agglomeration, at various spatial scales ranging from that of city neighbourhoods to that of city formation per se, and from that where industrial districts emerge to that where interregional disparities and the core-periphery dual structure of the global economy are generated [FUJITA & KRUGMAN, 2004]. In accordance with Marshall's *Principles of Economics* [MARSHALL, 1920], KRUGMAN, 1992, identifies labour market pooling, the supply of specialised intermediate goods and services, and technological spillovers as the main forces driving the process of agglomeration.

KRUGMAN, 1998, sees the reinstatement of space in economic theory which led to the emergence of the NEG in the 1990s as the fourth wave of the 'increasing returns/ imperfect competition revolution', following the modelling of imperfect competition by the 'New Industrial

Organisation', the modelling of international trade in the presence of increasing returns by the 'New Trade Theory', and the introduction of increasing returns in models of macroeconomic growth by the 'New Growth Theory' (i.e. endogenous growth theory). Krugman defines the NEG as "[a] genre: a style of economic analysis which tries to explain the spatial structure of the economy using certain technical tricks to produce models in which there are increasing returns and markets are characterised by imperfect competition" [Ibid.: 164].

Despite the claims for breaking away from economic orthodoxy, the NEG is still based on an extended neoclassical paradigm, similarly to all other 'waves' of the alleged revolution. All models of NEG, for instance, presented in one of its bibles, FUJITA *et al.*, 1999, are equilibrium-based,[7] and despite being macro-models, they implicitly share the neoclassical commitment to instrumental rationality and methodological individualism, as Krugman himself makes clear elsewhere [KRUGMAN, 1993].[8] As suggested in the previous chapter, increasing returns are not in principle inconsistent with the neoclassical paradigm but only with the specific model of competitive equilibrium, which however is not an indispensable feature of neoclassicism.[9] On the other hand, all three essential underpinnings of the neoclassical paradigm (individualistic-instrumental rationality, ex ante equilibration and reductionist aggregation) are reproduced explicitly in the general theory of location and implicitly in the NEG. The perception of space in the NEG is not very new either: Although this space is not the Euclidean isotropic continuum of regional science, but indeed a space with a variable topology largely shaped by agglomeration effects, it is still a predominantly abstract geometrical space with an a priori physical dimension.

Space in heterodox economic geographies

Despite its affinity to economic theory, economic geography retains a certain degree of autonomy vis-à-vis mainstream economics stemming from its eclecticism and cross-disciplinarity. This epistemological autonomy allows the discipline to be more open to paradigmatic change. Indeed, since the turn of the century a totally new genre of economic geography is emerging, which makes the NEG look like the last pièce-de-résistance of the neoclassical paradigm in economic geography.

Institutionalism and regulationism in economic geography

'Old' and 'new' institutionalism

In economics and political economy a sharp distinction should be drawn between two homonymous but diverging varieties of institutionalism: On the one hand the 'old' School founded on the works of Veblen, Commons, and Mitchell, is the precursor to contemporary institutional political economy and evolutionary institutional economics. This wide and heterogeneous strand includes economists (some of whom are also characterised as 'post-Keynesians') as diverse as Galbraith, Minsky, Myrdal, and more recently Hodgson, and Ha-Joon Chang. The 'old' institutionalist school of thought following the Veblenian tradition rejects the neoclassical paradigm, acknowledges the inherent instability of the financial markets and of capitalism [MINSKY, 1986], the influence of asymmetric corporate power in society and polity [VEBLEN, 1904; GALBRAITH, 1967], the disposition of socio-economic dynamics to generate uneven development through circular cumulative causation [MYRDAL, 1957], the bounded rationality of economic agents and their inclination to satisficing rather than optimising behaviour [SIMON, 1956], the fact that human choice is mostly based on norms and habits and adaptive learning rather than (global) rationality [HODGSON, 1998].

On the other hand the School of 'New Institutional Economics' embraces the neoclassical paradigm and extends it in the direction of the theory of the firm [COASE, 1937], the allocation of property rights in the face of externalities [COASE, 1960], transaction costs [CHEUNG, 1969; WILLIAMSON, 1979], the impact of institutions and institutional change on growth [NORTH, 1987; 1990], but also bounded rationality and asymmetric information, rent-seeking and public choice [KRUEGER, 1974; TULLOCK *et al.*, 2002], public goods and collective action [OLSON, 1965].

These two strands of institutionalism are fundamentally different: A central premise of 'old' institutionalism, in sharp contrast to neoclassicism, is the inseparability of the economy from the socio-political context in which it is embedded; as a result of this approach, even prices are treated as social conventions formed by institutions [HODGSON, 1998]. As HODGSON, 1998, notes, institutions provide the cognitive framework for interpreting sensory data and routines for transforming information into useful knowledge, while they ensure the stability of socioeconomic systems by constraining the diverse actions of many agents.

The 'old' School's preferred approach to economic phenomena is the historical and case-specific analysis as opposed to the reductionist, deductivist and formalist methodology of neoclassical economics. In sharp contrast to these, neo-institutionalism embraces methodological individualism and aims to explain the emergence of institutions on the basis of individualistic rational choice. As HODGSON, 1998, observes, this approach moves from an initial putative institution-free 'state of nature' in which individual preferences are considered as immutable towards the construction of institutions; institutions, therefore, result from the interactions of individuals, and the individual precedes society.

Institutional economic geography

MARTIN, 2008, identifies the 'institutional turn' in economic geography, i.e. the recognition of the importance of social institutions in conditioning and shaping economic activity in geographical space, as one of its major new directions following its revival in the last decade. Undoubtedly, the institutional turn in economic geography is not unrelated to the institutional turn in economic theory, which predated the former by almost a century. It can be argued, however, that institutions, both formal and informal, command a central position in mainstream economic geography unlike mainstream economics, and in that sense no separate institutional strand can be clearly identified in economic geography. Besides, identifying a clear-cut epistemological and methodological corpus of 'institutionalism' is difficult even within the discipline of economics, with the exception of the neo-institutional economic theory. In economic geography this task becomes even more complicated by the eclecticism of the discipline.

BOSCHMA & FRENKEN, 2006, consider that a common methodological trait of institutional economic geography is the rejection of formal modelling and econometrics, and the adoption of an inductive approach focusing on the local specificities of 'real places', and particularly on "place-specific institutions at different spatial scales". They observe that an institutional analysis aims at understanding how place-specific institutions determine local economic development starting from the differences between localities. MARTIN, 2008, considers that an institutionalist approach to economic geography would attempt to illuminate the question of how and to what extent institutional structures mediate and shape the process of geographically uneven capitalist economic development. He also associates the institutional turn in economic geography with the widespread adoption by economic geographers of regulationism, which, however, from a strict taxonomical perspective is a separate strand of theory.

Regulationism and 'flexible specialisation'

The 'Régulation' School of political economy is a variant of neo-Marxist structuralism, which has proven to be particularly influential among economic geographers.[10] Regulation theory aims to analyse the long-term, historically specific, dynamic regularities in the reproduction of the capitalist system, which is at least temporarily stabilised and made possible by its regulatory institutional framework, despite the inherent instability of its accumulation process, and its structural contradictions and natural proneness to crisis. Concepts commonly used by regulationists include the 'industrial (or techno-managerial) paradigm', the 'accumulation regime', and the 'mode of regulation'. As JESSOP, 2001, clarifies, an industrial paradigm is "a model governing the technical and social division of labour", and it is primarily a microeconomic concept. An accumulation regime is the long-term pattern of production and consumption, and it is primarily a macroeconomic concept. A mode of regulation is "an emergent ensemble of norms, institutions, organisational forms, social networks, and patterns of conduct that can stabilise an accumulation regime", and it is primarily a mesoeconomic concept, which however has extra-economic dimensions. It comprises the 'wage relation'; the enterprise form; the nature of money; the state; and international regimes, namely "the trade, investment, monetary settlements, and political arrangements that link national economies, nation states, and the world system". The combination of the other three elements in a way that secures "the conditions for a long wave of capitalist expansion" is the model of development.

The influence of regulationism on economic geography has mainly come through the literature on the Marshallian industrial districts supposedly found in 'Third Italy', a collection of Italian regions in the North-Northeast of Italy (e.g. Emilia-Romagna, Tuscany, Veneto), which, unlike the under-industrialised and largely agrarian South and the highly industrialised North (e.g. Lombardy, Piedmont, Liguria) supposedly dominated by Fordist large-scale mass production industrial conglomerates, exhibit a particular production structure characterised by economies of scope, which originate from a spatially embedded and locally specific division of labour. This structure is dominated by innovative SMEs with a specialised and skilled labour force. This idealised mode of industrial organisation is supposed to embody the post-Fordist 'flexible specialisation' techno-managerial paradigm. The theory, initially developed by a group of Italian social scientists and economists in the late seventies [BAGNASCO, 1977; BECATTINI, 1987], became very popular among economic geographers in the Anglosaxon academia mainly through the work of PIORE & SABEL, 1984. Since then the literature on industrial districts has undergone an explosive proliferation,[11] economic geographers have been scanning the globe for indications of geographical formations complying with the model, and, as MARTIN & SUNLEY, 2003, remark, the vocabulary of economic geography has been enriched with a plethora of neologisms, such as 'new industrial spaces', 'territorial production complexes', 'regional innovative milieux', 'innovative clusters', 'regional clusters', and the like. Many attempts to explain the 'miracle' of the Third Italy focus on contextual and institutional factors such as social capital [PUTNAM *et al.*, 1993], and 'untraded interdependencies' [STORPER, 1997], which together with regional learning and innovation [ASHEIM, 1995] became the new fad of the nineties in economic geography. From this point of view this corpus of literature can be considered as pertaining to the 'institutionalist' strand.

Although it does not propose an explicit model of geographical space – or maybe because of that – the broadly-defined 'institutionalist' strand in economic geography has enriched the sub-discipline with a fertile, realist conception of space, which has nothing to do with the abstract geometrical space of regional science and the NEG. This 'space of places' has a strong physical dimension, but it is also largely shaped by social norms and institutions. As we shall see in the next section, however, the 'relational' dimension of geographical space in this strand of theory is still dormant, or at least not explicitly and systematically treated.

Evolutionary economic geography

Similarly to the 'institutional' variant of economic geography, it is not very easy to define an evolutionary economic geography (EEG) independently from the corresponding strand of economics. EEG and evolutionary economics share essentially the same fundamental epistemological premises and methodological tools, which the former applies in the study of uneven geographical development [BOSCHMA & MARTIN, 2007], or, seen in the more specific context of the theory of evolutionary selection of organisational routines by NELSON & WINTER, 1982, in the study of the spatio-temporal distribution of these routines, their creation and diffusion in space, and the analysis of agglomerations in terms of the spatial concentration of organisational knowledge embedded in them [BOSCHMA & FRENKEN, 2006]. Under a broader definition, EEG studies the evolutionary dynamics of spatio-economic systems, i.e. systems emerging from the spatial interaction of the underlying populations of economic agents.

BOSCHMA & MARTIN, 2007, additionally identify as the subject-matter of an EEG "the spatialities of economic novelty", the emergence of the spatial structures of the economy from the micro-behaviours of economic agents, the self-organisation of the economic landscape, and the path-dependent shaping of geographies of economic development and transformation. Novelty, emergence, self-organisation and path-dependence are, however, typical systemic properties of complex adaptive systems without an explicit evolutionary tag,[12] and hence more associated with complexity theory rather than with evolutionary dynamics per se. The expansion of the scope of EEG in the direction of complexity theory, emergentism, connectionism, social network analysis, as well as institutionalism is not uncommon for this strand of the discipline [see, for instance, the diverse collection of articles in BOSCHMA & MARTIN, 2010].

BOSCHMA & FRENKEN, 2006, criticise, however, the tendency to convolute the evolutionary with the institutionalist approaches, and emphasise the epistemological and methodological autonomy of the former vis-à-vis the latter, while recognise that their cross-fertilisation is valuable for the discipline. They observe that EEG explains decision-making under bounded rationality in the context of organisational routines, while institutional approaches do that in the context of territorial institutions; as a result, the approach of the former to geographical phenomena is bottom-up, from the micro-dynamics of firms to the spatial macro-economy, while that of the latter is top-down, from the macro-perspective of institutions at the territorial level to the micro-behaviour of economic agents. The two approaches may converge when institutions are seen as co-evolving with technologies, markets and industrial organisation.

Still, the different conceptualisation of geographical space by the two approaches is harder to reconcile: BOSCHMA & FRENKEN, 2006: 289, note that the geographical space of formal evolutionary models is more similar to that of the neoclassical variants of economic geography, in that it is a 'neutral', abstract space, than that of the institutional variant, which is nothing but the space of the "real places in real-world cases". And while the latter approach implicitly takes these 'real places' as fixed or at least pre-existing ontologies determining spatio-economic processes, EEG "claims that real places emerge from actions of economic agents, rather than fully determining their actions" [Ibid.].

A generic modelling framework of economic development as an evolutionary branching process of product innovations, which allows to obtain firm and city size distributions as aggregates resulting from an evolutionary process, is proposed by FRENKEN & BOSCHMA, 2007. This generic model considers firm-level economies of scope and urban level Jacobs externalities as the principal feedback mechanisms in economic development, which generate path dependencies in the spatial concentration of industries and the specialisation of cities.

MARTIN & SUNLEY, 2006 critically examine the concept of path dependence as a persistent characteristic of and as an approach to economic phenomena in geographical space, and notably its potential meaning in a regional context as 'regional path dependence' (a possible interpretation of which is that of 'regional lock-in'), and its applicability to the study of regional economic evolution. SIMMIE & MARTIN, 2010, examine in a regional context a related systemic concept, that of resilience, which is interpreted as the ability of a regional economy to recover successfully from exogenous shocks threatening to throw it off its growth path, and the applicability of this concept to the study of the long-term evolutionary dynamics of urban and regional economies.

Relational economic geography

One more in a long list of turns in economic geography is the 'relational turn' [BOGGS & RANTISI, 2003; YEUNG, 2005].[13] This involves the adoption of a perspective "concerned with the ways social interactions between economic agents have shaped the geography of economic performance" [BOGGS & RANTISI, 2003: 109], or differently put, "an analytical focus on the complex nexus of relations among actors and structures that affect dynamic changes in the spatial organisation of economic activities" [YEUNG, 2005: 37].

Relational economic geography (REG) shifts the traditional focus of mainstream economic theory and of regional science from the individual economic agent who operates in an isotropic space of market-mediated interactions to the structure of (direct) interactions among economic agents on the basis of established social relationships.[14] BATHELT & GLÜCKLER, 2003: 123, argue that while regional science treats geographical space as an entity which exists independently from economic action, and which "confines and determines economic action", the relational approach "assumes that economic action transforms the localised material and institutional conditions of future economic action", and "emphasises that the economic actors themselves produce their own regional environments". They identify three conditions for this paradigmatic shift: 'contextuality', i.e. the recognition that economic actors are embedded in a social and institutional context, path-dependence, and 'contingency', i.e. the open-endedness of economic agents' strategies and actions, which remain not fully determined by their context or by path-dependence. They further identify four premises as an analytical basis for a REG: organisation, by which they essentially refer to industrial organisation and the internal (intra-firm) or external division of labour, evolution, innovation, and interaction, by which they refer to economic interactions between agents or groups of agents. In an attempt to define the epistemological scope of REG they contend that research in REG "focuses on processes, such as institutional learning, creative interaction, economic innovation, and interorganisational communication, and investigates these through a geographical lens, rather than uncovering spatial regularities and structures." [Ibid.: 125].

In his critical stance towards REG, YEUNG, 2005, warns against the 'anti-essentialist' tendencies of some (extreme) variants of REG ensuing from the fact that many generic relational concepts commonly used in REG, such as the concept of 'network', are merely descriptive and devoid of explanatory capacity. He proposes the reconsideration of the nature of relationality in REG on the basis of 'relational geometries', which he defines as "spatial configurations of heterogeneous power relations". In a similar vein, SUNLEY, 2008: 3, criticises REG for having "lost sight of many of the valuable insights of institutionalist and critical realist approaches", including the implications of emergence, and for failing "to offer analytical models that prioritise causes and identify causal mechanisms". He contends that "relational insights should be developed within an evolutionary institutionalism that is informed by critical and pragmatic realisms" [Ibid.].

Relational space, industrial organisation and the mesoeconomic plexus

Redefining the scope of economic geography: The relational dimension

Since the contemporary reincarnations of Marshall's industrial districts in the 'Third Italy' and throughout the eighties and nineties, economic geographers have been fascinated by this stylised geographical formation, which was seen as a paradigmatic materialisation of post-Fordist 'flexible specialisation' in space. These highly localised concentrations of economic activity seemed to exist and prosper in the face of increasing globalisation, or so it was thought. The paradigm started to lose some of its allure when it was soon realised, first, that it was not so easily reproducible outside the very specific institutional context in which it emerged, and second, that the most globally competitive production systems did not necessarily exhibit the level of regional closure found in the archetypical industrial districts [STORPER, 1997: 8]. Beyond the raw force of agglomeration, which is traditionally associated with localised economies of scale and production externalities assumed to be present in Marshallian industrial districts, economic geographers began to observe patterns in the internal as well as in the external linkages of these spatial formations, which they diversely described as 'neo-Marshallian nodes in global networks' [AMIN & THRIFT, 1992], 'sticky places in a slippery space' [MARKUSEN, 1996], 'regional motors of the global economy' [SCOTT, 1996], and so on.

Nevertheless, the attempts to present the industrial district as a generalisable model of industrial organisation have been inconclusive. I argue that this discourse has been largely misplaced: The problem here, to use critical realist terminology, is that the model of industrial district describes a 'constant conjunction of events' instead of a transfactual ontology, an isolated empirical regularity made into a stylised archetype, which however originates from a fundamentally open, ever-changing, constantly interacting with its environment, out-of-equilibrium, dynamically evolving complex production system. The patterns identified in an ad hoc manner by geographers are in reality instantiations of the deeper generative structures of the productive systems in question. These generative structures are not necessarily territorially contingent, even though their instantiations are. All production systems, from corporate organisations, through regional 'clusters', industries and national economies, to the global economy, have internal structures that articulate their micro-elements and external structures that integrate them in higher-level entities. These relational structures are neither isotropic nor random, but have a complex, nontrivial topology, whose study can yield a lot of insight into the deeper generative structures of the production systems.

The 'traditional' geographical approach commits the 'physicalist' fallacy by conceiving the physical space of economic geography as an ontological category in itself – as if this physical space has innate properties (affecting the economy) other than those emanating from the socio-economic ontologies it contains.[15] By reinstating the geographical space as a *relational space*, as a locus of socio-economic interactions, which also has a contingent physical dimension (the latter being a property of the socio-economic entities it contains rather than an innate property of the locus itself), the fallacy can be superseded. The relational space is what CASTELLS, 1991; 2011, calls a 'space of flows', an anisotropic, dynamic space-time with a variable, network-shaped geometry, as opposed to the 'space of places', the static and fragmented collection of physical spaces. It is only within the relational space where questions concerning the deeper generative structures of the production systems can be answered.

External division of labour and the nexus of interdependences

Interdependences as externalities

Externalities in production

In mainstream economic theory, externalities (or 'external economies') are economic effects not captured in the market prices of goods or of production factors. These effects drive a wedge between the private and the social value of a good or of a production factor, and therefore are considered to cause the failure of the first welfare theorem, since in the face of externalities a competitive equilibrium, even if it exists, it will not be Pareto-optimal. Externalities in the neoclassical context, therefore, are thought of as a leading cause of 'market failure' [MASKIN, 1994].

Another instructive definition of externalities is that they occur "whenever the well-being of a consumer or the production possibilities of a firm are directly affected by the actions of another agent in the economy", where 'directly' means "in a way not mediated by the price mechanism" [MAS-COLELL *et al.*, 1995: 352]. In a similar vain, SCITOVSKY, 1954: 144 (following an earlier definition by MEADE, 1952) defines 'technological external economies' as a type of direct (extra-market) interdependence among economic agents, by which the output of an individual producer depends "not only on his input of productive resources but also on the activities of other firms". He also distinguishes a type of interdependence which has, instead of direct extra-market effect, an effect through the market mechanism, and which he calls 'pecuniary external economies'. Scitovsky, as a matter of fact, replicates VINER, 1932, who distinguishes between technological and pecuniary externalities, of which the former corresponds to the modern concept, whereas the latter, a pseudo-externality, is the scale effect caused by a shift in the level of economic activity of an individual agent, capable of affecting other economic agents.

The concept of 'externality' is imbued with methodological individualism, as it considers the direct interaction of economic agents as an aberration from the norm and a source of market failure. As SCITOVSKY, 1954: 144, expressively observes, "in general equilibrium theory, direct interdependence is the villain of the piece and the cause for conflict between private profit and social benefit". Interestingly, a common theme in all definitions of 'externality' is the implicit assumption that the direct interaction of economic agents which affects their productive possibilities is, in a way, unintended and incidental. Here I propose an alternative explanation of the quantities characterised as 'externalities' within the neoclassical context, starting from the observation that these are phenomena pertaining to the meso domain, given that they involve micro-interactions of individual economic agents. I argue that 'externalities' are nothing but the 'residuals' from the artificial disaggregation at the micro level of otherwise irreducible, nonlinear interactions occurring at the meso level. 'Externalities' are therefore the unexplained (in the context of neoclassical theory) portion of the process of (weak) emergence, and can be considered as emergent phenomena per se.

Externalities as a causal mechanism of agglomeration

A conventional approach to local production systems of all types (including 'industrial districts', 'regional clusters', 'territorial production complexes', etc.), which is consistent with the stylised models of the NEG, is that they are territorial concentrations of economic activity induced by *agglomeration economies.* These accrue from factors exogenous to the agglomerated economic agents, such as physical infrastructure, favourable spatial planning provisions, other localised policy incentives (e.g. special tax regimes), low land rents, and most importantly, proximity to existing labour and consumer markets. The agglomerating factors that glue economic agents together in local production systems are, therefore, either the localised provision of public goods (physical infrastructure, enabling institutional framework, etc.) or territorially specific positive externalities. The former are usually the result of state intervention, while the latter are involuntary and incidental side-effects of economic activity. In this approach a local production system is, therefore, a territorial concentration of economic agents bound together by economic factors that do not result directly from their deliberate actions but are instead elements of the socio-economic environment in which they operate.[16]

In other strands of literature, *untraded interdependences* have been emphatically proclaimed as the major source of competitive advantage of localities, and, as a matter of fact, the very raison d'être of regional formations [STORPER, 1997].[17] The term 'untraded interdependences', coined by DOSI, 1984, refers, according to STORPER, 1997, to all "conventions, informal rules, and habits that coordinate economic actors under conditions of uncertainty" [Ibid.: 5]. Dosi himself defines untraded interdependences between sectors, technologies and firms as the "technological complementarities, 'synergies', and flow of stimuli and constraints which do not entirely correspond to commodity flows", but "represent a structured set of *technological externalities* which can be a collective asset of groups of firms/ industries within countries/ regions and/or tend to be internalised within individual companies". These untraded interdependences are "the *unintentional* outcome of decentralised (but irreversible) processes of environmental organisation and/or the result of *explicit strategies* of public and private institutions" (emphasis added) [DOSI, 1988: 226].

The nexus of interdependences as an external division of labour

The conventional 'agglomeration economies' approach to local production systems excludes their most important generative factor: the structured socio-economic relationships of economic agents. The 'untraded interdependences' approach improves on this deficiency, but still treats interdependences as a form of externality, i.e. as unintentional, extra-market side effects of economic activity which constitute elements of the socio-economic environment (despite the contradictory last line in Dosi's definition that untraded interdependences can be "the result of explicit strategies").

The approach adopted in this book is fundamentally different: I argue that the most important generative factor of local production systems, and by extension, the major source of their assumed competitive advantage, are the interdependences of economic agents (both traded and untraded, i.e. market-mediated and extra-market) induced by a locally stable *external division of labour.* This defines a *nexus of interdependences* (to paraphrase STORPER, 1995) generated by the interactions, both purposive and unintended, direct and indirect, pecuniary and untraded, of economic agents. In this approach 'traded interdependences', i.e. interdependences that involve pecuniary transactions and potentially formal, contractual relationships, are of utmost importance. On the other hand, the role of untraded interdependences in the form of conventions, informal rules, and habits, as well as formal institutions and mutual trust, is by no means underestimated: Untraded interdependencies are informational externalities accruing from and contributing to the external division of labour by supporting, as STORPER, 1997, suggests, the decentralised, local coordination of economic agents' actions in the presence of imperfect information and bounded rationality.

The external division of labour itself is not the unintended by-product of economic activity, a collection of externalities, but the result of "consciously pursued joint action" [SCHMITZ, 1999], even though joint action may benefit from existing agglomeration economies and give rise to externalities. According to SCHMITZ, 1999, joint action can be *horizontal,* taking the form of cooperation between competitors for the attainment of scale and scope economies, or *vertical,* in the form of coordination between producers of goods and services that are complementary in the production process, i.e. that belong to the same value-chain. Joint action can be *bilateral,* when individual firms cooperate to achieve a specific goal, such as the development of a new product, or *multilateral,* when groups of firms join forces to form producer consortia, cooperatives, etc. To these I add that joint action can also be *ad hoc,* when it takes place for the realisation of a specific project, or *repeated,* in the case of a cooperative scheme on a more permanent basis. Generally speaking, cooperation in this context does not exclude competition. Joint action is the basis of different forms of industrial organisation in the mesoeconomic domain examined in the next subsection.

The external division of labour generates a flexible form of industrial organisation, which in certain economic environments, for certain market niches and under certain operational conditions can be more efficient and competitive than the internal division of labour found in vertically integrated corporate organisations. This form of industrial organisation enables firms to specialise in specific segments of a complex production process, to product-differentiate and to innovate through gradual adaptation and learning. It also facilitates effective investment in small steps, since, for example, producers do not have to buy equipment or to train labour for the entire production chain but only for the segment in which they specialise. Moreover, it is a well-known risk-pooling device in economic environments of uncertainty, as it gives to smaller firms the opportunity to invest in innovative projects and to introduce relatively risky technical and organisational improvements in their field of specialisation with potential cascading effects on aggregate performance when the innovations in the whole production process become cumulative. It also reduces all types of entry barriers, thus facilitating the entry of newcomers irrespective of their size.[18] This observation shows the important role of this form of industrial organisation as 'enterprise incubator', and its ability to "help small firms to overcome well-known growth constraints and to sell to distant markets, nationally and internationally" [Ibid.: 466]. With regard to innovative activity, there is strong empirical evidence that it tends to agglomerate, and that this propensity is stronger in the early stages of the business life cycle, while it becomes more dispersed in the mature stages [AUDRETSCH & FELDMAN, 1996].

External division of labour and industrial organisation

Transaction and integration modes of industrial organisation

The nature of the external division of labour can be further elucidated by comparing it to the *internal division of labour* of a corporate organisation in the context of organisation theory. A corporation has a legal personality that secures and a hierarchical administrative structure that regulates intra-organisational transactions among its departments. Transactions take place in an extra-market framework. On the other hand, a local production system with an external division of labour has no legal personality. It is characterised by a heterarchical structure, in which the various production units are interdependent but autonomous. Inter-firm transactions are either governed by contractual arrangements, i.e. legally binding bilateral agreements, or are simply spot-market transactions coordinated through the market mechanism and regulated by the normative 'nexus of untraded interdependencies'.

The prevailing type of transaction arrangements among economic agents, which may take the form of *hierarchies, contracts* or *markets,* or indeed any mix of these three, define what I shall call the *transaction mode* of the economic system. The contract-based transaction mode is a 'hybrid' between extra-market and open-market transactions [WILLIAMSON, 2005].[19] With regard to the permanency of the arrangements, a transaction mode can be *perpetual, temporary* or *ad hoc,* depending on the types of joint actions it supports. A large complex local production system will most likely involve a multiplicity of coexisting transaction modes. Different mixes of hierarchical, contractual and open-market transactions is one aspect of what generates the variety of economic formations, such as corporate organisations and local production systems. Another aspect is the *integration mode.* By this term I refer to the way elementary or compound microeconomic entities become embedded in the division of labour of a (higher-order) production system. The implementation of an integration mode depends on the underlying *power structure* of the system, which may take the form of (formal) *authority, dominance* based on asymmetric dependence, or *interdependence.* The integration mode determines the way the *relational quasi-rent* is allocated and appropriated; this term, introduced by Aoki, 1986, refers to the quasi-rent that is generated by investment in 'relational assets'.[20] In the context of organisation theory the following integration modes can be distinguished:

Integration and dis-integration

Vertical integration refers to the expansion of corporate ownership into upstream or downstream activities. More specifically, downstream expansion is known as *forward integration* and upstream expansion as *backward integration. Horizontal integration* refers to the concentration of units belonging to the same level of the value-chain under a single ownership scheme by internal expansion of the firm or by external expansion through mergers and acquisitions. A vertically or horizontally integrated entity (a corporation) has a hierarchy-based transaction mode and an authority-based power structure. The generation and appropriation of relational quasi-rent is completely internalised.

Horizontal integration may generate economies of scale or scope, increase market power over suppliers and buyers or facilitate international transactions. Vertical integration may reduce transaction costs, stabilise and coordinate the supply chain, increase entry barriers to potential competitors, and internalise the risk of investment in specialised assets and activities, such as capital-intensive R&D activity, which normally would not be taken up by individual upstream or downstream actors. Vertical integration is intensified by adverse factors such as a restrictive tax regime, an unstable macroeconomic environment that increases uncertainty and risk, a weak institutional frame, inadequate social capital and lack of trust that make difficult the enforcement and monitoring of contracts, or just missing upstream or downstream markets. On the other hand, compared to alternative integration modes, vertical integration has a number of potential disadvantages: First, rigidities in the supply chain with regard to adapting to variable exogenous demand, which may cause excess upstream capacity building and bottlenecks; second, managerial diseconomies and potentially increased costs due to lack of supplier competition; third, inflexibility of the innovation-generating structure, which gives rise to diminishing returns to R&D investment. This last limitation is examined in more detail in the next section.

Vertical or *horizontal dis-integration* refers to the reverse process whereby, respectively, upstream or downstream segments of the value-chain or activities belonging to the same level of the value-chain are externalised. The process of disintegration leads to the reorganisation of the supply-chain of the firm by increasing outsourcing. It also leads to switches from hierarchy- to contract- or market-based transaction modes. The transition to the so-called post-Fordist 'flexible' regime of accumulation in the mid-1980s is associated with this tendency [LEBORGNE & LIPIETZ, 1992].

Quasi-integration

Quasi-integration is a decentralised but relatively stable inter-organisational division of labour with a network-like configuration. The power structure within quasi-integrated systems is not based on authority but on dominance or interdependence. The relational quasi-rent generated in the context of joint action schemes is allocated among the partners on the basis of their relative positions within the network. LEBORGNE & LIPIETZ, 1992, distinguish three forms of quasi-integration, namely 'vertical', 'horizontal' and 'oblique', explained below.

Vertical quasi-integration, a term attributed to BLOIS, 1972, is a production system consisting of a dominant firm and its (usually upstream) subcontractors. This corresponds to a hierarchical star-like network structure resembling the *hub-and-spoke* type of industrial district [MARKUSEN, 1996]. In this integration mode the dominant firm sets the rules and the specifications of production to its upstream suppliers and appropriates most of the relational quasi-rent. *Just-in-time* production methods favour this mode of integration over vertical integration. *Horizontal quasi-integration* occurs when there is no dominant partner in the network and the relational quasi-rent is allocated more-or-less evenly among the partners. The network is entirely decentralised, heterarchical, and the power structure is based on interdependence rather than on authority or dominance. Strategic alliances, joint ventures etc. are usual under this mode of integration. *Oblique quasi-integration* is an intermediate integration mode in which the suppliers preserve their autonomy vis-à-vis their customers in that they retain full control of their segment of the value-chain. The transaction mode of this scheme is predominantly contract-based, aiming at eliminating the moral hazard problem which is usual in principal-agent type of interactions with limited monitoring capacities.

Whereas the vertically integrated corporation is considered as an illustration of the Fordist-Taylorist techno-managerial paradigm, quasi-integrated production systems are seen as typical examples of post-Fordist, 'flexible' organisation [PIORE & SABEL, 1984; SABEL, 1989; LEBORGNE & LIPIETZ, 1992]. This mode (even partially) permits the mediation of the market mechanism and of inter-organisational competition. This introduces a local selection process potentially leading to the 'survival of the fittest', most efficient firms and entrepreneurial behaviour, at least within the boundaries of the system. At the same time it reduces the uncertainty and the coordination problems of open-market transactions. As a result, quasi-integrated production systems are supposed to combine flexibility with relative stability in their organisational structures. 'Globalisation' in the sense of increased trade openness is seen as a crucial factor inducing vertical dis-integration and the proliferation of the quasi-integration paradigm [MCLAREN, 2000].

Network representation of industrial organisation

The above descriptions of the integration and transaction modes of industrial organisation imply a network structure of the inter- and intra-organisational division of labour. This implicit reference can be taken further by approaching the different forms of industrial organisation from an explicit network-analytical perspective as instantiations of distinct network types.

A first step in this direction is the observation that in the post-Fordist knowledge-based economies traditional vertically integrated firms exhibit a tendency to transform into what is termed as 'network organisations' [JONES *et al.*, 1997; MILES & SNOW, 1992]. PODOLNY & PAGE, 1998: 59, define the network form of organisation as a "collection of actors that pursue repeated, enduring exchange relations with one another and, at the same time, lack a legitimate organisational authority to arbitrate and resolve disputes that may arise during the exchange". This definition corresponds to the specific modes of quasi-integration examined in the previous paragraph and clearly describes a *heterarchical* network structure. In a similar vein, POWELL, 1990: 313, sees the network as a hybrid form of industrial organisation between hierarchy and market that expands the boundaries of the firm "to encompass a larger community of actors and interests that would previously have either been fully separate entities or absorbed through merger".

I argue that the application of the powerful network paradigm in organisation theory can and should be generalised to encompass all types of organisational structures including the internal division of labour found in corporate organisations. By this approach the firm can be represented as a hierarchical network whose topology is subsumable to the same analytical methods as any other form of industrial organisation, whereas the industrial district as a complex heterarchical network which potentially also embeds various local hierarchies.

The network representation of the various forms of industrial organisation does not provide in itself, however, a complete explanation of how and why they occur and what makes them qualitatively distinct from one another: In the case, for instance, of a corporate organisation, its constituent micro-elements, i.e. individual economic agents, loose their 'ontological' autonomy (as economic agents) the moment they are incorporated in the organisational structure of the firm, unlike firms joining a quasi-integrated external division of labour, in which they retain their ontological autonomy. Moreover, the corporation itself, as already discussed in the previous chapter, is an emergent ontology which manages to exist independently from its constituent micro-elements. As it is more extensively discussed in a following section, technological knowledge and the processes of evolution and emergence are the crucial factors in binding micro-entities together in productive macro-systems and in shaping the network topologies of the latter.

The network is not only a means of structuring economic transactions but most importantly, a means for the diffusion of economically relevant information, and thus also of technological knowledge. In real economic systems the diffusion of information does not take place in an isotropic continuum, like the one implicit in neoclassical theory, but in an anisotropic space spanned by usually complex networks of variable architecture. Such networks often exhibit a capacity to diffuse information depending on their degree of connectivity: Some studies of social network models, for instance, find that by increasing connectivity, the information diffusion speed in a network also increases, though different types of connections may have different effects [e.g. MIDGLEY *et al.*, 1992; GOYAL & JANSSEN, 1996; CHWE, 2000].

Mesoeconomic plexus and economies of complexity

The mesoeconomic plexus defined

In Chapter 1 it was argued that the meso domain is an indispensable ontological level in a realist theory of economics, and by extension of economic geography: It is a relational space of micro-interactions which lies between and coheres the level of mereologically irreducible (either in the epistemological or in the ontological sense) macro-systems and the level of their constituent micro-parts, i.e. of individual economic agents, and the locus where emergence occurs par excellence.

I call the fundamental ontology of this domain 'mesoeconomic plexus', and I define this to be the cohesive set of all relatively stable micro-interactions which embodies a *complete* external division of labour in a *specific* production process.

This concise definition entails the following: The mesoeconomic plexus is a fundamental ontology in the same sense as individual economic agents are in the micro domain and macro-economic systems, such as national economies, are in the macro domain. The micro-interactions which make up the plexus are neither random nor unintended, but purposive joint actions induced by real and potentially lasting economic relationships. As a result, the plexus itself is a structured system, and as it is postulated in the following paragraph, a complex adaptive one. A mesoeconomic plexus embodies an entire external division of labour in a particular production process, and in that sense it is a superstructure that incorporates diverse forms of industrial organisation; as a matter of fact, given the possibility of network representation of these forms, the plexus can be conceived as a network of interlocking networks. A plexus is thus a scalable entity encompassing not only territorially embedded productive systems, such as regional clusters or industrial districts, but also various types of supralocal networks of economic activity, all of which are segments or layers of a specific division of labour. Its upper bounds are determined by the extension of the division of labour, by the nature of the production process, but also by the analytical perspective.

The mesoeconomic plexus is proposed as an analytical tool for the systemic paradigm in economic geography because, as it will be made clearer in the remaining of this chapter, it embodies the three proposed fundamental epistemological premises of this paradigm, complexity, evolution and emergence. But before any further development of this concept, the critical reader may justifiably ask what does this concept add to the very similar notions of 'relational space' and 'network' and why do we need to invent this theoretical construct in the first place. An advance answer to these legitimate questions is that 'relational space' is a term referring to the 'vessel' of economic interactions, the locus where they occur (and which is also shaped by them), not to the 'ontological' object itself. 'Network' is a generic term extensively used throughout this book, which does not specifically refer to economic phenomena, does not necessarily embody a complete division of labour, and is not necessarily part of the nested hierarchy of economic domains. A mesoeconomic plexus is an entity that resides in relational space but does not coincide with it. And while a plexus may have a network representation, a specific network need not be a plexus. An example of this last point is the interregional network of patent co-inventors, extensively analysed in Chapters 3 and 4: This knowledge network does not embody a complete external division of labour in itself – it merely is a particular aspect of the division of labour in technological knowledge production. Therefore, it is not a mesoeconomic plexus but merely a component of the 'knowledge plexus' (see below). Another legitimate question would be in what sense a mesoeconomic plexus, which is a complex system in itself, is ontologically distinct from the complex economic systems which reside in the macro domain. The answer is that macro-systems, such as national or regional economies, incorporate several intertwined production processes extending across several mesoeconomic plexuses, and therefore embody a multi-layered division of labour of a higher order of complexity than that of a single plexus.

Three types of plexuses span the macro-economy: the production-exchange (i.e. industry-trade) plexus, the financial plexus, and the knowledge (i.e. science-technology) plexus, which is the focal point of this book. As economic history amply demonstrates, these three types of plexuses are interdependent, and as a matter of fact, co-evolve. Each of these types of mesoeconomic plexuses has its own medium of accumulation, namely physical, financial and cognitive capital respectively, and a regulatory schema consisting in an explicit institutional and an implicit normative structure (of 'untraded interdependences', i.e. tacit rules, 'social capital', norms, etc.), which co-evolves with the plexus. The knowledge plexus, in particular, embodies the external division of labour in the production of economically relevant knowledge, and therefore supports its reproduction, accumulation and diffusion.

The mesoeconomic plexus as a complex adaptive system

Dissipation and self-organisation

The various instantiations of the mesoeconomic plexuses are open systems in constant exchange of factors of production, commodities and information with their socio-economic environments. During this process of exchange, and depending on their life-cycle stages, these entities become more organisationally complex as the number, the size and the interaction intensities of their constituent elements increase. At the early stages of their life cycle they endogenously expand their internal structure and increase their systemic complexity by developing more interdependences between their constituent elements. At the late stages, their decline, which comes as a result of cumulative diseconomies or technological lock-ins, is marked by their entropic degradation. For all these reasons, the instantiations of a mesoeconomic plexus are dissipative systems in a far-from-equilibrium state, exhibiting self-organisation.

In the process of self-organised expansion, the instantiations of the knowledge plexus, in particular, are able to transform information flows they receive from their environment into new technological knowledge and accumulate it as stocks of *relational cognitive capital* (defined and explained below).

Path dependence, nonlinearities and complex dynamics

An increasing number of studies in the field of economic geography identify path dependence as an essential feature of local production systems, such as industrial districts, regional clusters, regional networks, or, more generally, of the regions.[21] Dynamic increasing returns, the irreversibility of past investment and sunk costs, agglomeration economies, technological lock-ins, institutional inertia, and cumulative causation are among the factors that have been identified in related literature as sources of path dependence in economic geography, as well as in economic history [SAVIOTTI & METCALFE, 1991; KRUGMAN, 1991; STORPER, 1997; GARUD & KARNØE, 2001; FUCHS & SHAPIRA, 2005]. This rich theoretical and empirical evidence supports the view that the evolutionary trajectories of the various instantiations of the mesoeconomic plexuses exhibit the properties of nonergodicity and time-irreversibility.

The mesoeconomic plexus arises from the interactions of micro-parts which, unlike those of physical complex systems, are cognitive economic agents. These agents are heterogeneous, adaptive, and able to learn and even to consciously deliberate on their course of action on the basis of their bounded rationality and their constrained knowledge of their broader economic environment. An instantiation of a plexus is, therefore, a multiagent dynamical system consisting of a large number of heterogeneous adaptive agents.

The heterogeneity in the behavioural patterns of economic agents and their adaptability to their socio-economic environment implies that their set of interactions will be nonlinear. In that sense, the instantiations of the mesoeconomic plexuses are nonlinear dynamical systems. Agents' heterogeneity and systems' nonlinearities are potential sources of endogenous novelty. Of course nonlinear dynamics need not always be complex (class 4) dynamics; they can merely be chaotic (class 3). In the case of evolving mesoeconomic plexuses, however, the generation of new structure implies that their evolutionary trajectories exhibit complex dynamics 'between order and chaos' rather than chaotic ones.

Universality and phase transition

In complex socio-economic systems systemic fitness is not directly affected by or even associated with individual fitness. In the case of the various instantiations of mesoeconomic plexuses, an equivalent statement would be that the competitiveness of these entities as a whole remains unaffected by the competitiveness of their micro-parts: While individual economic agents such as firms may decline or cease to exist, the plexus lives on or even expands, as an illustration of Schumpeterian creative destruction. Moreover, while micro-interactions may be volatile and in a state of constant flux, the cohesion and aggregate properties of the plexus normally remain unaffected. This is a clear indication of the fundamental CAS property of universality, whereby the generic properties of a system are insensitive to variation in its micro-specification.

Phase transition occurs in a system when small shifts in its higher-order parameters cause drastic changes in its qualitative characteristics, such as leaps from one attractor basin to another or regime shifts. Economic history provides ample evidence of phase transitions in all forms of economic systems, including industrial districts, cities, regional or national economies, or even the global economy as a whole, reflected in their sudden wane and wax in terms of their growth dynamics or the discontinuous shifts in their techno-economic trajectories instigated by specific historical contingencies.

Emergence

A mesoeconomic plexus, as it can be directly deduced from the definition, is a mereologically complex entity whose properties supervene on and are irreducible to those of its micro-units: It is precisely the interdependences generated by the external division of labour which are responsible for the fact that the plexus cannot be fully decomposed into its micro-components.

In addition to the interdependences, a number of significant economic phenomena, which occur within the mesoeconomic plexus, such as *economies of complexity* (see definition below), collective efficiency, innovation, as well as various types of production and information externalities and spillovers, are not present at the level of the micro-units, i.e. the individual economic agents. These are clearly (at least weakly) emergent phenomena.

Moreover, the micro-units, the individual economic agents, exhibit behavioural patterns largely determined by their niche in the plexus, i.e. their position in the external division of labour that spans the plexus. This implies that the plexus also has a downward determinative influence on them. Finally, a mesoeconomic plexus is ontologically distinct from both the micro-units and the macro-systems, and its structure and properties are also qualitatively distinct from theirs, supervene on those of the former and subvene on those of the latter. All these characteristics imply that the plexus is an emergent ontology.

Economies of complexity

External economies of scale

The Marshallian concept of 'external economies of scale', i.e. scale economies external to (competitive, non-monopolistic) firms but internal to the entire industry, is a hybrid between externalities and traditional ('internal') economies of scale ingeniously devised by Marshall to reconcile Cournotian increasing returns with the competitive equilibrium framework [SRAFFA, 1926; STIGLER, 1941]. External economies of this kind are supposed to arise from the development of an industry as a whole, unlike internal economies which, according to Marshall, arise, among other reasons, from the intensification of the division of labour within a firm [MARSHALL, 1920].

Agglomeration economies is a territorially specific form of external economies of scale. However, Marshall's concept contains in latent form an idea beyond the traditional concept of externalities which has never been explored: Marshall's account of the sources of external economies of scale leaves out what may be considered as their principal source, namely the external division of labour itself. The 'extensification' of this division of labour (i.e. its deepening by expansion) is perfectly analogous to and has similar effects as the deepening by intensification of the division of labour within a firm in the case of internal economies of scale.

Scale versus complexity

Here I take this idea further by introducing the important new concept of 'economies of complexity', which bears some similarities to the Marshallian external economies of scale but also has two very fundamental differences: it distinguishes between *scale* and *systemic complexity*, and it is not an externality but the result of purposive joint action of economic agents within an external division of labour.

Consider the complete (industry-level) value-chain of a specific production process as an external division of labour among production units (firms), which has a natural network representation. This, in the terminology introduced in the previous paragraphs, would qualify as a mesoeconomic plexus. There are four ways of expanding the value-chain, and potentially generating increasing returns in the production process within the same technological set: (i) by increasing the scale of operation of the individual production units, i.e. their size in terms of the amount of physical capital and labour they employ; (ii) by increasing the number of the production units in the given value-chain, e.g. as new firms are created or integrated in the division of labour, which is equivalent to adding new nodes to the network; (iii) by establishing new relationships between existing but previously unrelated production units, e.g. through their participation in new joint ventures, which is equivalent to adding new ties between existing nodes in the network; and finally, (iv) by increasing the intensity of collaboration between units, equivalent to increasing the strength of existing ties. With the exception of case (i), which is a traditional internal expansion of scale, and possibly of case (ii), which is an external expansion of scale (but may have structural effects), the other expansions entail a quantitative but also a qualitative change in the structure of the mesoeconomic plexus. Case (i) is a linear physical expansion of the production scale ('physical' in that it involves an increase in tangible factor inputs), case (ii) is a nonlinear physical expansion, while the other cases are nonlinear structural ones. In cases (iii) and (iv), while the micro-units remain the same in terms of number and size (i.e. factor endowments), their interconnections are multiplied and their interactions are intensified; thus the plexus expands in the direction of increasing its internal structure, and hence its systemic complexity, not its scale. This process deepens the division of labour and, most probably, the degree of specialisation of its micro-units. This is a potential source of an increased 'collective efficiency' [SCHMITZ, 1999], which cannot be attributed either to agglomeration economies and network externalities or to increasing returns to scale internal to the constituent micro-units. This is an emergent phenomenon, which I refer to as *economies of complexity* (or equivalently 'increasing returns to complexity').[22] As a matter of fact, the concept of economies of complexity reflects much more faithfully than the concept of economies of scale the Smithian spirit with regard to the relationship between the division of labour and increasing returns as illustrated in the first three chapters of *The Wealth of Nations* [SMITH, 1776].

Similar conclusions also apply to the phenomenon of diminishing returns, whenever it occurs in this context: Beyond a certain threshold of systemic complexity the entropic degradation of the system begins, and *diseconomies of complexity* in the form of managerial diseconomies, coordination failures, etc., may set in.

Economies of complexity are distinct from 'network externalities' and 'network effects': Network externalities are consumption-side external economies occurring when the utility that a user derives from the consumption of a good increases with the number of other users consuming the same type of good [KATZ & SHAPIRO, 1985; FARRELL & SALONER, 1985], and therefore from the expansion of the scale of a consumer network. Network effects are production-side informational externalities or knowledge spillovers diffused through a network and affecting technological knowledge production [VARGA *et al.*, 2014], localised versions of which are 'Marshall-Arrow-Romer' (MAR) and 'Jacobs'-type externalities [GLAESER *et al.*, 1992].[23] None of these types of external economies is related to the internal structure of a network and the complexity of its division of labour.

In the knowledge economy where the most important factor of production, technological knowledge, is intangible and highly mobile, increasing returns are more likely to ensue from the increased degree of connectivity of the production units, and hence from the 'extensification' of the division of labour and the increased complexity of the network in which they are embedded, rather than from increasing their internal scale of operation. Economies of complexity are therefore particularly prominent in knowledge-intensive economic activities.

Economic cognition and the emergence of technological knowledge in the knowledge plexus

Typology of technological knowledge

Objectivist and constructivist construals of knowledge

Technological knowledge is here broadly defined as knowledge with actual or potential economic effects. By this definition the qualifier 'technological' does not signify 'technical' or 'applied', but rather any form of knowledge (including the purely 'scientific' one), which ultimately has some effect on the means and the process of production, and hence is economically useful.

In this book knowledge is considered to be the outcome of the process of cognition. This may sound as a tautology but the distinction and the causal relationship between cognition and knowledge is anything but trivial – as a matter of fact, it is a deep epistemological issue. Extending this proposition, it is further argued that technological knowledge is the outcome of the process of cognition by adaptive economic agents.

Technological knowledge is an intangible factor of production, which is at the micro level one of the most valuable assets of individuals and organisations, being the main source of their competitiveness, and at the macro level the principal generator of economic growth, being a source of 'absolute advantage' for national economies. The intensified deployment of technological knowledge in the production process in advanced industrial economies has led to an unprecedentedly rapid expansion of the global technological frontier and to the transition to today's 'knowledge-based economy'. Despite its exceptional importance in economic processes, the origins of technological knowledge and the way it determines micro and macro- economic competitiveness remain inexplicable in the context of neoclassical economics; technological knowledge is taken as given, trivially as a 'black box'. This is probably one of the major weaknesses of the theory.

In this section technological knowledge is examined under two different prisms, which I call the *objectivist* and the *constructivist*.

Under the objectivist prism technological knowledge is treated as a cumulable, capital-like asset, and, by extension, as a substance, a stock, and a fungible input in the production process comparable to physical capital. This approach is compatible with the concept of 'human capital'. In this context, the economic exploitation of knowledge necessitates its extraction from cognitive agents and its objectification, which is achieved by smoothing out its subjective and contextual elements [BONIFACIO *et al.*, 2004]. This approach does not connect technological knowledge with the process of cognition and so, in a way, misses its deeper generative structures.

Under the constructivist prism technological knowledge emerges as a result of the co-adaptation of reflective agents with internal cognitive schemata (explained in a following subsection). This approach draws heavily on Piaget's theory of cognitive development [PIAGET, 1971], and subsequent studies on artificial intelligence.

Types of technological knowledge

In this subsection I develop a taxonomy for classifying the various forms of technological knowledge according to the following criteria:

- the degree of its *embodiment* in economic agents, i.e. the degree to which knowledge may exist independently from its physical bearer or generator;
- its *codifiability*, which measures the degree of its 'objectifiability';
- its *contextuality*, i.e. the degree to which the valorisation of knowledge is context-dependent, and which determines its 'extractability';[24]
- the *appropriability* of its economic effects by individuals or organisations, which determines the degree of its economic exploitability [LEVIN, 1988; GRANT, 1996];

- its *embeddedness* in geographical space with regard to its generation and absorption, i.e. the degree to which it is produced or absorbed locally, respectively.

By these criteria I distinguish the following four types of technological knowledge:

Universal disembodied (also 'scientific', 'generic', 'theoretical', 'basic') knowledge is formal, codifiable, minimally contextual, with the characteristics of a public good (non-rivalry and non-excludability) and hence not directly appropriable on a private basis but with strong social spillovers and hence positive effects on overall economic activity. This type of knowledge constitutes the generic framework in which other types of knowledge are generated. It is produced and effortlessly diffused within global scientific communities and hence it is not territorially embedded. Due to its limited appropriability private economic agents have the tendency to under-produce it and, as a consequence, public investment is required to ensure its sufficient provision for the benefit of the society at large. This type of knowledge is typically contained in scientific publications resulting from basic academic research.

Instrumental disembodied (also 'technical', 'specific', 'applied') knowledge is also codifiable but more contextual than the previous type, as it is produced and deployed in specific techno-economic environments. This type of knowledge prior to the allocation of intellectual property rights (IPR) can be rival and excludable, but with the allocation of IPR it becomes publicly accessible even though its direct utilisation is restricted, while with the expiry of IPR in the longer run its excludability is lifted. It can be considered, therefore, as a 'quasi-private' good. It is not unusual for this type of knowledge to be produced by public institutions, in which case it can be considered as a quasi-public good.[25] The production of this type of knowledge is usually localised but its diffusion and utilisation need not be so. This knowledge is usually the result of applied research and can be found in patents.

Organisational knowledge is embodied in organisation structures [KOGUT & ZANDER, 1992]. Despite its collective production, this type of knowledge is owned, protected and exploited by the organisations which generate it, and therefore it is a private asset which in the short run confers technology rent to its proprietors. In the longer run it becomes accessible to competitors through imitation, reverse-engineering, etc. This type of knowledge is limitedly codifiable, 'discursive' and highly contextual. The generation of this knowledge is usually localised but organisational knowledge is to some extent transferable through intra- or inter-organisation networks or labour turnover, and as a result, its utilisation is not necessarily territorially embedded.

Individual knowledge is embodied in economic agents in the form of technical skills or know-how (as opposed to 'know-what'), and can be developed through learning-by-doing, vocational training or even formal education. This type of technological knowledge is both rival and excludable, and as a result, it is a private good. It is non-codifiable, 'non-discursive' or, according to POLANYI, 1967, 'tacit', and highly contextual. It is also territorially specific both in its generation and utilisation due to physical and institutional constraints in labour mobility. Table 2.1 summarises this taxonomical scheme.

Table 2.1: Types of technological knowledge

Type	**Embodiment**	**Objectifiability**		**Appropriability**	**Embeddedness**	
		Contextuality	**Codifiability**		**Generation**	**Absorption**
Universal	None	Low	High	Public	Global	Global
Instrumental	None	Medium	Medium-high	Quasi-public/private	Local	Global
Organisational	Collective	High	Medium-low	Private	Local	Local
Individual	Individual	High	Low	Private	Local	Local

Technological knowledge and industrial organisation

Knowledge-based theories of the firm

The corpus of economic and organisational literature known as 'theory of the firm' is actually a heterogeneous group of theories from diverse epistemological backgrounds, aiming to explain the origins, boundaries, structure, purpose and objectives of the firm as an extra-market formation with own internal structure which operates within the market. Certain strands of this corpus, for instance the neo-institutional transaction cost [COASE, 1937; WILLIAMSON, 1971; 1981], principal-agent, or contract [ALCHIAN & DEMSETZ,1972] theories of the firm, extend the rudimentary neoclassical theory of the firm by incorporating incentives, strategic considerations, asymmetric information and transaction costs, while others place the whole discourse in a different frame, such as the evolutionary neo-Schumpeterian.

A strand within the latter group, which distances itself from the neo-institutional approach and which is particularly relevant to the subject matter of this chapter, is that of the so-called *knowledge-based theory of the firm* [KOGUT & ZANDER, 1992; GRANT, 1996; SPENDER, 1996]. This theory postulates that the raison d'être of any corporate organisation is to combine, coordinate, integrate and structure on the basis of organising principles the 'social knowledge' found in stable relationships of individual economic agents [KOGUT & ZANDER, 1992]. This is considered as a function that the market mechanism by itself is incapable of accomplishing. Organisational knowledge is the most valuable asset of a firm; actually, the firm itself is a collection of cognitive assets embodied in individuals and social relationships, which however is not reducible to those of the individuals [Ibid.]. The firm has the ability to transform its cognitive assets into economic output by applying higher-order organising principles, which eventually determine its organisational capabilities. KOGUT & ZANDER, 1992, distinguish between a declarative and a procedural type of organisational knowledge, which they call *information* and *know-how based* respectively.

The model of organisation-level knowledge integration found in the knowledge-based theories of the firm is not intended to explain the whole range of knowledge-generating capabilities of economic agents and systems, and is compatible with the objectivist construal of technological knowledge.

Knowledge governance and integration modes

A common thread in the extensive literature of 'systems of innovation' shared by this book is that innovation, i.e. the generation of technological knowledge, is a strongly synergetic and systemic process [DOSI *et al.*, 1988; LUNDVALL, 1992; EDQUIST, 1997; et al.]. Synergetic innovation entails that economic agents combine and eventually integrate their heterogeneous cognitive assets in a common operational framework in order to produce new or to economically exploit existing technological knowledge, without necessarily sharing their ownership or management.

The cognitive assets of vertically or horizontally integrated corporations are under unitary ownership and management. These firms usually have specialised R&D departments and protect their cognitive assets by restricting their use within their confines or by patenting. Firms of this type have both the resources to invest in R&D and the incentives to assume the risk of their investment. The more they rely on own cognitive assets, the more heavily they will have to invest in R&D, but in the case of success, the higher will be the technological rent which they will appropriate.

The exponential growth in technological knowledge output in the second half of the last century and the rising complexity of technologies and of innovation systems make increasingly unaffordable for individual firms to keep the entire R&D process internalised. Moreover, internalisation of R&D also internalises the risk, increases the possibility of technological lock-ins and reduces exposure to technological spillovers. On the contrary, a quasi-integrated R&D process allows the dispersion of risk and of the cost of investment but reduces the fraction of appropriable technological rent for each partner. In a vertically quasi-integrated scheme the dominant partner, the 'hub', sets the rules and specifications of production to its upstream suppliers and has at its disposal the know-how of the subcontractor [LEBORGNE & LIPIETZ, 1992: 341]. As a consequence, the subcontractor may be locked-in in a particular technology and dependent on the dominant partner, the distribution of knowledge will be asymmetric and so will be the allocation of the technological rent. In an oblique quasi-integrated scheme the subcontractor possesses the know-how and the technology to produce according to customer's order autonomously. This allows a more even distribution of the technology rent according to the partner's position in the value chain. In a horizontally quasi-integrated scheme a group of firms linked by partnership jointly undertakes R&D projects and shares the risk. The cognitive assets of the partners are complementary, and the technological rent is allocated more-or-less symmetrically. The shift to flexible quasi-integrated schemes in R&D by participating in knowledge networks which exhibit collective efficiency in the generation and diffusion of innovation is supposed to transform the traditional firm into what has been termed a 'virtual', 'modular' or 'network' organisation.[26]

It seems reasonable to assume that different types of technological knowledge would favour different modes of organisational integration. Generic disembodied knowledge which is codified and non-contextual can be produced and diffused within globally networked scientific communities. Applied disembodied knowledge is produced in integrated or vertically quasi-integrated systems with centralised structures, but its diffusion can be assumed to be more open and decentralised. Organisational knowledge is produced and diffused within integrated systems that internalise the accruing technology rent. The correspondence of the knowledge governance regimes to the integration and transaction modes and the patterns of allocation of technology rent are summarised in Table 2.2.

Table 2.2: Knowledge governance regimes

Integration mode	Knowledge governance		Transaction mode	Power structure	Rent allocation
	Ownership	**Control**			
Vertical integration	Unitary	Unitary	Hierarchy	Authority	Full appropriation
Horizontal integration	Unitary	Unitary	Hierarchy	Authority	Full appropriation
Vertical quasi-integration	Principal	Principal	Contract	Dominance	Asymmetric
Oblique quasi-integration	Agent	Principal	Contract	Interdependence	Proportional
Horizontal quasi-integration	Distributed	Distributed	Contract / Market	Interdependence	Symmetric

Inevitably, the transition to the post-Fordist knowledge economy has increased the tendency of firms, including multinational corporations, to externalise entire R&D modules or sub-processes through R&D cooperation, with various degrees of externalisation of ownership and control. Cooperation may be equity-based (e.g. joint ventures, cross-equity holdings, etc.), contract-based (joint R&D agreements, customer-supplier relations, and bilateral or unilateral technology flows including cross-licensing, technology exchange agreements, licensing, etc.), or spot-market (or 'arms length') agreements [HAGEDOORN & SCHAKENRAAD, 1994; MOWERY *et al.*, 1996; NARULA & HAGEDOORN, 1999].

Even when large corporations have the resources to invest in R&D projects, radical innovations are sometimes introduced by small start-up firms with specialised cognitive assets occupying very specific technological niches, which are not locked-in in existing firm routines. Such firms may play a vital role in the innovation process and may also act as intermediaries between institutionalised research in universities and public research centres and large corporations. SAXENIAN, 1996, argues, for instance, that the small firms of the Silicon Valley have been more innovative than the large firms of the East Coast because of their ability to develop multiple connections in dense networks of knowledge, which allows rapid transfer of information and innovative ideas. However, there is also evidence that in some economic sectors quasi-integration, especially among low-tech SMEs, is not conducive to the generation of radical technological discoveries, and that technological lock-in is not an unusual phenomenon in mature quasi-integrated systems of this kind; incremental innovations in such cases are more usual than radical innovations.

Technological knowledge as capital

Forms of cognitive capital

The objectivist approach to technological knowledge entails its conception as a cumulable asset similar to physical capital. This approach implicitly assumes that technological knowledge is a divisible and fungible, albeit intangible, 'substance' rather than a context-specific process. The objectivist approach is currently dominant in economic theory, precisely because it allows the incorporation of technological knowledge in conventional economic models as a form of capital with familiar behaviour. It cannot be denied that the objectivist conception of technological knowledge in certain analytical contexts is useful, and it is partially adopted in the empirical models of Chapter 4 of this book.

From this point onward I shall use the term '*cognitive capital*' to refer to technological knowledge conceived as a cumulable factor input in the production process.

In mainstream economics cognitive capital, as defined here, is taken to be equivalent to 'human capital', namely "knowledge, skills, competences and other attributes embodied in individuals that are relevant to economic activity" [OECD, 1998: 9]. By this definition, human capital is a factor of production consisting in the stock of all forms of individual knowledge) embodied in economic agents (the labour force),[27] which enables them to create economic value. Human capital nevertheless represents only a fragment of the stock of cognitive capital in an economy. Previously we saw that individual knowledge, which is 'objectified' as human capital, is just one out of four types of technological knowledge. But how about the relational dimension of technological knowledge?

Social capital and relational cognitive capital

Definitions and varieties of social capital

BURT, 2001: 32, contends that "social capital is the contextual complement to human capital". In this vein, social capital in an economic context can be defined as an intangible resource consisting in the stock of collective intelligence embodied in social relationships (rather than in individuals), including institutions, norms, values and understandings, trust, reputation, etc., which contributes to the creation of economic value. This definition, however, is by no means agreed upon by everyone.

The vast literature on social capital which currently exists is predominantly sociological. The origins of the term 'social capital' can be traced back to Bourdieu's pioneering anthropological and ethnological work [BOURDIEU, 1972]. COLEMAN, 1988, popularises the term by reintroducing it in Anglosaxon literature in the context of social networks as a 'resource for action', an intangible, non-fungible relational asset embedded in social relationships, reproduced through social norms, trust and obligations, generated by 'network closure',[28] and contributing to the formation of human capital.

An opposite approach to Coleman's perception of social capital as a synergetic asset is found in BURT, 2007: 4, who refers to social capital as "the advantage created by a person's location in a structure of relationships". This is clearly a conception of social capital as an antagonistic asset, a "metaphor about advantage" [BURT, 2001: 31], which confers an exclusive competitive advantage to its possessor. From that perspective, Burt goes on to argue that social capital is formed around 'structural holes',[29] as network-embedded agents "broker connections between otherwise disconnected segments" of the network [Ibid.]. In a more neutral fashion, LIN, 2002: 19, defines social capital as "investment in social relations with expected returns in the marketplace" and also as "resources embedded in a social structure that are accessed and/or mobilized in purposive actions" [Ibid.: 29].

The following characteristics of social capital qualify it as a form of capital similar to physical:

- It is a manmade factor of production; it generates worth.
- Its production involves investment with expected returns.
- It is collectively produced and, often, individually owned. Moreover it is not necessarily owned by those who produce it but by those who are able to exploit it, i.e. to strategically access or mobilise it for their (pecuniary or otherwise) benefit.
- It is a cumulable asset; its locus of accumulation is the social structure.

Particular characteristics of social capital, which distinguish it from physical capital, are the following:

- It is intangible and disembodied.
- It is generated through joint rather than individual action.

However, on this last point the literature, as we already saw, is divided: In Coleman's synergetic perspective, social capital is the result of cooperation and sharing. In Burt's antagonistic perspective, it is the result of an advantage of an individual over others created by her position in a social structure.

Technological knowledge as individual and as relational cognitive capital

In all the above definitions the exact relationship of social capital to (technological) knowledge is not explicit. The reason is that the concept of social capital has not been devised in the first place specifically to refer to knowledge but rather more generally as a metaphor about the economic value of social relationships.

Here I introduce the concept of *relational cognitive capital*, the counterpart to *individual cognitive capital* (which is a different term for 'human capital'), as a specific type of social capital which embodies technological knowledge. This form of cognitive capital bears all the characteristics of social capital: it is an intangible asset embedded in social structures and the product of purposive joint action. In addition, it is an objectified representation of distributed knowledge (explained below). Since it is the product of micro-interactions, it resides in the meso domain and, more specifically, it is embedded in the knowledge plexus. In analogy to social capital, agents have differential access to it depending on their relative position in the structure of the knowledge plexus; agents connecting otherwise disconnected clusters of specific technological knowledge, i.e. structural holes, are in the particularly privileged position of the broker.

Relational cognitive capital is a clear manifestation of emergence: As a relational phenomenon it does not pertain to the level of micro-entities but to the meso level of the knowledge plexus. Contrary to human (or 'individual cognitive') capital it is non-decomposable, as it cannot be fully imputed to a single economic agent independently from others. Finally, it exercises downwardly causal influence on the micro-entities, by which it is also upwardly determined.

The concepts of individual and relational cognitive capital are extensively used in the empirical models developed in Chapter 4. There it is hypothesised that the relational form of cognitive capital may exercise an influence on the knowledge production process equal as or even stronger than the individual one, given that technological knowledge is systemically produced.

Technological knowledge as systemic phenomenon

The process of technological knowledge production is par excellence synergetic. In modern knowledge-based economies firms cannot conduct research exclusively by relying on own resources in isolation from their technological environment. Indeed, their innovative capacities are largely determined by their ability to position themselves in the knowledge plexus and to tap economies of complexity in knowledge production. As a result of this, firms increasingly adopt 'open innovation' practices [CHIAROMONTE, 2006; CHESBROUGH, 2003], and choose to collaborate with organisations, such as other private firms, universities, research institutes, public bodies, etc. Theoretical and empirical evidence points to the growing tendency among 'post-Fordist', knowledge-economy firms, including multinational corporations, to externalise their R&D functions by shifting from vertical integration to more flexible integration modes and to the 'network type of organisation' in knowledge production. In order to interpret these transitions and also to assess the wider role of technological knowledge in economic processes it is necessary to understand technological knowledge not only as an objectified factor of production but also through the 'constructivist' prism as a systemic phenomenon emerging from cognition by adaptive economic agents.

Cognition by adaptive agents

Structure of adaptive agents

The key to the 'black box' of technological knowledge as a systemic phenomenon is the intricate relationship between cognition and adaptation, first at the micro-level of individual adaptive agents and then at the macro-level of multiagent adaptive systems. Despite the significant progress in the field of artificial intelligence, cognitive theories of adaptive agents are still in their infancy. Here the causal relationship between adaptation and cognition is explored, without examining the ontological dimensions of knowledge.

An 'adaptive agent' is an entity that interacts with its environment and tries to accomplish a set of goals – such as the maximisation of his payoff function or the increase of his fitness; in other words, it is an entity that conducts *search in a fitness landscape* in order to optimise his objective function. The adaptive agent interacts with his environment in two fundamental ways: He can sense the environment through his 'detectors' and act upon the environment through his 'effectors' [BOOKER *et al.*, 1989]. These two functions are mediated by the agent's internal information-processing and decision-making mechanism. As the capacities of his information-processing apparatus are limited and the information signals he receives from his environment are noisy, the adaptive agent cannot function as a hyperrational global optimiser with perfect foresight. For this reason, the adaptive agent needs an internal, finite representation or 'model' of reality, which functions as an inference-making apparatus and provides him with anticipatory and predictive capacities. An element of this apparatus is the capacity to store structured information in 'memory', in the form of 'knowledge' that is recalled and used during the inference-making process and the formation of expectations. This apparatus is referred to as *internal model* by HOLLAND, 1996, or *schema* by GELL-MANN, 1994.

Schemata and constructivism

The notion of mental *schema* is essentially drawn from modern cognitive theory.[30] This strand of theory considers that knowledge stored in memory is structured as a set of discrete schemata, i.e. mental representations of types of objects or events of the environment reached through the sensory apparatuses. Knowledge is, therefore, an internalised representation of reality constructed by agents and not simply acquired from the environment – hence the term *constructivism* to refer to this strand of theory. The process of filtering sensory stimuli received from the environment, and structuring and storing in memory their information content is known as 'bottom-up processing'. The use of knowledge already stored in memory for inference-making purposes is known as 'top-down processing'. Schemata operate as top-down processing apparatuses that have been generated and are updated through bottom-up processing.

Schemata are internalised models of reality. These models are not necessarily 'correct' or optimal and for this reason they are constantly revised during the accumulation of new experiences and learning. Learning is the process by which the symbolic representations of reality become embedded into memory and by which new experiences are incorporated in existing cognitive structures. The updating of the schemata is the quintessence of the process of adaptation through learning: The agents' success in achieving their goals, in increasing their fitness and, eventually, in surviving depends on their ability to improve their internal models through the process of learning. According to HOLLAND, 1996, an agent's 'performance system' is a collection of rules with a given syntactic structure and a mechanism for updating the relative strength of the rules according to their payoffs, called 'credit assignment'. This is essentially a fundamental learning process based on trial-and-error.

Schemata are not exhaustive representations of reality but rather a set of generic rules that can be evoked and applied contingently to external stimuli. These schemata have a *modular structure*: they consist of simpler 'modules' or as HOLLAND, 1996, calls them, 'building blocks'. The updating of schemata is essentially a process of recombination of existing modules or, less frequently, the discovery of new ones.

In socio-economic systems the adaptation of an agent's schema by recombining existing modules would correspond to incremental innovation, while the introduction of new modules to radical innovation. In biological systems, the first process corresponds to crossover, while the second to mutation. The fitness of an agent endowed with a particular schema can be calculated by genetic algorithms that make use of the two genetic operators, namely the crossover and the mutation operator, together with a fitness function.[31] Cognition by an agent can also be represented by information processing models, whose updating rules are given by genetic algorithms.

Cognition in complex adaptive systems

Meta-agents' schemata and co-adaptation

Adaptive agents are often by themselves aggregations of lower-order adaptive agents, which can be modelled as multiagent systems or networks. When such compound entities are not simply resultant but emergent, they will be referred to as 'meta-agents'.[32] We have already seen, for instance, that corporate organisations can be conceived as emergent networks of individuals who themselves are reflective agents, while trivially, mesoeconomic plexuses and macro-economies also fall into this category when treated as entities.

Being adaptive agents in themselves, meta-agents should have their own schemata determining their operational regimes. Given that, by definition, meta-agents are ontologically distinct from the constituent lower-order agents, a meta-agent's schema cannot simply be an aggregation of the schemata of its lower-order components. A challenging issue in the study of complex adaptive systems is to understand and model the way these schemata and, more generally, the operational macro-regimes of meta-agents emerge from that of lower-order agents.

According to their internal architecture I distinguish two general types of meta-agents: First, hierarchical networks with unitary architecture and predetermined or fixed macro-structure, such as corporations, or, in biology, multicellular organisms, which I refer to as *integrated systems.* Lower-level agents in such systems are fully and irreversibly specialised with relatively fixed in-between links. Such systems have a unique centralised schema unrelated to the schemata of its constituent micro-units. Second, heterarchical networks with open architecture and evolving macro-structure, which I refer to as *distributed systems.* This type includes mesoeconomic plexuses, cities and industrial districts when considered as complex adaptive systems, or, in biology, colonial organisms and other localised symbiotic ecosystems. In these systems, lower-order agents are semi-specialised and semi-autonomous with relatively stable but flexible in-between links. These links are made possible by the development of complementarities in the schemata of the lower-order agents that favour symbiotic relationships. Systems of this type do not have a unitary, centralised schema, but instead their operational macro-regime is determined by a collective schema ensuing from the co-adapted schemata of their constituent micro-units.

Complementarities are the result of *co-evolution* and *co-adaptation.* In the case of biological systems, the development of complementarities is mainly a long-run inter-generational, inter- or intra-specific co-evolutionary process, which involves the mechanisms of selection and inheritance applied to whole populations rather than individuals. In the case of socio-economic systems, complementarities are mainly generated by the intra-generational process of co-adaptation applied to individual members of a population. Similarly to co-evolution, co-adaptation can be *competitive, mutualistic* or *exploitative*; as a matter of fact, mesoeconomic plexuses exhibit all three types of interactions. The co-adaptation process involves the exchange of large information flows between individual agents, ranging from simple sensory stimuli to structured knowledge; these information flows are processed by agents' schemata but also cause their updating, and hence the development of complementarities.

Heterarchies and distributed cognition

In the previous section we saw how knowledge is constructed within the schemata of adaptive agents. Technological knowledge, in particular, is the product of the schemata of economic agents. This cognitivist approach explains how knowledge accrues to individual agents; it does not explain, however, how knowledge accrues to multiagent systems. Since technological knowledge is by nature predominantly systemic and synergistic rather than individualistic, a theory that explains how it emerges in systems is essential for understanding its deeper generative mechanisms.

The concept of *distributed cognition* is directly relevant to the above question [ROGERS & ELLIS, 1994].[33] This concept stems from a relatively new branch of cognitive science, which examines how cognitive processes are distributed across social groups and how internal (such as schemata) and external (environment, artefacts, etc.) cognitive structures are coordinated. In the case of socio-economic systems, distributed cognition can be perceived as emanating from the integration of individual agents' 'intersubjective' knowledge through the division of labour.

Distributed systems are inherently capable of handling distributed cognition. The collective schemata of this type of systems are the results of emergence and self-organisation, and, as already noted, have decentralised and open-ended architectures. Knowledge generation in this type of systems is a multi-domain emergence process involving adaptive agents interacting at different ontological levels, from that of the neurons of the nervous system of individuals, to groups of individual researchers in organisations, up to the mesoeconomic plexus. Knowledge generation in these systems is, therefore, a genuinely synergetic, complex process shaped by the relational structure in which it emerges rather than by individuals.

Cognitive domains and intersubjective knowledge

The knowledge generated within an agent's schema can be partitioned in three distinct subsets, depending on its relevance to the agent as an individual or to the system where the agent belongs, which I refer to as *cognitive domains*: The cognitive domain in the agent's schema that is not reproduced in other agents' schemata and, therefore, is relevant exclusively to the agent as an individual will be called 'the domain of *subjective knowledge*'. The cognitive domain that is replicable in all agents' schemata within a system will be referred to as 'the domain of *objective knowledge*'; this is the subset of codifiable and reproducible knowledge. Finally, the cognitive domain in an agent's schema that is *isomorphic* to similar domains in other agents' schemata without being replicated in them will be referred to as 'the domain of *intersubjective knowledge*'.[34] This domain consists of tacit, imperfectly codifiable segments of the agents' schemata, which are systemically integrated despite the fact that they cannot be directly replicated and transmitted.

There is a certain correspondence between the three cognitive domains and the four types of knowledge identified previously: The universal and instrumental types generally fall in the domain of subjective knowledge; both 'embodied' types fall in the domain of intersubjective knowledge, with the exception of the segment of individual knowledge that is not directly relevant to the economic system in which the agent operates, and hence belongs to the domain of subjective knowledge. This correspondence is presented in Table 2.3.

Table 2.3: Cognitive domains and types of technological knowledge

COGNITIVE DOMAIN	TYPE OF TECHNOLOGICAL KNOWLEDGE	(OPTIMAL) LOCUS OF SYSTEMISATION
Objective	**Universal**	Distributed systems
	Instrumental	Integrated systems
Intersubjective	**Organisational**	Integrated systems
	Individual	Integrated / distributed systems
Subjective	**Individual**	

Systemic knowledge, according to this classification scheme, involves the domains of objective and intersubjective knowledge.

A fundamental question is how intersubjective knowledge of individuals becomes 'systemised', i.e. internalised in the schema of a multiagent system. The answer is that this happens through the process of mutualistic co-adaptation: It has already been observed that co-adaptive dynamics create complementarities among individual agents' schemata; these complementarities are *isomorphic mappings* between the corresponding domains of intersubjective knowledge of the adaptive agents.

Cognition as competitive co-adaptation

Of the three types of co-evolutionary relationships previously presented, namely competition, mutualism and exploitation, the synergetic generation of technological knowledge has been so far attributed mainly to one, namely mutualistic co-adaptation. In this paragraph the emphasis shifts to competitive co-adaptation as the driver of technological dynamics in the knowledge economy.

The frontier of inter-firm competition in the knowledge economy is continuously shifted through the intensification of product-differentiation by innovation and the shortening of the product life-cycle. By innovating, firms constantly create new niches of absolute advantage and temporarily secure their market power and share against potential imitators. This has become a generalised corporate strategy aiming at rendering mature products obsolete and thereby reducing

their profitability, so that potential market entrants would not be able to compete in terms of production costs with incumbent firms.

The phenomenon of innovation-based (instead of price-based) competition among firms in a continuous effort to simply maintain market shares and to avert product imitation by rivals evokes the *Red Queen principle* from evolutionary biology. This 'innovation arms race', as termed by BAUMOL, 2004, transforms the nature of competitive advantage and, consequently, the organisational structure of the firm: Traditional competition is based on cost reduction and economies of scale and scope. By contrast, innovation-based competition is based on flexibility and rapidity in searching, tracking down, tapping, transforming and utilising new knowledge, and on the ability to generate and exploit economies of complexity. Whereas the realisation of economies of scale and scope requires vertical and horizontal integration respectively, economies of complexity are better supported by quasi-integration, or more generally, by network organisational structures.

The Red Queen principle applied in the economic context provides an alternative explanation for the empirical failure of the R&D-based endogenous growth models [ROMER, 1990; GROSSMAN & HELPMAN, 1991; AGHION & HOWITT, 1992] demonstrated by JONES, 1995b. According to Jones' famous critique, the postwar exponential growth in R&D employment in the US is in sharp contrast to the stationarity of the US macroeconomic growth rates during the same period (and indeed the same applies to most other OECD countries), contrary to the predictions of the above models.[35] During the historical period studied by Jones, R&D investment in all industrialised countries follows a competitive arms race, which undeniably accelerates the global pace of scientific and technological progress (measured in R&D employment, as well as in knowledge output such as patents, scientific publications, technological products, etc.). This is, however, not translated in macroeconomic growth as technological competition erodes the margins of profit and the technology rent of the firms in a spiral of Red Queen dynamics. Moreover, radical innovations and shifts in technological paradigms, as the ones occurring in the postwar period, require heavy investment in the initial stages with uncertain economic outcomes – in many cases the research projects simply fail to have a market impact. In the case of mature technologies and established technological paradigms investment is less risky and its outcome more predictable. The postwar R&D arms race in industrialised economies, during which radically new technologies driven by scientific breakthroughs were explored and established, should be seen in this context.

Conclusion

The reinstatement of the relational space is the first step towards the establishment of the new systemic paradigm in economic geography based on the premises of complexity, evolution and emergence, as proposed in Chapter 1.

The second step is the recognition of the importance of the meso level as an ontological domain which articulates and coheres the nested hierarchy of domains of the economy from that of micro-economic agents to that of macro-economic systems. The meso domain is a relational space where the interactions of economic agents take place; as such, it is also the locus where the division of labour unfolds. Many essential economic processes occur there, but most importantly the production of technological knowledge.

The fundamental ontology of this domain is defined to be the 'mesoeconomic plexus'. This entity is a new analytical tool for systemic economic geography, representing the embodiment of a complete external division of labour in a specific production process. This entity exhibits many of the macro-properties of complex adaptive systems, and can also be conceived as an emergent heterarchical network of adaptive micro-units or, equivalently, as a meta-agent with the qualities of a distributed system. A specific type of mesoeconomic plexus is the *knowledge plexus*, which embodies the division of labour in the production of technological knowledge.

In mainstream economics and economic geography technological and informational externalities of various forms, including network effects, as well as external economies of scale, e.g. in the form of agglomeration economies, are thought of as typical economic phenomena occurring in local or supra-local formations of interconnected productive units, such as industrial districts, regional clusters, or various types of economic networks. All these are implicitly or explicitly treated as unintended 'by-products' of the economic activity. There is however a different dimension of the 'collective efficiency' exhibited by mesoeconomic plexuses which is not imputable either to traditional economies of scale and scope or to externalities but to the division of labour itself: the *economies of complexity*. In general these economies are common in distributed systems, and particularly prominent in knowledge-intensive industries.

The third step towards the systemic paradigm is the creation of a theory that explains how technological knowledge – probably the most important factor of production in modern economies – is generated in relational space, and, in turn, how it shapes geographical space. Technological knowledge may be treated as a capital-like *substance*, i.e. 'cognitive capital', or as a *systemic process*. As a substance, technological knowledge in its relational dimension is similar to social capital. As a process, technological knowledge emerges in multiagent systems through mutualistic as well as competitive co-adaptation of reflective (i.e. boundedly rational, adaptive and possessing own cognitive schemata) economic agents. The process of co-adaptation essentially connects, aligns and 'systemises' technological knowledge that belongs to the 'intersubjective domain' of individual agents' schemata (i.e. economically relevant individual knowledge).

Mesoeconomic plexuses can be modelled as 'meta-agents' possessing collective schemata with open, evolving architecture. From this perspective, the above described process of co-adaptation is instrumental in shaping the collective schemata of the mesoeconomic plexuses, which in turn determine the techno-economic trajectories of the macro-economies. In this context, competitive co-adaptation plays a crucial role in shaping the techno-economic trajectory of the 'post-Fordist' knowledge economy: This is characterised by a rapid expansion of the technological frontier and Red Queen-type of dynamics, which erode technological rent and push firms to compete in terms of innovation just for survival and for preserving their market shares. It is also characterised by the transition from the *closed* to the *open* model of innovation. Under the former the whole knowledge production process is internalised within the firm and protected; firms benefit only from rapidly exhaustible internal economies of scale. Under the latter the knowledge production process is externalised, and firms benefit from non-exhaustible economies of complexity.[36] In this context, strategic alliances, joint ventures and other forms of inter-firm collaboration are becoming increasingly important for the survival of the firms, and so collaboration happily co-exists with competition contrary to the mainstream perception of competition as the (only) primum mobile of the capitalist economy. The tendency towards the open model of innovation favours the flexible open architecture of heterarchical, quasi-integrated, network-shaped, distributed systems, over the closed and hierarchical architecture of integrated systems, such as the traditional 'Fordist' corporations, especially in the production of technological knowledge. Distributed systems are capable of internalising knowledge spillovers and generating economies of complexity more than integrated systems. However, their comparative efficiency in generating technological knowledge depends on the type of knowledge in question: Integrated systems may still perform relatively well in handling knowledge with limited spillovers and high degree of appropriability. In the modern knowledge economy, however, the main volume of knowledge produced does not fall under this category.

Supported by modern telecommunication technologies, the division of labour, which the mesoeconomic plexus embodies, may extend in geographical space almost without physical barriers. The plexus is not, therefore, a territorially embedded entity, but a supra-local heterarchical network, which occasionally incorporates locally embedded clusters of economic activity wherever territorial proximity is necessitated by the type of economic interaction – a structure which resembles the 'small-world' networks presented in Chapter 3. Relational rather than territorial proximity is, therefore, the determining geographical characteristic of the mesoeconomic plexus.

References

ACKERMAN, F. (2002): Still dead after all these years: interpreting the failure of general equilibrium theory. *Journal of Economic Methodology 9* (2): 119–139.

AGHION, P. & HOWITT, P. (1992): A model of growth through creative destruction. *Econometrica 60* (2): 323–351.

ALCHIAN, A.A , & DEMSETZ, H. (1972): Production, information costs, and economic organization. *American Economic Review 62* (5): 777–795.

AMIN, A. & THRIFT, N. (1992): Neo-Marshallian nodes in global networks. *International Journal of Urban and Regional Research 16* (4): 571–587.

AOKI, M. (1986): Horizontal versus vertical information structure of the firm. *American Economic Review 76* (5): 971–983.

ASHEIM, B. (1995): Industrial districts as 'learning regions'. A condition for prosperity? *STEP Report Series.*

AUDRETSCH, D.B. & FELDMAN, M.P. (1996): Innovative clusters and the industry life cycle. *Review of Industrial Organization 11* (2): 253–273.

BAGNASCO, A. (1977): *Tre Italie. La Problematica Territoriale dello Sviluppo Italiano.* Bologna: Il mulino.

BARRO, R.J., & X. SALA-I-MARTIN (1995): *Economic Growth.* New York, NY: McGraw-Hill.

BARTLETT, F.C. (1932): *Remembering.* Cambridge: Cambridge University Press.

BATHELT, H. & GLÜCKLER, J. (2003): Toward a relational economic geography. *Journal of Economic Geography 3* (2): 117–144.

BAUMOL, W.J. (2004): Red-Queen games: arms races, rule of law and market economies. *Journal of Evolutionary Economics 14* (2): 237–247.

BECATTINI, G. (1987): *Mercato e Forze Locali: Il Distretto Industriale.* Bologna: Il Mulino.

BELL, C.R. (1988): Economies of, versus returns to, scale: A clarification. *Journal of Economic Education 19* (4): 331–335.

BLOIS, K.J. (1972): Vertical quasi-integration. *Journal of Industrial Economics 20* (3): 253–272.

BOGGS, J.S. & RANTISI, N.M. (2003): The'relational turn' in economic geography. *Journal of Economic Geography 3* (2): 109–116.

BONIFACIO, M., BOUQUET, P., MAMELI, G. & NORI, M. (2004): Peer-mediated distributed knowledge management. In: VAN ELST, L., DIGNUM, V. & ABECKER, A., eds: *Agent-Mediated Knowledge Management*, pp. 31–47. Berlin: Springer-Verlag.

BOOKER, L.B., GOLDBERG, D.E. & HOLLAND, J.H. (1989): Classifier systems and genetic algorithms. *Artificial Intelligence 40* (1–3): 235–282.

BOSCHMA, R. & MARTIN, R. (2007): Editorial: Constructing an evolutionary economic geography. *Journal of Economic Geography 7* (5): 537–548.

BOSCHMA, R.A. & FRENKEN, K. (2006): Why is economic geography not an evolutionary science? Towards an evolutionary economic geography. *Journal of Economic Geography 6* (3): 273–302.

BOSCHMA, R.A. & MARTIN, R.L. (2010): *The Handbook of Evolutionary Economic Geography.* Cheltenham: Edward Elgar Publishing.

BOURDIEU, P. (1972): *Esquisse d'une Théorie de la Pratique (précédée de trois études d'ethnologie kabyle).* Genève: Librairie Droz.

BURT, R.S. (2007): *Brokerage and Closure. An Introduction to Social Capital.* Oxford: Oxford University Press.

BURT, R.S. (2001): Structural holes versus network closure as social capital. In: LIN, N., COOK, K. & BURT, R.S., eds: *Social Capital. Theory and Research*, pp. 31–56. New York, NY: Aldine de Gruyter.

CASTELLS, M. (1991): *The Informational City. Information Technology, Economic Restructuring, and the Urban-Regional Process.* Oxford: Blackwell.

CASTELLS, M. (2011): *The Rise of the Network Society. The Information Age: Economy, Society, and Culture.* Chichester: John Wiley & Sons.

CHESBROUGH, H.W. (2003): The era of open innovation. *MIT Sloan Management Review 44* (3): 35–41.

CHEUNG, S.N.S. (1969): Transaction costs, risk aversion, and the choice of contractual arrangements. *Journal of Law & Economics 12* (1): 23–42.

CHIAROMONTE, F. (2006): Open innovation through alliances and partnership: theory and practice. *International Journal of Technology Management 33* (2-3): 111–114.

CHRISTALLER, W. (1933): *Die zentralen Orte in Süddeutschland: eine ökonomisch-geographische Untersuchung über die Gesetzmässigkeit der Verbreitung und Entwicklung der Siedlungen mit städtischen Funktionen.* Jena: Gustav Fischer.

CHWE, M.S.-Y. (2000): Communication and coordination in social networks. *Review of Economic Studies 67* (1): 1–16.

COASE, R.H. (1937): The nature of the firm. *Economica 4* (16): 386–405.

COASE, R.H. (1960): The problem of social cost. *Journal of Law & Economics 3* (1): 1–44.

COLEMAN, J.S. (1988): Social capital in the creation of human capital. *American Journal of Sociology 94* (Suppl.): 95–120.

COMMONS, J.R. (1936): Institutional economics. *American Economic Review 26* (1): 237–249.

DAVIDOW, W.H. & MALONE, M.S. (1992): *The Virtual Corporation. Structuring and Revitalizing the Corporation for the 21st Century.* New York, NY: Harper Collins Publishers.

DOSI, G. (1984): *Technical Change and Industrial Transformation: The Theory and an Application to the Semiconductor Industry.* Basingstoke: Palgrave Macmillan.

DOSI, G. (1988): The nature of the innovative process. In: DOSI, G., FREEMAN, C., NELSON, R.R., SILVERBERG, G. & SOETE, L., eds: *Technical Change and Economic Theory,* pp. 221–238. London: Pinter.

EDQUIST, C., ed. (1997): *Systems of Innovation. Technologies, Institutions and Organizations.* London: Pinter.

FARRELL, J. & SALONER, G. (1985): Standardization, compatibility, and innovation. *RAND Journal of Economics 16* (1): 70–83.

FLAKE, G.W. (2000): *The Computational Beauty of Nature. Computer Explorations of Fractals, Chaos, Complex Systems and Adaptation.* Cambridge, MA: MIT Press.

FRENKEN, K. & BOSCHMA, R.A. (2007): A theoretical framework for evolutionary economic geography: industrial dynamics and urban growth as a branching process. *Journal of Economic Geography 7* (5): 635–649.

FUCHS, G. & SHAPIRA, P., eds (2005): *Rethinking Regional Innovation and Change: Path Dependency or Regional Breakthrough?* New York, NY: Springer.

FUJITA, M. & KRUGMAN, P. (2004): The new economic geography: Past, present and the future. *Papers in Regional Science 83* (1): 139–164.

FUJITA, M., KRUGMAN, P. & VENABLES, A.J. (1999): *The Spatial Economy. Cities, Regions and International Trade.* Cambridge, MA: MIT Press.

GALBRAITH, J.K. (1967): *The New Industrial State.* Princeton, NJ: Princeton University Press.

GARUD, R. & KARNØE, P., eds (2001): *Path Dependence and Creation.* Mahwah, NJ: Lawrence Erlbaum Associates.

GELL-MANN, M. (1994): *The Quark and the Jaguar. Adventures in the Simple and the Complex.* New York, NY: Freeman.

GLAESER, E.L., KALLAL, H.D., SCHEINKMAN, J.A. & SHLEIFER, A. (1992): Growth in cities. *Journal of Political Economy 100* (6): 1126–1152.

GOYAL, S. & JANSSEN, M. (1996): Interaction structure and social change. *Journal of Institutional and Theoretical Economics 152* (3): 472–495.

GRANT, R.M. (1996): Toward a knowledge-based theory of the firm. *Strategic Management Journal 17* (Special Issue: Knowledge and the Firm): 109–122.

GROSSMAN, G.M. & HELPMAN, E. (1991): Quality ladders in the theory of growth. *Review of Economic Studies 58* (1): 43–61.

HAGEDOORN, J. & SCHAKENRAAD, J. (1994): The effect of strategic technology alliances on company performance. *Strategic Management Journal 15* (4): 291–309.

HARRISON, B., KELLEY, M.R. & GANT, J. (1996): Innovative firm behavior and local milieu: Exploring the intersection of agglomeration, firm effects, and technological change. *Economic Geography 72* (3): 233–258.

HARVEY, D. (1973): *Social Justice and the City.* London: Edward Arnold Publishers.

HARVEY, D. (2006): *Spaces of Global Capitalism. Towards a Theory of Uneven Geographical Development.* London: Verso Books.

HODGSON, G.M. (1998): The approach of institutional economics. *Journal of Economic Literature 36* (1): 166–192.

HOFSTADTER, D.R. (1979): *Gödel, Escher, Bach: An Eternal Golden Braid.* Brighton: Harvester Press.

HOLLAND, J.H. (1996): *Hidden Order. How Adaptation Builds Complexity.* New York, NY: Basic Books.

HUTCHINS, E. & NORMAN, D.A. (1988): *Distributed cognition in aviation: A concept paper for NASA (Contract No. NCC 2-591).* University of California, San Diego, Department of Cognitive Science.

ISARD, W. (1956): *Location and Space-Economy: A General Theory Relating to Industrial Location, Market Areas, Land Use, Trade, and Urban Structure.* Cambridge, MA: MIT Press and Wiley.

JESSOP, B. (2001): Capitalism, the regulation approach, and critical realism. In: BROWN, A., FLEETWOOD, S., ROBERTS, J.M., eds: *Critical Realism and Marxism*, pp. 88–115. London: Routledge.

JONES, C., HESTERLY, W.S. & BORGATTI, S.P. (1997): A general theory of network governance: Exchange conditions and social mechanisms. *Academy of Management Review 22* (4): 911–945.

JONES, C.I. (1995a): R&D-based models of economic growth. *Journal of Political Economy 103* (4): 759–784.

JONES, C.I. (1995b): Time series tests of endogenous growth models. *Quarterly Journal of Economics 110* (2): 495–525.

KALDOR, N. (1972): The irrelevance of equilibrium economics. *Economic Journal 82* (328): 1237–1255.

KATZ, M.L. & SHAPIRO, C. (1985): Network externalities, competition, and compatibility. *American Economic Review 75* (3): 424–440.

KLEIN, B., CRAWFORD, R.G. & ALCHIAN, A.A. (1978): Vertical integration, appropriable rents, and the competitive contracting process. *Journal of Law and Economics 21*297–326.

KOGUT, B. & ZANDER, U. (1992): Knowledge of the firm, combinative capabilities, and the replication of technology. *Organization Science 3* (3): 383–397.

KRUEGER, A.O. (1974): The political economy of the rent-seeking society. *American Economic Review, 64* (3): 291–303.

KRUGMAN, P. (1998): Space: the final frontier. *Journal of Economic Perspectives 12* (2): 161–174.

KRUGMAN, P. (1993): On the relationship between trade theory and location theory. *Review of International Economics 1* (2): 110–122.

KRUGMAN, P. (1992): *Geography and Trade.* Cambridge, MA: MIT Press.

KRUGMAN, P. (1991): Increasing returns and economic geography. *Journal of Political Economy 99* (3): 483–99.

LAUNHARDT, W. (1885): *Mathematische Begründung der Volkswirtschaftslehre.* Leipzig: W. Engelmann.

LAUNHARDT, W. (1872): *The Theory of the Trace: Being a Discussion of the Principles of Location.* Madras: Lawrence Asylum Press.

LEBORGNE, D. & LIPIETZ, A. (1992): Conceptual fallacies and open questions on post-Fordism. In: STORPER, M. & SCOTT, A.J.: *Pathways to Industrialization and Regional Development,* pp. 332–348. London: Routledge.

LEVIN, R.C. (1988): Appropriability, R&D spending, and technological performance. *American Economic Review 78* (2): 424–428.

LIN, N. (2002): *Social Capital: A Theory of Social Structure and Action.* Cambridge: Cambridge University Press.

LÖSCH, A. (1940): *Die räumliche Ordnung der Wirtschaft. Eine Untersuchung über Standort, Wirtschaftsgebiete und internationalem Handel.* Jena: Fischer.

LUCAS, R.E. (1988): On the mechanics of economic development. *Journal of Monetary Economics 22* (1): 3–42.

LUNDVALL, B.-Å., ed. (1992): *National Systems of Innovation: Towards a Theory of Innovation and Interactive Learning.* London: Pinter.

LUNDVALL, B.-Å. & JOHNSON, B. (1994): The learning economy. *Journal of Industry Studies 1* (2): 23–42.

MARKUSEN, A. (1996): Sticky places in slippery space: A typology of industrial districts. *Economic Geography 72* (3): 293–313.

MARSHALL, A. (1920): *Principles of Economics.* 8th edition. London: Macmillan.

MARTIN, R.L. (2008): Institutional approaches in economic geography. In: SHEPPARD, E. & BARNES, T.J., eds: *A Companion to Economic Geography,* pp. 77–94. Oxford: Blackwell.

MARTIN, R.L. (1999): The new 'geographical turn' in economics: some critical reflections. *Cambridge Journal of Economics 23* (1): 65–91.

MARTIN, R.L. & SUNLEY, P. (2003): Deconstructing clusters: chaotic concept or policy panacea? *Journal of Economic Geography 3* (1): 5–35.

MARTIN, R.L. & SUNLEY, P. (2006): Path dependence and regional economic evolution. *Journal of Economic Geography 6* (4): 395–437.

MARTIN, R.L. & SUNLEY, P. (1996): Paul Krugman's geographical economics and its implications for regional development theory: A critical assessment. *Economic Geography 72* (3): 259–292.

MAS-COLELL, A., WHINSTON, M.D. & GREEN, J.R. (1995): *Microeconomic Theory.* New York, NY: Oxford University Press.

MASKIN, E.S. (1994): The invisible hand and externalities. *American Economic Review 84* (2): 333–337.

McClelland, J.L., & D.E. Rumelhart (1988): *Explorations in Parallel Distributed Processing.* Cambridge, MA: MIT Press.

McLaren, J. (2000): 'Globalization' and vertical structure. *American Economic Review 90* (5): 1239–1254.

Meade, J.E. (1952): External economies and diseconomies in a competitive situation. *Economic Journal 62* (245): 54–67.

Midgley, D.F., Morrison, P.D. & Roberts, J.H. (1992): The effect of network structure in industrial diffusion processes. *Research Policy 21* (6): 533–552.

Miles, R.E. & Snow, C.C. (1992): Causes of failure in network organizations. *California Management Review 34* (4): 53–72.

Minsky, H. (1986): *Stabilizing an Unstable Economy.* New Haven, CT: Yale University Press.

Minsky, M. (1985): *Society in Mind.* New York, NY: Simon & Schuster.

Mowery, D.C., Oxley, J.E. & Silverman, B.S. (1996): Strategic alliances and interfirm knowledge transfer. *Strategic Management Journal 17*: 77–91.

Myrdal, G. (1957): *Economic Theory and Underdeveloped Regions.* London: Methuen & Co.

Narula, R. & Hagedoorn, J. (1999): Innovating through strategic alliances: moving towards international partnerships and contractual agreements. *Technovation 19* (5): 283–294.

Nelson, R.R. & Winter, S.G. (1982): *An Evolutionary Theory of Economic Change.* Cambridge, MA: Belknap Press.

North, D.C. (1990): *Institutions, Institutional Change and Economic Performance.* Cambridge: Cambridge University Press.

North, D.C. (1987): Institutions, transaction costs and economic growth. *Economic Inquiry 25* (3): 419–428.

OECD (1998): *Human Capital Investment. An International Comparison.* Paris: OECD Center for Educational Research and Innovation.

OLSON, M. (1965): *The Logic of Collective Action. Public Goods and the Theory of Groups.* Cambridge, MA: Harvard University Press.

PIAGET, J. (1970): *Structuralism.* New York, NY: Harper & Row.

PIAGET, J. (1971): *Biology and Knowledge.* Chicago, IL: University of Chicago Press.

PIORE, M.J. & SABEL, C.F. (1984): *The Second Industrial Divide. Possibilities for Prosperity.* New York, NY: Basic Books.

PODOLNY, J.M. & PAGE, K.L. (1998): Network forms of organization. *Annual Review of Sociology 24*: 57–76.

POLANYI, M. (1967): *The Tacit Dimension.* New York, NY: Anchor Books.

POWELL, W.W. (1990): Neither market nor hierarchy: Network forms of organization. *Research in Organizational Behavior 12*: 295–336.

PUTNAM, R.D., R. LEONARDI, R., & R.Y. NANETTI (1993): *Making Democracy Work: Civic Traditions in Modern Italy.* Princeton, NJ: Princeton University Press.

ROGERS, Y. & ELLIS, J. (1994): Distributed cognition: An alternative framework for analysing and explaining collaborative working. *Journal of Information Technology* 9 (2): 119–128.

ROMER, P.M. (1990): Endogenous technological change. *Journal of Political Economy 98* (5, Part 2: The Problem of Development: A Conference of the Institute for the Study of Free Enterprise Systems): S71–S102.

SABEL, C. (1989): Flexible specialisation and the re-emergence of regional economies. In: HIRST, P. & ZEITLIN, J., eds: *Reversing Industrial Decline? Industrial Structure and Policies in Britain and Her Competitors*, pp. 17–70. New York, NY: Berg.

SANCHEZ, R. & MAHONEY, J.T. (1996): Modularity, flexibility, and knowledge management in product and organization design. *Strategic Management Journal 17*: 63–76.

SAVIOTTI, P. & METCALFE, J.S., eds (1991): *Evolutionary Theories of Economic and Technological Change. Present Status and Future Prospects.* Newark, NJ: Harwood Academic Publishers.

SAXENIAN, A. (1996): *Regional Advantage: Culture and Competition in Silicon Valley and Route 128.* Cambridge, MA: Harvard University Press.

SCHMITZ, H. (1999): Collective efficiency and increasing returns. *Cambridge Journal of Economics 23* (4): 465–483.

SCHUMPETER, J.A. (1954): *History of Economic Analysis.* London: Allen & Unwin.

SCITOVSKY, T. (1954): Two concepts of external economies. *Journal of Political Economy 62* (2): 143–151.

SCOTT, A.J. (1988): *New Industrial Spaces: Flexible Production Organisation and Regional Development in North America and Western Europe.* London: Pion.

SCOTT, A.J. (1996): Regional motors of the global economy. *Futures 28* (5): 391–411.

SIMMIE, J. & MARTIN, R.L. (2010): The economic resilience of regions: towards an evolutionary approach. *Cambridge Journal of Regions, Economy and Society 3* (1): 27–43.

SIMMIE, J. & SENNETT, J. (1999): Innovative clusters: global or local linkages? *National Institute Economic Review 170* (1): 87–98.

SIMON, H.A. (1956): Rational choice and the structure of the environment. *Psychological Review 63* (2): 129–138.

SMITH, A. (1776): *An Inquiry into the Nature and Causes of the Wealth of Nations.* London: Methuen & Co.

SPENDER, J.C. (1996): Making knowledge the basis of a dynamic theory of the firm. *Strategic Management Journal 17*: 45–62.

SRAFFA, P. (1926): The laws of returns under competitive conditions. *Economic Journal 36* (144): 535–550.

STIGLER, G.J. (1941): *Production and Distribution Theories.* New York, NY: Macmillan.

STORPER, M. (1997): *The Regional World. Territorial Development in a Global Economy.* New York, NY: Guilford Press.

Storper, M. (1995): The resurgence of regional economies, ten years later. The region as a nexus of untraded interdependencies. *European Urban and Regional Studies 2* (3): 191–221.

Storper, M. & Harrison, B. (1991): Flexibility, hierarchy and regional development: The changing structures of production systems and their forms of governance in the 1990s. *Research Policy 21*: 407–422.

Sunley, P. (2008): Relational economic geography: a partial understanding or a new paradigm? *Economic Geography 84* (1): 1–26.

Tullock, G., Brady, G., & Seldon, A. (2002): *Government Failure: A Primer in Public Choice.* Washington, DC: Cato Institute.

Uzawa, H. (1965): Optimum technical change in an aggregative model of economic growth. *International Economic Review 6* (1): 18–31.

Varga, A., Pontikakis, D. & Chorafakis, G. (2014): Metropolitan Edison and cosmopolitan Pasteur? Agglomeration and interregional research network effects on European R&D productivity. *Journal of Economic Geography 14* (2): 229–263.

Veblen, T. (1904): *The Theory of Business Enterprise.* New York, NY: Charles Scribner's sons.

Viner, J. (1932): Cost curves and supply curves. *Zeitschrift für Nationalökonomie 3* (1): 23–46.

Von Thünen, J.H. (1826): *Der isolierte Staat in Beziehung auf Nationalökonomie und Landwirtschaft.* Jena: Gustav Fischer.

Vygotsky, L.S. (1978): *Mind in Society. Development of Higher Psychological Processes.* Cambridge, MA: Harvard University Press.

Weber, A. (1909): *Über den Standort der Industrien. Erster Teil: Reine Theorie des Standorts.* Tübingen: Mohr.

Williamson, O.E. (1971): The vertical integration of production: Market failure considerations. *American Economic Review 61* (2): 112–123.

Williamson, O.E. (1979): Transaction costs economics: The governance of contractual relations. *Journal of Law and Economics 12* (2): 233–261.

WILLIAMSON, O.E. (1981): The economics of organization: The transaction cost approach. *American Journal of Sociology 87* (3): 548–577.

WILLIAMSON, O.E. (1985): *The Economic Institutions of Capitalism: Firms, Markets, Relational Contracting.* New York: Free Press.

WILLIAMSON, O.E. (2005): The economics of governance. *American Economic Review 95* (2): 1–18.

YEUNG, H.W. (2005): Rethinking relational economic geography. *Transactions of the Institute of British Geographers 30* (1): 37–51.

Notes

[1] As BARRO & SALA-I-MARTIN, 1995: 11, observe, "we end up with a model of growth that explains everything but long-run growth, an obviously unsatisfactory situation."
[2] Examples include UZAWA, 1965; LUCAS, 1988; ROMER, 1986; 1990; JONES, 1995a; AGHION & HOWITT, 1992.
[3] The Minkowskian space-time of special relativity is not a 'relative space', it is just a mathematical model of a physical space subject to the universal laws of classical (i.e. non-quantum) physics. Moreover, the typical relativistic phenomena, notably time dilation and Lorentz contraction, which characterise this space are perceivable when travelling close to the speed of light, and therefore are totally outside the scope of economic geography.
[4] Launhardt was a Hanoverian mathematician, whose work is considered as one of the earliest in mathematical economics [SCHUMPETER, 1954].
[5] The ratio of the weight of raw materials used in the manufacture of a product to the weight of the finished product.
[6] It should be noted that this has been an indispensable part of the Nazi state apparatus, which Christaller loyally served as a planner in Himmler's SS Planning and Soil Office, entrusted with the task of 'rationalising' spatial planning and reshaping and incorporating the annexed territories of the 'East' (Poland, Czechoslovakia and, as it was then envisaged, the USSR).
[7] To do justice to Krugman and his co-authors, a common characteristic in the collection of diverse models in FUJITA *et al.*, 1999, is the emphasis on adjustment dynamics, the existence of bifurcations in the dynamical systems describing agglomeration processes, and hence the possibility of multiple, unstable or punctuated equilibria, and phase transitions. Clearly, these characteristics are totally atypical of the neoclassical tradition, and in that respect the dynamic NEG models constitute a significant methodological (but not epistemological) departure from those of the static Walrasian general equilibrium.
[8] See MARTIN & SUNLEY, 1996, for a critique on this point.
[9] The presence of non-convexities in production, such as increasing returns to scale, makes even the *existence* of a Walrasian general equilibrium uncertain [ACKERMAN, 2002], and hence increasing returns is not a 'desirable' characteristic of 'well-behaved' economies. KALDOR, 1972: 1241, considers "the absence of increasing returns one of the basic axioms of the system" in the theory of general equilibrium.
[10] Aglietta, Boyer and Lipietz are prominent representatives of the Parisian School of 'Régulation'.
[11] Indicatively: SCOTT, 1988; STORPER & HARRISON, 1991; HARRISON *et al.*, 1996; SIMMIE & SENNETT, 1999.
[12] A CAS may or may not exhibit evolutionary dynamics (as defined in Chapter 1), and this ultimately depends on the internal structure of the lower-level adaptive agents, which may be much simpler and more 'primitive' than the minimum requirement for evolution to emerge. Conversely, a population in which evolutionary dynamics emerge may but need not be a CAS.
[13] Oddly, YEUNG, 2005, sees this turn as the enhancement with social actors and their network relations at different geographical scales of an earlier undercurrent

of 'relational thought' in economic geography, as he puts it, mainly expressed by the 'social relations of production framework', which he inadequately criticises for "overemphasising the structural determination" of spatial phenomena on the basis of class and division of labour. This misplaced critique seems to miss the point that the 'social relations of production framework' is in fact the centrepiece of Marxist political economy, whose fundamental ontology is social class, and whose epistemological and methodological foundations are, from a taxonomical perspective, totally unrelated to those of 'relational economic geography', by any tenable definition of the latter.

14 BOGGS & RANTISI, 2003: 110, wrongly, in the author's opinion, claim the exact opposite, namely that "the relational turn enters the structure-agency debate by ascribing a greater role to agency as opposed to structures in analyses of economic behaviour". They confusingly misidentify 'structure' as the immutable, teleological regularities allegedly found in a large number of heterogeneous theories, from Marxist political economy to neoclassical economics, naïvely subsumed under the banner of 'models sharing a teleological bent', which they then unjustifiably and vaguely criticise for neglecting "the range of socio-political constellations with which economic forces engage and by which varied outcomes develop".

15 Here a clarification is needed: I do not claim that the physical space *per se* does not have innate properties, I only argue that the physical space *of economic geography* should not be thought of as having innate properties other than those conferred to it by the economic entities and processes it contains. A similar view is expressed in BATHELT & GLÜCKLER, 2003.

16 Labour pooling and market size effects are, as clearly shown in NEG models, the results of cumulative causation, and hence self-reinforcing 'endogenous' processes; still, they are externalities, by-products of the economic activity, and hence elements of the socio-economic environment.

17 These roughly correspond to what Alfred Marshall called an 'industrial atmosphere' that was supposed to be present in the English industrial districts of Lancashire and Yorkshire, which he extensively studied.

18 The usual entry barriers are *product differentiation* and *economies of scope, absolute cost advantages*, and *economies of scale.*

19 Many concepts used in this subsection are drawn from the theory developed by WILLIAMSON, 1979; 1985; 2005 (which in turn has built on earlier work by COMMONS, 1936 and COASE, 1937). His approach is known as 'transaction costs economics', and in his more recent work as 'economics of governance'. The 'governance structure', according to him, depends on the frequency of transactions, uncertainty and the specificity of the assets involved. A 'hybrid governance structure' is one based on contractual arrangements.

20 *Quasi-rent* value of an asset is defined as "the excess of its value over its salvage value, that is, its value in its next best use to another renter" [KLEIN *et al.*, 1978: 298].

21 See MARTIN & SUNLEY, 2006 for a critical view on this topic.

22 Throughout this book the term 'economies of complexity' is used interchangeably with 'increasing returns to complexity', in analogy to the commonly in economic literature interchangeable use of 'economies of scale' and 'increasing returns to scale'. Nevertheless, the author is aware of the subtle

difference between the two terms, the former referring to cost savings due to increases in the scale of production, while the latter to output increases and hence productivity gains due to unspecified, usually exogenous, 'technological improvements' in relation to a (neoclassical) production function, ceteris paribus (see for instance, BELL, 1988, for a detailed account on the issue). Outside the neoclassical framework the distinction between the two terms is less meaningful, as 'technological improvements' can be identified, endogenised and thus associated with the scale of the factors of production.

[23] MAR-type externalities are dynamic localisation economies caused by intra-industry, vertical knowledge spillovers within the same value chain, while Jacobs-type externalities are dynamic urbanisation economies caused by inter-industry, horizontal knowledge spillovers between parallel value chains. Both types of externalities are induced by the collocation of economic agents in a specific locality.

[24] Universal, theoretical or generic knowledge is mostly non-contextual; instrumental, practical or applied knowledge is mostly contextual.

[25] I use the term 'quasi-private' to denote a good that in principle is rival and excludable, but with spillovers that in the longer run erode its excludability, and consequently, its private nature. In existing literature this term is sometimes used differently, to denote private goods provided by the government. 'Quasi-public' are publicly provided and socially beneficial goods, which however are neither fully non-rival nor non-excludable.

[26] See DAVIDOW & MALONE, 1992; MILES & SNOW, 1992; SANCHEZ & MAHONEY, 1996; JONES *et al.*, 1997.

[27] 'Know-what', 'know-why', 'know-how' and 'know-who', according to LUNDVALL & JOHNSON, 1994.

[28] This is similar to the network-analytical concept of *clustering* (see Chapter 3, Appendix 1, for a definition).

[29] See Chapter 3, Appendix 1, for a formal network-analytical definition of the term.

[30] In a different epistemological context, Kant first introduced the notion of *schema* in his *Kritik der reinen Vernunft*. This notion was later introduced in psychology by BARTLETT, 1932, and later used in a structuralist context by PIAGET, 1970; 1971. Modern cognitive theory is mainly based on Piaget's theory of cognitive development, and has also received strong influence from Gestalt psychology, Chomskyan linguistics and Broadbent's information processing model.

[31] FLAKE, 2000, gives the following definition for genetic algorithms (GA): "A method of simulating the action of evolution within a computer. A population of fixed-length strings is evolved with a GA by employing crossover and mutation operators along with a fitness function that determines how likely individuals are to reproduce. GAs perform a type of search in a fitness landscape." A simple genetic algorithm combining crossover with mutation is given by Holland's 'schema theorem' [HOLLAND, 1996].

[32] This term is originally found in HOLLAND, 1996: 11, without the distinction between resultant and emergent entities.

[33] The term 'distributed cognition' was introduced by HUTCHINS & NORMAN, 1988. A pioneer of the distributed cognition paradigm was VYGOTSKY, 1978, followed by

MINSKY, 1985. The *distributed processing model* is directly related to *parallel distributed processing* and to *connectionism*, the strand of cognitive science that treats cognitive processes as emergent phenomena of *neural networks*. A standard reference in parallel distributed processing is MCCLELLAND & RUMELHART, 1988.

[34] In algebraic topology *isomorphism* is a bijective morphism. In non-technical terms, this means that "two complex structures can be mapped onto each other, in such a way that to each part of one structure there is a corresponding part in the other structure, where 'corresponding' means that the two parts play similar roles in their respective structures" [HOFSTADTER, 1979: 49].

[35] JONES, 1995a proposes alternative, data-consistent model specifications, which offset the R&D scale effects of the ROMER, 1990 model by assuming 'diminishing technological opportunities'. In these quasi-endogenous models the steady-state growth rate of the knowledge stock is proportional to the population growth rate.

[36] Non-exhaustible because the open model favours the recombination of existing knowledge, the re-utilisation and marketisation of unused inventions, the involvement of exponentially more actors in the innovation process (including SMEs and academia), a better matching of research skills with problems, distributed cognition, etc.

Chapter 3

Mapping the knowledge plexus: The topological structure of interregional knowledge networks

Introduction

In the previous chapters I examined the epistemological foundations and some theoretical corollaries of a proposed 'systemic paradigm' in economic geography, placing particular emphasis on the fundamental issue of technological knowledge production. In this context I introduced the theoretical construct of the 'knowledge plexus', the fundamental ontology of the meso domain which embodies a complete division of labour in the production of technological knowledge. In this anisotropic and heterarchical network-like superstructure, which binds multiple knowledge networks together, economically relevant knowledge is collectively and 'distributedly' produced and accumulated. The purpose of this chapter is to analyse empirically specific aspects of the knowledge plexus focusing on its layers, namely interlocking knowledge networks, in which technological knowledge of various types is generated, diffused and accumulated.

Social networks are omnipresent in all forms of economic activity. This is particularly true in the processes of generation, diffusion and absorption of technological knowledge, and thus, in research and innovation. Knowledge networks are generated by real socio-economic interactions, as in the case of research collaborations, or are derived from conceptual associations between actors and artefacts, as in the case of academic and patent citations. Knowledge networks generated by real socio-economic relationships can be the open-ended result of spontaneous tie formation from ad hoc dyadic interactions, or the predetermined result of affiliation within an existing institutional setting. Knowledge networks can be policy-induced, as in the case of joint participations in the EU framework programmes for research and technological development, or self-organised, as in the case of joint ventures and strategic alliances in research. Knowledge networks may convey open, universal-type knowledge, as in the case of academic co-publication and citation networks, proprietary, instrumental-type technological knowledge, as in the case of the patent co-invention and citation networks, or even restricted organisational knowledge, as in the case of inter-firm joint-venture networks. It is reasonable to assume that in all cases the architecture of knowledge networks will differ according to the type of social relations which generate them (e.g. semantic association, exchange, cooperation, affiliation, membership, hierarchy); the reason of their existence and the institutional setting in which they operate (e.g. strategic choice in a self-organised market or policy-induced); and the type of knowledge they foster and convey (e.g. codified or tacit, open or proprietary, embodied or disembodied, and universal, instrumental or organisational).

My analysis focuses on a specific type of knowledge networks, the interregional networks of research collaboration in Europe. The nodes of these networks represent European regions where entities involved in the knowledge production process are located, namely higher education institutions, research organisations, as well as research-conducting private firms, public bodies, non-governmental or international organisations. Their ties represent their pairwise collaborative research efforts, notably their joint participation in the EU framework programmes for RTD, the joint filing of patent applications with EPO, and the forming of joint ventures and strategic alliances in research. This chapter examines the global and local topological characteristics of these networks, their longitudinal stability, their potential small-world or scale-invariant structures, the preferential attachment tendencies of their nodes, and their spatial dependence, and compares them in order to tell whether different types of technological knowledge generate different network topologies, to what extent they are interdependent and how they are interconnected.

The chapter is structured as follows: The second section reviews existing theoretical and empirical work on network analysis, with a particular focus on collaborative knowledge networks. The third section presents the methodology followed in this chapter, notably how the networks under study are constructed from the datasets and what types of network indicators are used in the analysis, and presents the datasets used in the present and following chapters, discussing data issues and the rationale for choosing the region as the unit of analysis. The last section presents the findings of network analysis, which consists in calculating a series of group and point measures of network topology, testing the hypotheses of small-worldliness, scale-invariance and assortativity, examining the rankings and correlations of topological attributes of regions as nodes, and probing to what extent and how interlocking knowledge networks are articulated.

Existing work on the topic

Network analysis

'Network science' as an emergent discipline, 'network theory' and 'network analysis' constitute a set of rapidly developing theories, methodologies and analytical techniques for the study of network representations of relational phenomena across a wide range of disciplines, notably physics, chemistry, biology, computer science, engineering, social sciences and economics. Network analysis employs graph theory, a branch of discrete mathematics, as well as matrix algebra, algebraic topology, set theory, probability theory and statistics. From the pioneering work of Erd s & Rényi, 1959, on random graphs to the small-world network model introduced by Watts & Strogatz, 1998, and the scale-free network model by Barabási & Albert, 1999, the mathematical and probabilistic network literature has proliferated immensely.

Social network analysis is the application of network theory in the social sciences and economics, which emerged as a methodological branch of sociometry and mathematical sociology in White *et al.*, 1976; Granovetter, 1973; Burt, 1987; White, 1992, among many others. This methodology is well developed and robust, admits mathematical formalism, permits quantitative as well as qualitative interpretation of the phenomena on which it is applied, and is covered by an extensive body of literature.

Compared to the sociological and anthropological applications of social network analysis, those in economics are recent and relatively underexplored. The main reason for that, from a theoretical perspective, is the incompatibility of the idea that economic relations among individuals, firms, or countries are embedded in a structured relational space with the isotropic continuum of the 'neoclassical' market and the independence and aggregativity of individual agents' actions implied by the precept of methodological individualism under the dominant paradigm in economic theory. From an empirical perspective, the existence of structural dependence, endogeneity, nonlinearities and circular causality in relational data describing network structure, and the consequent incompatibility of this type of data with the standard linear regression model, are additional factors which have held back the integration of network analysis with statistical and econometric models for inferential or predictive purposes. Dedicated statistical models for inferential analysis on networks have only relatively recently been developed or are still under development.

A plethora of papers on network analysis by economists of the 'deductivist' genre have contributed a series of stylised models of network formation, information diffusion, search, learning, coordination, and evolution [e.g. JACKSON & WOLINSKY, 1996; BALA & GOYAL, 2000; GOYAL & VEGA-REDONDO, 2000; GOYAL & JOSHI, 2003; GALEOTTI *et al.*, 2006; COWAN & JONARD, 2004]. Agent-based network simulation and dynamic network analysis constitute an emerging and, in the author's opinion, promising cognate, albeit methodologically distinct, field of research. This field originates from the econophysics and agent-based computational economics tradition, is inspired by the 'generative' method, and has a multitude of potential applications in economics and economic geography.

In an altogether different segment of literature, empirical studies on economic networks follow two distinct methodological directions: one applies network analysis in a descriptive manner, while the other is inferential, based on statistical modelling on networks. In the former methodological direction, BEARDEN *et al.*, 1975, a pioneering and influential conference paper, is one of the first to apply network-analytical methods, and in particular the concept of eigenvector centrality, on the study of interlocking directorates of corporate networks. In a similar line of research, MARIOLIS, 1975; MINTZ & SCHWARTZ, 1985; MARIOLIS & JONES, 1982; and MIZRUCHI & STEARNS, 1988, provide systematic insights in the socio-economic structure of corporate networks by means of network analysis. In a different strand of economic literature, the path-breaking paper by SNYDER & KICK, 1979, is an early empirical study aiming to explain differential economic growth of nations by applying blockmodel analysis on multiple international networks. The blockmodelling and structural equivalence approach to international trade flows is subsequently followed by many others, including NEMETH & SMITH, 1985; and SMITH & WHITE, 1992. It is interesting to observe here that even empirical studies using network analysis in economic topics have been dominated by sociologists rather than economists almost until the turn of the century, when the trend started to shift. The use of network analysis specifically in the economics of knowledge, innovation, and technology has seen in recent years an explosive proliferation. This strand of literature is reviewed in the following paragraphs.

Knowledge networks

An increasing number of studies are dedicated to the investigation of the causes and effects of knowledge networks from an economic perspective. VALENTE, 1995, highlights the importance of network ties and of network positioning in the diffusion and adoption of innovation, and presents a number of models supporting these hypotheses, including threshold and critical mass models of diffusion and adoption. LEONCINI *et al.*, 1996, compare the national technological systems of Italy and Germany conceived as four interlocking subsystems, the industrial, the innovative, the commercial and the institutional. In a rather sui generis fashion they apply basic network-analytical measures on 'intersectoral innovation flow matrices' inspired from input-output (I-O) analysis, mainly with data on R&D expenditure and employment. They find that the Italian technological system is more fragmented and exhibits a dual structure in which few high-tech sectors co-exist with many traditional and peripheral to the innovation flow network sectors, while the German system has more homogeneously distributed intersectoral innovation flows. SPENCER, 2003, suggest that the structure of knowledge diffusion networks and the existence of global knowledge brokers determine the competitiveness of firms and industries and, in turn, are determined by national institutional structures and firm-specific attributes. GIULIANI, 2007, in one of the first studies of this kind, explores knowledge creation and diffusion within 'cluster knowledge networks', i.e. knowledge networks territorially embedded in industrial districts – and more specifically three wine clusters in Italy and Chile. She uses social network analysis to measure structural properties of these networks concluding that, against what is commonly believed, knowledge is diffused within territorial clusters in a selective and uneven way not necessarily following the dispersed pattern of inter-firm interactions, and also that firm-level degree centrality positively correlates with innovative performance.

Networks of academic co-publications and citations

Bibliometric indicators have been rather successfully used as measures of knowledge output within and between scientific fields and geographical localities for decades, despite well-known biases and limitations in bibliometric data, such as the fact that scientific collaboration does not necessarily lead to co-authored articles [KATZ & MARTIN, 1997; LAUDEL, 2002], or the fact that the most widely used bibliometric databases have strong English-language bias and are proprietary, which means potentially not objective in the selection of journal titles. SUBRAMANYAM, 1983, lists several reasons why co-authorship is one of the most used indicators when examining scientific collaborations and knowledge flows: it is invariant and verifiable, it uses universal data sources, and the sample size is substantially larger than in any case study, thus giving more statistically significant results. Moreover, scientific collaborations that result in significant outcomes do in most cases lead to co-authored publications because of scientists' endeavour to be acknowledged for their contribution to science [MELIN & PERSSON, 1996].

Academic co-publication and citation networks are among the first and most extensively explored forms of knowledge networks. NEWMAN, 2001, analyses co-authorship networks in different scientific fields, and finds a high clustering coefficient combined with a small average path length indicating a degree distribution following a power-law and a small-world topology. Other studies obtain similar results: BARABÁSI *et al.*, 2002, characterise the co-authorship network as 'a prototype of complex evolving networks', study the longitudinal evolution of its topological properties and find that the network is scale-invariant and that its evolution is governed by preferential attachment. WAGNER & LEYDESDORFF, 2005b; 2005a, also regard the co-authorship network as a complex network, which exhibits dynamics based on competition and cooperation, and consider the growth of international co-authorships as a self-organising phenomenon governed by preferential attachment.

Networks of patent co-inventions and citations

Patents contain and convey knowledge which is codifiable, applied and appropriable, and hence mostly 'instrumental' rather than 'universal'. Counts of patent grants and citations are the most commonly used indicators of technological knowledge output. A large number of studies has established these indicators, most often in a 'knowledge production function' context in connection with (or without) endogenous growth theories, as a mainstream tool in the economics of innovation, technology and knowledge [e.g. GRILICHES, 1979, 1990; JAFFE, 1986, 1989; ARCHIBUGI & PIANTA, 1992, 1996; and in a regional context, ACS *et al.*, 2002].

Similarly to academic publications, there are well-known limitations of these indicators, which, however, do not deter the generalised use of patent counts and patent citations as measures of knowledge productivity and knowledge impact and diffusion respectively. With regard to counts of patent grants, it has been rightly argued that they may not fully reflect patents' real economic value for a number of reasons: The economic value and the technological impact of patents are by no means comparable and evenly distributed within their population, as the majority of patents is known to have limited marketability and to rarely represent radical innovations, while very few eventually have disproportional market or technological impact. For incumbent firms with market power, patenting may play a strategic, pre-emptive, hedging or hoarding role. The propensity to patent is largely dependent on institutional, cultural and ideological factors which determine the enforceability of intellectual property rights, inventors' access to markets and patent granting institutions, or even inventors' preferences with regard to openness to knowledge sharing; as a result, countries exhibit a highly differential propensity to patent [CANIËLS, 2000]. With regard to joint patent applications, it has been observed that they represent only a small percentage of total patenting activity due to the fact that collaborating firms prefer to divide patents among themselves than jointly applying and sharing patent ownership, because of the legal complexity of the ensuing intellectual property rights, especially when firms are based in different countries [HAGEDOORN, 2003; TER WAL & BOSCHMA, 2009]. With regard to the use of counts of patent citations as a measure of knowledge flows, it has been argued that they do not necessarily reflect the actual knowledge gain of the inventor from the cited patent, as citations often come from patent examiners (a common practice with EPO patent applications) or applicants' patent attorneys [BRESCHI & LISSONI, 2005]; that citations might be included for strategic reasons or due to legal considerations (e.g. to avert litigation); and that the average numbers of citations varies greatly from one patent office to another (e.g. between EPO and USPTO, the latter having a significantly higher rate of citations).[1]

Arguments in favour of the use of patent indicators include the following: Patent indicators are simply the best known and most easily and uniformly measurable proxies of technological knowledge output. Patentability requirements impose that applications be able to demonstrate their non-obviousness, novelty, and utility (US patent law) or industrial applicability (EU patent law), while the role of patent offices is precisely to guarantee that this is true. Patent applications involve considerable costs for filing and processing, which deter individuals from patenting economically irrelevant inventions. Even if some patents have limited marketability, they may have significant spillovers or be components of a wider innovation process with significant overall economic value. Highly cited patents most often represent important technological advances [CARPENTER *et al.*, 1981], and incorporate a high socio-economic value [TRAJTENBERG, 1990]. Counts of corporate patents and patent citations are excellent indicators of corporate technological strength [NARIN *et al.*, 1987]. Co-patent applications and citations are important sources of information on otherwise untraceable knowledge flows.

From a network-analytical perspective, joint patent applications and patent citations are two relationships which generate quite distinct network structures. BALCONI *et al.*, 2004, explore university-industry knowledge transfers by applying network analysis on an original dataset consisting of data on Italian academic inventors identified from patent applications registered with the EPO (i.e. university employees involved in patenting activity, in a country where patenting resulting from university research is individually managed by academics instead of the universities as legal entities). They find that networks generated by proprietary technologies are more fragmented than open science ones and that academic inventors are, on average, more central and better connected in the networks than non-academic inventors. BRESCHI & LISSONI, 2005, apply network analysis on patent citations to produce relational mappings between inventors and to measure relational proximity between cited and citing patents. They demonstrate with the use of logistic regressions that the probability of citation is positively influenced by relational proximity.

Networks of research collaboration under the EU framework programmes for RTD

The participation of research-conducting organisations in projects funded under the EU framework programmes for RTD (FP) has been analysed in a network-analytical context from several different perspectives.

A series of studies commissioned by the European Commission in the broader context of ex post evaluation of the FPs and their components indicate that network analysis is gradually making way into the domain of policy-making. In one of the first such studies, WAGNER *et al.*, 2005, apply network analysis on collaborative projects in the thematic area of Information Society Technologies (IST) under FP6. The report finds that participants are more tightly interconnected than in earlier FPs, and indeed than in any other type of knowledge network, and that, compared to other knowledge networks, the FP6 IST-RTD collaboration network is more likely to involve actors from diverse economic sectors and academic fields, bringing together academia and industry, patent holders and highly cited organisations, and SMEs more than any other (self-organised) knowledge network. In another commissioned study, MALERBA *et al.*, 2006, similarly apply network analysis on research collaborations under the FP6 IST-RTD programme to conclude that the programme has been successful in attracting key actors of the European ICT knowledge production system as network hubs, in generating and reinforcing connectivity among these hubs, and in creating and diffusing new knowledge effectively, despite the fact that only few European organisations are actually 'top-rated hubs' in the global ICT network. Finally, a large commissioned study on the whole spectrum of FP6 thematic areas [EC, 2009] confirms and extends the findings of previous studies by also examining the bibliometric performance of FP6 participants at the level of individual organisations and at the country level. It should be noted that common shortcomings of the above cited studies is their tendency to be complaisant towards European Commission policies, their descriptive approach adapted to the (perceived) needs of EU policy-makers, and the ensuing difficulty for the critical reader to justify their normative conclusions on the basis of their quantitative findings.

BRESCHI & CUSMANO, 2004, analyse the network of research collaboration under FP3 and partly FP4. The bipartite affiliation network is transformed into a unipartite participants' network by considering each project as a star structure where the central node is the project coordinator. They calculate standard graph indices and degree distribution, and they test the resilience of the network to random as well as targeted removals of nodes, to find that the network is dense, has a hierarchical, core-periphery structure with clear signs of preferential attachment on the basis of vertex degree, and exhibits small-world characteristics. Similar findings are provided by BARBER *et al.*, 2006. In their case, the collaboration network under all FPs from FP1 to FP4 is analysed as a unipartite graph, in which each project is represented as a clique. They find scale-free degree distribution, small diameter, and high and gradually increasing clustering coefficient, and they attempt to simulate the observed properties of the network structure in formal graph models. ALMENDRAL *et al.*, 2007, show that the collaboration network of research organisations under FP5 is also a scale-free complex network with accelerating growth, exhibiting hierarchical modularity (nested self-similarity), small-world properties and degree assortativity (i.e. preferential attachment on the basis of vertex degree). Information flows depend on the number of participants but there is no indication that they are dependent on geographical location or nationality. The analysis is based exclusively on standard graph-level indices. In a similar vein, GARAS & ARGYRAKIS, 2008, examine the scientific collaboration network of participant organisations in FP5 and FP6 by instrument and thematic area, again from the perspective of the graph-level characteristics, focusing in particular on the degree centrality of the country-level collaboration network. This analysis confirms, rather trivially, that larger countries play a more central role in the network.

Networks of joint ventures and strategic alliances

The transition to the knowledge economy is characterised by an unprecedented surge in R&D collaboration among organisations involved in the knowledge production process. Inter-firm cooperation occurring on ad hoc or strategic basis is the most common form of R&D collaboration. In terms of the degree of externalisation of ownership and control, inter-frim cooperation can be, in order of decreasing externalisation, equity-based, e.g. joint ventures, cross-equity holdings; contractual agreements, e.g. joint R&D agreements, customer-supplier relations, and bilateral or unilateral technology flows including cross-licensing, technology exchange agreements, licensing, etc.; and finally, spot-market or 'arms length' agreements [HAGEDOORN & SCHAKENRAAD, 1994; MOWERY *et al.*, 1996; NARULA & HAGEDOORN, 1999]. Firms engage in these forms of cooperation in order to exploit technological spillovers, to avoid technological lock-ins, to pool the risk of investment in new and often uncharted territories of technological knowledge, to share the high costs of research, but also to take advantage of the increased efficiency of networks in generating and diffusing new technological knowledge compared to internalised, vertically integrated organisational structures.

Another important type of inter-organisational collaboration is between universities or public research institutes and the private sector. The archetype of this form of collaboration is the MIT model of 'entrepreneurial university', later followed by Stanford and many others [ETZKOWITZ, 1998], first in the US and then gradually in Europe and the rest of the world with the institutionalisation of academia-industry knowledge transfer system [LEYDESDORFF & MEYER, 2003].

The tendency to collaborate in research is particularly strong among firms in knowledge-intensive or high-tech industries; it is also more prominent in some industrial sectors and technological fields than in others. For instance, the information and telecommunication technologies industry has been the leader in contractual R&D partnerships throughout the 90s closely followed by the pharmaceutical and biotech industry, while aerospace and defence, automotive and chemical industries do not seem to follow this trend [HAGEDOORN, 2002].

From a network-analytical perspective, ORSENIGO *et al.*, 1997; 2001, examine the dynamics of network formation and evolution in the case of collaborative R&D agreements in the pharmaceutical industry after the molecular biology revolution. They find a remarkable tendency of co-evolution between industrial organisation as reflected in the structure of the R&D agreements network on the one hand, and the emerging corpus of scientific knowledge and all related research activities on the other hand. They also find that the increase of network size does not affect its relatively stable topological properties and its core-periphery structure, and that inter-generational collaboration of firms is more significant than intra-generational collaboration. They conclude that the network itself is an evolutionary mechanism, which initially supports firm 'speciation' and then exposes firms to a selection process by capital markets. SOH & ROBERTS, 2003, examine how the co-evolution of technologies punctuated by change and the network of inter-firm alliances affect the development of emerging innovations. They specifically study strategic alliances in the US data communication industry to conclude that central positioning in the alliance network ensures better access to information on entrepreneurial opportunities and, therefore, that firms often engage into alliances in order to keep up with competitors' activities, and that incumbent firms are more likely to survive technological discontinuities by forming alliances.

Methodology and data

Variables and terminology

Relational data is intrinsically different from common non-relational data which I shall refer to as 'atomistic'. *Atomistic variables* are those which capture inherent properties or characteristics of an entity, from individuals to systems. *Relational variables* are those defined by the interaction between distinct entities. Within the group of relational variables a distinction must be drawn between *dyadic* and *systemic* variables [MIZRUCHI & MARQUIS, 2006], the former describing pairwise interactions while the latter system-wide ones. Another distinction, which is considered fundamental in social network analysis, must be drawn between relational variables defined in the context of *personal* or *egocentric*, and *complete* or *sociocentric* networks.[2] These types of networks are not only conceptually but also analytically different: the former consists in the ties formed between a specific node, the 'ego', and the 'alters', while the latter is the entire set of nodes and ties generated by a specific social relation. From an analytical perspective the methods employed in each case are not identical, mainly due to fundamentally different structural dependence assumptions underlying the formation of each type of network.

I further distinguish between variables referring to *global* and *local* topological characteristics of a network, and between *group* and *point* indices (or equivalently, *graph-* and *vertex-level* indices). The first two terms refer to whether the relational variable is determined by the entire structure of the network or merely by the structure of a neighbourhood of a node in the network; the other two terms refer to whether the indices characterise the network (or a substructure thereof) as a whole as opposed to individual nodes. A group variable can still be local if it is calculated as the average of local indices; similarly, a point variable can be global if its calculation requires knowledge of the entire structure of the network.

The terminology of network analysis is not fixed and consistent, due to its pluridisciplinary origins, and the fact that new concepts and indices emerge as the field develops. In this book I use the terms 'networks', 'nodes' and 'ties' to refer to the empirically observed entities, while I keep the terms 'graphs', 'vertices' and 'edges' for the abstract mathematical representation of these entities. Definitions of the network indices used in this book are provided in Appendix 1 in order to avoid the inconsistencies encountered in related literature.

Construction of the networks

Representation of organisation-level collaboration networks

The initial, organisation-level collaboration networks under study are conceived as bipartite, undirected, binary graphs $G_{\mathcal{A},\mathcal{P}}(V_{\mathcal{A}}, V_{\mathcal{P}}, E)$ with two partitions of the vertex set: $V_{\mathcal{A}}$, with bottom-level vertices representing actors $a \in \mathcal{A}$ (i.e. project participants, parent companies or researchers-inventors), and $V_{\mathcal{P}}$, with top-level vertices representing projects $P \in \mathcal{P}$ (i.e. FP projects, joint ventures and strategic alliances, or co-patents), where $\mathcal{A}$ is the set of actors and $\mathcal{P}$ is the set of projects. A number of attributes for each type of vertex is deducible from the existing dataset. The edge set E consists of edges $a \leftrightarrow P$ connecting vertices in $V_{\mathcal{A}}$ with vertices in $V_{\mathcal{P}}$.

For analytical purposes the initial bipartite graph $G_{\mathcal{A},\mathcal{P}}$ is transformed into a unipartite, undirected graph $G(V, E, W)$, whose top-level partition of the vertex set (the project-nodes) is dropped and only the partition of vertices representing actors is retained. This graph can be formed in three different ways, depending on the shape that will be given to the subgraph $g_P \subset G$ generated by each collaborative project $P \in \mathcal{P}$: It can be formed as a conventional binary (unweighted) graph G^B, in which g_P is conceived as a clique with unweighted edges,[3] implicitly assuming that all actors collaborate pairwise with equal intensity (their interaction is assumed to be equal to one), and, therefore, that they contribute to the project equally and that 'knowledge' flows uniformly in all directions within the project. In the other extreme, it can be assumed that only project 'coordinators' interact pairwise with project 'participants' or that only this interaction matters, and, therefore, that 'knowledge' flows exclusively and necessarily through them, in which case interaction between project participants is assumed to be equal to zero, and g_P is conceived as a star subgraph of a graph G^*.[4] I henceforth refer to these two alternative representations as the 'clique-project' and the 'star-project' graphs. Between these two extremes a middle solution is to represent the network as a weighted graph G^W, in which g_P is conceived as a clique with weighted edges.

Figure 3.1 illustrates the transformation of a hypothetical bipartite graph consisting of 3 projects and 5 participants, with one participant per project designated as coordinator (participant 4 for project A and participant 2 for projects B and C), into a clique-project and a star-project unipartite graph.

Figure 3.1: Clique-project and star-project transformations of a bipartite graph

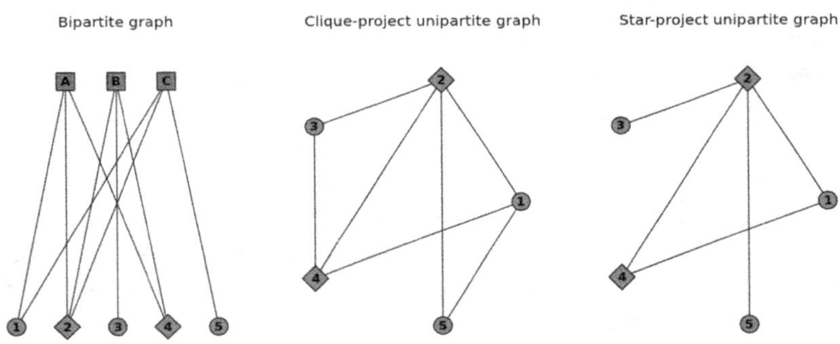

In this chapter all three approaches are applied on the derived interregional networks (where applicable) and the results are compared and interpreted accordingly. In addition to this, three weighting methods are tried in the case of the weighted graph G^W, namely weighting by *interaction frequency* – i.e. counts of interactions between pairs of regions; by *interaction propensity* – i.e. interaction frequency adjusted by within-project interaction propensities; and by *tie strength* – a composite indicator which combines interaction frequency, within-project interaction propensity and relative project weight, as explained in detail below.

Derivation of interregional collaboration networks

Each joint project generates a star-shaped or (binary or weighted) clique-like subgraph g_P of the organisation-level collaboration graph G_0. These graphs are subsequently transformed into regional-level collaboration graphs by superposing project subgraphs g_P and aggregating pairwise interactions. The ensuing interregional network will be a unipartite, undirected multigraph $G_M(V, E_M, W_M)$.[5] For analytical purposes this multigraph is eventually transformed into a regular weighted graph $G(V, E, W)$, consisting of a vertex set V of region-actors, and an edge set E of interregional collaborations, whose edges ij can be either binary or weighted with $w_{ij} \in W$. These weights are either simple counts of parallel edges (interaction frequencies) or sums of weights of parallel edges (interaction propensities or tie strengths as explained below).

While the nodes of the initial networks represent participations of individual actors of the knowledge economy (universities, research organisations, private firms, etc.), the nodes of the derived networks are poolings of participations at the NUTS-3 regional level. This way lower-level entities are substituted by higher-level entities on the basis of their geographical location. This shift of analytical level inevitably results in information loss. However, this transformation also has a number of significant advantages, already exposed in a previous section: the derived interregional networks consist of a computationally manageable number of longitudinally stable, fully comparable, consistently defined, geographically embedded entities. These entities are not so ontologically distant from local 'clusters' of individual organisations, are embedded in a dense relational space, and are well documented, as a good amount of statistical data on them is readily available from standard sources (e.g. OECD, EUROSTAT).

Interaction propensity and tie strength

Collaboration networks are commonly represented as binary, undirected, unipartite graphs, in which case the strength of ties is not taken properly into consideration. The implicit assumption of this approach that all participants in a collaborative project communicate and interact with equal frequency and intensity is not always a realistic hypothesis. Considering multiple collaborative ties between the same pair of nodes in a collaboration network as a single tie of uniform strength not only entails a significant loss of information but also a potential misspecification of the network model. In the case of the derived interregional collaboration networks studied in this book, such misspecification could be particularly distortionary: Here the networks are relatively tightly connected – for example, in the FP collaboration network most regions are found to collaborate with most others at least once – while the occurrence of repeated collaborations follows a fat-tailed probability distribution which is far from normal. It would be, therefore, highly problematic to implicitly treat a circumstantial collaboration between two regions, which occurs with low frequency or just once, as being of equal importance to multiple, recurring collaborations.

While the frequency of ties in between-project interactions can be derived directly from existing relational data, within-project interactions are virtually unknown, as the dataset does not provide any information on them. Thus the strength of ties within the project subnetworks will have to be deduced indirectly from other attributes of the projects. For this reason, I approach this issue in a probabilistic context, in which I assume that:

- interaction between project participants becomes more likely, the longer the duration of a project is;
- the cost of a project reflects the willingness of its participants to invest in a collaborative undertaking and, hence, is an indication of the value they attribute to their collaborative ties; therefore, interaction propensity is expected to increase with project costs;
- larger numbers of participants in a project make information flows and communication among them less efficient and, therefore, interaction with each other less likely;
- the importance of the project coordinator as information broker increases with the size of the project. Pairwise communication between common project participants becomes more difficult, and hence their interaction through the coordinator more likely, the larger the project subnetwork is. On the other hand, the participant-to-participant interaction propensity increases with project duration and with the number of prior joint projects;
- the existence of prior or recurrent collaborations in other projects between two project participants makes more likely their interaction in a subsequent project in which they jointly participate;

- the more 'similar' participants are, in terms of language, country of origin, disciplinary or geographical proximity, etc., the more likely is to collaborate.

Tie strength is therefore determined by the following factors:

- *brokerage*, deduced from the position of the node in the project subnetwork, which is determined by the participants' role in the project (i.e. coordinator or common participant), where relevant;
- *intimacy*, assumed to be inversely proportional to the number of project participants;
- *commitment*, as indicated by project duration and project cost;
- *precedent*, measured by counts of prior joint project participations;
- *homophily*, i.e. preferential attachment on the basis of typological similarity or geographical proximity.

In the actual construction of the composite tie strength measure I chose not to include homophily, since the influence of this factor on the formation of the networks is by itself a testable hypothesis explored in following paragraphs. Moreover, precedent, whose influence is also a testable hypothesis, can be replaced by an easily measurable indicator, namely *frequency*, measured by counts of joint project participations.

I assume that the interaction propensity between common project participants is inversely proportional to the number of participants in the project, while interaction propensity with the project coordinator is the highest possible, i.e. equal to one. More specifically, for any pair of participants i, j in project P their *within-project interaction propensity* is defined as:

$$\pi_{ij|P} = \begin{cases} 1, \text{if } i \text{ or } j \text{ is coordinator} \\ \frac{2}{|P|} \text{ otherwise} \end{cases}$$ **Equation 3.1**

Interaction propensity between nodes $i, j \in V$ is defined as the sum of their within-project interaction propensities in all projects $P \in \mathcal{P}$ in which they have jointly participated:

$$\pi_{ij} = \sum_{P \in \mathcal{P}} \pi_{ij|P}$$ **Equation 3.2**

A type of logistic normalisation ('softmax' method) is applied to the variables of project duration d and project cost c. This type of normalisation employs an inverse logistic function to transform data into an output, which follows a sigmoid curve in the range of $[0,1]$. The transformation is almost linear in the mid-range of the variable and non-linear, asymptotically reaching the extreme values at both ends. The procedure is as follows: First I calculate the standard scores (z-scores) of the above variables,

$$z_c = \frac{c - \bar{c}}{\sigma_c}, \qquad z_d = \frac{d - \bar{d}}{\sigma_d} \qquad \textbf{Equation 3.3}$$

where $\bar{x}$ is the mean and σ_x the standard deviation of the respective variables by instrument on a project-by-project basis. Then I transform the obtained z-scores via a hyperbolic tangent function, which is a type of inverse logistic function: $\tanh z_x = [1 + \exp(-z_x)]^{-1}$.

Relative project weight w_P is then defined as the geometric mean of $w_{c,P} = \tanh z_c$ and $w_{d,P} = \tanh z_d$:

$$w_P = \sqrt{w_{c,P} w_{d,P}} \qquad \textbf{Equation 3.4}$$

Within-project tie strength between participants i, j in project P is defined as the product of within-project interaction propensity and relative project weight of P:

$$s_{ij|P} = \pi_{ij|P} w_P = \pi_{ij|P} \sqrt{w_{c,P} w_{d,P}} \qquad \textbf{Equation 3.5}$$

Finally, *tie strength* between nodes i, j is defined as the sum of their within-project tie strengths in all projects $P \in \mathcal{P}$ in which they have jointly participated:

$$s_{ij} = \sum_{P \in \mathcal{P}} s_{ij|P} = \sum_{P \in \mathcal{P}} \pi_{ij|P} \sqrt{w_{c,P} w_{d,P}} \qquad \textbf{Equation 3.6}$$

Interregional FP participation network and theme-specific networks

From a longitudinal perspective, the FP participation network is examined on a FP-by-FP basis instead of on an annual basis, and so each FP corresponds to a cross-section of the entire network. The rationale for this choice is that FP participation networks are policy-induced, and the formation of collaborative ties largely depends on the timing of the respective calls for application and the timeline of the particular work programmes, which in turn depend on administrative decisions. The evolution of the FP participation network on an annual basis is, therefore, exogenously determined.

The thematic areas in which FP projects belong define a partition of the FP projects dataset, on the basis of which five thematic interregional networks are constructed in exactly the same manner as the cross-theme FP participation network, one for each of the following thematic groupings:

- life sciences and health; food and agriculture (BIO; 1.01, 1.02)
- information and communication technologies (ICT; 1.03)
- environment; energy (ECO; 1.06, 1.07)
- social sciences and humanities (SOC; 1.10)
- research infrastructures (RIS; 2.06)

The construction of interregional FP participation networks on the basis of the type of the participating organisation is not as straightforward as the construction of the theme-specific networks, because the regional aggregations of individual participants normally include participants of all organisation types, and also because the projects usually combine different types of participants. Even so, it is still feasible to construct an interregional network by aggregating at the NUTS-3 level dyads formed by same-type individual participants. In an ad hoc network structure of this type all ties between individual organisations of different types are excluded, and, for this reason the findings of network analysis should be interpreted cautiously. Without overlooking the limitations of this particular construction, I consider four type-determined interregional FP collaboration networks:

- academia (EDU)
- industry (PRC)
- research (RES)
- academia-industry (AIC)

The first three networks are formed as described above, while the fourth network is formed by aggregating dyads of individual organisations in which one side is from academia and the other side from industry.

Finally, the intersection graph $G_X = \bigcap_{k=1}^{3} G_k$ of the three instances of the interregional FP collaboration network (FP5, FP6 and FP7) produces a subgraph of the network consisting of edges, i.e. interregional collaboration ties, which remain stable from one FP to another. This intersection graph can be considered as the longitudinally stable 'core' of the respective network, and is also examined here.

Patent co-invention networks

The interregional network of patent co-inventors is constructed on the basis of inventor collaborations in patent applications filed with EPO, annually aggregated at the NUTS-3 regional level. The annual aggregation of the data is legitimate and meaningful given that the interregional patent co-invention network emerges spontaneously and in a bottom-up fashion without exogenous dependences, and remains dense and extensive even on an annual basis. The annual aggregation of the data permits the study of the temporal evolution of this specific network. A network of inventor collaborations in patent applications aggregated for the entire period of coverage (1990-2009) is also constructed and analysed, as well as an intersection network consisting of edges which persist throughout this period.

As the value of patents cannot be deduced from existing data or estimated otherwise, 'patent weight' cannot be defined in a similar way as the relative project weight w_P,[6] and tie strength is simply equivalent to interaction propensity, as defined in the previous subsection.

A star-project specification of the network is feasible if we consider the principal inventor of a patent, whose name is typically recorded first in the PATSTAT database, as the coordinator of the collaborative research project.

Joint ventures and strategic alliances networks

In the case of the joint ventures and strategic alliances (henceforth referred to as 'JVSA') network, there is no indication that exogenous deterministic dependence in tie formation exists, and so the network could in principle be analysed on an annual basis. The very limited number of observations at the level of NUTS-3 regions, however, makes this unworkable and requires the pooling of observations.

Given the prominence of collaborations with or between countries outside the European Union (in particular with the US and Japan) in this dataset, a network of collaborations at the country level, represented as a binary or unipartite, undirected, weighted graph, is also constructed and analysed.

Finally an alternative network configuration at the country level, as a unipartite, weighted, directed graph is also constructed and analysed. In this network the parent companies are represented as sending nodes, while the subsidiaries as receiving nodes. With this representation an additional piece of information is taken into account: the fact that a joint venture is a separate entity with own location and characteristics distinct from those of the parent companies. The aggregation of incoming and outgoing ties at the country level gives a clearer idea about the balance of international knowledge flows.

Data

Data quality issues

As already outlined above, the analysis focuses on three groups of research collaboration networks, namely networks formed through joint participation of all types of research-conducting entities in the EU framework programmes for RTD, networks of patent co-inventors who have filed applications with the EPO, and networks of joint ventures or strategic alliances for research formed predominantly by private firms.

In all cases the level of analysis is not that of the individual organisation but that of the geographical region in which research-conducting organisations and individuals are located, and more specifically, the NUTS-3 regional level. The choice of NUTS-3 regions as minimal units of analysis is justified both theoretically and practically: The original, raw datasets contain numerous duplications and errors related to the non-standardised way of registering individual organisations in the database; as a result, the same organisation may appear under several different names or variations of the same name and hence cannot be uniquely identified. The elimination of these inconsistencies requires a great amount of resources, including specialised data-mining software.

Even if practical data quality issues were resolved, the unique identification of individual organisations, and in particular of private firms, would still be obscured by frequent identity changes: in the course of the three framework programmes under study – a time span of more than 12 years – many organisations have been subject to mergers and acquisitions, splits, name changes, relocations, closures, or simply have ceased to participate in the framework programmes or participate intermittently. From a network perspective, longitudinal comparisons of the network at the level of individual organisations would be highly problematic, if not meaningless, given the frequent changes in the composition of the networks and the instability of their nodes along the time axis; on similar grounds, the simultaneous analysis of multiplex relations spanning the network(s) would be impossible, given the different node composition of the networks generated by each relation.

More substantially, not all individual entities appearing in the datasets belong to the same ontological level or are clearly and consistently delimitable: large, multi-department or multi-college universities, 'umbrella' research organisations with multi-disciplinary research activities, multinational corporations with many subsidiaries, often under different names, companies with complicated ownership and management structures, public bodies and government agencies, etc., cannot be subsumed under the same 'ontological' category as SMEs, individual research institutes, individual schools or university departments, or even individual research groups or scientists, and are therefore non-comparable entities.

The choice of NUTS-3 regions as units of analysis addresses all these issues: NUTS-3 regions are well-identified, comparable, longitudinally stable geographical entities. They are small enough to be close, in terms of atomistic and relational characteristics, to the urban agglomerations which they encompass, and large enough to have relatively comprehensive aggregate statistical data. Their scale also ensures that their geographical boundaries are not as arbitrary and unrelated to underlying real socio-economic and administrative processes as those of NUTS-1 and 2 regional levels. On the negative side, a study based exclusively on regional data is a priori limited to the meso domain of the knowledge plexus, with no possibility to directly observe and analyse micro-macro articulation and emergence.

Framework programmes participation data

The EU framework programs for research and technological development (FP) are the main research policy instruments of the EU with the objective of "strengthening its scientific and technological bases by achieving a European research area in which researchers, scientific knowledge and technology circulate freely, and encouraging it to become more competitive, including in its industry" (TFEU, Article 179).

The FPs are the biggest international research funding schemes in the world, accounting for a substantial part of European research funding; they involve practically all research-conducting organisations in Europe and the most important ones from the rest of the world; they are open to all types of research-conducting organisations, from academia and government to industry; they support a wide range of 'pre-competitive' research from basic to applied;[7] they fund research practically across the whole spectrum of disciplines and scientific and technological fields, from nanotechnologies to humanities; they have objective evaluation and selection processes for project proposals based on merit. Participation of research organisations in the FPs – which is open, competitive and usually requires mixed groups of actors from industry and academia and from several EU member-states, associated or third countries – generates its own research collaboration networks. These 'policy-induced' networks are essential elements of the European knowledge plexus. Moreover, the FP have complete longitudinal datasets on projects and participants, which permit detailed representation of the relational space where knowledge production takes place.

The FP database used here contains participation data from three consecutive framework programmes, 5, 6 and 7.[8] The coverage period is from the beginning of FP5 in 1998 until 2011, the fourth year of implementation of FP7.[9] The three framework programmes covered here do not have the same funding instruments, thematic areas, participants, etc. However, they remain quantitatively comparable and an effort has been made to organise the available data in a way that underlines the continuity of the knowledge networks formed by programme participants.

The data concerns signed contracts between the European Commission and organisations or individuals involved in scientific and technological research in a multiplicity of science and technology fields. 36,012 funded research projects are recorded in the dataset, of which 16,553 under FP5, 8,861 under FP6 and 10,598 under FP7 during the first four years of its implementation. 20,692 projects involve more than one participating organisations, 19,188 of which can be considered as collaborative, and 19,154 of which involve participants with registered NUTS-3 location. The maximum number of participants in a project is 119. The entirety of recorded projects involve 212,319 participations of organisations conducting scientific and technological research, although the actual number of distinct organisations should be considerably smaller but, as already explained, cannot be reliably estimated. The number of participations in collaborative projects with identifiable NUTS-3 location is 177,197.

The project participants come from 179 distinct countries of origin (EU member-states as well as associated and 'third' countries), including 35 European countries whose regional classification system complies with the NUTS convention. The biggest participants are the 4 largest in terms of population EU member-states followed by Spain, the Netherlands, Belgium, Sweden, Greece and Switzerland (see Figure 3.2 below for the top-50 country participants).

Figure 3.2: Top-50 FP participant countries in participation counts by FP

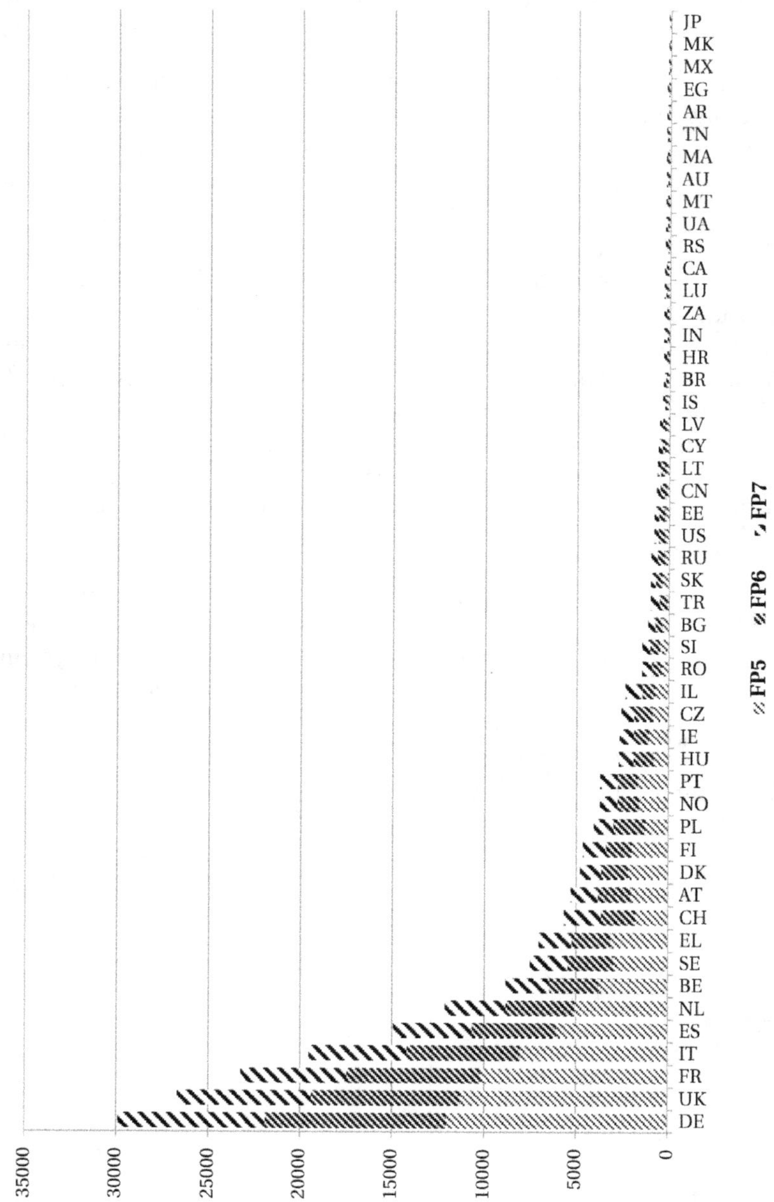

The total eligible cost of the projects funded under FP, which however is larger than the actual EU contribution to eligible project costs and, indeed, the budget of the corresponding framework programmes, is 19.6 billion euro in current prices for FP5, 22.6 billion for FP6, and 20.4 billion for the first four years of FP7. The biggest beneficiaries are the same abovementioned countries (see Figure 3.3 below for the top-50 country beneficiaries). It should be clarified here that FP projects are co-financed, instead of fully financed, by the EU with a contribution rate depending on the funding scheme, the legal status of the participants and the type of activity.[10] The standard contribution rate for research and technological development and for demonstration activities is 50% of the total project costs, which can go up to 75% for some types of legal entities, such as non-profit public bodies, SMEs, research organisations and higher education institutions.

Figure 3.3: Top-50 FP participant countries in FP funded project costs (current value M) by FP

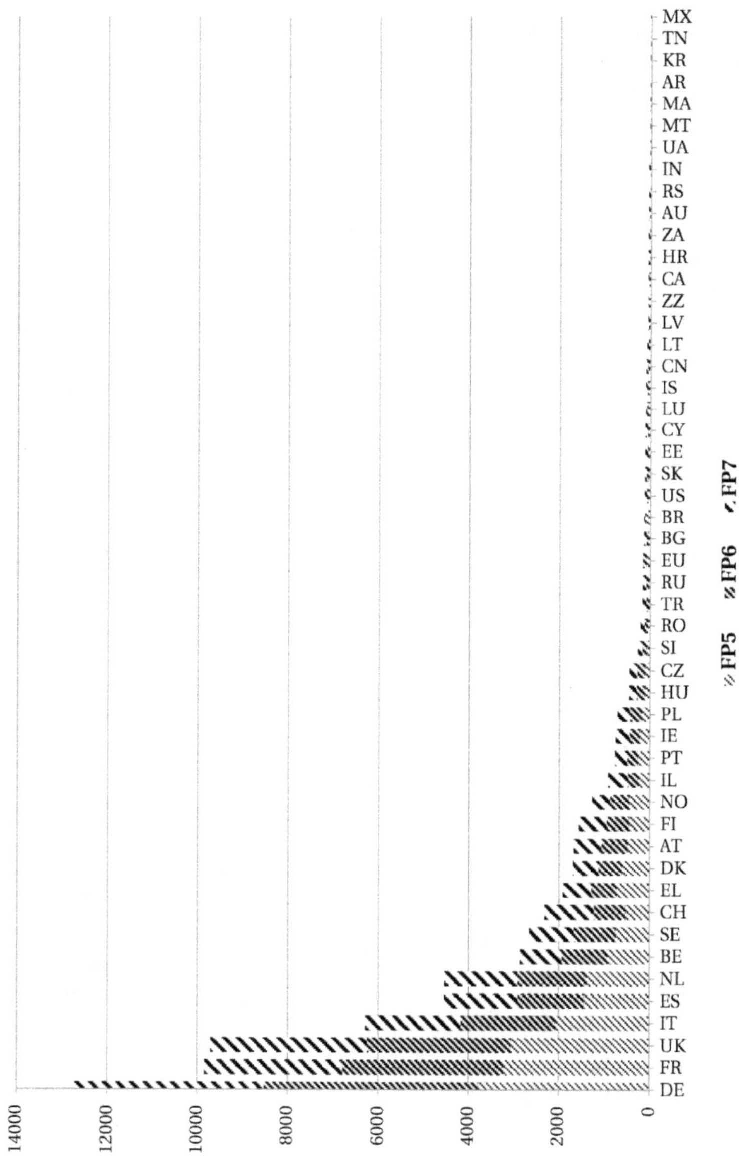

The NUTS-3 regions recorded in the database are 1,343 out of a total of 1,462 (excluding the ZZZ-coded 'extra-regio' territories), which indicates that the geographical coverage of Europe by the three framework programmes is almost complete, with the large majority of NUTS-3 regions hosting at least one participant organisation. The regions with the largest numbers of participations in the FP are the French department of Paris, the Spanish community of Madrid, the Italian province of Rome, West Inner London, the German district of the city of Munich, the Greek prefecture of Attica (which comprises the city of Athens), the Belgian region of Brussels, the Spanish province of Barcelona, the Finnish region of Uusimaa (which comprises the cities of Helsinki and Espoo), and the Italian province of Milan. In terms of costs of funded projects the list of the biggest beneficiaries also includes the Parisian department of Hauts-de-Seine, the Swedish county of Stockholm, and Oxfordshire.

Figures 3.4 and 3.5 below present the top 50 NUTS-3 regions in terms of participations and funded project costs respectively. Figure 3.6 presents a choropleth map coloured according to the amounts of the total eligible project costs partially or entirely funded by the EU under FP5, 6 and 7 in the period 1998-2011.

Figure 3.4: Top-50 participants NUTS-3 regions in participation counts by FP

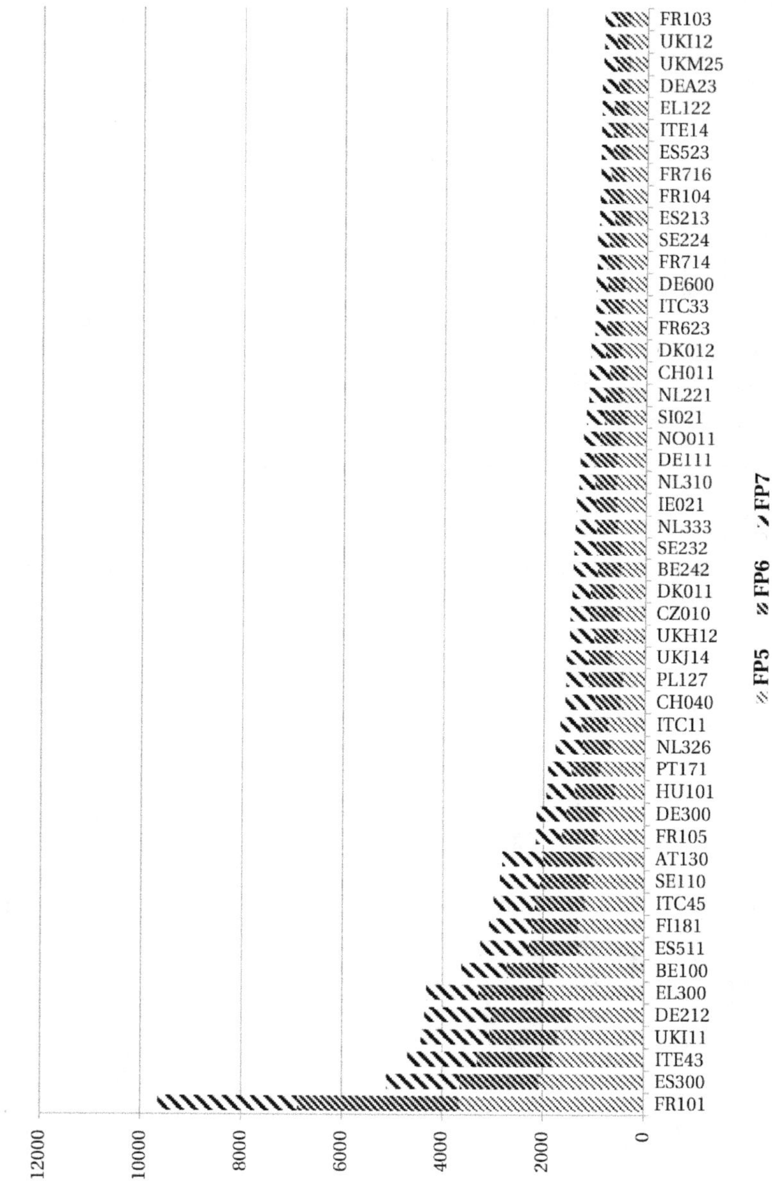

Figure 3.5: Top-50 FP participant NUTS-3 regions in FP funded project costs (current value M) by FP

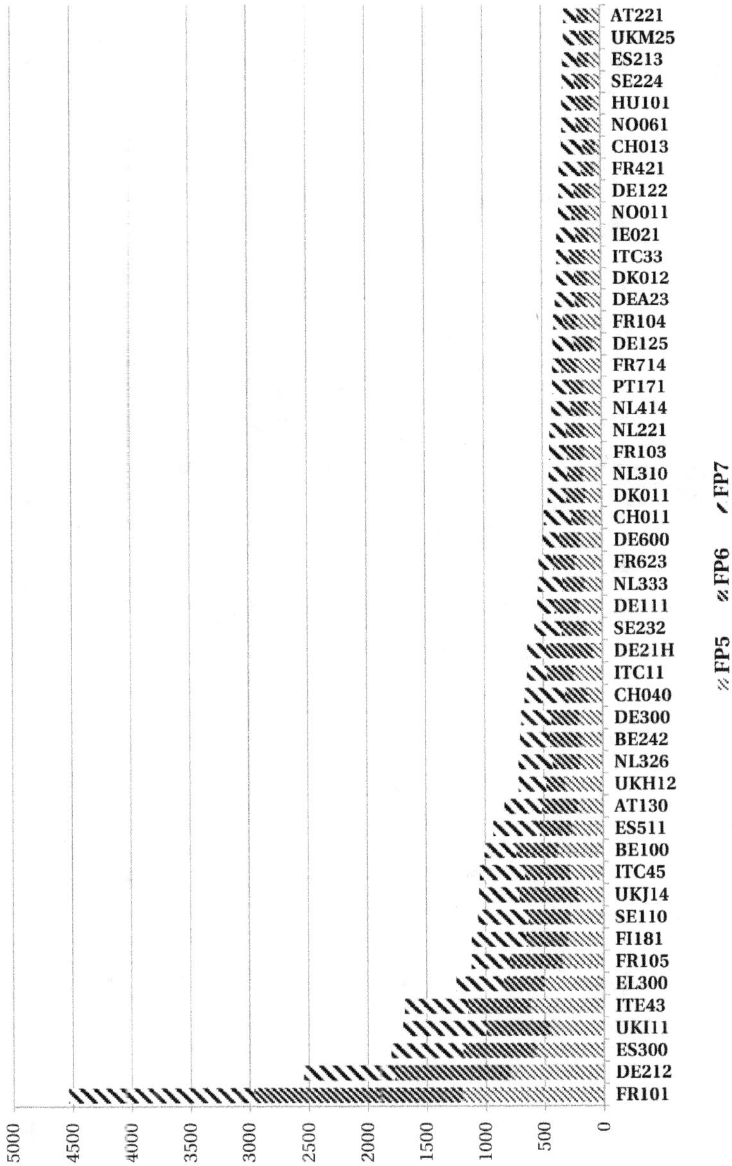

Figure 3.6: Funding to FP projects in NUTS-3 regions, 1998-2011 (total project costs)

For comparability purposes the thematic areas of the three framework programmes have been reclassified in a uniform scheme, which consists of 10 thematic and 7 horizontal clusters (see Table 4.1 in Appendix 2). Similarly the types of participating organisations have been reclassified into the following 7 categories: education (EDU), which includes institutions of secondary, vocational and higher education, research (RES), which includes all types of private and public organisations whose main function is scientific and technological research, private commercial (PRC), including SMEs, private non-profit (PNP), public bodies (PUB), including government, local authorities and public enterprises but excluding education and research-oriented public bodies, international bodies (INT), including international organisations, international professional associations but excluding multinational enterprises, and other (OTH), which includes individual researchers, some types of national or regional associations, some types of non-governmental organisations, etc.

Patent co-invention data

PATSTAT – EPO's Worldwide Statistical Patent database with bibliographic data on patents filed with more than 70 patent offices worldwide, including EPO itself – contains more than 60 million documents. These documents contain data on priority, application and publication dates,[11] technology classes, and applicants and inventors of the patents, as well as patent and non-patent citations. The OECD REGPAT database contains regionalised records of patent data from PATSTAT and the European PCT patents,[12] covering more than 5,000 regions from the 34 OECD member-countries, as well as China and Brazil. The process of 'regionalisation' was based on matching postcodes and/or locality names contained in the addresses provided in patents with the corresponding NUTS-3 regions.

The raw dataset contains 2,002,934 granted patent applications filed with EPO in the period 1990-2011, involving some 3,921,628 inventors (not necessarily distinct entities) from 204 countries, of which 34 follow the NUTS convention, and 4,914 micro-regions of which 1,444 NUTS-3. The total number of inventor participations in patent applications in this dataset is 5,199,505. The largest number of patent applications come from the US followed by Germany, Japan, France, the UK, Italy, the Netherlands, Switzerland, South Korea and Sweden in fractional counts, or with Japan at the second place above Germany, South Korea above the Netherlands and Switzerland, and Canada above Sweden in terms of whole counts. Among the non-EU countries China occupies the 13th and 14th place in the rankings in terms of fractional and whole patent counts respectively, while Israel the 19th and 17th, Australia the 20th, India the 22nd and 21st, and Russia the 24th and 23rd respectively (see Figure 3.7 below and Table 3.2 in Appendix 2 for a complete list of the top-50 countries).

Figure 3.7: Top-50 countries by fractional and whole patent application counts, 1990-2011 (log scale)

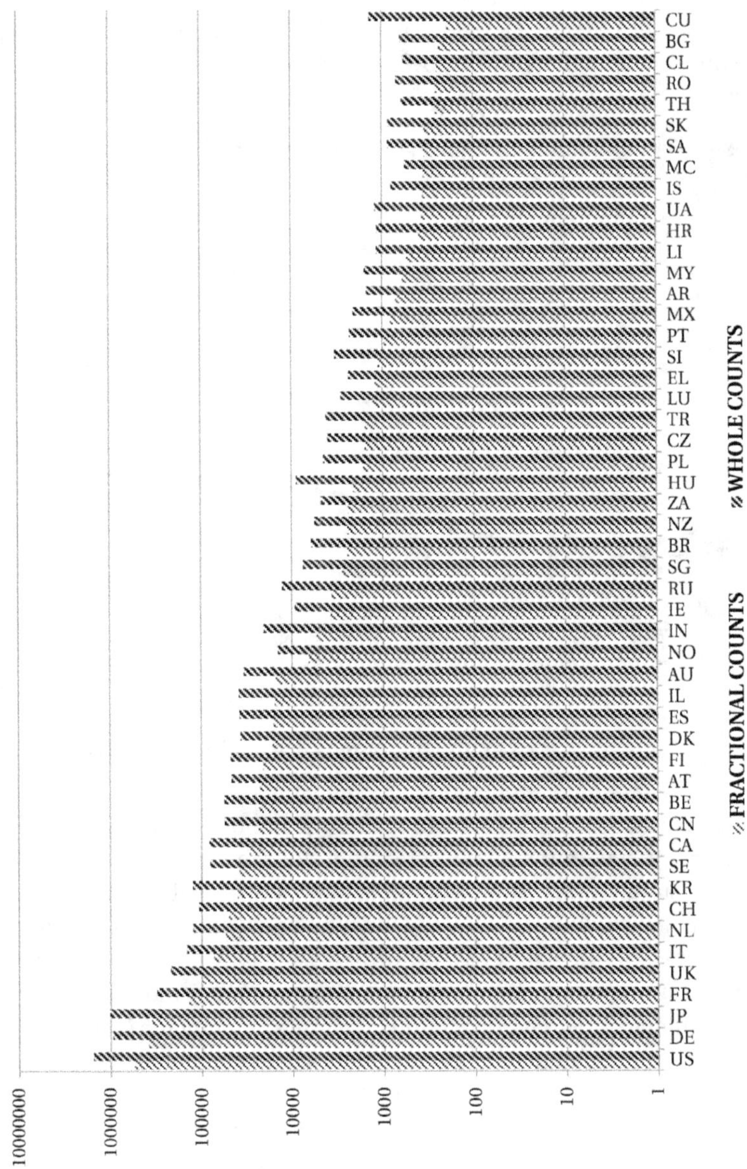

Patent application counts exhibit a strongly upward trend until 2006, then a decline in the subsequent years, and a sharp fall in 2010 and 2011, which is probably attributable to incomplete data for these last two years (see Figure 3.8 below and Table 3.4 in Appendix 2). For this reason, network analysis in following paragraphs covers only the period 1990-2009.

Figure 3.8: Trend in patent applications to EPO, 1990-2011

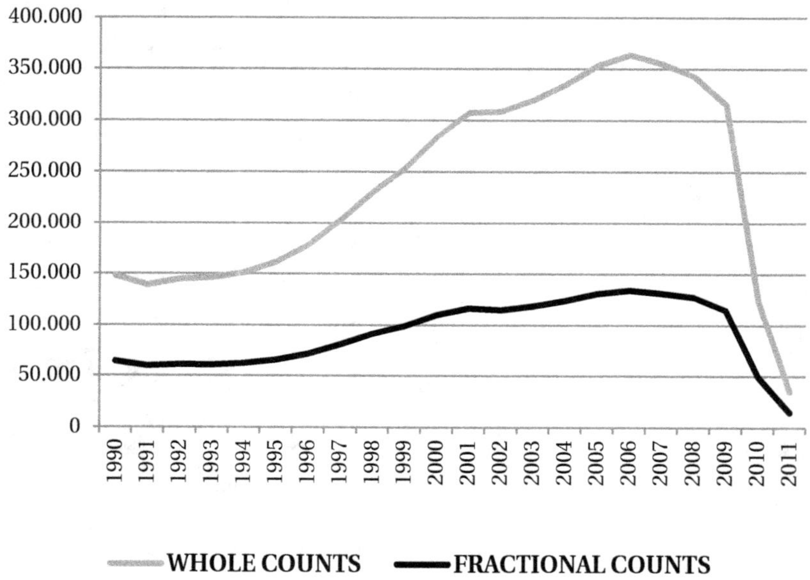

The dataset used in the present analysis is limited to the 34 countries which comply with the NUTS convention for the classification of their regional subdivisions. These countries consist of a total of 1,462 NUTS-3 regions (excluding the ZZZ-coded 'extra-regio' territories), of which 1,373 appear in the dataset as having at least one inventor in the patent applications filed with EPO between 1990 and 2011. In this sample the total number of patent applications is 981,268 of which 573,932 (58%) are co-invented patents, i.e. patents with more than one inventor from the group of NUTS-compliant countries, and the total number of inventor participations is 2,199,920, of which 1,792,584 (81%) are co-inventor participations from NUTS-compliant countries, corresponding to 1,559,515 inventors, of which 1,280,822 are co-inventors from NUTS-compliant countries. The Dutch region Zuidoost-Noord-Brabant which comprises the city of Eindhoven is consistently and by far the highest ranking NUTS-3 region in terms of both whole and fractional patent counts, followed by the German district of the city of Munich, the French department of Paris, the Italian province of Milan, and the French department of Hauts-de-Seine, which also forms part of the inner Parisian metropolitan area. The group of the top-10 NUTS-3 regions also include the Swedish county of Stockholm, the Swiss canton of Zurich, the German district of the city of Berlin, the Finnish region of Uusimaa, which comprises the cities of Helsinki and Espoo, and the German district of Ludwigsburg, which is part of the administrative region of Stuttgart. Figure 3.9 below and Table 3.3 in Appendix 2 provide a list of the top-50 NUTS-3 regions, while Figure 3.10 presents a choropleth map of Europe coloured according to the intensity of patenting activity (fractional counts) in the NUTS-3 regions.

Figure 3.9: Top-50 NUTS-3 regions by fractional and whole patent application counts, 1990-2011

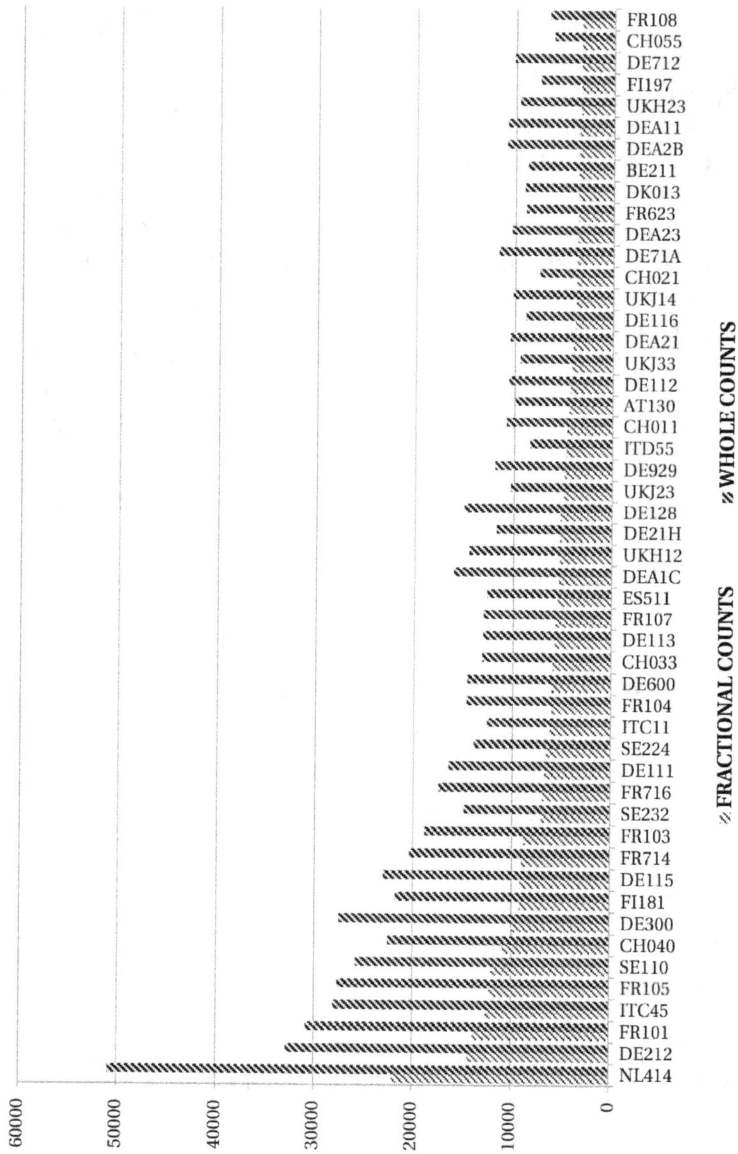

Figure 3.10: Intensity of patenting activity in NUTS-3 regions, 1990-2011 (fractional counts)

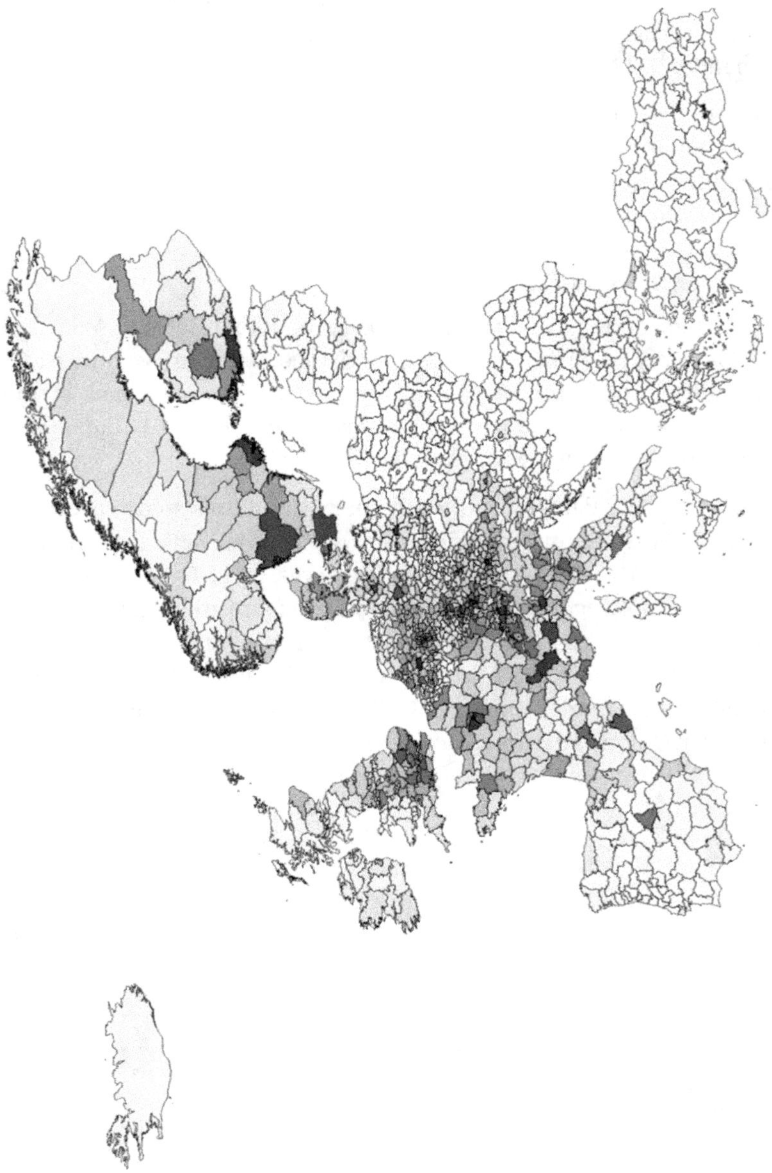

On a year-by-year basis, Zuidoost-Noord-Brabant, Milan, the Parisian metropolitan area (notably Paris and Hauts-de-Seine), and more recently the French department of Isère in the prefecture of Grenoble rank consistently first in patent counts (for details see Table 3.5 in Appendix 2).

For the purposes of the relational analysis only co-invented patents are taken into consideration. In the sample of co-invented patents the maximum number of co-inventors located in NUTS-compliant countries for a single patent is 94.

Joint ventures and strategic alliances data

The 'Thomson Financial Securities Data, Joint Ventures and Alliances' (TFSD), is a proprietary database with data on joint ventures and strategic alliances collected from announcements published in the financial press. Despite the weaknesses listed below, it is one of the most complete databases of its kind.

The particular dataset used for the purposes of this study covers the period 1990-2009 and contains data on strategic alliances in R&D services (11,544 records) and joint ventures in R&D services (2,637 records), involving 30,605 participations of more than 14,000 parent companies located in 100 distinct countries.[13] The majority of participations come from the US (17,745), Japan (3,517), UK (1,419), Canada (1,053), and Germany (1,025), while only 4,479 come from the European Union as a whole.

Figure 3.11: Top-50 countries as participants in joint ventures and strategic alliances, 1990-2009 (log scale)

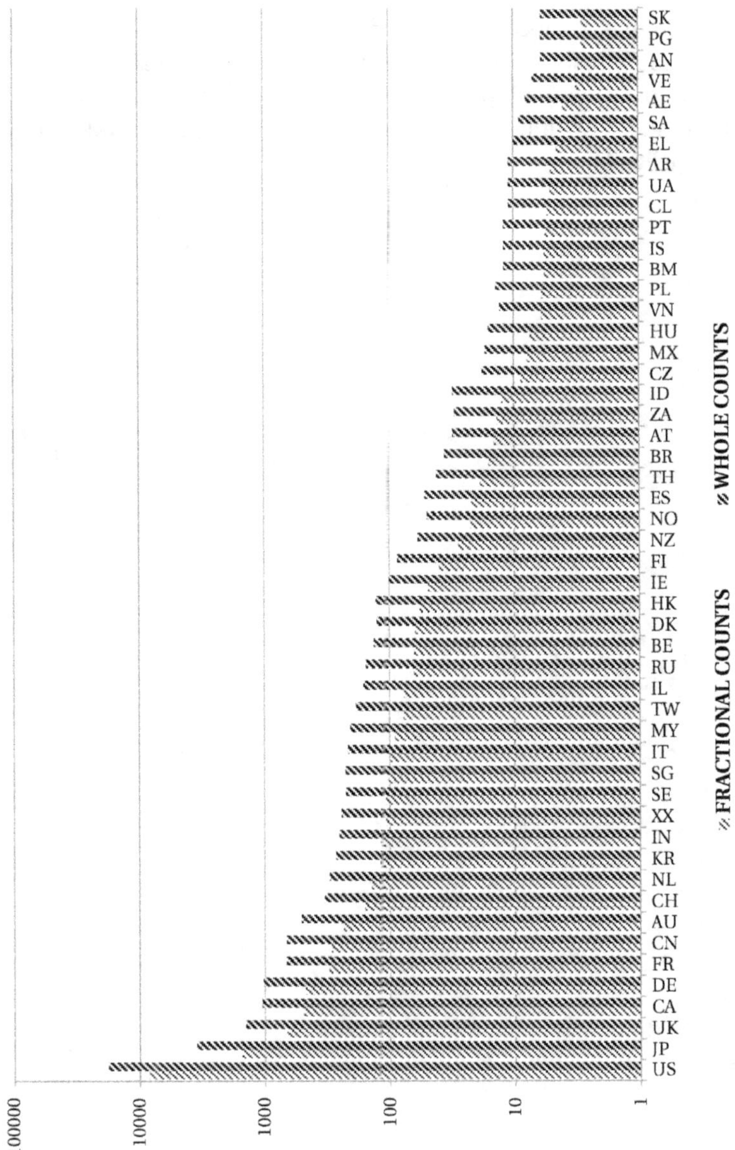

The dataset provides details on the localities, postcodes and addresses of the parent companies, which makes possible the identification of the NUTS-3 regions in which they are located (in the case of companies located in countries which have adopted the NUTS classification system). 397 NUTS-3 regions are represented in the dataset, corresponding to 679 localities (districts or municipalities and communities) of different scales, but mostly at the LAU-2 scale of municipalities.[14]

Figure 3.12: Top-50 NUTS-3 regions as participants in joint ventures and strategic alliances, 1990-2009

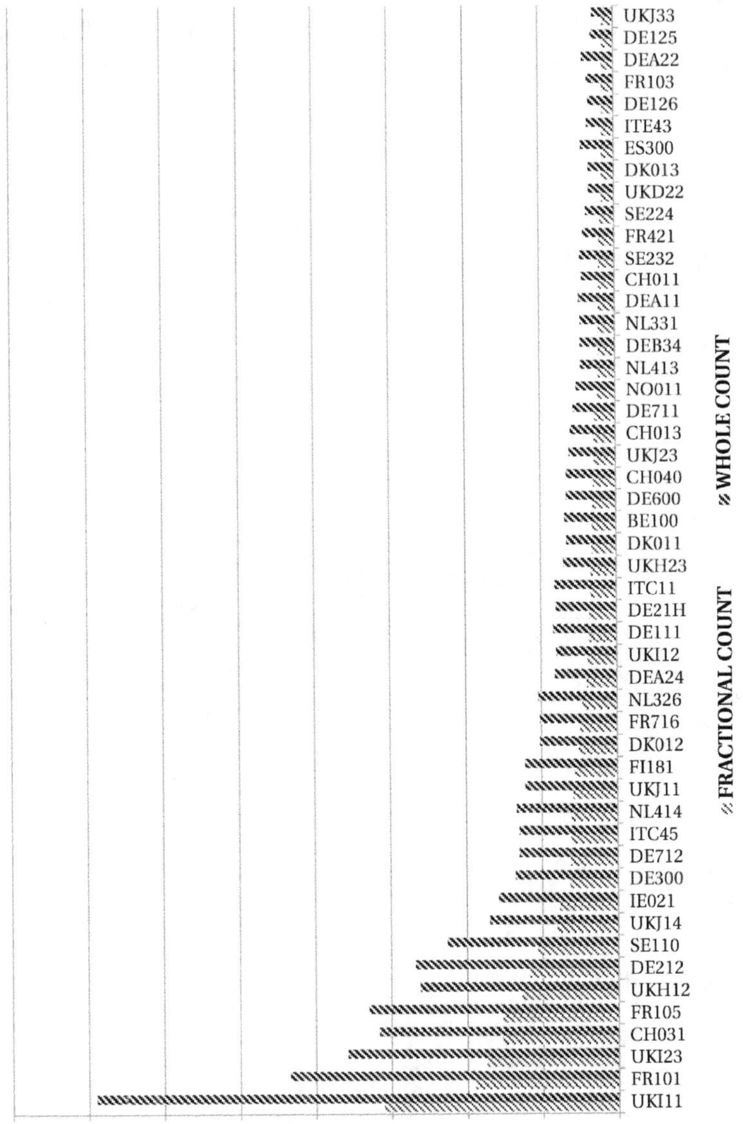

The joint ventures (subsidiary companies) themselves are located in 82 distinct countries – again the majority in the US (814), followed by China (286), Japan (274), the UK (130) and Germany (119), and 484 in the EU as a whole. Detailed data on localities or addresses of the joint ventures are not provided consistently, so the identification of the regions where the subsidiaries are established is not possible.

Figure 3.13: Top-50 countries as locations of joint ventures, 1990-2009 (log scale)

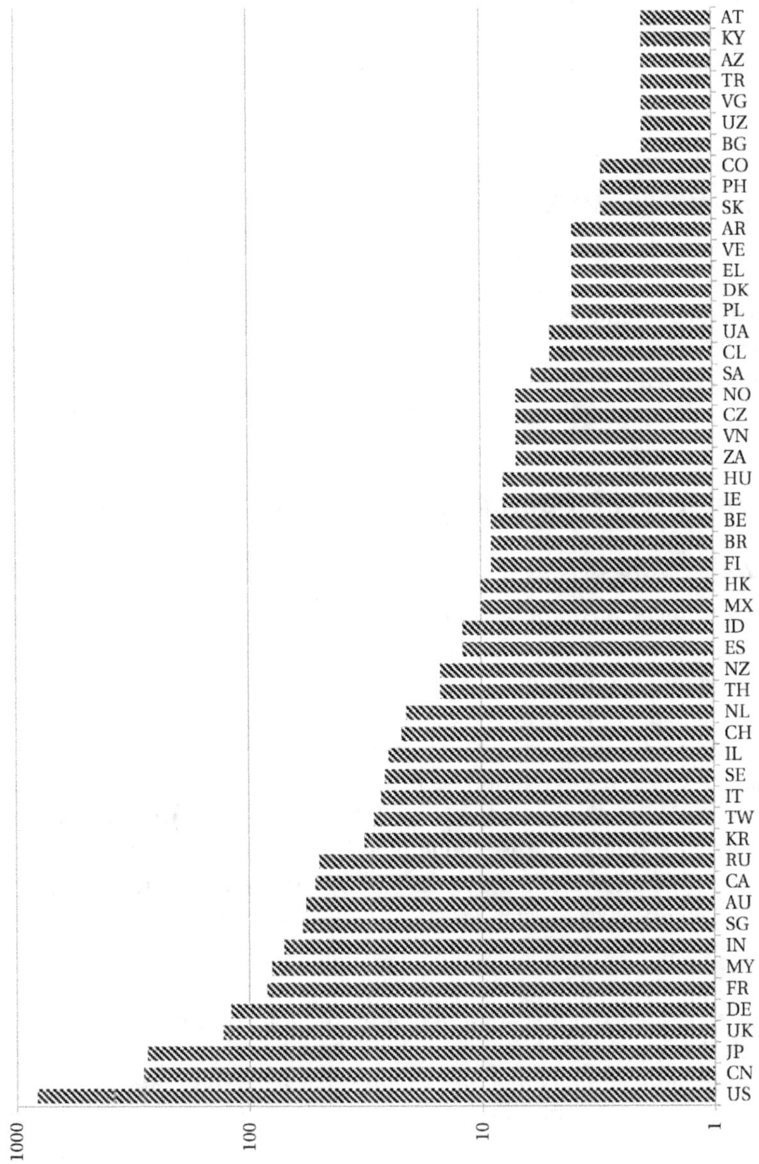

The limitations of the dataset have to do with its strong Anglosaxon bias, due to the fact that the data has been collected mainly from the English-speaking financial press, the (possibly related) not so extensive geographical coverage and the generally small presence of continental European firms, and the fact that the participants are mostly private firms.

Network analysis

The first subsection focuses on the analysis of graph-level (group) characteristics of the interregional knowledge network topologies, including standard network-analytical indicators, small-worldliness, scale invariance and assortativity. The second subsection examines and compares the vertex-level (point) characteristics of the networks and develops a regional typology on the basis of these relational attributes.

Graph-level topological characteristics

Connectedness

All instances of the interregional FP participation network (FP5, FP6 and FP7) in their 'clique-project' specifications consist of a single large connected component after excluding isolated nodes, and, interestingly, of a single large biconnected component after excluding trivial cases – namely pendant nodes and self-loops, which means that the network has no (nontrivial) articulation points or bridges. This indicates that the network is well-connected in a way that allows alternative routes of knowledge flow between all pairs of nodes, and hence no individual node is indispensable for preserving the connectedness of the whole. These conclusions are also confirmed by the analysis of the 'star-project' specifications of the network: the graphs here have the same order (number of vertices) as the clique-project graphs but just about a quarter of their size (number of edges), and, despite their much lower densities, also consist of single large components and bicomponents with no articulation points (see Table 3.6 in Appendix 2). From a longitudinal perspective, the intersection G_X of the three instances of the network produces a connected subgraph which consists of more than two thirds of the nodes and about a third of the edges of the main components of the initial graphs. In its star-project specification this common subgraph is less than half in order and about a quarter in size of the initial components.

All theme-specific networks exhibit similar structure in terms of connectedness: they consist of single large connected and biconnected components (with minor exceptions). The only remarkable feature of these networks, in particular in the thematic area of social sciences and infrastructures, is their very large ratio of isolated to connected nodes even after the exclusion of isolated self-loops, which reflects the low inter- and intra-regional collaboration propensity of many regions in these thematic areas.[15] The concentration of collaborative ties within specific thematic areas in small groups of regions indicates a tendency towards regional research specialisation.

Among the type-specific networks, the intra-industry and academia-industry collaboration networks are by far the most tightly connected: they have the smallest number of isolates, consist of giant components and, in most instances, of unique bicomponents of slightly smaller order than the components without non-trivial articulation points or bridges. This indicates that industry participation plays a crucial role in the formation of the interregional FP collaboration network, and academia-industry collaborative ties are the backbone of this structure. Having observed that, the examination of the intersection graphs G_X reveals that the largest such network in terms of size is the intra-academic one; this is even more clearly confirmed in the star-project specification of the intersection graphs, in which case the intra-academic network is also the largest in terms of order. These findings have the following interpretation: Intra-academic ties are the most temporally stable ties and constitute the lynchpin of the 'longitudinal core' of the FP participation network. Moreover, academic institutions participate in the network as coordinators, and hence moderators of knowledge flows, more frequently than any other type of organisation.

The interregional patent co-invention network for the entire 1990-2009 period is strongly connected, consisting essentially of single large connected and biconnected components with few isolated and pendant nodes. Similarly, the annual instances of this network are also relatively well-connected, all having single large connected and biconnected components. Interestingly, the order of these components as well as the size of the network and the number of self-loops steadily increase from year to year, while the number of isolates decreases (see Table 3.8 in Appendix 2). This indicates that collaborative activity is gradually intensified not only within but also between the regions, and that co-patenting activity becomes more geographically diffused as more regions join the interregional patent co-invention network.

By contrast, the intersection network G_X is much smaller in size, with just 1,483 ties (out of a total 86,073 of the entire network), and more fragmented, as it comprises several non-trivial connected and biconnected components, with the largest consisting of merely 13% and 8% of the nodes of the network respectively. This implies that the 'longitudinal core' of the network spans a much smaller group of regions compared to the FP participation network with an even more limited set of longitudinally stable interregional ties.

The interregional JVSA network has a considerably different structure compared to the FP participation network: It has significantly smaller order and size (with as little as 397 nodes forming 635 ties), and is therefore much sparser and less cohesive than the FP network. The network is fragmented, consisting of a large component (243 nodes) and several smaller ones, as well as a large biconnected component, whose order is about a third of the order of the whole network, and several smaller ones. As a result, the network has many articulation points and bridges (see Table 3.10 in Appendix 2).

By contrast, the international (country-level) JVSA network is better connected, with as many as 558 ties for 100 nodes, a single component, and a (non-trivial) bicomponent of 69 countries. An explanation for the increased connectedness of the international network, besides the fact that the level of aggregation of individual interactions is higher and therefore the cumulative probability of tie formation is also higher, is that the principal nodes which give cohesion to this network, notably the top participants US and Japan, are not present by construction in the interregional network which spans only European regions.

Distance

The diameters of the interregional FP collaboration network are generally small (ranging from 3 to 4 for the clique-project and from 5 to 6 for the star-project graphs). Theme-specific and type-specific networks have larger diameters (between 3 and 6, and 4 and 7 respectively) with the highest values attained by the intra-industry and the lowest by the intra-academia networks. Given that industry participation counts are comparable to that of academia, it can be deduced that industry participation is much more fragmented, and that the type of knowledge fostered by the FP participation network diffuses predominantly through academic institutions. The average graph distances for the entire interregional FP collaboration network are all low, close to 2 in the binary and the weighted-by-tie-strength specifications, and below 1 in the weighted-by-interaction-frequency specification.[16] In the weighted graphs, average distances increase dramatically in the cases of the thematic subnetwork of social sciences and humanities, as well as the network of academia-industry collaboration (see Table 3.7 in Appendix 2).

The diameters of the annual instances of the interregional patent co-invention network are significantly higher than those of the FP participation network (ranging from 6 to 9), and this is true even for the dense graph which corresponds to the 1990-2009 period (with a diameter of 6). This implies a slower technological knowledge diffusion process through this network as compared to the FP participation network, and is consistent with the view that instrumental-type technological knowledge, typically fostered by this network, tends to be less diffusive than the universal type. The average graph distance is also higher (when the binary specifications of the networks are considered),[17] but declines consistently over time, which implies that the interregional diffusion of technological knowledge, even of the instrumental type, is intensified in time. This is even more pronounced in the weighted graphs (see Figure 3.14 below and Table 3.9 in Appendix 2). Unsurprisingly given its order, size and degree of connectedness, the intersection network has an extremely large diameter and its main connected component has large average graph distances.

The diameter of the interregional JVSA network is high (8) as a result of its relatively high fragmentation, the heterogeneity of its actors, and the considerably smaller size of its graph. However, the diameter of the international JVSA network is half (4), precisely because of the presence of extra-European actors which account for more than two thirds of the total connectivity of the network. The average graph distances are 3.28 and 2.17 respectively, and much lower (2.37 and 0.94 respectively) in the weighted-by-interaction-frequency graphs (see Table 3.10 in Appendix 2).

Figure 3.14: Evolution of the interregional patent co-invention network topology, 1990-2009

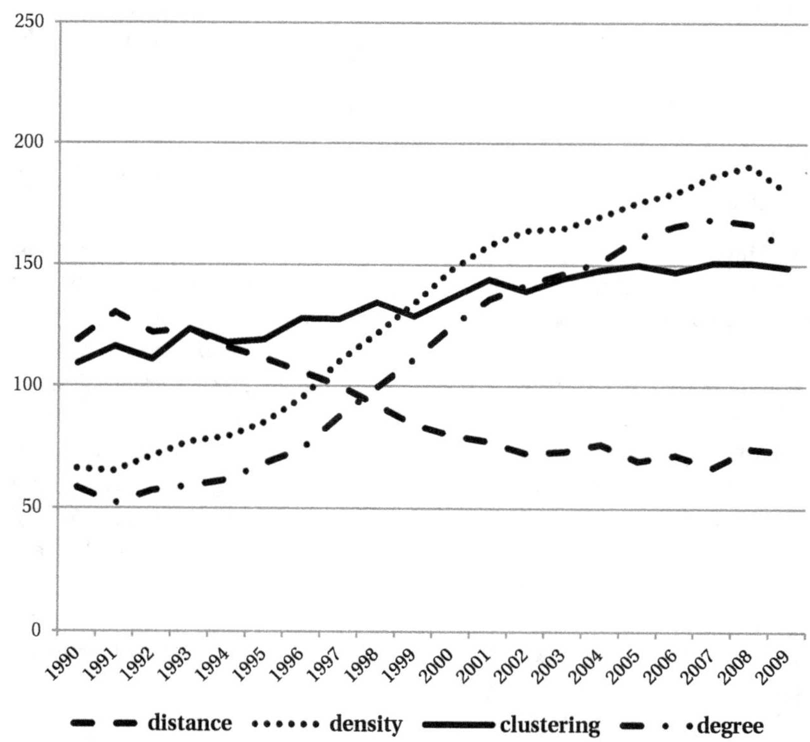

Degree centrality

FP participation network

In the clique-project binary and weighted-by-interaction-frequency specifications of the network, FP6 exhibits the highest average degree centrality, but in all other specifications the highest values are attained by FP5, which implies that while on average FP6 created more and more frequent interregional ties, those created by FP5 may have been qualitatively stronger and more stable. In the case of FP7, the low average degree centralities are justified by the fact that at the time of data extraction only half of the programme had been implemented, and therefore it is not directly comparable to completed FPs.

Among the thematic subnetworks, ICT exhibits by far the highest average degree centrality, especially in its weighted specifications, followed by ECO (environment and energy). Among the type-specific FP participation networks, PRC closely followed by EDU exhibit the highest values in almost all weighted specifications, while AIC exhibits the lowest in its weighted-by-tie-strength but one of the highest in its binary specifications. This indicates that academia-industry collaboration ties are not as strong and enduring, despite the fact that they are quite widespread and, as postulated in a previous paragraph, a key cohesion factor for the whole network.

The interregional patent co-invention network exhibits persistently high average degree centrality, which moreover steadily increases in time (Figure 3.14). This confirms that spontaneous (mostly inter-firm) collaboration, and therefore the extensive division of labour in the production of technological knowledge of the instrumental type is gradually intensifying – a conclusion consistent with the hypothesis that open innovation is becoming the dominant paradigm in technological knowledge production. However, in their binary specification all instances of the patent co-invention network exhibit lower average degree centralities than those of the FP participation network, even when measured for the entire 1990-2009 period of the former. This implies that interregional ties in the case of the former are much less diverse and more selective than in the case of the latter.

The interregional JVSA network exhibits a low average degree centrality which is indicative of the low connectivity of the network. The international JVSA network has a significantly higher average degree centrality, which however is still relatively low when compared to the other knowledge networks (see Appendix 2).

Density and clustering

The interregional FP collaboration network is highly dense in all instances (with densities ranging from 0.059 to 0.81 in its clique-project graphs and from 0.015 to 0.028 in its star-project graphs). As expected, the thematic subnetworks are less dense, with the highest scores attained by the ICT subnetwork. The inter-member-state FP collaboration network densities, which have been calculated specifically for this comparison, range from 0.186 to 0.254, and density increases from FP5 to FP7 as the programmes increasingly open to extra-EU participation. The average clustering coefficients of the interregional network are generally high, close to 0.6 in all binary clique-project graphs, and dropping to just below 0.4 in the star-project graphs. This is normal considering that the graphs become much less transitive with the removal of all within-project ties other than the coordinator-participant ones. Still, the clustering coefficients of these graphs remain quite high. The clustering coefficients calculated for the weighted graphs are lower by an order of magnitude (between 0.002 and 0.004), but this is due to the formula used in weighted graphs.[18]

The interregional patent co-invention network is sparser than the FP participation network, with only the density of the 1990-2009 period graph being comparable. Similarly to degree centrality, the density of the network increases with time (Figure 3.14). The clustering coefficient of the binary graph, and hence the transitivity of the network, is also increasing with time, although more moderately. However, in the weighted graphs, which also take into account the intensities of transitive ties, clustering appears to decrease and then stabilise. This can be interpreted as a tendency for more transitive ties but of decreasing importance in the knowledge diffusion process.

The interregional JVSA network is much sparser than the other two networks (density of 0.008). The international JVSA network is considerably denser (0.113) than the interregional one but still sparser than the inter-member-state FP participation network. For the interregional JVSA network the average clustering coefficient of the binary specification is comparably low (0.115), while of the weighted-by-interaction-frequency specification is 0.008. For comparison, the international JVSA is 0.535 and below 0.001 respectively.

Small-world structure and degree distribution

The graphs of all interregional FP collaboration network instances are far from complete,[19] but at the same time exhibit high clustering coefficients (in their binary specifications), and small diameters. These two characteristics typically indicate the presence of a small-world network structure. This is confirmed by the estimated small-world indices (SWI), all of which are significantly higher than one (see Table 3.7 in Appendix 2). The thematic and type-specific networks exhibit a more pronounced small-world structure with the exception of the inter-academia network.

Figure 3.15 presents the log-log histograms of the degree distributions of the interregional FP collaboration network instances. The first row of plots corresponds to the binary clique-project, the second to the weighted-by-interaction-frequency, the third to the weighted-by-tie-strength, and the fourth to the binary star-project specifications of the network. All graphs have an almost linear downward slope, more evident in the weighted and star-project graphs, which indicates the presence of a power-law distribution. The maximum likelihood fit indicates the possible existence of a truncated power-law (see Appendix 1 for an explanation of the procedure, and in Appendix 2 for the estimation results). In the case of the binary clique-project graphs, all likelihood ratio tests show that a lognormal distribution fits better to the sample, but distinguishing between lognormal and power-law distributions with certainty is not feasible for small samples and for segments of the probability mass function.

The annual instances of the interregional patent co-invention network exhibit even higher small-world indices, which however decline in the course of time as the network becomes increasingly denser (Table 3.9 in Appendix 2). The log-log histograms of the degree distributions (Figure 3.16) similarly indicate a probable power-law distribution. The results of the maximum likelihood tests are similar to those of the previous case (see Table 3.12 in Appendix 2).

The interregional and international JVSA networks also exhibit small-world structure but the former much more pronounced than the latter, which is better connected (in Appendix 2). The log-log histograms of the degree distributions (Figure 3.17) also reveal a possible power-law distribution.

Figure 3.15: Log-log histograms of interregional FP participation network degree distribution

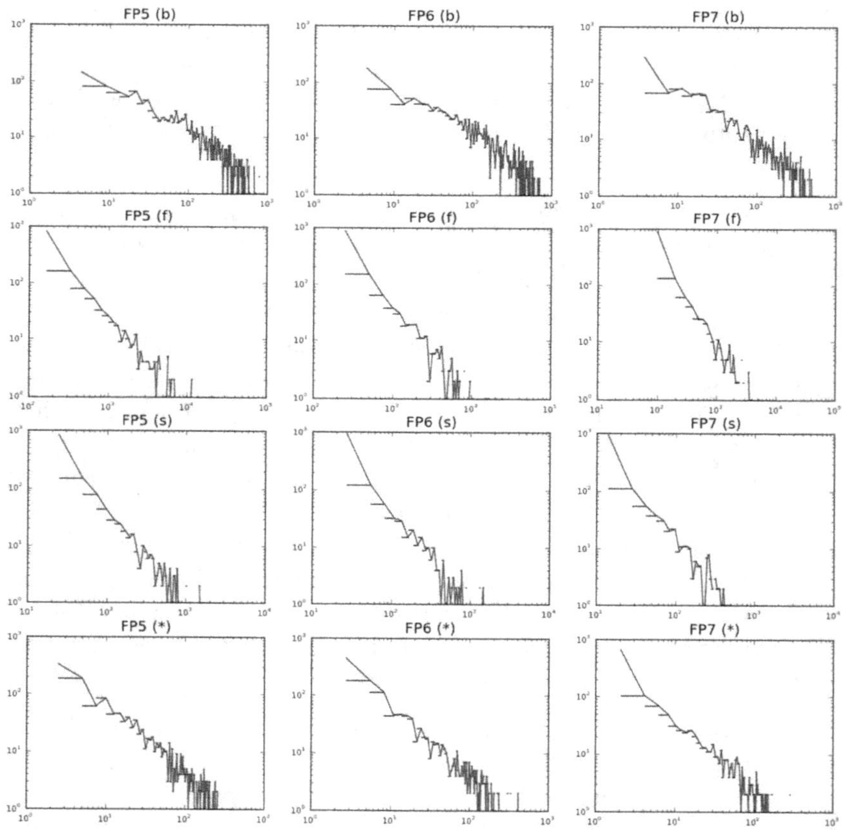

Figure 3.16: Log-log histograms of interregional patent co-invention network degree distribution

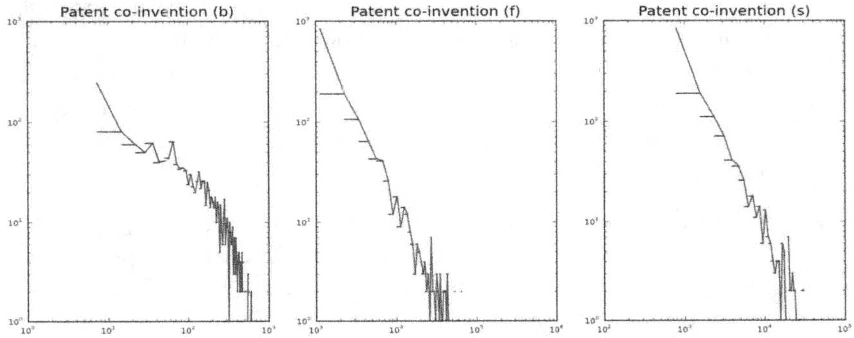

Figure 3.17: Log-log histograms of JVSA networks degree distribution

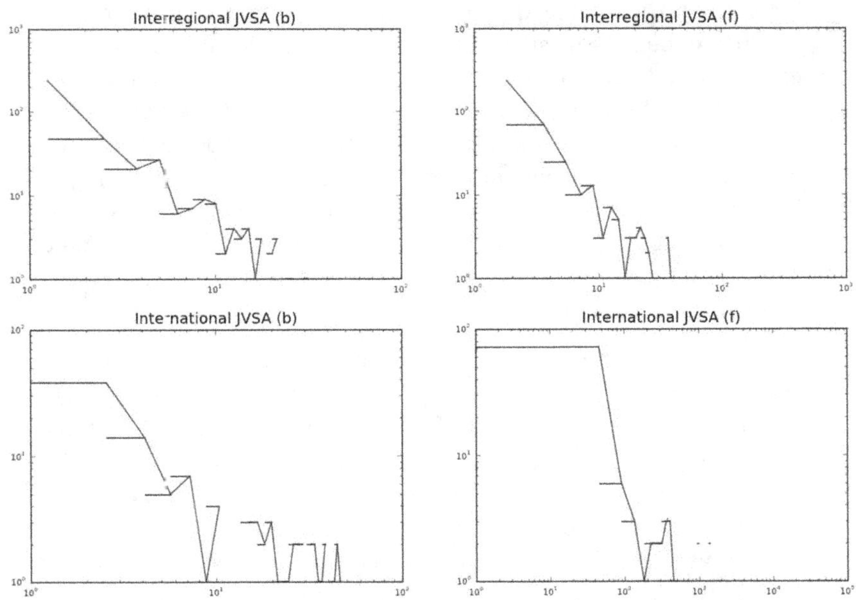

Assortativity

Several tests for assortativity in terms of various quantitative and categorical attributes of the nodes were conducted, including assortativity on the basis of regional income (examined in various quantiles, whereof only those corresponding to quartiles are presented here), the core-periphery divide measured by the eccentricity of individual regions as nodes, the North-South-East divides, national or regional groupings (i.e. NUTS-3 regions from the same country or NUTS-2 region), and vertex degree. The results of the assortativity hypotheses tests are quite different for the three interregional knowledge networks under study.

In the case of the FP participation network no systematic pattern of assortative mixing has been detected (see Table 3.16 in Appendix 2). More specifically, no network instance exhibits any significant tendency for preferential collaboration between NUTS-3 regions within the same NUTS-2 region or country. The calculated assortativity indices give no indication for preferential collaboration between regions belonging to the same quartile in the distribution of gross regional product either. Assortative mixing between regions from the same geographical 'bloc', i.e. 'North', 'South' and 'East', is also found to be insignificant. By contrast, there seems to be a statistically significant tendency towards disassortative mixing in terms of degree distribution of the nodes. This means that better-connected, more central regions have a tendency to collaborate more with less-connected ones. This is also confirmed by the weak disassortative tendency for collaboration between core and periphery regions (where 'core' and 'periphery' refer to the network structure).

A very different picture is painted by the results of assortativity analysis on the interregional patent co-invention network (Table 3.14 in Appendix 2). Here the tendency for preferential collaboration between NUTS-3 regions from the same country is strong and significant. The tendency for within-bloc preferential collaboration is even more pronounced than that of within-country, which indicates that assortative mixing in this network transcends country borders. A similar tendency is detected in the preferential mixing of regions belonging to the same income quartiles. By contrast, degree assortativity is either weak or negative, which indicates that the choice of partner is not influenced by the partner's position in the network. Interestingly, all significant assortativity values are declining in the course of time, which once again confirms that the innovation process is becoming more inclusive and diffusive even in the case of instrumental technological knowledge. Assortative mixing is also significant in the case of the interregional and international JVSA networks, but the effect here is weaker than in the previous case.

Vertex-level topological characteristics

In this subsection four point indicators of network topology are used for the assessment and ranking of the regions, namely eigenvector centrality (more specifically 'page rank') as an indicator for overall connectivity, current-flow betweenness centrality for positional influence, closeness centrality for structural proximity, and clustering for network embeddedness.[20]

Regional rankings

The ten top-ranking regions in terms of eigenvector, betweenness, and closeness centralities in the interregional FP participation network for the period 1998-2011 (FP5, 6 and 7) include combinations of the following NUTS-3 regions: the department of Paris, the province of Rome, the city-district of Munich, the community of Madrid, the prefecture of Attica (which comprises the city of Athens), West Inner London, the region of Brussels, the region of Uusimaa (which comprises the cities of Helsinki and Espoo), the province of Milan, the province of Barcelona, the district of Vienna, the county of Stockholm, and the Parisian department of Hauts-de-Seine. Figures 3.18 and 3.19 below present the choropleth maps of NUTS-3 regions coloured according to their eigenvector and betweenness centrality measures in the interregional FP participation network.

Figure 3.18: Eigenvector centralities in interregional FP participation network

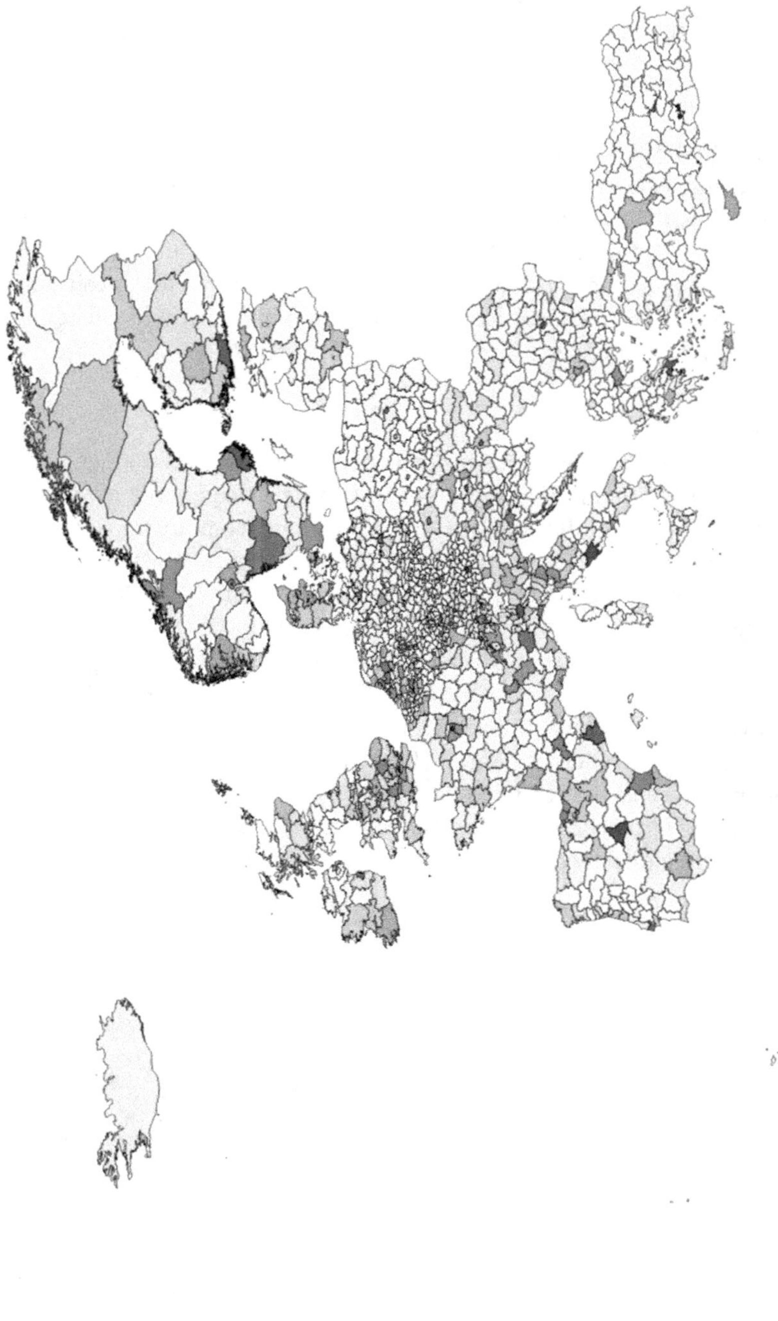

Figure 3.19: Current-flow betweenness centralities in interregional FP participation network

The rankings of NUTS-3 regions in the case of the interregional patent co-invention network (for the period 1990-2009) are significantly different. In terms of eigenvector centrality, the top-10 group consists in the province of Milan, the city-districts of Berlin and Munich, the department of Paris, the region of Uusimaa, the county of Stockholm, the German district of Ludwigsburg (in the administrative region of Stuttgart), the Parisian department of Hauts-de-Seine, the Dutch region of Southeast-North-Brabant, and the county of Budapest. In terms of betweenness centrality, 5 out of the top-10 regions are German, in addition to Stockholm, Milan, Paris, the French department of Rhône, and the Swiss canton of Basel, while in terms of closeness centrality, all top-50 regions with one exception (the French department of Rhône) are German. Figures 3.20 and 3.21 present two choropleth maps of NUTS-3 regions coloured according to their eigenvector and betweenness centrality measures in the interregional patent co-invention network for the period 1990-2009.

Figure 3.20: Eigenvector centralities in interregional patent co-invention network

Figure 3.21: Current-flow betweenness centralities in interregional patent co-invention network

In the interregional JVSA network for the period 1990-2009 the top-10 group includes combinations of West Inner, East Inner and West-Northwest Outer London, Cambridgeshire, Oxfordshire, Paris and Hauts-de-Seine, Munich, Berlin, Basel, Stockholm, Milan, Turin, and Madrid, depending on the type of centrality measure.[21] Figures 3.22 and 3.23 below present the choropleth maps for two centrality measures of NUTS-3 regions in the interregional JVSA network.

Figure 3.22: Eigenvector centralities in interregional JVSA network

Figure 3.23: Current-flow betweenness centralities in interregional JVSA network

Dyads of regions with the highest scores in terms of *edge betweenness centrality* can be considered as the most influential interregional ties in the network and as connectors of network *communities*.[22] Most dyads in the top-100 group of interregional ties in the FP participation network include the department of Paris, while in the patent co-invention network there is a strong presence of German regions but the overall picture is more diverse (see Tables 3.20 and 3.21 in Appendix 2).

Inter-network relationships

Rank correlations

The empirical evidence presented in the previous subsections indicates that the three interregional knowledge networks under study are not only dissimilar in some of their general topological characteristics but also with regard to the structural positions of the regions. This is evident in the different composition and rankings of the groups of top-50 regions by various vertex-level centrality measures. A more general test for this purpose is the estimation of the pairwise correlation of the same centrality measures between interlocking networks. For this purpose the Kendall rank correlation coefficient is calculated for four types of centrality measures (degree, eigenvalue, current flow betweenness and closeness) and for clustering on the weighted-by-tie-strength graphs of the interregional FP participation and patent co-invention networks.[23] The latter has been specifically constructed with patent data aggregated for the three FP time-periods in order to be directly comparable to the former. The correlation coefficients of all centrality measures, and in particular of betweenness and closeness centralities, are found to be relatively low, and of clustering even lower (see Table 3.22 in Appendix 2).

Correlations of structural and spatial distances

The Mantel test [MANTEL, 1967] is a non-parametric (Monte-Carlo) statistical test for matrix correlation based on repeated random permutations of the row and columns of the matrices, designed to deal with the inherent problem of structural dependence in this type of data. The logic of this test is similar to that of the quadratic assignment procedure, and it is typically applied on distance or dissimilarity matrices. The correlations of the permutated cells are normally measured by Pearson's product-moment method.

This test applied on the (graph) distance matrices[24] of the interregional FP participation and patent co-invention networks safely leads to the rejection of the null hypothesis (i.e. that correlation is zero), and yields a Mantel statistic of 0.207 (after 1,000 permutations), whose interpretation is that the interdependence of the two networks explains roughly a fifth of the relational distance of the regions. Using a distance matrix of regional centroids to control for spatial dependence, the correlation of the two networks is again found to be statistically significant, and actually of a slightly larger magnitude (0.22), which implies that proximity in physical space cannot explain this correlation.

Interestingly, the correlation between the distance matrix of the patent co-invention network and the spatial matrix of regional centroids is found to be statistically significant with a Mantel statistic of 0.274. By contrast, in the FP participation network this correlation is not significant (the null hypothesis cannot be rejected), and in any case the Mantel statistic is marginally below zero (-0.017).

Multiplexity and inter-network articulation points

The knowledge plexus consists of various overlaid and interlocked knowledge networks. *Multiplexity* is therefore an essential feature in the articulation of the knowledge plexus.[25] This subsection specifically focuses on the articulation of the interregional FP participation and patent co-invention networks. For this purpose an intersection graph of the two networks is constructed for each FP time-period and the longitudinally stable principal connected component is extracted from the three instances. This graph consists of 770 vertices (about half of those of the interlocking graphs) and 3,562 edges (a small fraction of those of the initial graphs). After removing the self-loops, the graph consists of 595 vertices and 3,274 edges, which can be considered as the stable articulation points of the two networks. This is a large and diverse group of regions (it comprises about 40% of the entire population of regions).

Hierarchical agglomerative clustering

I conduct hierarchical agglomerative clustering with the Ward method on the scaled values of the three centrality measures (eigenvector, current-flow betweenness, and closeness) in the two networks combined. I partitioned the sample into 8 clusters, which seemed reasonable from the dendrogram. The cluster of leading regions in both dimensions (FP participation and patents), which interestingly has always the same membership in all meaningful partitions of the sample, consists of 14 regions, namely those of Vienna, Brussels, Munich, Berlin, Attica, Madrid, Barcelona, Uusima, Paris, Hauts-de-Seine, Milan, Rome, Stockholm and West Inner London, all of which also belong to the group of stable articulation points of the two networks.

Conclusion

In this chapter three different interregional knowledge networks were examined, which correspond to an equal number of technological knowledge types. The FP funds predominantly 'pre-competitive' research of a public good nature, and therefore the ensuing participation network can be considered as a medium for the creation and diffusion of universal-type technological knowledge. The network of patent co-inventors corresponds to technological knowledge of the instrumental type, while the network of joint ventures and strategic alliances, which consists of stable inter-firm collaborations in the production of technological knowledge, supports technological knowledge of the organisational type.

The first two networks are very extensive, and relatively dense and well-connected. By contrast the third network is much more sparsely populated, and considerably fragmented. This is consistent with the theory: inter-organisational knowledge is proprietary, embodied, protected, and its diffusion much more restricted than the other two types of knowledge. All three networks have small-world and core-periphery structures. While the FP participation network clearly exhibits this core-periphery structure with a degree distribution which appears to follow a truncated power-law, it is more 'egalitarian' and geographically spread, with no detectable assortative bias along the regional 'core-periphery divide'. Undoubtedly, the participation of academia is the backbone of this network, the factor which coheres its structure and facilitates the supra-regional diffusion of knowledge. Academic institutions in that sense play the role of interregional knowledge brokers. Academia-industry ties have a very crucial function in this context, but they are still relatively weak and ad hoc.

The 'core' does not have the same composition in the three networks: In the case of the FP participation network, it is a group of predominantly urban regions with large academic communities from the European 'North' and 'South' (although less from the 'East'). Although industry participation in the FPs is of an equal magnitude in quantitative terms as that of academia, it does not seem to be a determinant of the geographical distribution of 'universal' knowledge production in the European Research Area. The lack of a North-South divide in this network is reflected in that the South is well-represented in the core group, which largely consists of urban regions containing national or large regional capitals. By contrast, the structure of the patent co-invention network reproduces the North-South divide, and this is also true in the case of the JVSA network. The core of the former predominantly consist of regions with strong industrial bases and is dominated by the North, and in particular by German regions.

The networks also differ substantially with respect to the tendency of their nodes to assortative mixing: The FP participation network does not exhibit any such tendency, and this implies that it is a truly transnational network in the spirit of the European Research Area, which the FP has been designed to support. By contrast, the patent co-invention network exhibits strong tendencies for preferential attachment in terms of country, higher-order region, regional income and regional bloc.

Another interesting difference of the two networks is their relationship to physical space: The interregional patent co-invention network exhibits significant spatial dependence, while the FP participation network does not. Moreover, the two networks exhibit a certain degree of interdependence, which is sustained by a group of regions in the 'longitudinal core' and a relatively small number of stable ties among them. This group plays a prominent role in the articulation of the knowledge plexus.

With regard to the temporal evolution of the networks, while in the FP participation network no significant structural differences from one programming period to another are apparent, the patent co-invention network seems to evolve in the direction of increasing extensification of the division of labour in knowledge production, which is consistent with the hypothesis that open innovation is becoming the dominant paradigm.

Appendix 1: Measures of network topology

The definitions provided here have been drawn from multiple print and web sources, including WASSERMAN & FAUST, 1994, SCOTT, 2000, CARRINGTON *et al.*, 2005, YANG & KNOKE, 2007, JACKSON, 2010, and the online version of HANNEMAN & RIDDLE, 2005. Unless the origins of a concept or definition can be unequivocally attributed to a specific article or author, these sources are not individually cited. Most of the definitions have been extensively re-synthesised with consistent notation and adapted to the style and needs of the present text.

Connectedness

A graph $G(V,E)$ is *connected* if every node of G is reachable from every other node of the graph, i.e. if for every pair of nodes $i,j \in V$, there is a path from i to j, $\{i \dots j\} \in G$.

(*Connected*) *component* of a graph $G(V,E)$ is a connected subgraph $G'(V',E')$ of G, whose vertices are not connected to any other vertex of G not belonging to G', formally:

$$G' \neq \emptyset,\ G'\text{: connected},\ V' \subseteq V, E' \subseteq E, \text{ and } \forall i \in V', ij \in E \Rightarrow ij \in E'$$

Components, therefore, define a partition of a graph into connected subgraphs. A connected graph is considered to trivially consist of a single component.

Cut-vertex or *articulation point* is any vertex whose removal increases the number of connected components of a graph. *Cut-edge* or *bridge* is any edge whose removal has the same effect; incidence on a cut-vertex is a necessary but not sufficient condition for an edge to be a cut-edge.

Bicomponent (or *biconnected component*) is a maximal connected subgraph G'' of G, which remains connected even after the removal of any one of its vertices and of the edges incident on that vertex; therefore, a bicomponent by definition does not have any cut-vertices or cut-edges.

Clique $Q(V_Q, E_Q)$ is a complete subgraph of graph $G(V,E)$, formally:

$$V_Q \subseteq V, E_Q \subseteq E : \forall i,j \in V_Q, \exists\ ij \in E_Q$$

A clique is defined by at least three nodes and edges; the smallest possible clique is, therefore, a complete triad (a triangle).

Maximum clique of a graph G is the largest clique of G. *Clique number* $\omega(G)$ is the order of the maximum clique in G.

Maximal clique is a clique which is not subgraph of a larger clique. A maximum clique is also maximal, but the converse does not hold.

Clique problems, such as the detection of all maximal cliques or of the maximum clique and clique number of a graph, are all computationally intensive problems (belonging to the NP-complete complexity class) with no guaranteed algorithmic solution in finite time, which makes the calculation of these indices in large and complex graphs not always feasible.

Distance

(*Geodesic*) *distance* $\delta(i, j)$ of a pair of vertices $i, j \in V$ in a graph $G(V, E)$ is the length $\|\gamma(i, j)\|$ of the *geodesic* (or *shortest path*) $\gamma(i, j)$ connecting the two vertices, measured in terms of a *graph metric* $\| \ \|$.

In binary graphs this quantity is a positive integer. In weighted graphs it is a nonnegative real number, typically calculated as the sum of edge weights along the shortest path, which in turn is defined as the path between two vertices with the minimum sum of edge weights. This calculation, which is also implemented in the widely used Dijkstra algorithm, interprets edge weights as 'costs' or 'resistances': higher edge weights along the path entail higher path lengths and geodesic distances. In the case of our collaboration knowledge networks, however, the cost interpretation of edge weights is inappropriate: higher edge weights should entail stronger ties, which in turn mean easier diffusion of knowledge, and hence shorter geodesic distances. For this reason here I consider edge weight as a measure of *closeness* and, consequently, I define as *edge length* $\|ij\|$ the inverse of edge weight: $\|ij\| = w_{ij}^{-1}$. It then follows naturally that the geodesic distance of any pair of path-connected vertices is the minimum sum of edge lengths along some path connecting the pair.

Vertex distance $\delta(i), i \in V(G)$ is the sum of geodesic distances between vertex i and all other vertices in the graph:

$$\delta(i) = \sum_{j \in V} \delta(i,j)$$ **Equation 3.7**

Together with vertex degree, vertex distance is the most fundamental local attribute of a vertex. *Average vertex distance* is the normalised vertex distance defined as:

$$\langle\delta(i)\rangle = \frac{1}{|V|}\sum_{j \in V} \delta(i,j)$$ **Equation 3.8**

Graph distance (or *total (shortest) path length*) $\delta(G)$ is a global attribute of graph $G(V,E)$ defined as the sum of all pairwise vertex distances in that graph:

$$\delta(G) = \sum_{i \in V}\sum_{j \in V} \delta(i,j)$$ **Equation 3.9**

Average graph distance (or *average (shortest) path length*) $\langle\delta(G)\rangle$ of a graph $G(V,E)$ is the normalised graph distance:[26]

$$\langle\delta(G)\rangle = \frac{\delta(G)}{|V|(|V|-1)} = \frac{\sum_{i \in V}\sum_{j \in V}\delta(i,j)}{|V|(|V|-1)}$$ **Equation 3.10**

Distance matrix $\mathbf{\Delta}(G)$ of a graph $G(V,E)$ is a square (and symmetric for undirected graphs) $|V| \times |V|$ matrix, whose elements are the pairwise distances of the vertices of the graph:

$$\mathbf{\Delta}(G) = \left[\delta_{ij}\right]_{i,j \in V}, \text{ where } \delta_{ij} = \delta(i,j)$$

This type of matrix will be used in the statistical models of the next chapter, along with the *adjacency matrix* of the graph:

$$\mathbf{A}(G) = \left[\alpha_{ij}\right]_{i,j \in V}, \text{ where } \alpha_{ij} = \begin{cases} w_{ij}, \text{if } ij \in E \\ 0 \text{ otherwise} \end{cases}$$

and $w_{ij} \in \mathbb{R}_+$ is the weight of edge $ij \in E$ (equal to 1 in the case of binary graphs).

Eccentricity of a vertex $\epsilon(i), i \in V(G)$ is the maximum geodesic distance of that vertex from any other vertex in the graph:

$$\epsilon(i) = \max_{j \in V} \delta(i,j) \qquad \textbf{Equation 3.11}$$

Diameter $D(G)$ of a graph $G(V,E)$ is its maximum eccentricity, i.e. the maximum distance between any pair of vertices in the graph, and it is a global attribute of the graph:

$$D(G) = \max_{i \in V} \left[\max_{j \in V} \delta(i,j) \right] \qquad \textbf{Equation 3.12}$$

Radius $R(G)$ of a graph $G(V,E)$ is its minimum eccentricity:

$$R(G) = \min_{i \in V} \left[\max_{j \in V} \delta(i,j) \right] \qquad \textbf{Equation 3.13}$$

Centre $C(G)$ of a graph $G(V,E)$ is the subset of the graph's vertex set, consisting of vertices with minimum eccentricity (i.e. eccentricity equal to the graph radius):

$$C = \{i \in V : \epsilon(i) = R(G)\} \subset V$$

Periphery $P(G)$ of a graph $G(V,E)$ is the subset of the vertex set with vertices of maximum eccentricity (i.e. eccentricity equal to the graph diameter):

$$P = \{i \in V : \epsilon(i) = D(G)\} \subset V$$

Coreness is a global vertex index, first defined in BORGATTI & EVERETT, 2000, which represents the Euclidean distance of the vertex from the centroid of the graph measured in the vector space spanned by its adjacency matrix. It is related to the notion of *core-periphery structure*, namely the structure generated by a partition of the graph vertex set into two subsets with the following properties: the first subset spans a highly cohesive subgraph, the *core*, in which vertices are maximally connected; the second subset spans a non-cohesive structure attached to the core, the *periphery*, in which vertices are loosely connected among themselves, while being relatively more tightly connected to the core.

With the exception of coreness, a particularity of distance indices that has to be taken into consideration in graph comparisons, is that they are calculated on the largest connected component of the graph, as in the opposite case the distance between non-connected vertices or subgraphs would be infinity and their sum would not converge. The average graph distance index is normalised by the order of the graph (more precisely, by the order of its largest component) but the diameter is non-normalised.

Centrality

Centralities are the main analytical tools of network analysis. They measure the prominence, influence and obsolescence of a node in the network structure. They refer to individual vertices, and hence they are point indices; group centrality indices are constructed as averages of the respective point indices. Some types of centrality are local metrics of the vertices while others are global.

Degree (or *degree index*) $\deg(i)$ of vertex $i \in V(G)$ is the number of edges $ij \in E(G)$ incident on i, or differently phrased, the number of nearest neighbouring vertices. It is the simplest and most fundamental local attribute of the vertex. If the edges are weighted, then degree is equal to the sum of their weights:

$$\deg(i) = \sum_{j \in V: ij \in E} w_{ij}$$ **Equation 3.14**

Degree centrality $C_D(i)$ of a vertex $i \in V(G)$ is the simplest and most commonly used local measure of vertex centrality, defined as vertex degree normalised by graph order:[27]

$$C_D(i) = \frac{\deg(i)}{|V| - 1}$$ **Equation 3.15**

In weighted graphs, vertex degree is normalised by the total sum of weights in the graph:

$$C_D^W(i) = \deg(i)\left[\sum_{j \in V} \deg(j)\right]^{-1} = \sum_{j \in V} w_{ij} \left(\sum \sum_{i,j \in V} w_{ij}\right)^{-1}$$ **Equation 3.16**

Degree centrality provides only limited information on the local topological structure of a graph and on the structural position of a vertex. Alternative, arguably more sophisticated, indicators of centrality are Bonacich's eigenvector and Freeman's betweenness and closeness centralities.

Eigenvector centrality $C_E(i)$ of a vertex $i \in V(G)$ is the sum of all centrality scores of its adjacent vertices given by this (forward) iterative formula:

$$C_E(i) = \frac{1}{\lambda} \sum_{j \in V(G)} \alpha_{ij} C_E(j)$$ **Equation 3.17**

where α_{ij} is the *ij*th element of the adjacency matrix **A** of the graph and λ is a scaling constant. This equation in vector notation becomes:

$$\lambda \mathbf{v} = \mathbf{A}\mathbf{v}$$ **Equation 3.18**

Eigenvector centrality $C_E(i)$ is then equal to the v_i component of the eigenvector **v** of the adjacency matrix **A** which corresponds to its largest eigenvalue λ [BONACICH, 1972; 1987]. This centrality index is a global measure of vertex centrality, essentially determined by the centralities of all neighbouring vertices of the vertex in question. The algorithm for the calculation of eigenvector centrality is computationally intensive and not guaranteed to converge for large networks. An alternative measure which gives similar results to eigenvector centrality and is more efficient to calculate is *page rank* $C_{PR}(i)$, initially a Google algorithm for search engine optimisation conceived for webpage ranking now used in network analysis.

Betweenness centrality $C_B(i)$ is a global measure of vertex centrality, and specifically of the influence of a vertex on information flows between other vertices, assuming that information follows the shortest path [GIRVAN & NEWMAN, 2002]; it is therefore a measure of brokerage power. If $\Gamma(j,k)$ is the set of all geodesics (shortest paths) $\gamma(j,k)$ between $j,k \in V(G)$ and $\Gamma(j,k|i)$ is the set of all geodesics $\gamma(j,k|i)$ between j and k through i, the *betweenness index* of vertex $i \in V(G)$ is the fraction of all geodesics of G through i:

$$b(i) = \sum_{j,k \in V - \{i\}} \frac{|\Gamma(j,k|i)|}{|\Gamma(j,k)|} = \sum_{j,k \in V - \{i\}} \frac{\|\gamma(j,k|i)\|}{\|\gamma(j,k)\|}$$ **Equation 3.19**

In weighted graphs, shortest path length $\|\gamma(j,k)\|$ is defined as the sum of (inverse) edge weights along the geodesic $\gamma(j,k)$. The maximum value of the index is attained when i lies on all geodesics of the graph (e.g. when i is the central vertex in a star graph):

$$\max_{i \in V} b(i) = \frac{1}{2}(|V| - 1)(|V| - 2)$$ **Equation 3.20**

The normalisation of the index by its maximum attainable value gives the betweenness centrality of the vertex:

$$C_B(i) = \frac{2b(i)}{(|V| - 1)(|V| - 2)}$$ **Equation 3.21**

Load $C_L(i)$ and *flow (betweenness)* $C_F(i)$ *centralities* are two global vertex indices suitable for weighted graphs very similar to betweenness centrality, based on calculations of current flows instead of shortest paths.[28]

Gatekeeping of j on i (or *pair-dependency*) [WASSERMAN & FAUST, 1994: 191], is defined as:

$$GK(i,j) = \sum_{k \in V - \{i,j\}} \frac{\|\gamma(j,k|i)\|}{\|\gamma(j,k)\|}$$ **Equation 3.22**

Closeness centrality $C_C(i)$ is essentially the *closeness index* of the vertex (i.e. inverse vertex distance) normalised by graph order, and it is also a global measure of vertex centrality:

$$C_C(i) = \frac{|V| - 1}{\delta(i)}$$ **Equation 3.23**

Information centrality $C_I(i)$ (or *flow closeness centrality*) is a variant of closeness centrality suitable for weighted networks, based on the current flow model.[29]

Integrated centrality index [BONCHEV, 2009], is the ratio of the two most fundamental vertex attributes, degree and distance, which is equivalent to the product of degree and closeness centralities, combined in a single indicator:

$$C_{INT}(i) = \deg(i)[\delta(i)]^{-1} = C_D(i)C_C(i)$$ **Equation 3.24**

This index can also be used as an indicator of topological complexity and small-worldliness of a graph when aggregated over all vertices in the vertex set:

$$C_{INT}(G) = \sum_{i \in V} \frac{\deg(i)}{\delta(i)}$$ **Equation 3.25**

Density

Density $\rho(G)$ is a global attribute of graph $G(V, E)$ defined as the ratio of the number of existing edges in the graph $|E|$ over the maximum possible number of edges $\frac{1}{2}|V|(|V| - 1)$, formally:

$$\rho(G) = \frac{2|E|}{|V|(|V| - 1)}$$ **Equation 3.26**

Triadic structure

Transitivity (or *triadic closure*) is a property of a graph $G(V, E)$ whereby any triple $\{i, j, k\}$ of vertices in the vertex set V forms a complete triad, i.e. a triangle with all edges in the edge set E of the graph, formally:

$$\forall i, j, k \in V: ij \in E \wedge jk \in E \Rightarrow ik \in E$$

Clustering coefficient $\kappa(i)$ of a vertex $i \in V(G)$ measures *cliquishness*, and more specifically the extent to which neighbouring vertices of i are pairwise connected. It is a local property of the vertex, defined as the fraction of the number of complete (or 'transitive') triads (i.e. triangles) $\tilde{\tau}(i)$ over the total number of connected triads $\tau(i)$ (i.e. triads with at least two edges). It can be easily demonstrated that:

$$\tau(i) = \binom{\deg(i)}{2} = \frac{1}{2}\deg(i)[\deg(i) - 1]$$ **Equation 3.27**

where $\deg(i) \geq 2$ is the degree of node i. The vertex clustering coefficient then becomes:

$$\kappa(i) = \frac{2\tilde{\tau}(i)}{\deg(i)[\deg(i) - 1]}$$ **Equation 3.28**

In weighted graphs the clustering coefficient is defined as the geometric average of the edge weights of all incident triads:

$$\kappa(i) = \frac{1}{\deg(i)[\deg(i) - 1]} \sum_{j,k \in V} \sqrt[3]{w_{ij} w_{ik} w_{jk}}$$ **Equation 3.29**

The graph clustering coefficient $\kappa(G)$ is just the average of this value over all vertices of the graph with $\deg(i) \geq 2$, namely:

$$\kappa(G) = \frac{1}{|V|} \sum_{i \in V : \deg(i) \geq 2} \kappa(i)$$ **Equation 3.30**

The clustering coefficient of an unweighted complete graph is equal to 1.

This type of cliquishness is also known as *triangle clustering* in distinction to *square clustering*, whose coefficient measures the fraction of the number of actual squares formed by edges incident on *i* and on its neighbours over the number of all possible ones, and shows the extent to which neighbours of vertex *i* share a common neighbour other than *i*.

Figure 3.24 shows all sixteen possible non-isomorphic configurations of a triadic relationship in a directed graph coded by three digits.[30] The *triad census* [HOLLAND & LEINHARDT, 1976] measures the frequency of occurrence of these configurations in a directed graph. In the case of undirected graphs there are only four isomorphism classes, namely the null triad (003), the disconnected triad (102), the intransitive triad (201), and the complete (or transitive) triad (300).[31] Of particular interest to our study is the intransitive triad, which essentially contains a structural hole.

Figure 3.24: Triad isomorphism classes in directed graphs

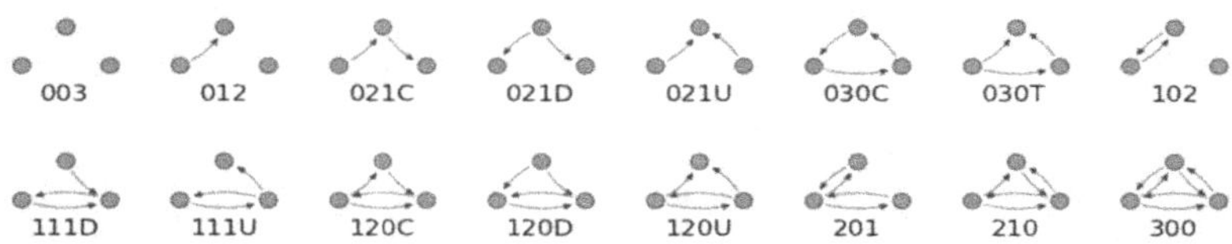

Structural hole is the connection gap existing between two unconnected nodes in a network, which however are (potentially) connected via a third node. BURT, 1995, where the concept originates, considers structural holes to be great sources of economic opportunity and leverage, as they represent the 'opportunity to broker the flow of information between people, and control the projects that bring together people from opposite sides of the hole' [BURT, 2001: 35].

Brokerage, in a social network context, is the exploitation of the opportunity represented by a structural hole, and more specifically the opportunity for an actor (a node) to mediate between otherwise disconnected nodes by bridging the gap to her own benefit. I introduce here a measure of brokerage, the *brokerage coefficient*, calculated similarly to the clustering coefficient as the fraction of intransitive triads over all connected triads:

$$\beta(i) = \frac{\hat{\tau}(i)}{\tau(i)} = \frac{2\hat{\tau}(i)}{\deg(i)[\deg(i) - 1]}$$ **Equation 3.31**

where $\hat{\tau}(i)$ is the count of intransitive triads incident on vertex i. The graph brokerage coefficient is then defined as:

$$\beta(G) = \frac{1}{|V|} \sum_{i \in V:\deg(i) \geq 2} \beta(i)$$ **Equation 3.32**

Community structure

Community structure [GIRVAN & NEWMAN, 2002] is the result of groups of nodes clustering together in network substructures larger than that of the triad; the term refers, therefore, to network topology examined at a level higher than that of the triadic structure.

Modularity measures the extent to which a graph is divided into *modules* or *communities*. It is a global graph index defined as the number of edges in a graph falling within cohesive groups after subtracting the expected number of edges in an equivalent random graph generated from the same vertex set. High modularity in a network indicates a stronger tendency of the nodes to form within-community rather than between-community ties.

Formally, modularity of a graph $G(V, E)$ partitioned in two communities c_1, c_2, as defined in NEWMAN, 2006, is:

$$M(G) = \frac{1}{4|E|}\mathbf{s}'\mathbf{M}(G)\mathbf{s}$$ **Equation 3.33**

where $\mathbf{s} = [s_1 \quad \cdots \quad s_n]'$ is a vector of $s_i = \begin{cases} 1, \text{if } i \in c_1 \\ -1, \text{if } i \in c_2 \end{cases}$, and $\mathbf{M}$ is the *modularity matrix* of graph G defined as:

$$\mathbf{M}(G) = [m_{ij}]_{i,j \in V(G)}$$

where $m_{ij} = a_{ij} - \frac{\deg(i) \cdot \deg(j)}{2|E(G)|}$, and a_{ij} are the elements of the adjacency matrix $\mathbf{A}(G)$.

Modularity optimisation with spectral decomposition of the modularity matrix as proposed by NEWMAN, 2006, yields a partition of the graph into communities of this type. Similar results are obtained by one of the most efficient algorithms for community detection (based on 'greedy optimisation'), the so-called 'Louvain algorithm' [BLONDEL *et al.*, 2008].

Small-world structure

The term *small-world network* is usually associated with the WATTS & STROGATZ, 1998 (WS) model, which demonstrates a process of rewiring randomly selected edges of a regular lattice to produce a graph combining high clustering coefficient, typical in regular lattices, with small average path length, common in random graphs.[32] A broader definition of a small-world network is that it is a graph whose average path length increases sufficiently slowly (e.g. logarithmically) as a function of its order, or in other words a network whose growth does not affect detrimentally the reachability of its nodes.

Figure 3.25 illustrates three types of graphs generated from the same vertex set in order of increasing randomness, from regular lattice (with uniform vertex degree 4), to a random graph with a 25% probability for edge creation. The small-world graph has been generated according to the WS model from the initial lattice with a 25% rewiring probability.

Figure 3.25: Regular lattice, small-world graph (WS), and random graph

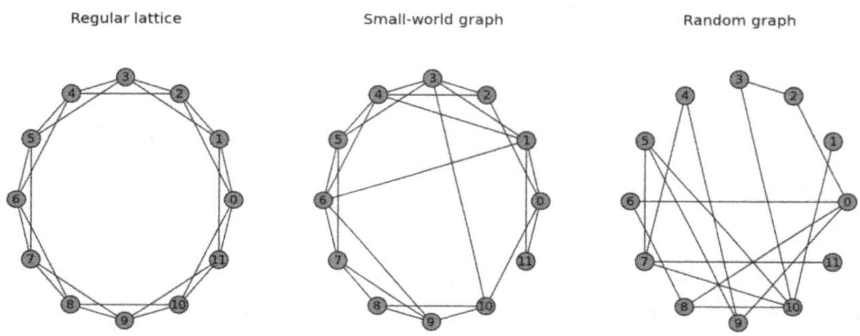

Small-world networks are considered as appropriate models for the interactions of real-world complex systems, including social, economic, biological, neuronal, computer and chemical ones. Many empirically observed social networks, including knowledge, and in particular research collaboration networks, exhibit small-world characteristics. Small-worldliness is generally regarded as a desirable property of knowledge networks, because in its presence the network is supposed to be more efficient in the global diffusion of knowledge produced locally in highly connected, cohesive, and often territorially embedded, clusters.

There is no commonly agreed formula-based measure of small-worldliness. An often used empirical indicator, the *small-world index*, is the ratio of clustering coefficients over average path lengths $\lambda_G = \frac{q(G)}{\langle \delta(G) \rangle}$ between the observed graph $G(V, E)$ and a random graph $G_R(V, E_R)$ with the same vertex set:

$$s(G) = \lambda_G \lambda_R^{-1} = \frac{q(G)}{\langle\delta(G)\rangle}\left[\frac{q(G_R)}{\langle\delta(G_R)\rangle}\right]^{-1}$$ **Equation 3.34**

If after repeated measures of the index for a number of random graphs of the same order, the index remains on average significantly above one, then it is probable that the graph has a small-world structure.

Degree distribution

In random graphs the degrees of the vertices usually follow a Poisson or binomial probability distribution, while in regular lattices degree distribution is uniform. A class of graphs exhibits a degree distribution which follows a *power law* (also known as *Pareto distribution*) with density function (in continuous form):

$$p(x) \sim cx^{-\gamma}$$ **Equation 3.35**

where the exponent $\gamma > 0$ is a constant known as *scaling parameter* of the distribution and c is a constant adjustment factor. Power laws are ubiquitous in physical, biological and socio-economic systems. Fat-tailed, Pareto-like, power law degree distributions in networks imply preferential attachment to high degree nodes. However, as CLAUSET *et al.*, 2007, note, empirical data rarely obey a pure power law for the whole range of the variable under study, but most often the power law applies to the tail of the distribution above a lower bound $x_{\min}$, what is often called a *truncated power-law* distribution.

The most rudimentary test for the presence of a power law in a distribution is to examine the extent to which the log-log plot of the distribution fits a downward sloping straight line, since the density function equation under a log-transformation becomes:

$$\log p(x) = -\gamma \log x + c$$

The graphical test, however, cannot be conclusive for the presence of a power law. For this reason I test for the power law hypothesis and estimate its parameters following the procedure described in CLAUSET *et al.*, 2007: First, I estimate the lower bound $x_{\min}$ of the power-law tail by minimising the Kolmogorov-Smirnov distance (KSd) between observed and theoretical cumulative distributions; second, I estimate the scaling exponent γ by fitting a power-law distribution with maximum likelihood; and finally I conduct a series of goodness-of-fit tests, including the calculation of the p-value of the sample in a Monte Carlo procedure, and the calculation of likelihood ratio tests between the (truncated) power-law model and alternative distributions (lognormal, exponential, gamma).[33]

A distinctive characteristic of power laws is *scale-invariance*.[34] It is interesting to note that scale-free networks are also small-world networks [AMARAL *et al.*, 2000], although the converse does not always hold.[35]

Complexity

There is no standard, commonly agreed definition of network complexity in the literature. To begin with, complexity is not equivalent to connectivity. If that were the case, degree centrality would be an appropriate measure of graph complexity. The highest values of degree centrality are attained by the vertices of *complete graphs*. These vertices have a uniform maximum degree $n-1$, where n is the order of the graph. However, complete graphs, especially when they are binary, have trivial topologies as all nodes share the same structural characteristics, and therefore, from an informational perspective, they exhibit the highest entropy indices. Clearly, complexity cannot be conceived as degree centrality. BONCHEV, 2009 and BONCHEV & BUCK, 2010 propose the *integrated centrality index* as a measure of graph complexity.[36] Potentially appropriate approaches to graph complexity is to treat it as *informational* or *computational complexity*, which, however, can only refer to the complexity of the graph as a whole.

Assortativity

Assortativity (also known as *assortative mixing* or in the social sciences as *homophily*) is a type of preferential attachment based on perceived similarities.

Degree assortativity is the preferential attachment of high-degree nodes of a network to other high-degree nodes [NEWMAN, 2003].

Multiplexity

The term *multiplexity* refers to the (co-)existence of multiple, overlapping relationships among a set of entities constituting a system. Since a network is defined by a single relationship among its nodes, multiplexity entails the overlaying and interlocking of a multiplicity of networks, which share a common vertex set.

Despite the fact that this is a crucial property of complex, multi-layered systems, and in particular of social and biological systems, it has not been sufficiently developed either theoretically or methodologically, and indeed, there are no standard network-analytical tools for modelling multiplex networks.

References

ACS, Z., ANSELIN, L. & VARGA, A. (2002): Patents and innovation counts as measures of regional production of new knowledge. *Research Policy 31*: 1069–1085.

ALMENDRAL, J.A., OLIVEIRA, J.G., LÓPEZ, L., MENDES, J.F.F. & SANJUÁN, M.A.F. (2007): The network of scientific collaborations within the European framework programme. *Physica A: Statistical Mechanics and its Applications 384* (2): 675–683.

AMARAL, L.A.N., SCALA, A., BARTHÉLÉMY, M. & STANLEY, H.E. (2000): Classes of small-world networks. *PNAS 97* (21): 11149–11152.

ARCHIBUGI, D. & PIANTA, M. (1996): Measuring technological change through patents and innovation surveys. *Technovation 16* (9): 451–468.

ARCHIBUGI, D. & PIANTA, M. (1992): Specialization and size of technological activities in industrial countries: The analysis of patent data. *Research Policy 21* (1): 79–93.

BALA, V. & GOYAL, S. (2000): A noncooperative model of network formation. *Econometrica 68* (5): 1181–1229.

BALCONI, M., BRESCHI, S. & LISSONI, F. (2004): Networks of inventors and the role of academia: an exploration of Italian patent data. *Research Policy 33* (1): 127–145.

BARABÁSI, A.-L. & ALBERT, R. (1999): Emergence of scaling in random networks. *Science 286* (5439): 509–512.

BARABÁSI, A.-L., JEONG, H., NÉDA, Z., RAVASZ, E., SCHUBERT, A., *et al.* (2002): Evolution of the social network of scientific collaborations. *Physica A: Statistical Mechanics and its Applications 311* (3–4): 590–614.

BARBER, M.J., KRUEGER, A., KRUEGER, T. & ROEDIGER-SCHLUGA, T. (2006): Network of European Union-funded collaborative research and development projects. *Physical Review E (Statistical, Nonlinear, and Soft Matter Physics) 73* (3): 036132–13.

BEARDEN, J., ATWOOD, W., FREITAG, P., HENDRICKS, C., MINTZ, B., *et al.* (1975): The nature and extent of bank centrality in corporate networks. Paper presented at the annual meeting of the American Sociological Association in San Francisco, CA, 1975.

BLONDEL, V.D., GUILLAUME, J.-L., LAMBIOTTE, R. & LEFEBVRE, E. (2008): Fast unfolding of communities in large networks. *Journal of Statistical Mechanics: Theory and Experiment 2008*: P10008.

BONACICH, P. (1972): Factoring and weighting approaches to status scores and clique identification. *Journal of Mathematical Sociology 2* (1): 113–120.

BONACICH, P. (1987): Power and centrality: A family of measures. *American Journal of Sociology 92* (5): 1170–1182.

BONCHEV, D. (2009): A simple integrated approach to network complexity and node centrality. In: DEHMER, M. & EMMERT-STREIB, F., eds: *Analysis of Complex Networks*, pp. 47–53. Weinheim: Wiley-VCH Verlag.

BONCHEV, D. & BUCK, G.A. (2010): Quantitative measures of network complexity. In: BONCHEV, D. & ROUVRAY, D., eds: *Complexity in Chemistry, Biology, and Ecology*, pp. 191–236. New York, NY: Springer.

BORGATTI, S.P. & EVERETT, M.G. (2000): Models of core/periphery structures. *Social Networks 21* (4): 375–395.

BRANDES, U. (2008): On variants of shortest-path betweenness centrality and their generic computation. *Social Networks 30* (2): 136–145.

BRANDES, U. & FLEISCHER, D. (2005): Centrality measures based on current flow. In: *Proceedings of STACS 2005*, pp. 533–544.

BRESCHI, S. & CUSMANO, L. (2004): Unveiling the texture of a European Research Area: emergence of oligarchic networks under EU framework programmes. *International Journal of Technology Management 27* (8): 747 – 772.

BRESCHI, S. & LISSONI, F. (2005): Knowledge networks from patent data. In: MOED, H.F., GLÄNZEL, W. & SCHMOCH, U., eds: *Handbook of Quantitative Science and Technology Research*, pp. 613–643. Dordrecht: Kluwer Academic Publishers.

BURT, R.S. (1987): Social contagion and innovation. Cohesion versus structural equivalence. *American Journal of Sociology 92* (6): 1287–1335.

BURT, R.S. (2001): Structural holes versus network closure as social capital. In: LIN, N., COOK, K. & BURT, R.S., eds: *Social Capital. Theory and Research*, pp. 31–56. New York, NY: Aldine de Gruyter.

BURT, R.S. (1995): *Structural Holes. The Social Structure of Competition.* Cambridge, MA: Harvard University Press.

CANI LS, M.C.J. (2000): *Knowledge Spillovers and Economic Growth: Regional Growth Differentials across Europe.* Cheltenham: Edward Elgar Publishing.

CARPENTER, M.P., NARIN, F. & WOOLF, P. (1981): Citation rates to technologically important patents. *World Patent Information 3* (4): 160–163.

CARRINGTON, P.J., SCOTT, J. & WASSERMAN, S. (2005): *Models and Methods in Social Network Analysis.* Cambridge University Press.

CLAUSET, A., SHALIZI, C.R. & NEWMAN, M.E.J. (2007): Power-law distributions in empirical data. *SIAM Review 51* (4): 661–703.

COWAN, R. & JONARD, N. (2004): Network structure and the diffusion of knowledge. *Journal of Economic Dynamics and Control 28* (8): 1557–1575.

EC (2009): *Structuring effects of Community research: The impact of the Framework Programmes for RTD on network formation.* A study produced in the context of the ex post evaluation of FP6 for DG RTD of the European Commission. Brussels: European Commission.

ERD S, P. & RÉNYI, A. (1959): On random graphs I. *Publicationes Mathematicae 6*: 290–297.

ETZKOWITZ, H. (1998): The norms of entrepreneurial science: cognitive effects of the new university–industry linkages. *Research Policy 27* (8): 823–833.

GALEOTTI, A., GOYAL, S. & KAMPHORST, J. (2006): Network formation with heterogeneous players. *Games and Economic Behavior 54* (2): 353–372.

GARAS, A. & ARGYRAKIS, P. (2008): A network approach for the scientific collaboration in the European framework programs. *Europhysics Letters 84* (6): 68005.

GIRVAN, M. & NEWMAN, M.E.J. (2002): Community structure in social and biological networks. *PNAS 99* (12): 7821–7826.

GIULIANI, E. (2007): The selective nature of knowledge networks in clusters: evidence from the wine industry. *Journal of Economic Geography 7* (2): 139–168.

GOYAL, S. & JOSHI, S. (2003): Networks of collaboration in oligopoly. *Games and Economic Behavior 43* (1): 57–85.

GOYAL, S. & VEGA-REDONDO, F. (2000): Learning, network formation and coordination. *Tinbergen Institute Discussion Paper,* TI 2000-093/1.

GRANOVETTER, M.S. (1973): The strength of weak ties. *American Journal of Sociology 78* (6): 1360–1380.

GRILICHES, Z. (1979): Issues in assessing the contribution of research and development on productivity growth. *Bell Journal of Economics 10*: 92–116.

GRILICHES, Z. (1990): Patent statistics as economic indicators. A survey. *Journal of Economic Literature 28* (4): 1661–1707.

HAGEDOORN, J. (2002): Inter-firm R&D partnerships: an overview of major trends and patterns since 1960. *Research Policy 31* (4): 477–492.

HAGEDOORN, J. (2003): Sharing intellectual property rights—an exploratory study of joint patenting amongst companies. *Industrial and Corporate Change 12* (5): 1035–1050.

HAGEDOORN, J. & SCHAKENRAAD, J. (1994): The effect of strategic technology alliances on company performance. *Strategic Management Journal 15* (4): 291–309.

HANNEMAN, R. & RIDDLE, M. (2005): *Introduction to Social Network Methods.* Riverside, CA: University of California, Riverside.

HOLLAND, P.W. & LEINHARDT, S. (1976): Local structure in social networks. *Sociological methodology 7* (1): 1–45.

JACKSON, M.O. (2010): *Social and Economic Networks.* Princeton, NJ: Princeton University Press.

JACKSON, M.O. & WOLINSKY, A. (1996): A strategic model of social and economic networks. *Journal of Economic Theory 71* (1): 44–74.

JAFFE, A. (1989): Real effects of academic research. *American Economic Review 79*: 957–970.

JAFFE, A. (1986): Technological opportunity and spillovers of R&D: Evidence from firm's patents, profits and market value. *American Economic Review 76*: 984–1001.

KATZ, J.S. & MARTIN, B.R. (1997): What is research collaboration? *Research Policy 26* (1): 1–18.

LAUDEL, G. (2002): What do we measure by co-authorships? *Research Evaluation 11* (1): 3–15.

LEONCINI, R., MAGGIONI, M.A. & MONTRESOR, S. (1996): Intersectoral innovation flows and national technological systems: network analysis for comparing Italy and Germany. *Research Policy 25* (3): 415–430.

LEYDESDORFF, L. & MEYER, M. (2003): The Triple Helix of university-industry-government relations. *Scientometrics 58* (2): 191–203.

MALERBA, F., VONORTAS, N.S., BRESCHI, S. & CASSI, L. (2006): *Evaluation of progress towards a European Research Area for Information Society Technologies.* A study produced for DG INFSO of the European Commission. Brussels: European Commission.

MANTEL, N. (1967): The detection of disease clustering and a generalized regression approach. *Cancer Research 27* (2): 209–220.

MARIOLIS, P. (1975): Interlocking directorates and control of corporations: The theory of bank control. *Social Science Quarterly 56* (3): 425–439.

MARIOLIS, P. & JONES, M.H. (1982): Centrality in corporate interlock networks: Reliability and stability. *Administrative Science Quarterly 27* (4): 571–585.

MELIN, G. & PERSSON, O. (1996): Studying research collaboration using co-authorships. *Scientometrics 36* (3): 363–377.

MINTZ, B.A. & SCHWARTZ, M. (1985): *The Power Structure of American Business.* Chicago, IL: University of Chicago Press.

MIZRUCHI, M.S. & MARQUIS, C. (2006): Egocentric, sociocentric, or dyadic?: Identifying the appropriate level of analysis in the study of organizational networks. *Social Networks 28* (3): 187–208.

MIZRUCHI, M.S. & STEARNS, L.B. (1988): A longitudinal study of the formation of interlocking directorates. *Administrative Science Quarterly 33* (2): 194–210.

MOWERY, D.C., OXLEY, J.E. & SILVERMAN, B.S. (1996): Strategic alliances and interfirm knowledge transfer. *Strategic management journal 17* (Special Issue: Knowledge and the Firm): 77–91.

NARIN, F., NOMA, E. & PERRY, R. (1987): Patents as indicators of corporate technological strength. *Research Policy 16* (2–4): 143–155.

NARULA, R. & HAGEDOORN, J. (1999): Innovating through strategic alliances: moving towards international partnerships and contractual agreements. *Technovation 19* (5): 283–294.

NEMETH, R.J. & SMITH, D.A. (1985): International trade and world-system structure. A multiple network analysis. *Review (Fernand Braudel Center) 8* (4): 517–560.

NEWMAN, M.E.J. (2003): Mixing patterns in networks. *Physical Review E (Statistical, Nonlinear, and Soft Matter Physics) 67* (2): 026126.

NEWMAN, M.E.J. (2006): Modularity and community structure in networks. *PNAS 103* (23): 8577–8582.

NEWMAN, M.E.J. (2001): The structure of scientific collaboration networks. *PNAS 98* (2): 404–409.

NEWMAN, M.E.J. & WATTS, D.J. (1999): Renormalization group analysis of the small-world network model. *Physics Letters A 263* (4–6): 341–346.

ORSENIGO, L., PAMMOLLI, F. & RICCABONI, M. (2001): Technological change and network dynamics: Lessons from the pharmaceutical industry. *Research Policy 30* (3): 485–508.

ORSENIGO, L., PAMMOLLI, F., RICCABONI, M., BONACCORSI, A. & TURCHETTI, G. (1997): The evolution of knowledge and the dynamics of an industry network. *Journal of Management and Governance 1* (2): 147–175.

SCOTT, J. (2000): *Social Network Analysis: A Handbook.* London: Sage Publications.

SMITH, D.A. & WHITE, D.R. (1992): Structure and dynamics of the global economy. Network analysis of international trade 1965-1980. *Social Forces 70* (4): 857–893.

SNYDER, D. & KICK, E.L. (1979): Structural position in the world system and economic growth, 1955-1970. A multiple-network analysis of transnational interactions. *American Journal of Sociology 84* (5): 1096–1126.

SOH, P.-H. & ROBERTS, E.B. (2003): Networks of innovators: a longitudinal perspective. *Research Policy 32* (9): 1569–1588.

SPENCER, J.W. (2003): Global gatekeeping, representation, and network structure: a longitudinal analysis of regional and global knowledge-diffusion networks. *Journal of International Business Studies 34* (5): 428–442.

SUBRAMANYAM, K. (1983): Bibliometric studies of research collaboration. A review. *Journal of information Science 6* (1): 33–38.

TER WAL, A. & BOSCHMA, R. (2009): Applying social network analysis in economic geography: framing some key analytic issues. *Annals of Regional Science 43* (3): 739–756.

TRAJTENBERG, M. (1990): A penny for your quotes: patent citations and the value of innovations. *Rand Journal of Economics 21* (1): 172–187.

VALENTE, T.W. (1995): *Network Models of the Diffusion of Innovations.* New York, NY: Hampton Press.

WAGNER, C.S., CAVE, J., TESCH, T., ALLEE, V., THOMSON, R., *et al.* (2005): *Evaluation of networks of collaboration among participants in IST research and their evolution to collaborations in the European Research Area.* A study produced for DG INFSO of the European Commission. Brussels: European Commission.

WAGNER, C.S. & LEYDESDORFF, L. (2005a): Mapping the network of global science: comparing international co-authorships from 1990 to 2000. *International Journal of Technology and Globalisation 1* (2): 185–208.

WAGNER, C.S. & LEYDESDORFF, L. (2005b): Network structure, self-organization, and the growth of international collaboration in science. *Research policy 34* (10): 1608–1618.

WASSERMAN, S. & FAUST, K. (1994): *Social Network Analysis. Methods and Applications.* Cambridge: Cambridge University Press.

WATTS, D.J. & STROGATZ, S.H. (1998): Collective dynamics of 'small-world' networks. *Nature 393* (6684): 440–442.

WHITE, H.C. (1992): *Identity and Control.* Princeton, NJ: Princeton University Press.

WHITE, H.C., BOORMAN, S.A. & BREIGER, R.L. (1976): Social structure from multiple networks. I. Blockmodels of roles and positions. *American Journal of Sociology 81* (4): 730–780.

YANG, S. & KNOKE, D. (2007): *Social Network Analysis.* London: Sage Publications.

Notes

[1] There are some fundamental differences with regard to citation practices prevalent among different patent offices, which explain, for instance, the significant differences in the numbers of citations found in patents filed with USPTO and EPO: USPTO imposes full disclosure of all prior art known to the applicant ('Duty of Candour'); as a result, USPTO patent applications often come with large volumes of citations, which are subsequently reviewed and filtered during the patent examination process. EPO regards citing of prior art by the applicant as optional; 'references' (rather than citations) are added ex post by the examiner.

[2] 'Complete networks' in this particular context should not be confused with 'complete graphs', i.e. graphs in which all vertices are connected.

[3] Clique is a complete subgraph, i.e. a graph generated by a subset of the vertex set of a graph, every pair of vertices of which is connected by an edge.

[4] This solution is also found in Breschi & Cusmano, 2004. Clearly, this solution is relevant only when a partition of the actor node set into 'coordinators' and 'participants' is feasible and supported by the data, as in the case of FP participation networks. This solution is also partly feasible in the case of the joint ventures and strategic alliances dataset, where a partition of the actor node set into 'holding' and 'subsidiary' companies already exists.

[5] *Multigraph* is a graph whose edge set is a multiset, i.e. a graph with multiedges (parallel edges) and self-loops. This type of graph can represent multiple connections between pairs of nodes in a network.

[6] The relative weight of a patent could potentially be estimated through citation counts by various methods, but this is open to future research on the topic.

[7] 'Pre-competitive research' is a term used in the context of EU research policy to refer to the type of research whose knowledge outcome is not directly appropriable, and therefore it is rather of the 'universal' type.

[8] FP7 is covered here up until the year of last data extraction from the CORDA database for the purposes of this study, namely 25 April 2011.

[9] FP5 covers the period 1998-2002, FP6 the period 2002-2006 and FP7 the period 2007-2013. In practice all framework programmes continue the funding of selected projects beyond their coverage period, and it is not uncommon for the starting date of a project to be later than the end date of the FP under which the project is funded.

[10] Exceptions are some activities, such as consortium management, networking, training, coordination, and dissemination, as well as 'frontier research' actions under the European Research Council, in which cases the EU contribution can go up to 100% of the eligible costs.

[11] 'Filing' and 'priority' date are terms often used interchangeably without being exactly identical: The former is the date when a patent application is first filed at a patent office, while the latter is the date after which the invention under question is established as 'prior art', and may be earlier than the filing date of an application. Patent applications are published 18 months (exactly in the case of EPO, and depending on whether it is an international application in the case of USPTO) after the earliest priority date; a 'search report' is published, usually with

the application, which determines the patentability of the invention and the existence of relevant prior art.

[12] Patent Co-operation Treaty allowing inventors to file pre-applications to many collaborating offices worldwide, managed by the World Intellectual Property Organisation (WIPO).

[13] Again here, similarly to the framework programme participants, the unique identification of parent companies is not guaranteed due to data quality issues, such as multiple entries with variations of the same name, as well as name changes, mergers, acquisitions, closures, etc. The number of distinct parent companies is, therefore, not accurate. This does not affect the analysis at the regional level.

[14] 'Local Administrative Units' in Eurostat terminology, previously known as NUTS-5.

[15] In the case of isolated nodes, the possibility of a preference for intra-regional collaboration is also excluded, because self-loops are not counted as isolates.

[16] Cross-comparisons of average graph distances between different network specifications are meaningless, with the only exception being those between binary and weighted-by-interaction-frequency graphs.

[17] Distances measured on the weighted specifications of the three networks (FP participation, patent co-invention and JVSA) are not directly comparable given the different specification of the weights in each case.

[18] The formula uses geometric means of edge weights, which are often below one (especially in the case of tie strengths). As edge weights are entered in the formula multiplicatively, the weighted clustering coefficient can be lower than the binary clustering coefficient by orders of magnitude (see 'Triadic structure' in Appendix 1).

[19] Their size is much smaller than the square of their order: $|E| \ll |V|^2$.

[20] For definitions see 'Centrality' in Appendix 1.

[21] It should be noted, however, that the over-representation of British regions in this sample may be partially due to the Anglosaxon bias of the JVSA dataset.

[22] See 'Community structure' in Appendix 1.

[23] It is a non-parametric rank correlation statistic similar to the Pearson's but more appropriate for comparisons of variables drawn from different and not necessarily normal distributions.

[24] See 'Distance' in Appendix 1.

[25] See 'Multiplexity' in Appendix 1.

[26] In the case of weighted graphs containing self-loops, $\delta(i, i) > 0$ and the denominator becomes $|V|^2$.

[27] *Order* $|V(G)|$ is the cardinality of the vertex set, i.e. the number of vertices in the graph. *Size* $E(G)|$ is the cardinality of the edge set, i.e. the number of edges in the graph.

[28] The idea behind current flow-based centrality measures, and their fundamental difference with shortest path-based centrality measures, such as closeness and betweenness centralities, is that information does not necessarily propagate in networks only through shortest paths; instead, information flow can be modelled similarly to the flow of electrical current in an electrical network obeying Kirchhoff's circuit laws. See BRANDES, 2008, for an excellent account of

the variants of betweenness centrality and their algorithmic computation, and BRANDES & FLEISCHER, 2005, for complete definitions and explanations of current flow-based centrality measures.

[29] Ibid.

[30] The first digit is the number of reciprocated pairs in the triad, the second is the number of asymmetric pairs, the third is the number of null pairs, while the letter refers to the orientation of asymmetric pairs [HOLLAND & LEINHARDT, 1976].

[31] In undirected graphs, in practical terms, the triad census is applied on a transformation of the graph into symmetrically directed by replacing its undirected edges with symmetric pairs of directed ones.

[32] The 'NW model' introduced in NEWMAN & WATTS, 1999, achieves similar results by adding a 'shortcut' edge in a regular lattice.

[33] For the maximum likelihood estimation, the Kolmogorov-Smirnov test for the estimation of the p-value, and the visualisation of the fitted distribution I use the package *powerlaw* in the programming language Python.
[ALSTOTT, J., 2012: Powerlaw package for Python.
pypi.python.org/pypi/powerlaw]

[34] A function f is said to be invariant under dilation of its argument x, if for all dilations λ: $f(\lambda x) = \lambda^{\gamma} f(x)$.

[35] AMARAL *et al.*, 2000, distinguish three classes of small-world networks: scale-free networks, whose degree distribution decays according to a pure power law; broad-scale networks with only truncated power-law degree distribution; and single-scale networks whose degree distribution decay is faster (e.g. exponential or Gaussian).

[36] For the definition of integrated centrality see 'Centrality' in Appendix 1.

Chapter 4

Analysing the knowledge plexus: The production of technological knowledge in relational space

Introduction

On a world scale the economic geography of knowledge production exhibits a local-global duality, a paradox also reflected in the neologism 'glocalisation' [SWYNGEDOUW, 2004], which stems from the fact that local economic systems increase, albeit selectively, their interconnection and their degree of integration in the global production of technological knowledge, while they retain their local embeddedness. On the one hand, the increased tendency to interconnect is confirmed by the increased internationalisation of R&D activities, the intensification of collaboration in scientific publications and patent applications [GLÄNZEL & DE LANGE, 1997; GLÄNZEL & SCHUBERT, 2005], the proliferation of R&D joint ventures and strategic alliances [HAGEDOORN, 2002], as well as other forms of inter-firm or academia-industry research collaboration, and, in general, the increasing success of the 'open innovation' paradigm in the business sector. On the other hand, the persistence of local embeddedness, as confirmed in various studies, is demonstrated in the fact that the spatial distribution of cognitive capital and of technological knowledge production remains highly uneven, as it concentrates in a very selective club of localities which constitute the core of the global knowledge economy. Membership in this club is not immutable: the well-documented rise of until recently peripheral economies to rapid industrialisation status has caused the expansion of the club beyond its traditional borders, the old industrial powers; even so, the process of concentration which reinforces the uneven distribution of knowledge production in geographical space is still at work.

These processes are not unrelated to the dualities of technological knowledge itself as an embedded and at the same time transmissible intangible asset, and as a private good and very valuable factor of production, and at the same time a non-excludable and non-rival public good, which generates considerable (positive) externalities and spillovers. At a theoretical level they are also reflected in another duality which until recently escaped the attention of 'mainstream' economic geographers: the duality of geographical space per se. Today we have serious indications that (physical) space does matter, but this statement tells only a small part of the whole story. Even though economic geographers and regional scientists had already captured aspects of geographical duality in figurative schemes and metaphors such as the 'sticky places in a slippery space' [MARKUSEN, 1996], or the 'neo-Marshallian nodes of global networks' [AMIN & THRIFT, 1992], the discipline remained for years trapped both theoretically and methodologically in the frame of the discourse on clusters, industrial districts, agglomeration, and (physical) proximity. Only recently geographers – particularly those studying the intricacies of the economic geography of knowledge creation and diffusion – have begun to systematically turn their attention from issues stemming from the traditional conception of geographical space as a 'space of places' – a static and fragmented collection of physical spaces – to issues related to the 'space of flows' – the unifying, dynamic, relational space of variable, network-shaped geometry [CASTELLS, 1991; 2011].

The knowledge plexus, as defined in Chapter 2, is a typical entity residing in this anisotropic 'space of flows' where knowledge is generated and diffused. In the previous chapter several topological aspects of this entity were examined. This chapter focuses on the knowledge production process inside the knowledge plexus and links the empirical findings of the previous chapter to this process. Here the specific interregional knowledge networks that make up the plexus are examined from two distinct albeit related perspectives: on the one hand as a medium supporting the emergence of *distributed knowledge*, which is a key intangible factor input in the technological knowledge production process, and as a source of economies of complexity, and on the other hand as a medium constraining and channelling technological knowledge production. In the context of the former, measures of the knowledge network topology are treated as indicators of *relational cognitive capital*, which is a direct result of purposive, often strategic, joint action of economic agents. In the context of the latter, network structure is treated as source of structural dependence in relational space, in analogy to physical space as source of spatial dependence. By this approach, agglomeration and network effects are considered as manifestations of externalities and spillovers – the unintended by-products of economic processes and, from a statistical perspective, the observable results of spatial and structural dependence respectively.

Some of the research questions touched upon in this chapter pertain to the traditional domain of economic geography: Does physical proximity influence knowledge productivity? Are agglomeration economies important in the production of certain types of technological knowledge more than others? Other questions are gradually coming to the focus of the discipline: How important are network effects in knowledge production? How do they compare to agglomeration effects in their magnitude of influence and for which types of produced knowledge? Finally, other questions posed here are novel: How do emergence and complexity manifest themselves in knowledge production? How are they related to physical and, most importantly, relational geographical space? How do *economies of complexity* affect the production of knowledge and compare to traditional economies of scale and scope?

The remainder of this chapter consists in three sections structured as follows: The second section is a review of existing literature on localised knowledge spillovers, on the role of networks and of relational space in knowledge production, as well as on the role of social capital (a notion very closely related to that of 'relational cognitive capital' introduced in Chapter 2) in the generation and diffusion of knowledge. The third section sets the general context and develops the theoretical models for assessing the relative impact on the knowledge production process, and more specifically on knowledge output, (i) of agglomeration and connectivity effects – the latter quantified by measures of network topology, and (ii) of relational cognitive capital associated with economies of complexity, in comparison to individual cognitive capital associated with more conventional localised economies of scale. The fourth section introduces the specific statistical models, discusses data issues, and presents the findings of the empirical analysis.

Existing work on the topic

The process of technological knowledge production is a diverse topic which has come to the attention of mainstream economists mainly through endogenous growth theory. An indispensable tool for analysing the knowledge production process in this context is the *knowledge production function* (KPF), which has been used extensively in a variety of contexts in a plethora of academic papers. The literature on *localised knowledge spillovers* stems from the same tradition but is even more empirically oriented, and increasingly resorts to spatial econometric methods – a tendency with a more explicit 'geographical' flavour. *Network effects* in technological knowledge production is a recent and less explored topic, for the simple reason that it requires the combination of two, until recently separate, analytical methodologies, namely econometrics traditionally used by economists, and social network analysis, which still remains largely in the hands of sociologists. Finally, another relevant strand of theory and research is on the effect of *social capital* on knowledge production. Despite the popularity of the notion of social capital, especially in sociological circles, its use in an empirical economic context is limited to its 'institutionalist' conception, whereby it is treated as a contextual control variable instead of a capital-like factor of production.

The knowledge production function framework

The generic knowledge production function (henceforth KPF) is a standard tool for empirical estimation of the effects of various types of knowledge inputs, most commonly R&D expenditure or R&D employment, and knowledge stock, on the creation of new knowledge,[1] or on economic growth.[2] The concept builds on the idea that knowledge (or 'ideas') is a factor of production in its own right, and a cumulable asset that resembles physical capital (although not constrained by the usual assumption of constant returns). The most common measures of knowledge output in the context of the KPF are counts of patent grants as indicators of technological change,[3] and counts of scientific publications as indicators of scientific progress.[4]

Specific functional forms of the KPF have been proposed in the context of various stylised models of endogenous growth theory, whence the KPF draws its origins. Endogenous growth models, which came as a significant improvement to the failure of neoclassical growth theory to account for technological change, incorporate in the production function important determinants of economic growth through technological change, such as human capital and R&D investment.[5] The reference model for R&D-driven macroeconomic growth by ROMER, 1990, conceives the steady-state growth rate of the knowledge stock and of per capita output as proportional to the accumulated stock of past ideas and the amount of labour employed in the R&D sector of the economy. The model has stirred considerable academic debate (e.g. the widely cited JONES, 1995b, critique), which however will not receive more attention here, as it is deemed to be misplaced, if not irrelevant (see Chapter 2 for an alternative 'systemic' interpretation of the empirical failure of the ROMER, 1990 model).

It should be clarified that in subsequent sections the generic KPF is used purely as a tool for empirical exploratory or inferential analysis, devoid of its endogenous growth connotations.

Space in knowledge production

A common thread in the literature of the economic geography of knowledge is the hypothesis that physical space does matter in the generation and diffusion of knowledge, with the most obvious justification being that it mediates face-to-face contacts of economic agents involved in the knowledge production process.

Localised knowledge spillovers

A segment of the economics of innovation and technology literature focuses on the localisation patterns of knowledge spillovers. In their seminal and highly cited paper, JAFFE *et al.*, 1993, compare the geographic locations of citing and cited patents in order to test the extent to which knowledge spillovers are localised after controlling for pre-existing patterns of territorial concentration of technologically related activities. They find that citations are more likely to come from the same state and metropolitan statistical area as the cited patents, and that territorially localised knowledge spillovers are statistically significant but their localisation effect fades over time. They also find little evidence for an effect of the technological field on localisation, or for differences in localisation patterns between the citations of academic and corporate patents. In another highly cited paper, AUDRETSCH & FELDMAN, 1996, measure the spatial concentration of industrial activity and link it to knowledge externalities using data from the US small business administration innovation database at the state level. After controlling for the territorial distribution of production, they conclude (somehow trivially) that innovative activity tends to cluster more in industries where knowledge spillovers play a decisive role. In a dissonant paper, ZUCKER *et al.*, 1998, analyse relational data on the biotech academia-industry nexus in California to conclude that knowledge transfers from research universities to co-located firms is not the result of localised knowledge spillovers but of identifiable market transactions between 'star' scientists affiliated to universities and firms within commuting distance – a phenomenon due to the appropriable, rival, and excludable nature of the exchanged knowledge. In a similar spirit, ALMEIDA & KOGUT, 1999, focus on the relationship between the mobility of individual patent holders and the localisation of technological knowledge using a selected sample of patent citations on semiconductor technology. They find that there are regional variations in the degree of localisation of patentable knowledge, with high levels of localisation attained only in a limited group of regions in the US (notably the Silicon Valley, New York and Southern California), and that ideas spread largely through the mobility of patent holders. They conclude that inter-firm mobility of engineers influences local knowledge transfer, and therefore that knowledge flows are embedded in regional labour networks. PACI & USAI, 2000, examine the spatial distribution of innovative activity in a sample of NUTS-1 and NUTS-2 EU regions with patent counts, to confirm that technological activity is highly concentrated (albeit with a tendency to disperse in the 1980s), that the regional distribution of innovative activity and of labour productivity are positively correlated, and, contrary to JAFFE *et al.*, 1993, that spatial and sectoral specialisation in innovative activities are also correlated.

The above papers all agree in that technological activity, as well as knowledge spillovers tend to be territorially concentrated. It should be noted, however, that these results stem from empirical analyses limited to 'instrumental' and 'organisational' types of knowledge (according to the classification scheme introduced in Chapter 2). Another common element in this strand of literature is the treatment of knowledge flows as externalities transmitted in an unspecified spatial continuum. This approach not only overlooks the relational structure that generates and diffuses knowledge, but also, paradoxically, does not treat physical space and spatial dependence explicitly.

Spatial models of knowledge spillovers

This last issue is addressed by a number of papers in the spatial econometric tradition. ANSELIN *et al.*, 1997, examine the spillover effects of university R&D on the innovative capacity of regions, either directly or indirectly through its interaction with private R&D, using a modified Griliches-Jaffe KPF framework [GRILICHES, 1979; JAFFE, 1989] applied on innovation counts at the US state, MSA and county level. They propose and test several new indices of spatial interaction (co-location, gravity and covering indices) instead of Jaffe's 'geographic coincidence index', and introduce spatial lag variables in the empirical model. They find strong evidence of spatial externalities which transcend county boundaries, and conclude that there is a positive and significant relationship between university R&D and innovative activity, directly as well as indirectly through private R&D, and estimate that the spillovers of university R&D diffuse over a range of 50 miles around the innovating areas, though not through their effect on private R&D. In a technical paper, LESAGE *et al.*, 2007, extend the spatial interaction model with latent spatially structured origin and destination effects, whose parameters are estimated on the basis of spatial autoregressive priors in a Bayesian hierarchical framework. The model is applied on counts of citations among high-technology EPO patents in a mix of NUTS-2 European regions and countries. Four spatial separation variables are considered, namely geographical distance between regional economic centres, country border and language barrier effects, and technological proximity. They find that distance and borders have negative effects of comparable magnitude on knowledge flows, language differences have even more negative and significant effects, while technological proximity has a significant positive effect. They conclude that high-technology knowledge flows more easily within than between countries, that knowledge flows are industry-specific and most often occur between technologically proximate regions, and interestingly, that technological proximity matters more than geographical proximity. GREUNZ, 2003, is lead to similar findings through a model based on a regionalised Griliches-Jaffe KPF enhanced with spatial and technological distances (Jaffe's measure of technological distance calculated on patent applications). The dependent variable of this model is patent counts and the explanatory variable R&D expenditure in a mixed sample of European NUTS-2 and NUTS-1 regions. The paper finds that interregional knowledge spillovers exist between territorially proximate regions, as well as between regions with similar technological profiles, and interestingly, that these spillovers are mainly driven by private sector R&D, and are significantly hampered by national borders.

The above papers are all based on corporate and patent data, which, as already noted, correspond to instrumental- and organisational-type knowledge. The spatial diffusion of universal-type knowledge is also treated by a number of papers in this direction. SCHERNGELL & BARBER, 2009, study interregional research collaboration projects under FP5 (at the NUTS-2 level) using a spatial interaction model for count data. Similarly to the above papers they use standard separation variables of geographical distance, country border, regional border, language area and technological distance on the basis of (dis)similarities of regional patenting profiles, but unlike the above papers, they do not treat spatial dependence explicitly. Their findings confirm those of the others, namely that geography is an important determinant of interregional collaboration, but the effect of technological proximity is more significant. HOEKMAN *et al.*, 2010, study the interregional effects of the same spatial separation measures, but include a 'cognitive' separation variable based on an index of (dis)similarity in disciplinary specialisation on the basis of scientific co-publications across NUTS-2 European regions and countries, and add the time dimension to the variables. They find that the propensity to collaborate within territorial borders is decreasing over time, but the importance of spatial proximity is not. This tendency is interpreted as an indication that the process of European integration does indeed positively affect research collaboration, despite the significant heterogeneity in the propensity to collaborate among regions and countries due to differences in size, quality of research and accessibility.

Structural effects in knowledge production

The conception of space as a structureless continuum in pure spatial models of knowledge spillovers does not paint the whole picture of the knowledge production process and of the underlying interactions of cognitive agents. The integration of relational variables or of network effects in econometric models, alone or in combination with spatial effects, as an answer to this limitation is a recent practice, and for this reason the treatment of structural dependence in a knowledge production context has not yet reached the level of methodological maturity found in the econometric treatment of spatial dependence.

MAGGIONI & UBERTI, 2005, analyse four types of information and knowledge flows across NUTS-2 regions of the five largest EU countries, namely internet hyperlinks of academic webpages, participation in FP5 projects, EPO co-patent applications, and Erasmus student exchange, which are assumed to cover the whole range of knowledge types. Network analysis is conducted on the basis of density, clustering coefficients, and degree centrality measures on both binary and weighted ties. A gravity model is proposed, whereby knowledge flows represented by these network measures are regressed on spatial distance (shortest path between regional capitals), 'functional' distance (based on a regional innovation index), and 'sectoral' distance (based on the sectoral composition of the regional patent profile). The study finds a hierarchical centre-periphery structure largely conditioned by physical, but also by functional and sectoral distances. Similarly, MAGGIONI *et al.*, 2007, use FP5 participation data and EPO co-patent applications from a sample of NUTS-2 regions in the 5 largest EU countries in a gravitation and in a spatial econometric model to investigate the determinants of patenting activity allowing for spatial and structural spillover effects. AUTANT-BERNARD *et al.*, 2007, analyse a binary affiliation network formed from a sample of FP6 project proposals by private-firm participants in the thematic area of nanotechnologies. They calculate basic network measures at the level of individual firms, namely degree centrality and geodesic distances, and test the significance of structural and spatial effects in the formation of collaborative ties in R&D using logistic regression with atomistic and relational explanatory variables, such as research potential, absorptive capacity, relational and physical proximity. They find that despite the high concentration of firms in the European 'core', network effects play an important role, while spatial effects are not significant, which leads to the conclusion that physical proximity is not a principal determinant of knowledge spillovers. They also find a certain size-dependent assortativity. PONDS *et al.*, 2007, test the hypothesis that collaboration between different types of organisations is more geographically localised than between institutionally proximate organisations. Using data on co-publications in a gravitation model, collaborations patterns are analysed and the hypothesis is confirmed. BRESCHI & LISSONI, 2009, study the localisation of knowledge flows measured by patent citations in a dataset of EPO-registered US inventor patents in the fields of drugs, biotechnology and organic chemistry using the methodology developed in JAFFE *et al.*, 1993, augmented with network-analytical tools. After controlling for inventors' mobility and for the co-inventor network effects, they find that the effect of spatial proximity on knowledge diffusion is significantly reduced. They conclude that physical space constrains the diffusion of knowledge across firms and within cities or states mainly because mobile inventors rarely relocate and their co-invention network thus becomes locally embedded. VARGA *et al.*, 2014, examine the relative influence of static and dynamic agglomeration effects and of interregional network effects on R&D productivity in EU regions with an empirically estimated Romerian KPF, whose dependent variables are counts of patents and scientific publications, and the explanatory variables are regional R&D expenditures and patent stocks. The agglomeration effects are measured by regional concentration of employment in knowledge-intensive sectors, and the interregional network effects are captured by an adjacency matrix whose elements are collaborative project costs under FP5. In this paper we find that the degree of agglomeration is a good predictor of R&D productivity in market-oriented research, while network effects are important determinants of R&D productivity in science-driven research. However, the two determinants are never jointly significant, which means that they are neither substitutes nor complements but affect different segments of the knowledge production process. We also explore counterfactual scenarios of policy interventions in a forward-looking simulation of the dynamic effects of FP6 funding on regional R&D productivity, which shows that these will be greater in highly agglomerated regions.

The above papers follow a mixed approach to knowledge spillovers, whereby both structural and spatial effects are considered and compared. Other papers focus exclusively on the relational dimension of the economic geography of knowledge. AHUJA, 2000, studies from a theoretical and empirical perspective the impact of direct and indirect ties and of structural holes in firms' R&D joint-ventures ego-networks on their innovation output measured by patent counts, and concludes that direct and indirect ties both have a positive impact on innovation, unlike structural holes. HAGEDOORN *et al.*, 2006, look at 'centrality-based' and 'efficiency-based' network capabilities of firms as determinants of formation of R&D joint ventures and strategic alliances in the pharmaceutical biotechnology industry. They combine logistic regression for panel data with network-analytical measures (more specifically betweenness centrality and measures of hierarchy) to find that these network capabilities positively affect the formation of new partnerships and enable firms to continue to interact with other firms. SINGH, 2005, using patent citation data to measure probabilities of knowledge flows between inventors in a logistic regression setting based on 'weighted exogenous sampling maximum likelihood' estimation [introduced in MANSKI & LERMAN, 1977], finds that intra-regional and intra-firm knowledge flows are stronger than those between regions or firms. He examines the extent to which this can be explained by past collaboration ties among inventors, and finds that the prior existence of ties increases the probability of knowledge flow, while this probability decreases with network distance. He also finds that being located in the same region has little additional effect on the probability of knowledge flow among inventors who already are connected with network ties. He concludes that interpersonal networks are important in determining patterns of knowledge diffusion.

SCHILLING & PHELPS, 2007, postulate that local clustering fosters communication and cooperation and that firms embedded in 'alliance networks' exhibiting high clustering and short average path lengths (i.e. small-world properties) should be expected to have improved innovative performance, as these characteristics give the network greater reach to a wider range of knowledge resources. They test and confirm this hypothesis in a longitudinal study of the patenting activity in a number of industry-level alliance networks. FLEMING *et al.*, 2007, test empirically the hypothesis that the small-world structure of networks enhance innovation and creativity in a patent collaboration network. They report that they fail to find evidence that small-world structure enhances innovative productivity within regions, although they confirm that shorter path lengths and larger connected components correlate with increased innovation.

Social capital in knowledge production

Measuring the economic significance of social capital and estimating its impact on factor productivity and growth, or, more specifically, assessing its role in the knowledge production process in an empirical setting, are issues less commonly dealt with in existing literature.

The 'institutionalist' approach to the topic treats social capital as a contextual factor determining the normative environment in which socio-economic relationships take shape, and therefore, as a collection of social institutions, norms of civic cooperation, interpersonal trust, etc. conducive to socio-economic development [KNACK & KEEFER, 1997]. In this spirit, PUTNAM *et al.*, 1993, attribute in their widely acclaimed analysis the divergent regional socio-economic performances of northern and southern Italy to social capital differentials of the 'institutionalist' type.[6] A common issue with this approach is the quantification of the effect of social institutions, civic norms, and trust associated with social capital, which are by nature incommensurable and intangible. Common empirical proxies for this purpose are various indicators of the institutional setting of the economy and the society, e.g. the indices of 'civic community' and institutional performance proposed by Putnam [Ibid.],[7] the 'corruption perceptions index', freedom and democracy indices, indicators of collective action and social inclusion, etc. Such proxies are often value-laden, and subject to strong ideological bias, opinion judgements, and significant observational errors. Moreover, their potential correlation with macroeconomic indicators cannot be interpreted as genuinely causal in the absence of a theoretical model of causal relationship between 'good' institutions and norms (such as 'freedom', 'democracy', etc.) and economic performance, and also in the absence of global and diachronic empirical evidence in support of this position; thus a conjunctural correlation cannot be irrefutably claimed not to be spurious.

A totally different approach to the representation and measuring of social capital is the 'structuralist' approach (already discussed in Chapter 2), which consists in the direct quantification of socio-economic relationships by means of appropriate measures of network topology. In this approach the notion of social capital is devoid of ideological connotations and subjective opinion bias. In one of the few empirical studies on the impact of social capital of this type on economic performance, WALKER *et al.*, 1997, examine joint ventures in biotechnology start-ups and find that social capital significantly and positively influences network formation and industry growth.

Theoretical context and models

This section introduces the general context and presents the theoretical models that will be used to analyse the effects of the knowledge plexus topology, and specifically of the structure of interregional knowledge networks, on regional knowledge output. The models proposed here combine two distinct aspects of the social relationships which govern the knowledge production process: On the one hand, these social relationships are seen as sources of distributed knowledge in themselves, and are treated as capital-like assets capable of generating knowledge output. In this context two models are proposed: in the first one, knowledge-network topology measures are used as proxies for distributed knowledge and introduced in an empirical KPF as explanatory variables; in the second one, the structure of the knowledge network itself (its adjacency matrix) is used in the calculation of stocks of relational cognitive capital which are introduced in the KPF as explanatory variables. Non-relational factors, which are already known from existing literature to significantly affect knowledge output, such as R&D expenditure, are tried in these models as control variables. This approach is a hybrid of the 'constructivist' and the 'objectivist' construals of technological knowledge in that it assumes that technological knowledge is collectively generated through structured interactions of cognitive agents in the frame of 'symbiotic' socio-economic relationships, while at the same time it treats technological knowledge as a capital-like asset in the KPF framework. On the other hand, the social relationships governing the knowledge production process are seen as sources of structural dependence, and are introduced in the empirical KPF as 'structural autocorrelation effects' along with the conventional spatial autocorrelation effects. In this case the dependence structure generated by social relationships is treated as a 'nuisance' (in the statistical sense), which needs to be controlled for, instead of 'substance' [SNIJDERS, 2011].

Measuring distributed knowledge

The term *relational cognitive capital* introduced in Chapter 2 denotes the capital-like aspect of distributed knowledge, i.e. of collectively produced and embedded in social relationships technological knowledge – in other words, it is an 'objectivist' representation of an otherwise 'constructivist' concept. By its definition, relational cognitive capital resembles, and as a matter of fact is a specific variant of, social capital. The use of the term 'social capital' in the knowledge production context is, however, avoided in this book for a number of reasons: First, the term has been employed in so many different contexts that it has become imprecise, all-encompassing, and in the end elusive. On the contrary, in my empirical analysis relational cognitive capital is an empirically quantifiable and measurable concept, which specifically refers to the process of technological knowledge production. Second, the term 'social capital' bears strong institutionalist, and often ideological connotations, which commonly result in social capital being construed as an a priori positive quality of socio-economic systems. In my analysis, relational cognitive capital is intended to be ideologically neutral and devoid of any a priori assumptions of this type. The methodology developed here follows the 'structuralist' approach, which favours measuring the generative relationships per se over measuring aspects of the institutional environment in which they occur, especially since the analytical focus is on their economic effects rather than on their socio-cultural origins.

In this chapter I consider and test five network topology measures as potential proxies for network effects associated with distributed technological knowledge. The different sociological conceptions of social capital can give us some ideas for the direction of this investigation on the basis of the analogies between social and relational cognitive capital. Following the conception of social capital as a result of *network closure* [COLEMAN, 1988], we are allowed to assume that the existence of dense social ties indicates the presence of Coleman-type social capital. The *local density* of a node's egocentric network is, therefore, a prima facie candidate.[8] This proxy, however, can be shown to be inadequate: In the hypothetical case of an intransitive (i.e. with a clustering coefficient of zero), purely star-shaped, egocentric network, as the order of the network increases (i.e. as more nodes are attached to the central node), density will asymptotically tend to zero.[9] Considering local density in knowledge networks as proxy for distributed knowledge would thus entail that as the intransitive egocentric network of a node grows bigger, its distributed knowledge potential diminishes, which is clearly counterintuitive. *Cliquishness* measured by the clustering coefficient of a node is a second candidate. This index, however, again has the limitation that it does not take into account the number of ties incident to a node, and only informs about the extent to which these ties are transitive. A third candidate is *brokerage* related to *structural holes.* This is essentially the opposite of clustering (with some minor differences),[10] and of network closure, and, as such, it would fit the antagonistic conception of social capital found in BURT, 2007. This measure is not unproblematic either, as its use as proxy would entail that a denser local neighbourhood of a node in a knowledge network corresponds to lower levels of distributed knowledge, which again does not seem to be intuitively right. A fourth candidate is *betweenness centrality,* and more specifically current flow betweenness. A node with high (current flow) betweenness centrality can be thought of as being the privileged broker of information flows, fitting Burt's antagonistic conception of social capital. On the other hand, higher connectivity is usually associated with higher current flow betweenness, which is intuitively consistent with the perception of social capital as the product of network connectivity. Betweenness centrality is, therefore, a strong candidate. Finally, the *integrated centrality index* represents the ratio of two fundamental structural measures of connectivity and position, namely vertex degree and distance (equivalent to the product of degree and closeness centralities of a vertex in a binary graph).[11] Moreover, BONCHEV, 2009, proposes integrated centrality as a measure of vertex-level network complexity. This is, therefore, another strong candidate as proxy for network effects related to distributed technological knowledge.

Theoretical models

KPF with agglomeration and network effects (Model A)

The basic model described in this subsection assumes a standard Romerian Cobb-Douglas KPF specification as follows:

$$\dot{K} = \alpha H^{\theta} K^{\phi} \quad \textbf{Equation 4.1}$$

where K is the stock of accumulated knowledge, i.e. the stock of 'cognitive' capital, H is a policy variable, which in its most generic configuration represents the resources devoted to the production of knowledge, normally human resources, i.e. human capital or labour, and $\dot{K}$ is the time derivative of K, which is interpreted as the flows of new knowledge generated by the application of H on K. In empirical terms K is the national or regional patent or R&D stock. H can be either employment in the R&D sector (headcounts of researchers) or the equivalent measure of R&D investment, which is preferred here.[12] The exponent ϕ captures returns to the stock of knowledge – the path-dependent effect of knowledge accumulation on the production of new knowledge; I call this effect *returns to experience*. The exponent θ captures returns to research efforts given the existing stock of knowledge. The total returns are said to be *diminishing* if $0 < \theta + \phi < 1$, *constant* if $\theta + \phi = 1$, and *increasing* if $\theta + \phi > 1$. In the specific empirical model developed below, θ is the main parameter of interest.

In log-linear form Equation 4.1 becomes:

$$\log Y = \alpha_0 + \theta \log H + \phi \log K \quad \textbf{Equation 4.2}$$

and its empirical specification:

$$\log Y_{it} = \alpha_0 + \theta_{it} \log H_{it-\tau} + \phi \log K_{it-\tau} + \zeta' \log Z_{it} + \varepsilon_{it} \quad \textbf{Equation 4.3}$$

where Y_{it} is a measure of new knowledge produced in region i at time t, $H_{it-\tau}$ is a lagged measure of investment in the production of new knowledge similarly indexed but with a time lag which represents the time needed for the effect of investment to generate results, $K_{it-\tau}$ is a lagged measure of the stock of cognitive capital at the regional level, and Z a matrix of additional control variables.

This traditional formulation leaves little space for modelling network effects and relational cognitive capital. A strategy to get round this problem, in the spirit of VARGA *et al.*, 2014, is the 'expansion method' [CASETTI, 1972], whereby ϑ is modelled as a variable itself dependent on other (measurable) quantities related to network effects. Here I propose modelling ϑ as a composite index expressing the joint influence of traditional local returns to scale generated by the localised accumulation of H, measured by an *agglomeration factor* γ, and returns to complexity generated by the relational structure of H, represented by a *complexity factor* ψ. While H is an observable quantity and ϑ can be directly estimated, γ and ψ are latent effects, which however can be estimated from other observable quantities. The coefficient ϑ can be estimated from Equation 4.3 and subsequently used as the response variable in a two-step estimation of the relative influence of the agglomeration and complexity factors γ and ψ in the equation:

$$\theta_{it} = \alpha_1 + \alpha_2 \gamma_i + \alpha_3 \psi_{it-\tau} + u_{it} \quad \textbf{Equation 4.4}$$

Alternatively, Equation 4.4 can be substituted into Equation 4.3, which after rewriting the log-transformed variables with lowercase letters becomes:

$$y_{it} = \alpha_0 + \alpha_1 h_{it-\tau} + \alpha_2 \gamma_i h_{it-\tau} + \alpha_3 \psi_{it-\tau} h_{it-\tau} + \phi k_{it-\tau} + \zeta' z_{it} + \tilde{\varepsilon}_{it} \quad \textbf{Equation 4.5}$$

This is the generic form of Model A, in which network and agglomeration effects are introduced in the empirical equation through interaction terms. The limitation of this specification is that distributed knowledge is not explicitly present in the specification but only proxied by the complexity factor ψ.

KPF augmented with relational cognitive capital (Model B)

An alternative specification begins with the same Cobb-Douglas KPF, this time augmented with relational cognitive capital as follows:

$$\dot{K} = \alpha H^{\theta} S^{\kappa} K^{\phi}$$ **Equation 4.6**

where S is relational cognitive capital and H is human capital conceived as a flow of individual cognitive resources. In this specification S is assumed to be directly observable, and can be interpreted in two different ways, which determine the way it is modelled and measured:

(i) S as a capital stock similar to K. In this case, K represents own ('domestic') cognitive capital stock, while S is conceived as the sum of the segments of cognitive capital stocks owned by other entities j, to which entity i has access through its network connections:

$$S_i = \prod_j K_j^{\gamma_i \alpha_{ij}}$$ **Equation 4.7**

where K_j is the cognitive capital stock of any other unit j to which unit i has access through a network tie of strength α_{ij}, and the exponent γ_i measures the absorptive capacity of unit i, i.e. its capacity to tap and benefit from the cognitive capital stock of the others. Equivalently in log-linear form with suppressed capital letters this equation becomes:

$$s_i = \gamma_i \sum_j \alpha_{ij} k_j$$ **Equation 4.8**

and in matrix notation:

$$s_i = \gamma_i \hat{e}_i' \mathbf{A} k$$ **Equation 4.9**

where $\mathbf{A}$ is essentially the $N \times N$ adjacency matrix of the knowledge network in which unit i is embedded, γ_i a scalar, $\hat{e}_i$ a unit vector (i.e. the

i-th column of identity matrix I_N), and k the N-dimensional vector of the (logarithms of) cognitive capital stocks of all units in the network. This formulation takes into account only direct ties between units. Alternatively, assuming the existence of additional spillover effects through the indirect ties of unit i which decay with (network) distance, relational cognitive capital will be:

$$S_i = \prod_j K_j^{g[\delta(i,j)]\gamma_i}$$ **Equation 4.10**

which in log-linear form becomes:

$$s_i = \gamma_i \sum_j g[\delta(i,j)]k_j = \gamma_i \hat{e}_i' \mathbf{W} k$$ **Equation 4.11**

where $\delta(i,j)$ is the geodesic distance of units i and j in the knowledge network where they are embedded, g a distance-decay ('separation') function,[13] and $\mathbf{W} = g(\mathbf{\Delta})$ a proximity matrix, where is the distance matrix of the network.[14]

(ii) S as a flow similar to H. In this case, S represents the sum of knowledge spillovers from (mainly R&D investment of) other entities with which the entity under study interacts through the network.

The main difference between sub-models (i) and (ii) is that the former takes into account the cumulative effect of knowledge creation in other units, while the latter only the contemporaneous effect. The latter is similar to Model A (Equation 4.5), but here the 'cognitive' capacities of other units, namely R&D investment by other units, are explicitly integrated in the model.

The idea behind these two sub-models is that while technological knowledge contained in patents is in principle accessible to anyone for general inspiration, its specific use in a way that allows the extraction of technological rent is restricted to the owners of the property rights and indirectly to those who have the capacity to tap and exploit the knowledge spillovers of the invention through the innovation networks. Similarly, R&D investment also has spillover effects, which do not propagate in the air but rather through structured social relationships. Social networks allow access to other agents' cognitive resources, and in that sense they, and by extension the knowledge plexus, are the locus of accumulation of relational cognitive capital.

The empirical specification of Equation 4.6 in log-linear form with suppressed capital letters is the following:

$$y_{it} = \alpha_0 + \theta h_{it-\tau} + \kappa(\gamma_i \hat{e}_i' \mathbf{A} k_{t-\tau}) + \phi k_{it-\tau} + \zeta' z_{it-\tau} + \varepsilon_{it} \qquad \textbf{Equation 4.12}$$

This is the most general formulation of Model B. Here the main parameters of interest are θ, κ and ϕ, which express the respective returns to the factors of knowledge production, namely *H*, *S* and *K*, while the *z*'s are additional control variables. The region-specific parameter γ_i, which as defined above represents *regional absorptive capacity*, can in turn be assumed to depend on individual attributes of the region, such as its comparative level of human capital measured by relative educational attainment or its relative concentration of human resources in the knowledge-intensive sectors of the economy, similar to the agglomeration factor in Model A (Equation 4.4).

Empirical analysis

Variables

Knowledge output

The response variable y_{it} of the proposed models is the measurable knowledge output of unit *i* at time *t*. Unlike the majority of papers on this topic, in which the unit of analysis is the individual organisation involved in the knowledge production process, here the unit of analysis is the NUTS-3 region.

Knowledge output in the models of this chapter corresponds to the production of two distinct types of technological knowledge, the instrumental and the universal types (according to the typology proposed in Chapter 2). Patents embody technological knowledge of medium contextuality and medium-to-high codifiability, which has been made appropriable with the allocation of IPR through the patent grant itself, while it remains publicly accessible and replicable under conditions. This clearly corresponds to the instrumental type of technological knowledge. Competitive funding of research projects under the EU FP is here taken as an indicator of regional technological knowledge output of the universal type. This requires some clarification: As discussed in the previous chapter, the EU FP for RTD not only are the biggest research funding instruments internationally, but they support 'pre-competitive', mostly collaborative research in the widest possible range of thematic areas. The knowledge output of this programme is predominantly of a public good nature, not directly appropriable and marketable (hence 'pre-competitive' in EC jargon), and mostly non-contextual, given the international and networked character of the funded consortia. Most importantly, FP funding comes only after an exhaustive international research proposal selection procedure, which is widely recognised as being highly competitive and meritocratic In that sense, it is fair to consider that the amounts of FP funding received by countries or regions, after controlling for potential exogenous sources of heterogeneity, reflect rather objectively real outputs of technological knowledge of the universal type, much more than, for instance, GERD, given that the latter is largely determined by policy choices.

In the case of instrumental knowledge, output is measured in whole or fractional counts of granted patent applications registered with EPO (variable PAT), while in the case of universal knowledge, in amounts of costs of FP-funded projects (variable COST). Patent output is a count variable, which would be reasonable to model as a Poisson, (overdispersed) quasi-Poisson or negative binomial process, depending on the presence of overdispersion. However, in practice, as patent counts are aggregated at the regional level, modelling the data as a (log-normalised) Gaussian distribution is a legitimate alternative. FP project costs are modelled as a Gaussian distribution.

Explanatory and control variables

Knowledge stocks

The knowledge stock K of region i may represent either the stock of R&D expenditures in the region (KRD), or the regional stock of fractional patents (KPAT). While these two alternative specifications are usually statistically interchangeable, the inclusion of R&D stocks in some regressions as an explanatory variable results to strong collinearity with variable *H*, and in these cases patent stock is preferred.

Knowledge stocks are typically calculated according to the 'perpetual inventory method' either without depreciation [PORTER & STERN, 2000; FURMAN *et al.*, 2002], or with a 5%, 13%, or 15% annual depreciation rate [PARK & PARK, 2006], according to the following recursive formula:

$$K_{it} = R_{it} + (1 - \delta)K_{it-1}$$ **Equation 4.13**

where R_{it} is current knowledge output (patent counts or annualised FP funding) in region i in year t, and is the depreciation rate. The choice of depreciation rate does not affect the regression results. In this study, the 13% depreciation rate has been chosen. The initial value of the knowledge stock is calculated by the following formula:

$$K_{i0} = R_{i0}(g_i + \delta)^{-1}$$ **Equation 4.14**

where g_i is the compound annual growth rate of knowledge output in region *i* for the period under study.[15]

Attributive variables

It is well documented in related literature that R&D expenditure has a major impact on the knowledge production process. Actually, many studies involving regressions based on the KPF specification use it as the main or unique explanatory variable. In the present study, regional gross expenditure in R&D (variable RD) is introduced in both models as explanatory variable, alone or in interaction terms, for the analysis of patent data. In the case of FP participation data, regional employment in R&D in full-time equivalent headcounts (variable RDEMP) is used instead of RD, due to multicollinearity issues.

Other attributive (i.e. non-relational) control variables introduced in the regressions are gross regional product per capita (GRP), population (POP), which controls for the size of the region, as well as two categorical variables, one reflecting the degree of urbanisation of the region (URB), which is particularly relevant in patent production, and one describing the EU status of the national entity where the region belongs (EUST), which is highly relevant in FP funding.

Relational variables

In Model A the network effects in the production of technological knowledge are captured as interactions of sociocentric, vertex-level measures of network topology with the policy variable *H*, which represents R&D expenditure or employment (variables RD or RDEMP). In this model I have specifically tested eigenvector centrality (EIGEN), current flow betweenness centrality (LOAD), integrated centrality (INTEG), and brokerage (BROK). Confirming the initial assumptions, integrated centrality is found to be the most appropriate for the purposes of this study, not only from a theoretical but also from an empirical perspective, as the regressions in which it was tried exhibited the best fit to the data and the lowest AIC and BIC scores.

In Model B the stock of relational cognitive capital is introduced as a factor of production along with the policy variable *H*, which again here represents flows of R&D expenditure or employment (RD or RDEMP), and the stock of individual (domestic) cognitive capital *K*. Relational cognitive capital (SPAT, SRD) is calculated according to Equation 4.9 by multiplying the adjacency matrix of the interregional patent co-inventor network or of the interregional FP collaboration network with the vector of regional knowledge stocks.

Agglomeration and connectivity factors

Crucial elements of Model A are the agglomeration and complexity factors γ and ψ. The former is an adapted version of the agglomeration index of knowledge-intensive employment introduced in VARGA *et al.*, 2014 (which in turn is inspired by the indices of geographic concentration discussed in ELLISON & GLAESER, 1997):

$$\gamma_i = \left[\frac{L_i^K}{L_T^K}\left(\frac{L_i}{L_T}\right)^{-1}\right]\left[\left(1-\frac{L_i}{L_T}\right)\prod_k\left(1-\frac{L_{ik}^K}{L_{T,k}^K}\right)\right]^{-1}$$ **Equation 4.15**

where L_i^K, L_T^K are employment in the knowledge intensive sectors of the economy in region i and in the EU respectively, L_i, L_T are total employment in region i and in the EU respectively, and L_{ik}^K, $L_{T,k}^K$ are employment in the k-th knowledge-intensive sector of the economy in region i and in the EU respectively. This agglomeration index (corresponding to variable LQHT) is essentially a size-weighted *location quotient*. The left-bracket component of this index is the typical location quotient which has the property of taking a value of 1 in regions with a level of agglomeration equal to the EU average, while the right-bracket component rewards larger regions by taking higher values in the case of higher ratios of regional to total employment.

The complexity factor does not simply capture the connectivity of an entity (i.e. its 'degree') but the overall structural influence of this entity in its relational space. After exhaustive testing, the integrated centrality index (INTEG) presented in Chapter 3 was found to be the most appropriate . This measure is equivalent to the ratio of vertex degree to distance:

$$\psi_i = \frac{\deg(i)}{\delta(i)} = \sum_j w_{ij} \left[\sum\nolimits_j \delta(i,j)\right]^{-1} \qquad \textbf{Equation 4.16}$$

where w_{ij} is the strength of the tie between regions i and j and $\delta(i,j)$ their network distance.

An element of Model B is the regional absorptive capacity coefficient , which determines the extent to which the region is capable of tapping knowledge spillovers from its partners' cognitive capital stock through its involvement in interregional knowledge networks. Similarly to the - index (Equation 4.15) used in Model A, this is calculated as a size-weighted location quotient of employed population with tertiary and upper-secondary education compared to total employment in the region and in the EU (variable LQEDU).

Data issues

Counts of granted patents corresponding to applications filed with the EPO during the period 1990-2009 are calculated at the NUTS-3 and NUTS-2 levels (variable PAT). The data source is the OECD REGPAT database. Each patent application can be considered as a Poisson (or negative binomial) process. These Poisson processes are aggregated at the regional level, and given that the sum of independent Poisson processes is also a Poisson process with parameter equal to the sum of the parameters of the underlying processes, the aggregate regional counts would also follow a Poisson process. The data are nonnegative integers. Due to the aggregated nature of the data and the considerable regional heterogeneity it is possible that the sample exhibits overdispersion – a hypothesis subject to testing.

The frequent occurrence of zero values is very common in samples of firm-level patent data. However, in the sample under study with regionally aggregated count data, zero values are much more limited: as we saw in Chapter 3, only a small percentage of NUTS-3 regions do not participate at all in either the FP collaboration or the patent co-inventor networks, which is within the acceptable limits of a regular Poisson or negative binomial distribution without the need to resort to a zero-inflated model.

Data on patent counts is available on an annual basis but this is not the case for FP-funded projects, for which only the start and the expected end dates are known. Financial data concerning total project costs and costs per participant in the project consortium are only available for the entire duration of the individual project. The imputation of regional aggregations of project costs (COST) on a year-by-year basis using this piece of information has been tested and found to be non-satisfactory due to the exogenous time dependence of the FP participation data on administrative decisions. The use of such data in econometric analysis without accounting for the exogenous time trend would yield spurious results. For this reason, a preferred alternative is the aggregation of the data in the three periods corresponding to the duration of the FPs (namely 1998-2002, 2002-2006, and 2007-2013). As the cross-sectional units of reference are the same in all time periods, the observations can be easily structured as a short panel.

With the exception of data on gross regional product (GRP) and population (POP), which are available at the NUTS-3 level, most Eurostat regional data, such as gross R&D expenditure (RD), employment in R&D (RDEMP), human resources in S&T (HRST), etc., are only available at the NUTS-2 level and above. Moreover, the regional time-series are often incomplete. In this study, missing data on the crucial variable RD have been imputed at the NUTS-2 level, and then calculated at the NUTS-3 level proportionally to the NUTS-2-to-NUTS-3 regional employment ratios.

The control variable URB is a dummy following the urban-rural Eurostat classification of NUTS-3 regions on the basis of their shares of rural population.[16] It receives 3 categorical values: (predominantly) urban regions (1), in which the rural population is less than 20% of the total, intermediate regions (2), in which the rural population is 20-50% of the total, and (predominantly) rural regions (3), in which the rural population is 50% or more of the total. An additional criterion for this classification is the population size and share of the cities in the region.[17] The EUST dummy takes a value of 1 for pre-2004 ('old') EU member states, 2 for post-2004 ('new') EU member states, and 3 for non-members.

Node-specific relational variables are calculated at the NUTS-3 level after removing the self-loops of the corresponding networks. The rationale for the exclusion of self-loops (which were included in all network analyses in Chapter 3) is that they represent intra-regional collaboration ties, whereas in the models estimated here we are predominantly interested in the impact of interregional collaboration. More importantly, if self-loops were kept, the topological measures of the networks used as explanatory variables would be simultaneously determined with the response variable, namely knowledge output. By considering only the interregional network effect on knowledge output a source of endogeneity is removed.

The proximity (or 'weights') matrices used in the models with spatial and structural effects are constructed on the basis of two types of proximity measures, physical and relational (WGEO, WNET). The former is measured as the inverse distances of NUTS-2 regional centroids, calculated from the geodata shapefiles of the Eurostat GISCO database. The latter is measured as the inverse geodesic distances of the regional nodes in the interregional patent co-inventor and FP participation networks. These networks are derived from the aggregations of all patent and FP project collaborations during the periods 1990-2009 and 1998-2009 respectively. Both matrices are row-normalised.

Statistical models

Baseline models

The baseline statistical models used in this section are generalised linear mixed effects models in a KPF setting, in which some of the explanatory variables are relational.[18] The direct introduction of relational variables as regressors in a KPF estimated as a count data (Poisson) panel model is also found in AHUJA, 2000. Unlike that model, however, the relational elements of the two models presented here are either node-specific network measures introduced in the regressions as interaction terms with knowledge flows, i.e. R&D expenditures or employment (Model A), or the interactions of the entire adjacency matrices of the underlying networks with knowledge stocks (Model B). The models proposed here have some crucial advantages over those in which network measures are included as raw regressors [e.g. in AHUJA, 2000]: they are theoretically more meaningful, the relationship of their regressors to the response variables is more naturally interpretable and explicit, and so are their estimated coefficients.

A general framework for linear mixed-effects models for longitudinal data is introduced in LAIRD & WARE, 1982 as an extension of the traditional linear model with the incorporation of random effects accounting for within-group dependence of the observations. Panel data can be seen as particular cases of this general modelling framework, in which the grouping factors are the cross-sectional units (e.g. regions, countries, individuals, etc.) and within-group dependence occurs essentially as the (serial) autocorrelation of observations on a cross-sectional unit. The linear mixed-effect model in matrix notation is:

$$y_i = X_i\beta + V_i\xi_i + \varepsilon_i$$ **Equation 4.17**

or equivalently in vector notation, in the particular case of within-group time variation:

$$y_{it} = \beta' x_{it} + \xi_i' v_{it} + \varepsilon_{it}$$ **Equation 4.18**

where $i = 1, \dots N$ are the cross-sectional units, $t = 1, \dots T$ the within-group observations, the fixed effects, $\xi_i \sim \mathcal{N}(0, \Sigma)$ the (unit specific) random effects, V_i a (known) $T \times N$ random-effect regressor matrix, and $\varepsilon_i \sim \mathcal{N}(0, \sigma^2 I)$ the within-group error terms assumed to have a spherical Gaussian distribution. Typically (although not necessarily) panel data models have invariable between-group coefficients and assume $v_{it} = \iota_T$, i.e. the random effect is merely a group-specific intercept, in which case Equation 4.18 becomes:

$$y_{it} = \xi_i' + \beta' x_{it} + \varepsilon_{it}$$ **Equation 4.19**

This linear model is used throughout this chapter with the exception of the analysis of FP participation data, where the longitudinal dimension is very short compared to the cross-sectional (only 3 periods), and grouping of observations along this dimension can affect the regression results. For this reason an additional period-specific random effect is added to Equation 4.19:

$$y_{it} = \tau_t + \xi_i + \beta' x_{it} + \varepsilon_{it}$$ **Equation 4.20**

The models presented here are estimated and tested under three alternative assumptions on the conditional distributions of the response variables, namely a Gaussian (after being log-normalised), a Poisson and a negative binomial distribution. In the latter two cases, following the influential paper by HAUSMAN *et al.*, 1984, the general specification of the models expresses the mean of the response y_{it} conditional on region-specific random effects ξ_i as a function of a linear predictor η_{it}:

$$E[y_{it} | \xi_i] = g^{-1}(\eta_{it})$$ **Equation 4.21**

where g is the link function (identity for the Gaussian distribution, and logarithmic for the Poisson and negative binomial distributions). The linear predictor η_{it} is a linear combination of vectors of explanatory variables x_{it}, v_{it}, corresponding to fixed and random effects respectively:

$$\eta_{it} = \beta' x_{it} + \xi_i' v_{it}$$ **Equation 4.22**

In the case of a Poisson process without random effects the mass function will be:

$$\Pr(y_{it} = y) = \mu_{it}^{y} \exp(-\mu_{it}) \, (y!)^{-1}$$ **Equation 4.23**

where μ_{it} is the Poisson parameter equal to the conditional mean and variance:

$$\mu_{it} = E[y_{it}] = Var[y_{it}] = \exp(\beta' x_{it})$$ **Equation 4.24**

In the presence of individual (region-specific) random effects ξ_i the Poisson parameter $\tilde{\mu}_{it}$ of the augmented model becomes:

$$\tilde{\mu}_{it} = E[y_{it} | \xi_i] = \exp(\beta' x_{it} + \xi_i)$$ **Equation 4.25**

As observed in HAUSMAN *et al.*, 1984, while the parameter μ_{it} is a deterministic function of η_{it}, due to the inclusion of the random effect, $\tilde{\mu}_{it}$ becomes a stochastic function of η_{it}, for which equidispersion no longer holds. Assuming, for instance, that $\xi_i \sim \Gamma(\alpha, \alpha)$:

$$Var[y_{it} | \xi_i] = \tilde{\mu}_{it} (\tilde{\mu}_{it} + \alpha) \alpha^{-1}$$ **Equation 4.26**

Models augmented with spatial and structural effects

The above models are further tested for the presence of spatial and structural effects not captured by their relational regressors, and which may manifest themselves in the form of residual spatial or structural (cross-sectional) dependence.

In order to control for these two types of dependence the models are augmented by including a spatial lag of the response variable in the regressors (a 'spatial autoregressive' term according to ANSELIN, 1988) as follows:

$$y_{it} = \lambda \hat{e}_i' \mathbf{W} y_{it} + \beta' x_{it} + \varepsilon_{it}$$ **Equation 4.27**

or equivalently in full matrix notation:

$$y = \lambda (I_T \otimes \mathbf{W}) y + X\beta + \varepsilon$$ **Equation 4.28**

or by assuming a 'spatial error' component as follows:

$$\varepsilon_{it} = \rho \hat{e}_i' \mathbf{W} \xi_i + u_{it}$$ **Equation 4.29**

or equivalently:

$$\varepsilon = \rho(\iota_T \otimes \mathbf{W})\xi + u$$ **Equation 4.30**

where X is the matrix of regressors, is an individual (region-specific), time-invariant, spatially or structurally induced component of the error term, **W** is a $N \times N$ normalised proximity matrix, $u \sim IID(0, \sigma_u^2)$ is the remaining uncorrelated spherical error, I_T and ι_T are a $T \times T$ identity matrix and a $T \times 1$ vector of ones respectively, and N and T are the numbers of spatial units and of years in the panel respectively.

The spatial lag and the spatial error component can be jointly included in the model, while the proximity matrices **W** in each term need not be the same. Here two types of proximity matrices are tested: one of physical proximity measured as the inverse of the physical distance of regional centroids, and one of relational proximity measured as the inverse of geodesic distance of regional nodes in the interregional network.

In the case of the count data statistical models discussed above, the Poisson parameter introduced in Equation 4.25 can be reformulated by adding spatial or structural effects as individual random effects as follows:

$$\log \tilde{\mu}_{it} = \beta' x_{it} + \rho \hat{e}_i' \mathbf{W} \xi_i$$ **Equation 4.31**

or even a spatial lag of the response variable as follows (in matrix notation):

$$\log \tilde{\mu} = [I_T \otimes (I_N - \lambda \mathbf{W})^{-1}] X\beta + \iota_T \otimes \xi$$ **Equation 4.32**

Unfortunately, existing statistical software is not capable of estimating these novel generalised linear models, and inevitably this task is deferred to future research.

In this chapter only the Gaussian versions of the augmented models are estimated, but even this task is practically not feasible in the case of NUTS-3 regions due to computational limitations of both software and hardware, given the very large size of the ensuing spatial weights matrices **W**.[19] For this reason these models are only estimated and tested at the NUTS-2 regional level, where **W** has a more manageable size. Of course the patterns of spatial and structural dependence at this higher level of aggregation cannot be assumed to be comparable to those of the NUTS-3 level. Still some useful insights can be drawn from their study.

Estimation and tests

Statistical tests and diagnostics

Collinearity

The pairwise Pearson product-moment correlation coefficients of the attributive variables show that some of these variables are so highly correlated that they are practically interchangeable, e.g. human resources in S&T (HRST) and R&D employment (RDEMP), gross (GERD) and business (BERD) expenditure in R&D, and most importantly, RDEMP and GERD (see Appendix).

The variance inflation factor (VIF) is an indicator of multicollinearity.20 Multicollinearity is present when VIF is large for at least one independent variable – as a rule of thumb when VIF > 5. In panel data, a VIF below 10 is usually acceptable. The variables used in this analysis were selected so that multicollinearity is minimised. GERD (RD) and R&D stocks (KRD) are highly multicollinear in both models, and so the equivalent variable of patent stocks (KPAT) is used instead of KRD. RD is also found to be multicollinear with respect to the interaction term of the location quotient LQHT with RD (see Table 4.9 in Appendix). For this reason only lagged values of RD can be considered in model A. However, these are found to be non-significant, while their presence also reduces the significance of the interaction term, which is the main variable of interest in the model. For this reason, the standalone RD variable is finally not included in the estimation of model A. This way the effect of R&D expenditure on knowledge output is assumed to take place through its interaction with the agglomeration and connectivity factors, which is perfectly consistent with model A – it merely implies that the intercept $\boldsymbol{\alpha_1} = \mathbf{0}$ (Equation 4.4).

Normality

The histograms of the untransformed PAT variable are strongly skewed to the right – an indication that the normality assumption is not applicable here. The quantile-quantile plot of the standardised PAT variable against the standard normal distribution clearly shows that the data is not normally distributed (Figure 4.1 in Appendix). This is also confirmed by the Shapiro-Wilks normality test applied to annual cross-sections of the data: the test statistic is between 0.38 and 0.46 and the *p*-values close to zero. The lack of normality is to be expected in count data, and the log-normalisation of the variables is necessary when they are included in a Gaussian model instead of a count data model.

Overdispersion

Overdispersion occurs when the observed variance in the sample is larger than the predicted variance. In the case of a count variable assumed to be Poisson-distributed, its variance equals its conditional mean. If this condition is violated, a situation very common in real-world count data, the pure Poisson model is not appropriate, but an overdispersed Poisson or the negative binomial may be. The simplest test for overdispersion is to check whether the index of dispersion, the *variance-to-mean ratio,* is significantly larger than 1. Indeed this test confirms that the patent count variable PAT exhibits significant overdispersion, and for this reason a negative binomial regression, instead of the pure Poisson, is fitted to the patent data.

Spatial and structural autocorrelation

Moran's I autocorrelation coefficient is a standard measure of spatial autocorrelation. It is essentially a pairwise-weighted variant of Pearson's product-moment correlation coefficient, where the weights typically represent spatial proximity of the units of observation. The value of the statistic ranges from -1 in the case of perfect spatial dispersion of observations to 1 in the case of perfect clustering, while a value of 0 indicates that the spatial distribution of observations is random. The expected value of the statistic, $E(I) = (1 - N)^{-1}$, only depends on the number of the units of observation N. I use this statistic to test not only for spatial autocorrelation in the dependent variables (PAT, COST) due to physical proximity (measured as the inverse distance of NUTS-3 regional centroids), but also for structural autocorrelation, i.e. correlation resulting from the relational proximity of the units, measured as the inverse graph distance of the regions as nodes in the respective interregional knowledge networks. Spatial autocorrelation is found to be generally low but statistically significant in all network instances, but considerably higher in the patent co-invention than in the FP participation network. Structural autocorrelation is also found to be significant in all network instances. Interestingly, compared to spatial autocorrelation it is about twice as high in the case of the patent network, and higher by almost an order of magnitude in the FP network, while comparing the two networks, structural autocorrelation is about twice as high in the latter (see Tables 4.7 and 4.8 in Appendix).

I also use Moran's *I* statistic to test for autocorrelation in the residuals of OLS regressions estimated for this purpose, with both spatial and structural proximity matrices, all of which lead to the rejection of the no-autocorrelation null hypothesis.

Lagged regressors

The effect of one- to eight-year lagged values of regional GERD (RD) on regional patent output (PAT) is examined in three distinct statistical models, a linear (Gaussian) panel data model with random effects fitted by generalised least squares (GLS) with heteroskedasticity-robust standard errors, and two generalised linear (Poisson and negative binomial) panel data models with random effects estimated by maximum likelihood. The Poisson model is found to be inappropriate due to the large overdispersion of the response variable. Lagged RD is not found to be significant in any (valid) model with the possible (but implausible) exception of the 8-year lag (Table 4.10 in Appendix). This, despite the different model specification and nature of the data, is also consistent with the results in Hausman et al., 1984, where the inclusion of organisation-specific random effects makes the lagged effects of R&D difficult to detect. This is also confirmed in the case of lagged values of individual and relational cognitive capital stocks measured in terms of patents and of R&D expenditures (the results are not presented here). For this reason only current values of the explanatory variables are included in the main regressions.

Estimation and results

Patent co-invention

Theoretical models A and B are fitted to patent data at the NUTS-3 and NUTS-2 levels. The variables of interest here are patent counts (PAT), regional gross expenditure in R&D (RD), alone or in interaction terms with integrated centrality (INTEG) and the agglomeration factor (LQHT), and 'domestic' (KPAT) and 'relational' (SPAT) patent stocks. A series of nested statistical models is estimated by restricted maximum likelihood (REML) assuming individual random effects along the cross-sectional dimension. Structural and spatial effects captured by the graph proximity matrix (WNET) of the interregional patent co-invention network, and the spatial proximity matrix (WGEO), are used in spatial lags of the response variable, as well as in spatial error components at the NUTS-2 level. The regression results and the ANOVA-based comparisons of the nested models are presented in Table 4.11 NUTS-3 level, Gaussian regressions), Table 4.12 (NUTS-3 level, negative binomial regressions) and Table 4.13 (NUTS-2 level, Gaussian regressions with spatial and structural effects) in the Appendix.

As expected, regional GERD and domestic cognitive capital stock are found to be significant in all models and at both NUTS levels.

In model A the network measure taken as proxy for the connectivity effect ψ, which gives the best fit to the regression when inserted in the interaction term with RD, is integrated centrality (INTEG). This effect is twice as large as that of agglomeration. Brokerage (BROK) in the interaction term is also significant, but its effect much reduced compared to INTEG, while current flow betweenness (LOAD) has a very weak effect.

In model B relational cognitive capital is found to be significant at both NUTS levels, but its influence appears to be much weakened at the NUTS-2 level. This implies that interregional collaboration is more intensive among NUTS-3 regions than NUTS-2 regions, which in turn may imply that intra-regional collaboration at the NUTS-2 level is substantial.

At the NUTS-2 level, in general, the influence of all relational variables on patent output is weak compared to that of the agglomeration factor γ. However, structural dependence captured by the network proximity matrix is generally stronger than spatial dependence. This is reflected in the λ-coefficients of the spatial lag of patent output ($W \times \log PAT$), while the ρ-coefficients of the spatial error components are about the same. Moreover, the model with the network proximity matrix is better fitted (as shown by the log-likelihoods and the AIC).

The sum of the coefficients of H, K, S in the Gaussian model appear to be around 1.2. Of this, the influence of relational cognitive capital stock appears to be almost equal to that of R&D flows and higher than individual cognitive capital. Since the variables are log-normalised, this may indicate the presence of increasing returns, and by extension, of increasing returns to complexity, given the prominence of the relational variables in the model.

FP participation

Models A and B are also applied on FP participation data at the NUTS-3 and NUTS-2 level, notably on the main variables of interest: FP-funded project costs (COST), employment in R&D in full-time equivalent headcounts (RDEMP), alone or in interaction terms with INTEG and LQHT, and domestic (KRD) and relational (SRD) stocks of R&D investments. Other relational measures (e.g. LOAD, EIGEN, BROK) are also tested here, but INTEG is found to be the most appropriate both theoretically and statistically. Two-way random effects, along the cross-sectional and longitudinal dimensions, are assumed in this case. Adding longitudinal random effects is found to improve the fit of the models, and it also makes theoretical sense, as in the case of FP participation data it is reasonable to assume that observations are not only grouped by region but also by FP. Matrices WNET and WGEO, the former measured on the interregional FP participation network, are also used here in spatial lags and in spatial error components.

At the NUTS-3 level R&D employment as a standalone regressor is found to be significant only at the 5% level, while similarly to domestic cognitive capital stock, it loses its significance when population size and regional (per capita) income effects are controlled for. The general picture is that domestic investment in R&D, which is directly related to

R&D employment, is not a determinant of FP participation performance.

In all sub-models of model A the complexity factor outperforms the agglomeration factor . As a matter of fact, the effect of the latter on FP-related output is found to be negative and significant at the 5% level, while the former is positive and significant at all levels. This implies that the concentration of cognitive resources (and in particular of knowledge intensive employment) is not a determining factor in the production of 'universal-type' knowledge. Interestingly, EU status does not seem to affect FP participation performance either.

In model B, relational cognitive capital is always significant. Model comparison, however, shows that 'regional absorptive capacities' measured as the size-weighted location quotient of the region in terms of education levels, does not add explanatory power to the model. EU status does not increase the explanatory power of the model either (according to the ANOVA model comparisons), despite the fact that it is found to be significant on the basis of p-values.

At the NUTS-2 level most variables become significant. The agglomeration effect remains negative and the network effect positive and substantial, although their magnitude of influence is somehow reduced compared to the NUTS-3 level. At this regional scale population size has a steadily negative effect on knowledge output, which is another indication that there are no economies of scale in this type of knowledge production. Domestic knowledge stock has a certain effect but only a fraction of that of interregional knowledge flows through the network and relational cognitive capital.

The ρ-coefficient of the spatial error term is always significant at 0.1%, but the spatially lagged dependent variable is only significant in the case of the network proximity matrix (sub-model 4.A.N), not in that of the spatial proximity matrix (4.A.S). The combined use of the two matrices in a regression with a spatial lag and error components, however, gives the best fit, and in that case they are jointly significant.

In model B the spatial lag is found not to be significant, while the error component still is with both matrices. This indicates that spatial and structural dependence stem from the general clustering and grouping of the regions rather than the direct influence of the neighbours. The insignificance of the spatial lag coefficient, however, may be due to the fact that this type of effect is already captured by the relational cognitive capital variable. Population size effect and absorptive capacities are also shown to be insignificant by the ANOVA specification tests.

Conclusion

This chapter focused on the collaborative production of two types of technological knowledge, the *universal* and the *instrumental*. An underlying assumption in Chapter 3 is that FP-funded research projects typically contribute to the creation of the former (given the commitment of the FP to support 'pre-competitive' research, and its meritocratic project selection and evaluation procedures), whereas the collaboration of patent inventors results in the creation of the latter. In both cases collaboration does not occur randomly in an isotropic relational space but is based on highly structured synergetic relationships, which generate knowledge networks with interesting, non-trivial topologies.

This chapter has studied the direct and indirect effects of these topologies on the production of technological knowledge by extending the empirical network analysis on the European knowledge plexus performed in Chapter 3 with the use of econometric methods in an enhanced knowledge production function framework. In this context the direct effects are modelled as 'relational cognitive capital', and the indirect effects as structural dependence, which may co-exist with spatial dependence. The findings of the inferential statistical analysis conducted here are largely consistent with the theoretical hypotheses formulated in Chapter 2, and also with the empirical findings of Chapter 3.

A first finding is that the collaborative production of technological knowledge of the universal type is not affected by physical distance in geographical space, and that, by contrast, it is strongly dependent on relational proximity in the knowledge plexus, i.e. in the corresponding interregional knowledge networks. Interregional collaboration in the production of instrumental knowledge, on the other hand, is clearly affected by physical distance, but even in this type of knowledge production, the spatial effects are not necessarily stronger than the relational effects. The direct relational effects become much weaker at the NUTS-2 level, which implies that collaboration among NUTS-3 regions in the production of instrumental knowledge is spatially clustered within NUTS-2 regions. With regard to the indirect effects, structural dependence seems to be more significant, and spatial dependence emanates from geographical clustering rather than from neighbours' influence.

In the case of FP-funded interregional research collaboration, agglomeration in the knowledge economy, measured as concentration of labour in knowledge-intensive sectors of the economy, is found to have a statistically significant negative effect on the productivity of R&D investment after controlling for connectivity (integrated and eigenvector centralities) and brokerage, although this effect ceases to be significant after controlling for positional influence (betweenness centrality). There is an indication, therefore, that investment in the production of universal knowledge is more efficient away from 'highly-agglomerated' regions, probably due to a substitution effect between universal and instrumental knowledge production in these regions. In general, the production of universal technological knowledge appears to be more dispersed in physical space and less attracted to localised economies of scale. The statistical analysis also indicates the potential presence of economies of complexity in the technological knowledge production process, especially in the production of universal-type knowledge, but this tentative conclusion needs to be tested further. In the case of instrumental-type knowledge, the agglomeration factor becomes more significant, and so does the region's domestic knowledge stock compared to its relational cognitive capital. This may indicate that the production of instrumental technological knowledge is attracted by agglomeration economies. The implications of the above findings not only are important from a theoretical perspective, but are also crucial for policy-making, as the following chapter shows.

Some of the research questions posed in the introduction to this chapter have only been partially answered due to computational limitations, but also due to the fact that other analytical methods are needed in addition to those employed here. For example, a full investigation of the question of emergence would require non-inferential, generative methods, such as agent-based simulation. These directions for future research are discussed in the general conclusion of the book.

Appendix: Statistical tables

Table 4.1: Variables used in the study

Name	Description	Sources
PAT	Annual whole or fractional counts of patents registered with EPO and granted to inventors in region *i*, aggregated at the NUTS-3 or NUTS-2 levels.	Own calculations from OECD REGPAT / EPO PATSTAT database
COST	Project costs by FP participant in region *i* funded under the FP, aggregated at the NUTS-3 or NUTS-2 levels for each FP period.	Own calculations from DG RTD CORDA database
CT	Counts of FP participations in region *i*, aggregated at the NUTS-3 or NUTS-2 levels for each FP period.	Own calculations from DG RTD CORDA database
RD	Annual regional gross expenditures in R&D (GERD) in region *i* available at the NUTS-2 level, and imputed at the NUTS-3 level.	Eurostat data
RDEMP	Full-time equivalent headcounts of employment in R&D in region *i* available at the NUTS-2 level, and imputed at the NUTS-3 level.	Eurostat data
HRST	Headcounts of human resources in S&T in region *i* available at the NUTS-2 level, and imputed at the NUTS-3 level.	Eurostat data
KPAT	Domestic knowledge stock of region *i*, calculated from fractional counts of patents registered with EPO and granted to inventors in region *i* by the perpetual inventory method at the NUTS-3 or NUTS-2 levels.	Own calculations from OECD REGPAT / EPO PATSTAT database
SPAT	Relational knowledge stock of region *i* calculated from patent knowledge stocks of regions interacting with region *i* through the interregional patent co-inventor network at the NUTS-3 or NUTS-2 levels.	Own calculations from OECD REGPAT / EPO PATSTAT database
KCOST	Domestic knowledge stock of region *i* calculated from annualised participant costs of projects funded under the FP by the perpetual inventory method at the NUTS-3 or NUTS-2 levels.	Own calculations from DG RTD CORDA database
SCOST	Relational knowledge stock of region *i* calculated from FP-related knowledge stocks of regions interacting with region *i* through the interregional FP participation network at the NUTS-3 or NUTS-2 levels.	Own calculations from DG RTD CORDA database
KRD	Domestic knowledge stock of region *i* calculated from annual regional gross expenditures in R&D (GERD) by the perpetual inventory method at the NUTS-3 or NUTS-2 levels.	Own calculations from Eurostat data
SRD	Relational knowledge stock of region *i* calculated from R&D stocks of regions interacting with region *i* through the interregional patent co-inventor or the FP participation networks at the NUTS-3 or NUTS-2	Own calculations from Eurostat data

	levels.	
INTEG	Integrated centrality for weighted networks (equal to degree:distance ratio) of region *i* in the interregional patent co-inventor or FP participation networks.	Own calculations from DG RTD CORDA, and OECD REGPAT / EPO PATSTAT databases
EIGEN	Page rank for weighted networks (equivalent to eigenvector centrality) of region *i* in the interregional patent co-inventor or FP participation networks.	Own calculations from DG RTD CORDA, and OECD REGPAT / EPO PATSTAT databases
LOAD	Load centrality for weighted networks (equivalent to current flow betweenness centrality) of region *i* in the interregional patent co-inventor or FP participation networks.	Own calculations from DG RTD CORDA, and OECD REGPAT / EPO PATSTAT databases
BROK	Brokerage of region *i* in the interregional patent co-inventor or FP participation networks.	Own calculations from DG RTD CORDA, and OECD REGPAT / EPO PATSTAT databases
LQEDU	Weighted location quotient of employed population with ISCED 3 to 6 qualification in region *i*, averaged over time at the NUTS-3 or NUTS-2 level.	Own calculations from Eurostat data
LQHT	Weighted location quotient of employment in high-technology sectors in region *i*, averaged over time at the NUTS-3 or NUTS-2 level.	Own calculations from Eurostat data
URB	Urbanisation index of region *i* at the NUTS-3 level (dummy)	Eurostat data
EUST	Index of EU status of the country to which region *i* belongs (dummy)	Own calculation
POP	Headcounts of population in region *i* at the NUTS-3 or NUTS-2 levels.	Eurostat data
GRP	Gross domestic product (EUR at current prices) in region *i* at the NUTS-3 or NUTS-2 levels.	Eurostat data
WGEO	Physical proximity matrix calculated as row-normalised inverse physical distances of regional centroids at the NUTS-3 or NUTS-2 levels.	Own calculations from Eurostat GISCO database
WNET	Relational proximity matrix calculated as row-normalised inverse graph distances of regions in the interregional patent co-inventor or FP participation networks for the entire time-period of the sample at the NUTS-3 or NUTS-2 levels.	Own calculations from DG RTD CORDA, and OECD REGPAT / EPO PATSTAT databases

Table 4.2: Pearson correlation coefficients of Eurostat variables

	PAT (w)	PAT (f)	POP	GRP	ED U	HRST	RDEM P	(GE)R D	BER D
PAT (w)	1.00	0.99	0.33	0.52	0.25	0.34	0.39	0.42	0.40
PAT (f)	0.99	1.00	0.32	0.51	0.25	0.34	0.39	0.42	0.40
POP	0.33	0.32	1.00	0.83	0.00	0.28	0.21	0.04	0.00
GRP	0.52	0.51	0.83	1.00	0.27	0.37	0.34	0.23	0.17
EDU	0.41	0.39	0.93	0.89	1.00	0.35	0.30	0.14	0.10
HRST	0.34	0.34	0.28	0.37	0.27	1.00	0.88	0.77	0.70
RDEM P	0.39	0.39	0.21	0.34	0.34	0.88	1.00	0.93	0.88
(GE)R D	0.42	0.42	0.04	0.23	0.39	0.77	0.93	1.00	0.98
BERD	0.40	0.40	0.00	0.17	0.39	0.70	0.88	0.98	1.00

Table 4.3: Pearson correlation coefficients of FP participation network-related variables

	COST	RD	DEG	EIGEN	LOAD	CLOSE	INTEG	CLUST	BROK
COST	1.00	0.67	0.95	0.93	0.76	0.35	0.95	0.15	0.05
RD	0.67	1.00	0.68	0.69	0.37	0.42	0.68	0.14	0.04
DEG	0.95	0.68	1.00	0.99	0.73	0.41	1.00	0.17	0.05
EIGEN	0.93	0.69	0.99	1.00	0.72	0.41	0.99	0.18	0.05
LOAD	0.76	0.37	0.73	0.72	1.00	0.12	0.73	0.09	0.06
CLOSE	0.35	0.42	0.41	0.41	0.12	1.00	0.39	0.51	0.27
INTEG	0.95	0.68	1.00	0.99	0.73	0.39	1.00	0.17	0.05
CLUST	0.15	0.14	0.17	0.18	0.09	0.51	0.17	1.00	0.43
BROK	0.05	0.04	0.05	0.05	0.06	0.27	0.05	0.43	1.00

Table 4.4: Pearson correlation coefficients of FP participation variables

	COST	KCOST	SCOST	CT	KCT	SCT	RD	KRD	SRD	POP	GRP (pc)
COST	1.00	0.84	0.84	0.93	0.83	0.87	0.65	0.62	0.93	0.48	0.35
KCOST	0.84	1.00	0.94	0.73	0.96	0.94	0.62	0.65	0.89	0.49	0.37
SCOST	0.84	0.94	1.00	0.80	0.98	1.00	0.67	0.68	0.95	0.57	0.39
CT	0.93	0.73	0.80	1.00	0.79	0.83	0.64	0.60	0.94	0.57	0.31
KCT	0.83	0.96	0.98	0.79	1.00	0.98	0.65	0.66	0.93	0.58	0.37
SCT	0.87	0.94	1.00	0.83	0.98	1.00	0.68	0.68	0.96	0.58	0.38
RD	0.65	0.62	0.67	0.64	0.65	0.68	1.00	0.97	0.68	0.61	0.38
KRD	0.62	0.65	0.68	0.60	0.66	0.68	0.97	1.00	0.68	0.60	0.39
SRD	0.93	0.89	0.95	0.94	0.93	0.96	0.68	0.68	1.00	0.58	0.38
POP	0.48	0.49	0.57	0.57	0.58	0.58	0.61	0.60	0.58	1.00	0.02
GRP (pc)	0.35	0.37	0.39	0.31	0.37	0.38	0.38	0.39	0.38	0.02	1.00

Table 4.5: Pearson correlation coefficients of patent inventor network-related variables

	PAT	RD	DEG	EIGEN	LOAD	CLOSE	INTEG	CLUST	BROK
PAT	1.00	0.74	0.71	0.80	0.67	0.46	0.15	0.07	0.26
RD	0.74	1.00	0.56	0.67	0.58	0.40	0.12	0.06	0.22
DEG	0.71	0.56	1.00	0.95	0.70	0.41	0.12	0.18	0.23
EIGEN	0.80	0.67	0.95	1.00	0.76	0.46	0.14	0.16	0.25
LOAD	0.67	0.58	0.70	0.76	1.00	0.28	0.12	0.03	0.16
CLOSE	0.46	0.40	0.41	0.46	0.28	1.00	0.05	0.32	0.59
INTEG	0.15	0.12	0.12	0.14	0.12	0.05	1.00	-0.01	0.02
CLUST	0.07	0.06	0.18	0.16	0.03	0.32	-0.01	1.00	0.17
BROK	0.26	0.22	0.23	0.25	0.16	0.59	0.02	0.17	1.00

Table 4.6: Pearson correlation coefficients of patent-related variables

	PAT (w)	PAT (f)	RD	KPAT	KRD	SPAT	SRD
PAT (w)	1.00	0.99	0.73	0.97	0.73	0.63	0.61
PAT (f)	0.99	1.00	0.74	0.97	0.74	0.61	0.61
RD	0.73	0.74	1.00	0.76	0.99	0.55	0.60
KPAT	0.97	0.97	0.76	1.00	0.76	0.64	0.64
KRD	0.73	0.74	0.99	0.76	1.00	0.56	0.61
SPAT	0.63	0.61	0.55	0.64	0.56	1.00	0.95
SRD	0.61	0.61	0.60	0.64	0.61	0.95	1.00

Table 4.7: Moran's *I* test results for COST variable

		WGEO			WNET		
FP	**EXPECTED**	**OBSERVED**	**STD**	**p-VALUE**	**OBSERVED**	**STD**	**p-VALUE**
5	-0.0007	0.0202	0.0015	< 2.2e-16	0.2807	0.0005	< 2.2e-16
6	-0.0007	0.0203	0.0014	< 2.2e-16	0.2498	0.0005	< 2.2e-16
7	-0.0007	0.0159	0.0015	< 2.2e-16	0.2663	0.0005	< 2.2e-16

Table 4.8: Moran's *I* test results for PAT variable

		WGEO			WNET		
YEARS	**EXPECTED**	**OBSERVED**	**STD**	**p-VALUE**	**OBSERVED**	**STD**	**p-VALUE**
1990	-0.0007	0.0701	0.0016	< 2.2e-18	0.1447	0.0008	< 2.2e-18
1991	-0.0007	0.0718	0.0016	< 2.2e-19	0.1518	0.0008	< 2.2e-19
1992	-0.0007	0.0694	0.0016	< 2.2e-20	0.1477	0.0008	< 2.2e-20
1993	-0.0007	0.0690	0.0016	< 2.2e-21	0.1437	0.0008	< 2.2e-21
1994	-0.0007	0.0695	0.0016	< 2.2e-22	0.1469	0.0008	< 2.2e-22
1995	-0.0007	0.0694	0.0016	< 2.2e-23	0.1481	0.0008	< 2.2e-23
1996	-0.0007	0.0649	0.0016	< 2.2e-24	0.1430	0.0008	< 2.2e-24
1997	-0.0007	0.0623	0.0016	< 2.2e-25	0.1341	0.0008	< 2.2e-25
1998	-0.0007	0.0590	0.0016	< 2.2e-26	0.1321	0.0008	< 2.2e-26
1999	-0.0007	0.0573	0.0016	< 2.2e-27	0.1296	0.0008	< 2.2e-27
2000	-0.0007	0.0545	0.0016	< 2.2e-28	0.1228	0.0008	< 2.2e-28
2001	-0.0007	0.0492	0.0015	< 2.2e-29	0.1134	0.0008	< 2.2e-29
2002	-0.0007	0.0398	0.0015	< 2.2e-30	0.0927	0.0008	< 2.2e-30
2003	-0.0007	0.0472	0.0015	< 2.2e-31	0.1061	0.0008	< 2.2e-31
2004	-0.0007	0.0510	0.0015	< 2.2e-32	0.1149	0.0008	< 2.2e-32
2005	-0.0007	0.0508	0.0016	< 2.2e-33	0.1170	0.0008	< 2.2e-33
2006	-0.0007	0.0510	0.0016	< 2.2e-34	0.1185	0.0008	< 2.2e-34
2007	-0.0007	0.0484	0.0016	< 2.2e-35	0.1143	0.0008	< 2.2e-35
2008	-0.0007	0.0518	0.0016	< 2.2e-36	0.1255	0.0008	< 2.2e-36
2009	-0.0007	0.0513	0.0016	< 2.2e-37	0.1210	0.0008	< 2.2e-37

Table 4.9: Variance inflation factor (VIF) tests for multicollinearity (NUTS-3 level)

logPA T	logRD	logRD x INTEG	logRD x LQHT	logKP AT	logSP AT	logSP AT x LQED U	logP OP	logG RP
A	1.770			1.770				
	107.871	3.147	117.332	2.346				
		3.007	2.620	2.329				
		3.052	5.162	2.353			1.903	4.099
B	2.139			2.345	2.551			
	2.136			2.346		2.548		
	4.840			2.164		2.472	2.335	3.952

logCO ST	logRDE MP	logRDE MP x INTEG	logRDE MP x LQHT	logKR D	logSR D	logSR D x LQED U	logP OP	logG RP
A	2.049			2.049				
	41.562	1.371	65.698	8.124				
		1.357	5.762	5.471				
		1.493	15.093	20.869			2.833	5.377
B	2.085			2.149	1.221			
	2.085			2.150		1.221		
	2.891			6.337		1.323	2.430	4.094

Figure 4.1: Q-Q plot of response variable PAT (w)

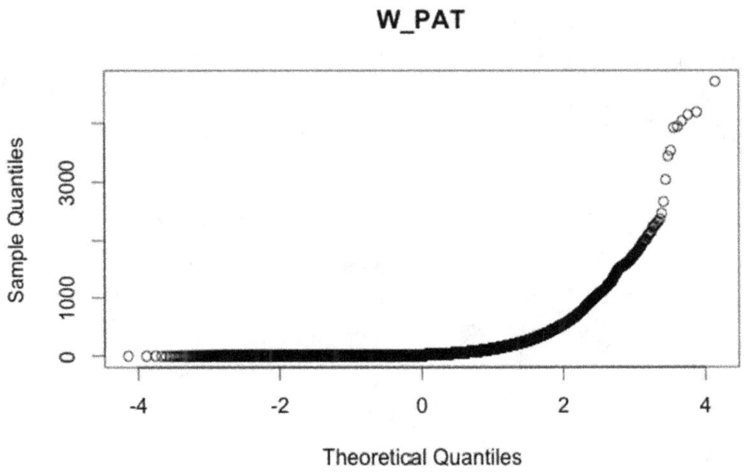

Table 4.10: Estimated coefficients of lagged regional GERD as explanatory variables for regional patent output

	logPAT (Gaussian)	**PAT (Poisson)**	**PAT (Negbin)**
(Intercept)	-17.676 ***	1.073 ***	-0.449 ***
	(0.369)	(0.037)	(0.044)
$logRD_t$	1.766 ***	0.360 ***	0.337 ***
	(0.345)	(0.010)	(0.024)
$logRD_{t-1}$	-0.050	0.066 ***	0.059 *
	(0.458)	(0.012)	(0.029)
$logRD_{t-2}$	0.478	0.098 ***	0.065 *
	(0.466)	(0.012)	(0.029)
$logRD_{t-3}$	0.141	0.012	0.025
	(0.466)	(0.012)	(0.030)
$logRD_{t-4}$	0.847	0.086 ***	0.094 **
	(0.473)	(0.012)	(0.031)
$logRD_{t-5}$	-2.008 ***	0.030 *	0.014
	(0.448)	(0.012)	(0.029)
$logRD_{t-6}$	0.285	-0.036 **	-0.058 *
	(0.413)	(0.011)	(0.027)
$logRD_{t-7}$	1.241 **	-0.028 *	-0.006
	(0.409)	(0.012)	(0.029)
$logRD_{t-8}$	1.698 ***	0.088	0.150 ***
	(0.307)	(0.010)	(0.025)

$^{***}p < 0.001$, $^{**}p < 0.01$, $^{*}p < 0.05$

Table 4.11: Regression results for patent data (NUTS-3 level – Gaussian distribution)

logPAT	Model 1	Model 2	Model 3.A.1	Model 3.A.2	Model 3.A.3
(Intercept)	-21.13 ***	-11.54 ***	-0.67 ***	-4.98 ***	-9.61 ***
	(0.30)	(0.24)	(0.17)	(0.23)	(0.27)
logRD	4.93 ***	2.23 ***			
	(0.07)	(0.06)			
logRD x LQHT			0.15 ***	1.18 ***	2.03 ***
			(0.04)	(0.05)	(0.06)
logRD x INTEG			0.54		
			(0.00)		
logRD x BROK				0.25 ***	
				(0.00)	
logRD x LOAD					0.03 ***
					(0.00)
logKPAT		0.57 ***	0.39 ***	0.49 ***	0.54 ***
		(0.01)	(0.01)	(0.01)	(0.01)
logSPAT					
logSPAT x LQEDU					
logGRP					
logPOP					
URB1					
URB2					
URB3					
AIC	182175.08	174962.22	120918.66	127501.76	130061.77
BIC	182207.8 6	175003.2 0	120966.24	127549.34	130109.35
logLik	- 91083.54	- 87476.11	-60453.33	-63744.88	-65024.89
Deviance	182167.0 8	174952.2 2	120906.66	127489.76	130049.77
No. obs.	26820	26820	20540	20540	20540
No. groups: n	1341	1341	1027	1027	1027
ANOVA χ^2		7224 ***	54057 ***	47472 ***	44911 ***

logPAT	Model 4.A	Model 3.B	Model 4.B	Model 5.B	Model 6.B
(Intercept)		-5.10 ***	-5.16 ***	-12.47 ***	
		(0.14)	(0.14)	(1.52)	
logRD		0.46 ***	0.46 ***	0.28 ***	0.24 ***
		(0.04)	(0.04)	(0.07)	(0.07)
logRD x LQHT	0.05 ***				
	(0.08)				
logRD x INTEG	0.57				
	(0.01)				
logRD x BROK					
logRD x LOAD					
logKPAT	0.35 ***	0.38 ***	0.38 ***	0.35 ***	0.34 ***
	(0.01)	(0.00)	(0.00)	(0.01)	(0.01)
logSPAT		0.44 ***			
		(0.00)			
logSPAT x LQEDU			0.44 ***	0.47 ***	0.47 ***
			(0.00)	(0.00)	(0.00)
logGRP	0.71 ***			0.68 ***	0.73 ***
	(0.16)			(0.14)	(0.14)
logPOP	-0.21 ***			0.21 *	0.23 *
	(0.11)			(0.10)	(0.11)
URB1	-6.42 ***				-13.01 ***
	(1.83)				(1.60)
URB2	-5.84 ***				-12.60 ***
	(1.80)				(1.57)
URB3	-6.12 ***				-13.01 ***
	(1.79)				(1.56)
AIC	76339.66	161707.85	161692.61	108852.30	105440.83
BIC	76414.41	161757.03	161741.79	108914.64	105518.47
logLik	-38159.83	-80847.92	-80840.30	-54418.15	-52710.42
Deviance	76319.66	161695.85	161680.61	108836.30	105420.83
No. obs.	13023	26820	26820	17895	17397
No. groups: n	875	1341	1341	1218	1176
ANOVA χ^2	44593 ***	13269 ***	15.2 ***	52848 ***	3419 ***

*** $p < 0.001$, ** $p < 0.01$, * $p < 0.05$

Table 4.12: Regression results for patent data (NUTS-3 level - Negative binomial distribution)

PAT	Model 1	Model 2	Model 3.A.1	Model 3.A.2	Model 3.A.3
Intercept	-1.783 ***	-1.784 ***	0.824 ***	-1.553 ***	-1.655 ***
	(0.028)	(0.023)	(0.039)	(0.028)	(0.026)
logRD	0.797 ***	0.184 ***			
	(0.006)	(0.006)			
logRD x LQHT			-0.145 ***	0.127 ***	0.144 ***
			(0.007)	(0.007)	(0.007)
logRD x INTEG			0.217 ***		
			(0.003)		
logRD x BROK				0.011 ***	
				(0.001)	
logRD x LOAD					0.004 ***
					(0.000)
logKPAT		0.709 ***	0.569 ***	0.714 ***	0.725 ***
		(0.006)	(0.005)	(0.006)	(0.006)
logSPAT					
logSPAT x LQEDU					
logGRP					
logPOP					
URB1					
URB2					
URB3					
r	1.019	10.046	39.366	10.870	11.939
	(0.039)	(0.492)	(2.477)	(0.606)	(0.683)
s	3.161	38.018	68.396	43.296	48.086
	(0.157)	(1.971)	(4.173)	(2.528)	(2.890)
logLik	-96238	-88756	-68897	-71661	-71744
No. of obs.	26820	26820	20540	20540	20540
No. of groups: n	1341	1341	1027	1027	1027
Wald χ^2	17803 ***	41181 ***	57897 ***	30928 ***	33409 ***
L-ratio vs pooled	35000 ***	14000 ***	8452 ***	11000 ***	9539 ***

PAT	Model 3.B	Model 4.B	Model 5.B	Model 6.B
Intercept	-1.454 ***	-1.461 ***	-2.427 ***	
	(0.023)	(0.023)	(0.179)	
logRD	0.159 ***	0.160 ***	-0.002	0.001
	(0.006)	(0.006)	(0.010)	(0.010)
logRD x LQHT				
logRD x INTEG				
logRD x BROK				
logRD x LOAD				
logKPAT	0.614 ***	0.613 ***	0.664 ***	0.666 ***
	(0.006)	(0.006)	(0.008)	(0.008)
logSPAT	0.045 ***			
	(0.001)			
logSPAT x LQEDU		0.045 ***	0.041 ***	0.041 ***
		(0.001)	(0.001)	(0.001)
logGRP			0.158 ***	0.163 ***
			(0.017)	(0.017)
logPOP			0.028 *	0.050
			(0.014)	(0.015)
URB1				-2.717 ***
				(0.189)
URB2				-2.606 ***
				(0.187)
URB3				-2.545 ***
				(0.186)
r	10.899	10.987	9.966	9.323
	(0.527)	(0.531)	(0.575)	(0.561)
s	36.145	36.469	26.414	24.694
	(1.805)	(1.822)	(1.640)	(1.615)
logLik	-87420	-87419	-59072	-57748
No. of obs.	26820	26820	17895	17397
No. of groups: n	1341	1341	1218	1176
Wald χ^2	35937 ***	35959 ***	26299 ***	51148 ***
L-ratio vs pooled	16000 ***	16000 ***	10000 ***	10000 ***

$^{***}p < 0.001$, $^{**}p < 0.01$, $^{*}p < 0.05$

Table 4.13: Regression results for patent data (NUTS-2 level - Spatial and structural effects)

logPAT	Model 1	Model 2	Model 3.A.1	Model 3.A.2	Model 3.A.3	Model 3.A.S	Model 3.A.N
(Intercept)	-0.97 ***	-2.45 ***	-2.21 ***	-2.26 ***	-2.31 ***	-2.67 ***	-2.97 ***
	(0.10)	(0.05)	(0.05)	(0.05)	(0.05)	(0.06)	(0.06)
logRD	0.91 ***	0.14 ***					
	(0.01)	(0.01)					
logRD x LQHT			0.11 ***	0.11 ***	0.12 ***	0.08 ***	0.08 ***
			(0.01)	(0.01)	(0.01)	(0.01)	(0.01)
logRD x INTEG			0.01 ***			0.01 ***	0.01 ***
			(0.00)			(0.00)	(0.00)
logRD x BROK				0.00 ***			
				(0.00)			
logRD x LOAD					0.00 ***		
					(0.00)		
logKPAT		0.87 ***	0.86 ***	0.87 ***	0.87 ***	0.83 ***	0.82 ***
		(0.01)	(0.01)	(0.01)	(0.01)	(0.01)	(0.01)
logSPAT							
logSPAT x LQEDU							
logGRP							
logPOP							
W x logPAT						0.18 ***	0.25 ***
						(0.03)	(0.04)
ρ						0.75 ***	0.75 ***
						(0.04)	(0.04)
AIC	4150.63	694.78	643.90	667.07	717.95		
BIC	4175.83	726.28	681.69	704.86	755.74		
logLik	-2071.32	-342.39	-315.95	-327.53	-352.97	-24.11	-13.91
Deviance	4142.63	684.78	631.90	655.07	705.95		
No. obs.	4020	4020	4020	4020	4020	4020	4020
No. groups: n	201	201	201	201	201	201	201
ANOVA χ^2		3469.3 ***	64.6 ***	42.8 ***	0		

logPAT	Model 3.A.SN	Model 4.A	Model 3.B	Model 3.B.N	Model 3.B.S	Model 3.B.SN	Model 4.B	Model 5.B
(Intercept)	-2.97 ***	-3.55 ***	-2.39 ***	-2.79 ***	-3.07 ***	-2.97 ***	-2.39 ***	-3.52 ***
	(0.06)	(0.31)	(0.05)	(0.06)	(0.06)	(0.06)	(0.05)	(0.32)
logRD			0.14 ***	0.10 ***	0.09 ***	0.07 ***	0.14 ***	0.03 *
			(0.01)	(0.01)	(0.01)	(0.01)	(0.01)	(0.02)
logRD x LQHT	0.07 ***	0.00						
	(0.01)	(0.01)						
logRD x INTEG	0.01 ***	0.01 ***						
	(0.00)	(0.00)						
logRD x BROK								
logRD x LOAD								
logKPAT	0.82 ***	0.89 ***	0.85 ***	0.84 ***	0.82 ***	0.01 ***	0.85 ***	0.89 ***
	(0.01)	(0.01)	(0.01)	(0.01)	(0.01)	(0.00)	(0.01)	(0.01)
logSPAT			0.01 ***	0.01 ***	0.01 ***	0.82 ***		
			(0.00)	(0.00)	(0.00)	(0.01)		
logSPAT x LQEDU							0.01 ***	0.01 ***
							(0.00)	(0.00)
logGRP		0.13 ***						0.11 ***
		(0.03)						(0.03)
logPOP		0.07 ***						0.06 **
		(0.02)						(0.02)
W x logPAT	0.25 ***			0.17 ***	0.24 ***	0.25 ***		
	(0.04)			(0.03)	(0.04)	(0.04)		
ρ	0.75 ***			0.75 ***	0.76 ***	0.75 ***		
	(0.04)			(0.04)	(0.04)	(0.04)		
AIC		-100.90	627.72				627.99	-102.06
BIC		-53.78	665.52				665.78	-54.94
logLik	-12.35	58.45	-307.86	-22.60	-12.68	-11.72	-307.99	59.03
Deviance		-116.90	615.72				615.99	-118.06
No. obs.	4020	2670	4020	4020	4020	4020	4020	2670
No. groups: n	201	182	201	201	201	201	201	182
ANOVA χ^2		760 ***	81.3 ***				0	744.9 ***

*** $p < 0.001$, ** $p < 0.01$, * $p < 0.05$

Table 4.14: **Regression results for FP participation data (NUTS-3 level)**

logCOST	**Model 1**	**Model 2**	**Model 3.A**	**Model 4.A**
(Intercept)	-17.48 *	-23.86 **	15.79 **	
	(2.48)	(2.73)	(1.21)	
logRDEMP	3.56 ***	1.22 ***		
	(0.21)	(0.26)		
logRDEMP x LQHT			-1.11 ***	-1.14 *
			(0.23)	(0.46)
logRDEMP x INTEG			1.36 ***	1.35 ***
			(0.01)	(0.01)
logKRD		3.81 ***	0.36 *	0.14
		(0.27)	(0.18)	(0.45)
logSRD				
logSRD x LQEDU				
logGRP				0.84 *
				(0.42)
logPOP				0.27
				(0.25)
EUST1				7.51
				(4.35)
EUST2				8.11
				(4.21)
EUST3				6.52
				(4.58)
AIC	29818.72	29625.03	24132.34	21548.78
BIC	29849.66	29662.16	24175.56	21615.46
logLik	-14904.36	-14806.51	-12059.17	-10763.39
Deviance	29808.72	29613.03	24118.34	21526.78
No. obs.	3597	3597	3549	3173
No. groups: n	1329	1329	1299	1176
No. groups: t	3	3	3	3
ANOVA χ^2		196.3 ***	5505.9 ***	2589.8 ***

logCOST	Model 3.B	Model 4.B	Model 5.B	Model 6.B
(Intercept)	-1.74	-1.83	-16.73 **	
	(1.17)	(1.17)	(3.67)	
logRDEMP	0.26 *	0.27 *	0.08	0.09
	(0.12)	(0.12)	(0.15)	(0.15)
logRDEMP x LQHT				
logRDEMP x INTEG				
logKRD	0.35 **	0.35 **	-0.19	-0.23
	(0.11)	(0.11)	(0.20)	(0.21)
logSRD	1.03 ***			
	(0.01)			
logSRD x LQEDU		1.03 ***	1.01 ***	1.01 ***
		(0.01)	(0.01)	(0.01)
logGRP			1.24 ***	1.29 **
			(0.34)	(0.41)
logPOP			1.31 ***	1.33 ***
			(0.23)	(0.24)
EUST1				-17.14 **
				(4.23)
EUST2				-17.21 **
				(3.97)
EUST3				-18.00 **
				(4.44)
AIC	24566.32	24576.12	21942.33	21942.86
BIC	24609.64	24619.44	21997.03	22009.72
logLik	-12276.16	-12281.06	-10962.17	-10960.43
Deviance	24552.32	24562.12	21924.33	21920.86
No. obs.	3597	3597	3221	3221
No. groups: n	1329	1329	1206	1206
No. groups: t	3	3	3	3
ANOVA χ^2	5073.4 ***	0	2639.4 ***	1.1

$^{***}p < 0.001$, $^{**}p < 0.01$, $^{*}p < 0.05$

Table 4.15: Regression results for FP participation data (NUTS-2 level - Spatial and structural effects)

logCOST	**Model 1**	**Model 2**	**Model 3.A**	**Model 4.A**	**Model 4.A.N**	**Model 4.A.S**	**Model 4.A.SN**
(Intercept)	9.03 ***	8.86 ***	15.15 ***	15.97 ***	5.96 ***	16.69 ***	6.48 ***
	(0.40)	(0.40)	(0.26)	(0.28)	(0.26)	(0.26)	(0.25)
logRDEMP	0.98 ***	0.61 ***					
	(0.05)	(0.09)					
logRDEMP x LQHT			-0.80 ***	-0.67 ***	-0.66 ***	-0.68 ***	-0.66 ***
			(0.06)	(0.06)	(0.06)	(0.06)	(0.06)
logRDEMP x INTEG			0.75 ***	0.76 ***	0.69 ***	0.76 ***	0.70 ***
			(0.02)	(0.02)	(0.02)	(0.02)	(0.02)
logKRD		0.39 ***	0.30 ***	0.26 ***	0.24 ***	0.26 ***	0.24 ***
		(0.08)	(0.04)	(0.04)	(0.04)	(0.04)	(0.04)
logSRD							
logSRD x LQEDU							
logPOP				-0.23 ***	-0.22 ***	-0.23 ***	-0.21 ***
				(0.04)	(0.03)	(0.04)	(0.04)
W x logCOST					0.57 ***	-0.05	0.54 ***
					(0.14)	(0.13)	(0.15)
ρ					0.92 ***	0.91 ***	0.90 ***
					(0.04)	(0.03)	(0.04)
AIC	994.10	978.25	296.07	266.47			
BIC	1016.11	1004.66	326.89	301.68			
logLik	-492.05	-483.12	-141.04	-125.23	-105.56	-103.93	-98.09
Deviance	984.10	966.25	282.07	250.47			
No. obs.	603	603	603	603	603	603	603
No. groups: n	201	201	201	201	201	201	201
No. groups: t	3	3	3	3	3	3	3
ANOVA χ^2		20.7 ***	692.5 ***	36.9 ***			

logCOST	Model 3.B	Model 3.B.N	Model 3.B.S	Model 3.B.SN	Model 4.B	Model 5.B
(Intercept)	2.28 ***	-1.84 ***	4.60 ***	-1.37 ***	2.58 ***	2.57 ***
	(0.20)	(0.20)	(0.19)	(0.19)	(0.24)	(0.29)
logRDEMP	-0.12 ***	-0.13 **	-0.12 **	-0.12 **	0.00	0.00
	(0.04)	(0.04)	(0.04)	(0.04)	(0.05)	(0.06)
logRDEMP x LQHT						
logRDEMP x INTEG						
logKRD	0.17 ***	0.16 ***	0.17 ***	0.16 ***	0.11 **	0.11 **
	(0.03)	(0.03)	(0.03)	(0.03)	(0.04)	(0.04)
logSRD	0.99 ***	0.94 ***	0.99 ***	0.95 ***		
	(0.02)	(0.02)	(0.02)	(0.02)		
logSRD x LQEDU					0.92 ***	0.92 ***
					(0.03)	(0.03)
logPOP						0.00
						(0.05)
W x logCOST		0.27	-0.13	0.24		
		(0.18)	(0.12)	(0.18)		
ρ		0.78 ***	0.78 ***	0.76 ***		
		(0.09)	(0.08)	(0.09)		
AIC	257.65				345.16	351.37
BIC	288.47				375.97	386.58
logLik	-121.83	-110.03	-106.46	-106.20	-165.58	-167.68
Deviance	243.65				331.16	335.37
No. obs.	603				603	603
No. groups: n	201				201	201
No. groups: t	3				3	3
ANOVA χ^2	733.1 ***				0	0

***p < 0.001, **p < 0.01, *p < 0.05

References

AGHION, P. & HOWITT, P. (1992): A model of growth through creative destruction. *Econometrica 60* (2): 323–351.

AHUJA, G. (2000): Collaboration networks, structural holes, and innovation: A longitudinal study. *Administrative Science Quarterly 45* (3): 425–455.

ALMEIDA, P. & KOGUT, B. (1999): Localization of knowledge and the mobility of engineers in regional networks. *Management science 45* (7): 905–917.

AMIN, A. & THRIFT, N. (1992): Neo-Marshallian nodes in global networks. *International Journal of Urban and Regional Research 16* (4): 571–587.

ANSELIN, L. (1988): *Spatial Econometrics. Methods and Models.* Dordrecht: Kluwer Academic Publishers.

ANSELIN, L., VARGA, A. & ACS, Z. (1997): Local geographic spillovers between university research and high technology innovations. *Journal of Urban Economics 42* (3): 422–448.

AUDRETSCH, D.B. & FELDMAN, M.P. (1996): R&D spillovers and the geography of innovation and production. *American Economic Review 86* (3): 630–640.

AUTANT-BERNARD, C., BILLAND, P., FRACHISSE, D. & MASSARD, N. (2007): Social distance versus spatial distance in R&D cooperation: Empirical evidence from European collaboration choices in micro and nanotechnologies. *Papers in Regional Science 86* (3): 495–519.

BONCHEV, D. (2009). A simple integrated approach to network complexity and node centrality. In: DEHMER, M. & EMMERT-STREIB, F., eds: *Analysis of Complex Networks*, pp. 47–53. Weinheim: Wiley-VCH Verlag.

BRESCHI, S. & LISSONI, F. (2009): Mobility of skilled workers and co-invention networks: an anatomy of localized knowledge flows. *Journal of Economic Geography 9* (4): 439–468.

BURT, R.S. (2007): *Brokerage and Closure. An Introduction to Social Capital.* Oxford: Oxford University Press.

CASETTI, E. (1972): Generating models by the expansion method. Applications to geographical research. *Geographical Analysis 4* (1): 81–91.

CASTELLS, M. (1991): *The Informational City. Information Technology, Economic Restructuring, and the Urban-Regional Process.* Oxford: Blackwell.

CASTELLS, M. (2011): *The Rise of the Network Society. The Information Age: Economy, Society, and Culture.* Chichester: John Wiley & Sons.

COE, D.T. & HELPMAN, E. (1995): International R&D spillovers. *European Economic Review 39* (5): 859–887.

COE, D.T., HELPMAN, E. & HOFFMAISTER, A.W. (1997): North-South R&D spillovers. *Economic Journal 107* (440): 134–49.

COLEMAN, J.S. (1988): Social capital in the creation of human capital. *American Journal of Sociology 94* (3-Supplement): 95–120.

EATON, J. & KORTUM, S. (1996a): Trade in ideas. Patenting and productivity in the OECD. *Journal of International Economics 40* (3-4): 251–278.

EATON, J. & KORTUM, S. (1996b): Measuring technology diffusion and the international sources of growth. *Eastern Economic Journal 22* (4): 401–410.

ELLISON, G. & GLAESER, E.L. (1997): Geographic concentration in U.S. manufacturing industries: A dartboard approach. *Journal of Political Economy 105* (5): 889–927.

FAGERBERG, J. (1994): Technology and international differences in growth rates. *Journal of Economic Literature 32* (3): 1147–1175.

FAGERBERG, J. (1987): A technology gap approach to why growth rates differ. *Research Policy 16* (2-4): 87–99.

FAGERBERG, J., VERSPAGEN, B. & CANIËLS, M. (1997): Technology, growth and unemployment across European regions. *Regional Studies 31* (5): 457–466.

FLEMING, L., KING, C. & JUDA, A.I. (2007): Small worlds and regional innovation. *Organization Science 18* (6): 938–954.

FURMAN, J.L., PORTER, M.E. & STERN, S. (2002): The determinants of national innovative capacity. *Research Policy 31* (6): 899–933.

GLÄNZEL, W., & C. DE LANGE (1997): Modelling and measuring multilateral co-authorship in international scientific collaboration. Part II. A comparative study on the extent and change of international scientific collaboration links. *Scientometrics 40* (3): 605–626.

GLÄNZEL, W., & SCHUBERT, A. (2005): Analysing scientific networks through co-authorship. In: MOED, H.F., GLÄNZEL, W. & SCHMOCH, U., eds: *Handbook of Quantitative Science and Technology Research*, pp. 257–276. Dordrecht: Kluwer Academic Publishers.

GREUNZ, L. (2003): Geographically and technologically mediated knowledge spillovers between European regions. *Annals of Regional Science 37* (4): 657–680.

GRILICHES, Z. (1990): Patent statistics as economic indicators. A survey. *Journal of Economic Literature 28* (4): 1661–1707.

GRILICHES, Z. (1979): Issues in assessing the contribution of research and development on productivity growth. *Bell Journal of Economics 10:* 92–116.

GROSSMAN, G.M. & HELPMAN, E. (1991): Quality ladders in the theory of growth. *Review of Economic Studies 58* (1): 43–61.

HAGEDOORN, J. (2002): Inter-firm R&D partnerships: an overview of major trends and patterns since 1960. *Research Policy 31* (4): 477–492.

HAGEDOORN, J., ROIJAKKERS, N. & VAN KRANENBURG, H. (2006): Inter-firm R&D networks: the importance of strategic network capabilities for high-tech partnership formation. *British Journal of Management 17* (1): 39–53.

HAUSMAN, J., HALL, B.H. & GRILICHES, Z. (1984): Econometric models for count data with an application to the patents-R&D relationship. *Econometrica 52* (4): 909–938.

HOEKMAN, J., FRENKEN, K. & TIJSSEN, R.J.W. (2010): Research collaboration at a distance: Changing spatial patterns of scientific collaboration within Europe. *Research Policy 39* (5): 662–673.

JACKSON, M.O. (2005): A survey of network formation models: Stability and efficiency. In: DEMANGE, G. & WOODERS, M., eds: *Group Formation in Economics: Networks, Clubs and Coalitions*, pp. 11–57. Cambridge: Cambridge University Press.

JACKSON, M.O. (2010): *Social and Economic Networks*. Princeton, NJ: Princeton University Press.

JACKSON, M.O. & WOLINSKY, A. (1996): A strategic model of social and economic networks. *Journal of Economic Theory 71* (1): 44–74.

JAFFE, A. (1989): Real effects of academic research. *American Economic Review 79*: 957–970.

JAFFE, A., TRAJTENBERG, M. & HENDERSON, R. (1993): Geographic localization of knowledge spillovers as evidence from patent citations. *Quarterly Journal of Economics 108*: 577–598.

JONES, C.I. (1995a): R&D-based models of economic growth. *Journal of Political Economy 103* (4): 759–784.

JONES, C.I. (1995b): Time series tests of endogenous growth models. *Quarterly Journal of Economics 110* (2): 495–525.

KNACK, S., & P. KEEFER (1997): Does social capital have an economic payoff? A cross-country investigation. *Quarterly Journal of Economics 112* (4): 1251–1288.

KRACKHARDT, D. (1988): Predicting with networks: Nonparametric multiple regression analysis of dyadic data. *Social Networks 10* (4): 359–381.

KRACKHARDT, D. (1987): QAP partialling as a test of spuriousness. *Social Networks 9* (2): 171–186.

LAIRD, N.M. & WARE, J.H. (1982): Random-effects models for longitudinal data. *Biometrics 38* (4): 963–974.

LESAGE, J.P., FISCHER, M.M. & SCHERNGELL, T. (2007): Knowledge spillovers across Europe: Evidence from a Poisson spatial interaction model with spatial effects. *Papers in Regional Science 86* (3): 393–421.

LUCAS, R.E. (1988): On the mechanics of economic development. *Journal of Monetary Economics 22* (1): 3–42.

MAGGIONI, M.A., NOSVELLI, M. & UBERTI, T.E. (2007): Space versus networks in the geography of innovation: A European analysis. *Papers in Regional Science 86* (3): 471–493.

MAGGIONI, M.A. & UBERTI, T.E. (2005): International networks of knowledge flows: an econometric analysis. *Papers on economics and evolution, Max-Planck-Institut für Ökonomik,* no. 0519.

MANSKI, C.F. (1993): Identification of endogenous social effects: The reflection problem. *Review of Economic Studies 60* (3): 531–542.

MANSKI, C.F. & LERMAN, S.R. (1977): The estimation of choice probabilities from choice based samples. *Econometrica 45* (8): 1977–1988.

MARKUSEN, A. (1996): Sticky places in slippery space: A typology of industrial districts. *Economic Geography 72* (3): 293–313.

NOWICKI, K. & SNIJDERS, T.A.B. (2001): Estimation and prediction for stochastic blockstructures. *Journal of the American Statistical Association 96* (455): 1077–1087.

ORD, K. (1975): Estimation methods for models of spatial interaction. *Journal of the American Statistical Association 70* (349): 120–126.

PACI, R. & USAI, S. (2000): Technological enclaves and industrial districts: An analysis of the regional distribution of innovative activity in Europe. *Regional Studies 34* (2): 97–114.

PARK, G., & PARK, Y. (2006): On the measurement of patent stock as knowledge indicators. *Technological Forecasting and Social Change 73*: 793–812.

PATTISON, P. & ROBINS, G. (2002): Neighborhood–based models for social networks. *Sociological Methodology 32* (1): 301–337.

PONDS, R., VAN OORT, F. & FRENKEN, K. (2007): The geographical and institutional proximity of research collaboration. *Papers in Regional Science 86* (3): 423–443.

PORTER, M.E. & STERN, S. (2000): Measuring the 'ideas' production function: evidence from international patent output. *NBER Working Papers,* no. 7891.

PUTNAM, R.D., LEONARDI, R. & NANETTI, R.Y. (1993): *Making Democracy Work: Civic Traditions in Modern Italy.* Princeton, NJ: Princeton University Press.

ROBINS, G., PATTISON, P., KALISH, Y. & LUSHER, D. (2007): An introduction to exponential random graph (p*) models for social networks. *Social networks 29* (2): 173–191.

ROMER, P.M. (1990): Endogenous technological change. *Journal of Political Economy 98* (5, Part 2: The Problem of Development: A Conference of the Institute for the Study of Free Enterprise Systems): S71–S102.

ROMER, P.M. (1986): Increasing returns and long-run growth. *Journal of Political Economy 94* (5): 1002–1037.

ROY, J.R. & THILL, J.-C. (2004): Spatial interaction modelling. *Papers in Regional Science 83* (1): 339–361.

SCHERNGELL, T. & BARBER, M.J. (2009): Spatial interaction modelling of cross-region R&D collaborations: empirical evidence from the 5th EU framework programme. *Papers in Regional Science 88* (3): 531–546.

SCHILLING, M.A. & PHELPS, C.C. (2007): Interfirm collaboration networks. The impact of large-scale network structure on firm innovation. *Management Science 53* (7): 1113–1126.

SCHWEINBERGER, M. & SNIJDERS, T.A.B. (2003): Settings in social networks. A measurement model. *Sociological Methodology 33* (1): 307–341.

SEN, A. & SMITH, T.E. (1995): *Gravity Models of Spatial Interaction Behavior.* Heidelberg: Springer-Verlag.

SHAN, W., WALKER, G. & KOGUT, B. (1994): Interfirm cooperation and startup innovation in the biotechnology industry. *Strategic management journal 15* (5): 387–394.

SINGH, J. (2005): Collaborative networks as determinants of knowledge diffusion patterns. *Management Science 51* (5): 756–770.

SNIJDERS, T.A.B. (2002): Markov chain Monte Carlo estimation of exponential random graph models. *Journal of Social Structure 3* (2): 1–40.

SNIJDERS, T.A.B. (2011): Statistical models for social networks. *Annual Review of Sociology 37* (1): 131–153.

SNIJDERS, T.A.B., PATTISON, P.E., ROBINS G.L. & HANDCOCK, M.S. (2006): New specifications for exponential random graph models. *Sociological Methodology 36* (1): 99–153.

SWYNGEDOUW, E. (2004): Globalisation or 'glocalisation'? Networks, territories and rescaling. *Cambridge Review of International Affairs 17* (1): 25–48.

UZAWA, H. (1965): Optimum technical change in an aggregative model of economic growth. *International Economic Review 6* (1): 18–31.

VAN DUIJN, M.A.J., SNIJDERS, T.A.B. & ZIJLSTRA, B.J.H. (2004): p2: a random effects model with covariates for directed graphs. *Statistica Neerlandica 58* (2): 234–254.

VAN RAAN, A.F.J. (2004): Measuring science. Capita selecta of current main issues. In: MOED, H.F., GLÄNZEL, W. & SCHMOCH, U., eds: *Handbook of Quantitative Science and Technology Research*, pp. 19-50. Dordrecht: Kluwer Academic Publishers.

VARGA, A., PONTIKAKIS, D. & CHORAFAKIS, G. (2014): Metropolitan Edison and cosmopolitan Pasteur? Agglomeration and interregional research network effects on European R&D productivity. *Journal of Economic Geography 14* (2): 229–263.

WALKER, G., KOGUT, B. & SHAN, W. (1997): Social capital, structural holes and the formation of an industry network. *Organization science 8* (2): 109–125.

ZUCKER, L.G., DARBY, M.R. & ARMSTRONG, J. (1998): Geographically localized knowledge: spillovers or markets? *Economic Inquiry 36* (1): 65–86.

Notes

[1] e.g. GRILICHES, 1979; JAFFE, 1989; EATON & KORTUM, 1996a; PORTER & STERN, 2000.
[2] e.g. FAGERBERG, 1987; 1994; FAGERBERG *et al.*, 1997; COE & HELPMAN, 1995; EATON & KORTUM, 1996b; COE *et al.*, 1997.
[3] See GRILICHES, 1990 for a review.
[4] See VAN RAAN, 2004 for a review.
[5] Endogenous growth literature includes UZAWA, 1965; ROMER, 1986; 1990; LUCAS, 1988; GROSSMAN & HELPMAN, 1991; AGHION & HOWITT, 1992; JONES, 1995b; 1995a.
[6] Emilia-Romagna, the economic geographers' darling, and the archetype of industrial district, is unsurprisingly the best-performing region in this analysis.
[7] Based on indicators as diverse as newspaper reading, cultural associations, referendum turnout, cabinet stability, legislative innovation, day-care centres, industrial policy instruments, housing and urban development, bureaucratic responsiveness, etc.
[8] For a definition see Chapter 3, Appendix 1, section 'Density'.
[9] The minimum attainable local density in the first-order neighbourhood of any node is $\rho_{\min} = \frac{2}{n-1}$ and $\lim_{n\to\infty} \frac{2}{n-1} = 0$.
[10] For a definition of 'brokerage' and its relation to clustering and structural holes see Chapter 3, Appendix 1, section 'Triadic structure'.
[11] See Chapter 3, Appendix 1, section 'Centrality'.
[12] Gross expenditure in R&D and R&D employment exhibit an extremely high correlation coefficient at the national and regional levels (see

Table 4.2), which makes these two variables practically interchangeable in empirical studies.
[13] The distance-decay function can be of the form $g(x) = x^{-1}$, $g(x) = x^{-2}$, or even $g(x) = \exp(-x)$.
[14] As defined in Chapter 3, Appendix 1, section 'Distance'.
[15] *Compound annual growth rate* is the average annual geometric growth rate: $g = \left(\frac{R_T}{R_0}\right)^{\frac{1}{T}} - 1$, where R_0 is the start value and R_T is the finish value of the variable under study and *T* the number of years of the period.
[16] i.e. the share of the population living in rural grid cells of 1 km². Grid cells are classified either as urban or as rural according to the following criteria: a grid cell is defined as 'urban' if it has a population density of at least 300 inhabitants per km², and a minimum population of 5,000 inhabitants in contiguous cells above the density threshold.
[http://epp.eurostat.ec.europa.eu/statistics_explained/index.php/Glossary:Urban-rural_typology]
[17] A region classified as predominantly rural becomes intermediate, if it contains a city of more than 200,000 inhabitants representing at least 25% of the regional population. A region classified as intermediate by the above criteria becomes predominantly urban, if it contains a city of more than 500,000 inhabitants representing at least 25% of the regional population.
[18] In conventional econometric terminology this is equivalent to a generalised linear panel data model with individual random effects.

[19] With 1,462 NUTS-3 regions the square spatial weights matrix will have 2,137,444 elements. Together with the other regression terms the total number of observations becomes unmanageable for existing statistical software. On the contrary, in the case of the 312 NUTS-2 regions the spatial weights matrix is within the computational limits of existing software.
[20] The VIF for a predictor i is equal to $(1 - R_i^2)^{-1}$, where R_i^2 is the R^2 of the regression of predictor i against the remaining predictors.

Chapter 5

Governing the knowledge plexus: Policy myths, realities and dilemmas in a regionally divided Europe

Introduction

Chapters 1 and 2 of this book proposed and outlined a 'systemic' paradigm in economic geography founded on the theories of complexity and evolution and the epistemological premise of emergence. The concept of 'knowledge plexus', a particular type of mesoeconomic plexus, was developed as a metaphor for the division of labour in technological knowledge production, conceived as a multi-layered, emergent, self-organised, evolving, heterarchical, complex network. Chapters 3 and 4 examined empirical aspects of the knowledge plexus, notably the topological structure of interregional knowledge networks, which constitute particular layers of the European knowledge plexus, their formation and their effects on the knowledge production process. This chapter examines potential normative implications of the theory and of the empirical findings presented in the previous chapters, and in their light scrutinises the underpinnings of research, technological development and innovation (RTDI) policy in conjunction with regional, cohesion and industrial policies, in a regionally divided European Union.

The history of the common European RTDI policy is relatively brief. Since the establishment of the European Economic Community in 1957 and through the introvert post-war period of stable macroeconomic growth under the 'Fordist regime of accumulation' [AGLIETTA, 1982], relative financial stability under the international Bretton Woods monetary system [EICHENGREEN, 2008], and the reign of the Keynesian welfare state [JESSOP, 2002], and of state-led capitalism, science and technology matters remained a strictly domestic affair of sovereign European states: RTDI policies were tightly combined with interventionist and dirigiste industrial policies promoting 'national champions' and national strategic priorities in a period of a revived 'techno-nationalism' [PETERSON & SHARP, 1998].

With the exception of the Euratom treaty of 1957, the first elements of a common European RTDI policy were put in place not earlier than the 1980's. The perceived widening technology gap with the US and Japan led to the launch of ESPRIT in 1983,[1] a programme for shared-cost, collaborative research, whose priorities were set by the EEC in consultation with a group of European 'national champions' in the IT industry (the 'Big Twelve'). The programme, which is considered to be a precursor to the Framework Programme for RTD (FP), was criticised for sustaining existing oligopolies at the expense of much needed 'creative destruction' leading to genuine technological progress [GUZZETTI, 1995]. The FP was launched in 1984, and ever since it has been the main RTDI policy instrument of the European Community. The Single European Act in 1986 established for the first time Community competences in RTDI policy. The Maastricht Treaty in 1992 enhanced these competences significantly and attached to them a cohesion objective, aiming at the creation of a 'common technological space' as a means for further European integration, a vision which later transformed into the 'European Research Area' (ERA), and more recently into the 'Innovation Union' flagship initiative.

The FPs were designed to support 'pre-competitive', collaborative, international and multidisciplinary research. The first requirement ensures that scientific and technological knowledge generated under Community support retains its public good nature and has the potential to spill over, while R&D funding, consistently with the competition principles of the Common Market, is not used as a tacit form of industrial subsidy to which the Union is avowedly avert; the second and third requirements aim at the reinforcement of European scientific and technological integration by building networks of RTDI actors from the whole range of academia, industry and the public sector, while ensuring meritocracy and equal opportunities of participation to EU member-states and the associated countries; the last feature intends to broaden the range of targeted research thus promoting scientific and technological diversity with potential cross-fertilisation effects and avoiding exclusive concentration of resources in a limited number of sectors and disciplines. The successful participation of member-states with less developed national RTDI systems, despite the competitive and merit-based selection procedures for fund allocation established by the FP, is considered as a safe indication that its a priori 'distributional neutrality' does not undermine the cohesion objective of the Community.

Since its inception, EU RTDI policy has been traditionally moulded on a 'mechanistic' construal of knowledge production based on neoclassical textbook economics – including welfare economics of the neoclassical variety [CHORAFAKIS & PONTIKAKIS, 2011]. It can be argued, however, that since the mid-1990s European RTDI policy has begun to undergo a partial paradigmatic shift towards a more 'systemic' paradigm with neo-Schumpeterian and evolutionary influences eclectically co-existing with relics of mainstream mechanistic thinking [Ibid.; PELLEGRIN, 2007]. The 'systemic' turn in European RTDI, however, came to a halt in recent years with the emergence of a new policy discourse under the banner of 'smart specialisation' [FORAY & VAN ARK, 2007; FORAY, 2009], which envisages a policy-induced redistribution of knowledge-related resources, and in particular of research funding, among EU regions according to existing patterns of revealed comparative advantage. This purportedly aims at generating economies of scale as a solution to Europe's perceived technological lag vis-à-vis its principal industrial competitors, and at making Europe an attractive destination for R&D investment [FORAY & VAN ARK, 2007]. This essentially naïve recasting of worn-out mechanistic arguments, which paradoxically combines the neoliberal narrative with 'old Europe'-style dirigisme under a pseudo-systemic guise, has already found willing ears among EU policy-makers, becoming one of the principal policy objectives of the EU 'Innovation Union' flagship initiative, which is expected to guide the design and implementation of EU RTDI policy until 2020 [EC, 2010a; EC, 2010b].

The fundamental normative questions discussed in this chapter are whether RTDI policies should favour the regional concentration of cognitive resources, instead of being distributionally neutral as they were until recently, or pro-cohesion; whether diversity in the technological knowledge production process is desirable or, instead, whether RTDI and regional policies should promote a 'planned' specialisation aiming at the inducement of economies of scale and improved 'competitiveness' at the expense of diversity; whether, from a developmental perspective, RTDI and regional policies are sufficient substitutes for a proper industrial policy in peripheral regions; and whether the revealed comparative advantage of a regional (or national) economy should guide its technological development strategy.

The remainder chapter is split in three parts: The second section contrasts the rationales for policy intervention from the perspective of efficiency under two different systems of thought, the neoclassical and a broadly defined 'Schumpeterian', and discusses the nature of the 'social planner', and in particular her cognitive restrictions, purpose of intervention and political stance with regard to 'social welfare' and 'public interest'. The third section critically examines the mechanistic underpinnings of EU technological knowledge-related policies, starting from the 'mechanistic construal' of the innovation process, and continuing with the exposition of nine recurrent myths in policy discourse related to the mechanistic construal, the new tenet of 'smart specialisation', and the neoliberal ideology which is gradually making headway in all facets of EU policy. The last section proposes an alternative framework for EU knowledge governance based on the systemic paradigm, in the light of the theory developed in Chapters 1 and 2 of this book, raising the case for new robust and coherent, bottom-up techno-industrial strategies in the periphery on systemic underpinnings as a much needed complement to EU RTDI, regional and cohesion policies.

Rationales for policy intervention

Neoclassical versus 'neo-Schumpeterian' rationale

Two divergent schools of thought provide contrasting theoretical justifications for policy intervention in the economy: Neoclassical welfare economics sees scope for policy intervention in the case of 'market failures', i.e. aberrations from the competitive market norm leading to the non-applicability of the first welfare theorem. By contrast, a broadly-defined 'neo-Schumpeterian' strand treats these aberrations as necessary conditions for the performance of economic systems and, therefore, as indispensable features of their 'dynamic efficiency'.

EU RTDI policy has been very eclectic with regard to these two rationales, and at the same time quite pragmatic: While the neoclassical jargon of 'market failure' is broadly adopted and conveniently used to justify policy intervention, the discourse on the need to promote innovation, to accelerate the pace of technological change and to restore Europe's position as a global technological leader, embedded, for instance, in the Lisbon strategy, reveals its Schumpeterian influences.

Market failures

The first theorem of welfare economics postulates that in the absence of externalities any competitive equilibrium will lead to a Pareto-optimal allocation of resources. Any deviation from the conditions of the competitive market leads to Pareto sub-optimal allocations, which admit of 'Pareto improvements', i.e. the re-allocation of resources in a way that no economic agent is made worse-off while some economic agents are made better-off. Deviations from the Walrasian equilibrium conditions are termed 'market failures', and justify government intervention in the market. 'Market failures' are of many different types: They may involve the concentration of market power in the form of monopolies or oligopolies; non-convexities in production related to increasing returns; externalities and spillovers; missing markets and incomplete contracts requiring the allocation of property rights; transaction costs; under-provision of pure and quasi- public goods; the depletion of collective goods ('the tragedy of the commons'); incomplete information; uncertainty deterring economic agents from participating in the market; etc.[2] On the margin of the neoclassical paradigm, government intervention is also justified (although this view is strongly contested by neoliberal-minded theorists as well as neoclassical purists) in the provision of 'merit goods', i.e. private goods under-provided by the market, which are deemed to be socially beneficial (e.g. social housing, education, health services); in cases where national interest is involved; and, finally, in (extreme) cases where social equity concerns are involved.[3]

It is evident that what is perceived in the neoclassical context as an aberration from the norm and defined as a 'market failure' *is* the norm in real socio-economic systems. Technological knowledge production, being a genuinely systemic, complex, dynamic and out-of-equilibrium process, is inevitably assumed in this reductionist context to involve numerous 'market failures' which make the case for government intervention. ARROW, 1962, identifies three typical sources of market failure in the knowledge production process: *indivisibilities* linked to increasing returns, *inappropriability* related to externalities, and *uncertainty* inherent in investment in research and innovation. In Chapter 2 we saw that some forms of technological knowledge indeed are inappropriable because of their strong spillover effects, which bestows them (quasi-) public good characteristics. All these market failures result in the under-provision of technological knowledge by the market and justifies intervention through public funding of research – especially 'basic' research aiming at the creation and diffusion of technological knowledge of the 'universal' type, which is the least appropriable type.

Paretian versus Schumpeterian efficiency

In the strongly reductionist neoclassical framework government intervention is justified only as long as it restores Pareto efficiency under the *existing* competitive equilibrium. This is a *static* type of efficiency which takes the production technology set of the economy as given. Moreover, the Pareto efficiency concept, despite the claims to the opposite, is essentially a value-laden normative principle, based on a strong version of the liberal premise of non-interference (the 'do-no-harm' canon), which a priori excludes any equity concerns and prohibits wealth redistribution after the initial allocation of endowments [VAN STAVEREN, 2012]. Clearly, this restrictive definition of efficiency is inadequate in real economic systems with complex techno-economic dynamics characterised by multiple attractors (the dynamic equivalent to a fixed-point equilibrium) and out-of-equilibrium phase transitions, and endogenous novelty. As METCALFE, 1997: 269, contends, "innovation and Pareto optimality are fundamentally incompatible". It is also inadequate for policy design (including the design of RTDI policy), where equity concerns are not uncommon, and where some types of wealth redistribution may be conducive to the improvement of allocative efficiency [BOWLES & GINTIS, 2000].

An alternative concept is that of *dynamic efficiency* in the Schumpeterian/evolutionary context, which I call 'Schumpeterian efficiency'. From the Schumpeterian perspective, market power, increasing returns, information asymmetries, and other deviations from the competitive market norm, are driving forces of innovation-based competition instead of market failures.[4] The open-ended nature of technological change and the discontinuities, anisotropies, path-dependences, nonlinearities and endogenous novelties of complex evolving techno-economic systems make impossible the ex ante identification of their *global* optima, and therefore the definition of dynamic efficiency on the basis of global optimality criteria (as in the case of Pareto efficiency). Schumpeterian efficiency is therefore a much more elusive and hard-to-define concept compared to the simple, strongly reductionist Pareto principle. Still, some characteristics can be identified: It is a dynamic, and therefore intertemporal property; it is systemic, in the sense that it characterises the state of the system as a whole instead of the state of its micro-elements, the individual economic agents; it involves the comparison of a multiplicity of *local* optima which the system may attain through 'adaptive walk' in a technological 'fitness landscape', and around which the system may settle (in which case they become the system's attractors); and it concerns the allocation of productive resources rather than the interpersonal distribution of utility or income [VAN STAVEREN, 2012].

As a normative basis for policy intervention, its fundamental difference from the Paretian rationale for policy intervention is that it is *proactive* (enabling), while the latter is *counteractive* (corrective). Proactive policy interventions aim to support and accelerate the process of technological development rather than to restore competitive market conditions, and hence are justified as means to offset technological lock-in caused by path dependence, to facilitate transition between technological trajectories, and to accelerate shifting techno-economic paradigms [SMITH, 2000].

The 'social planner' conundrum

Limitations to the social planner's knowledge

The neoclassical rationale for government intervention in the face of market failures implicitly assumes that the social planner, similarly to all neoclassical economic agents and to the Walrasian auctioneer – the omniscient 'hyper-computational demon', possesses full and perfect information on market structure, unbounded rationality, and infinite computational capacities, ensuring that her choices are fully consistent with the maximisation of her objective function. In addition to omniscient, this fictitious being is also implicitly assumed to be 'benevolent': her objective function is fully and exclusively defined by 'social welfare' criteria, and therefore she is assumed to represent 'public interest'.

Taking the assumptions of the neoclassical paradigm at face value, there should be no market failures in the first place, as the invisible hand seamlessly restores perfectly competitive market conditions. Neoliberal theorists, who devotedly believe in the infallibility of the invisible hand doctrine, and especially those associated with 'public choice theory', prefer to attribute any observed economic failure to excessive and ill-conceived state intervention in the functioning of the market, which they call 'government failure' [KRUEGER, 1990; TULLOCK *et al.*, 2002]. In the 'public choice' approach to government, which admittedly is more realistic than the idealised model of the benevolent, hyper-rational social planner outlined in the first paragraph, government is not a unitary agent with a simple objective function but an aggregation of individual (political) agents with objective functions determined not only by public but also by private interests. The objective functions of social planners, therefore, do not necessarily coincide with public interest: 'budget-maximising' [NISKANEN, 1971], 'regulatory capture' [STIGLER, 1971], and 'rent-seeking' [KRUEGER, 1974] are some of the causes of this discrepancy. Moreover, social planners neither are unboundedly rational nor possess perfect and full information on market conditions. The fact that policy-makers can only have very limited knowledge of the micro-structure of the market is often evoked as a demonstration of the inferiority of any centrally planned solution vis-à-vis the decentralised and self-organised 'catallactic' mechanism of the market [HAYEK, 1982].[5]

In an evolutionary context, the social planner, conceived for the moment as a unitary reflective agent with a simple objective function similarly to any other real economic agent, is faced with two types of cognitive limitations: a *contingent* limitation to her capacity to know the actual state of the economy, due to incomplete information and to her inherent computational constraints, and a *structural* limitation to know (or to predict) the economy's evolutionary trajectories and, therefore, the whole set of future technological opportunities.[6] This latter limitation is not contingent on the social planner's cognitive capacities but related to the non-deterministic, open-ended nature of the innovation process which is marked by complexity, emergence, and endogenous novelty, and to the nonlinear 'undecidable' dynamics of self-organised techno-economic systems. Even if the social planner were benevolent, fully rational, and possessed complete information on the state of the economy, and policy implementation were frictionless and costless, it would still be impossible for her to determine the optimal path of technological evolution [METCALFE, 1997; METCALFE & RAMLOGAN, 2005].

The social planer's purpose of intervention

In the neoliberal/public choice discourse, the limitations to the social planner's ability to know are evoked as a demonstration that the social planner's choices are a priori inferior from a welfare perspective to the decentralised market solution, and hence as an argument against policy intervention. Public choice theory, while it demystifies the social planner's capacities and intentions, dogmatically espouses the idealised model of the neoclassical competitive market and takes for granted the infallibility of its decentralised allocation mechanism.

By contrast, a systemic approach recognises the fact that the unfettered market mechanism not only often fails to coordinate individual agents' plans (an informational failure), but also when it does so, it may lead to dynamically inefficient, developmentally inferior or socially undesirable resource allocations. One of the most important sources of this problem is the inherent disposition of the unregulated market mechanism to generate uneven development, which in the longer run undermines its proper functioning and stability. It is well-documented, to the point of becoming trivial, by a plethora of empirical and theoretical analyses from various theoretical perspectives, from Marxist to evolutionary, and from the econometric literature on convergence to the models of the New Economic Geography, that the process of unfettered capitalist development not only leads to uneven inter-class, interregional and international distribution of wealth, but also is a self-reinforcing process following a spiral of 'cumulative causation'.

In this context, policy intervention has two potential purposes:

(i) In the presence of a multiplicity of local optima in the evolutionary fitness landscape, policy intervention may function as a 'signalling instrument', which leads the economic system to a particular local optimum by coordinating the move of individual economic agents in this direction, despite the social planner's inability to know the agents' exact micro-states.[7] The social planner may thus intervene to improve market and non-market coordination of economic agents, reduce their uncertainty [ALBIN, 1998; COLANDER & VAN EES, 2006: 208], and ensure the overall stability, and eventually the dynamic efficiency of the system.

(ii) In the case where the spontaneous coordination of the agents' plans has already led the system to settle in a socially undesirable or a developmentally inferior attractor basin – what in development theory is termed a 'low-level equilibrium' [NELSON, 1956; BARDHAN, 1993], policy intervention may be aimed at shifting the system from that attractor basin to a superior one. In this case policy intervention is of a much more complex nature, as it requires the combination of several policy instruments for a longer period of time, the mobilisation of a multiplicity of resources, and the existence of a strategic plan. It is also more contestable as it may affect various social groups asymmetrically, disrupt socio-economic norms, and uproot established economic interests.

The instruments the social planner has at her disposal for the above purposes include the provision of regulation, or more generally of the institutional framework which guides individual choice and governs agents' interactions [COLANDER & VAN EES, 2006: 208], the provision of incentives, the redistribution of resources (through taxation, subsidies, provision of public and quasi-public goods, etc.), or even the steering of the 'primary accumulation' process (mostly in developing economies) through state control of strategic resources.

The social planner's objectivity hypothesis

We saw that public choice theory puts in question not only the social planner's capacity to know but also her motives. As a rational agent she is self-interested, she can act against public interest, and she can be biased or even corrupt. The perception of government as an aggregation of rational, self-interested individuals is a common theme in public choice theory. Despite the fact, however, that this model of government, and by extension of the state, is overtly reductionist, individualistic, ahistorical, and most importantly, apolitical, in the sense that it lacks a social class perspective, it still makes an interesting point, namely that it is naïve to assume that the social planner's construal of public interest is neutral and 'objective'.

So far I have avoided issues pertaining directly to the subject-matter of political economy like the one above, given the actual size limits of this book and the vastness of the field. However, the naïve, apolitical perception of the social planner as a benevolent and objective social welfare optimiser is clearly unsatisfactory when policy impacts are assessed, and in particular when distributional issues come in question.

From a diametrical point of view, in the (early) instrumentalist Marxist conception of the state, there are no socially optimal policy solutions, only solutions determined by specific class interests. The capitalist state serves the class interests of the capitalist class.[8] This view is moderated by Gramsci with the concept of (cultural) 'hegemony', later extended and reworked by POULANTZAS, 1968, who views the state as relatively autonomous from the ruling class but institutionally inscribing the political and ideological dominance of the latter, while ensuring the conditions of its reproduction, i.e. the continuity of the capitalist system. Following Poulantzas's structural-functionalist approach, JESSOP, 1990; 2007, sees the state as an overdetermined social relation,[9] relatively independent from the 'circuit of capital' and the specific, potentially conflicting, interests of the various fractions of the capitalist class, but at the same time as the apparatus for the imposition and the legitimisation of a 'hegemonic project' usually combined with an 'accumulation strategy'.

The radical structural-functionalist view of the state is consistent with the systemic paradigm developed in the previous chapters. The state, conceived as a strongly emergent relational ontology, supervenes on class interests, reconciles them favouring some of them (those of the ruling class) but without merely being reducible to them, while at the same time has significant downwardly causal powers ensuring the coherent and continuous reproduction of the subvenient socio-economic relations, and co-evolves with the economy. The reified state apparatus (the 'government') is per se a complex multiagent hierarchical system composed by, but irreducible to, individual 'political' agents (its political and administrative personnel), and can be conceived as a meta-agent with its own internal schema shaped through the co-adaptation of diverse group interests external to the apparatus itself, and in particular those with systemic socio-economic power, rather than exclusively by individuals from inside.

These views imply that public interest cannot be defined outside its political context. It is not uncommon in EU policy discourse, however, to assume that particular policies are to the benefit of the EU as a whole, or of the society at large, when in fact they promote specific class, sectoral or even national interests within the EU. The distributional implications of these policies are conveniently concealed by a rhetoric based on elusive and generic notions, such as 'competitiveness', 'excellence', 'freedom', etc., while the neoclassical fallacy of the 'trickle-down' argument is often evoked as a response to their distributional bias, namely that the benefits from development or growth will spontaneously diffuse within the economy as a result of the equilibrating forces of the market, and hence that no compensating policy intervention is needed.

The next section examines how the rationales for policy intervention analysed here are interpreted and implemented under two contrasting approaches to knowledge governance, the mechanistic and the systemic.

Mechanistic versus systemic construal of knowledge governance

EU knowledge governance in historical perspective

The term 'mechanistic' is used here to refer to the dominant way of thinking about the process of technological knowledge production, mainly in the context of RTDI policy, inspired by mainstream economics and the 'market failure' rationale. Its early success in academic as well as in policy discourse can be attributed to its simplicity, its tractability and, most importantly, its epistemological affinity with the neoclassical paradigm [CHORAFAKIS & PONTIKAKIS, 2011]: Mechanistic thinking is strongly reductionist, implicitly embraces methodological individualism, fails to treat knowledge production as a synergetic and systemic process, is infused with a 'naïve' determinism which ignores complexity in the process of technological knowledge production, and is aspatial and atemporal, i.e. it is devoid of any geographical and historical dimensions. Given the remarkable lack of an actual model of technological knowledge production in this context, I refer to it as a 'construal' rather than as a 'paradigm' or a 'model'. In historical perspective, mechanistic thinking has shaped the origins of European RTDI policy but also relapses from time to time in contemporary policy discourse.

The linear model of innovation

The mechanistic archetype of knowledge production is the nowadays largely discredited 'linear model' of innovation. This model conceives the innovation process from the phase of basic and applied research through the product development and production phases to the phase of product marketing and diffusion as a linear sequence of actions. As a corollary, it postulates a deterministic relationship between R&D expenditure and macroeconomic growth assuming that increases in the level of R&D investment cause commensurate increases in the level of technological innovation and a predictably matching rate of economic growth [MALECKI, 1997: 115].

The reductionist 'assembly line' perception of the knowledge production process, which underlies this sketchy model, fits well with the dominant in the 1950s and 60s Fordist-Taylorist techno-managerial paradigm, and has been present in a large number of policy documents and related academic articles of the time [see, for instance, BUSH, 1945; MACLAURIN, 1953; GRILICHES, 1958; NELSON, 1959]. However, as the model has lost completely its relevance in the post-Fordist knowledge economies, so it has become obsolete in the theory of technological change and has eventually been purged from academia.

Since then, according to FREEMAN, 1996: 27, "no model of the innovative process has been more frequently attacked and demolished than the so-called 'linear model of innovation'. At one time it was almost impossible to read a book or an article on technology policy or technological forecasting that did not begin or end with such a polemic". More provokingly, EDGERTON, 2004, asserts that the linear model has never existed as such, but rather as an ex post historical construct used as the academic 'straw man' in science and technology studies.

Despite the irreversible demise of the 'linear model' in academia, many relics of the mechanistic construal of technological knowledge production still survive in contemporary EU policy discourse.

The systemic turn

Already in the early 1990s the increasingly dominant in technology and innovation studies neo-Schumpeterian paradigm began to sway European RTDI policy.[10] This was part of an incomplete 'systemic' turn in EU RTDI policy, characterised by the gradual espousal of the ideas of 'national systems of innovation',[11] 'regional innovation systems',[12] the 'triple helix' [ETZKOWITZ & LEYDESDORFF, 1997], etc. Several years later this turn was evident in the Lisbon Agenda [EC, 2005], to whose formulation several prominent neo-Schumpeterian economists contributed,[13] but also in earlier policy documents which helped shape the modalities of the RTDI policy instruments, in particular those of the Framework Programmes in the context of the 'European Research Area' [EC, 2000].

Today the 'systemic framework' of EU knowledge governance remains underdeveloped in two respects: It is yet to be formulated in a fully systemic language free from the relics of the mechanistic construal; and it lacks a proactive developmental perspective sensitive to territorial heterogeneity, which would aim at closing the technological gap and reinforcing the dynamic efficiency of the European knowledge plexus by strengthening the techno-economic periphery. The underdeveloped state of the systemic framework is aggravated by the recent advance of the pseudo-systemic 'smart specialisation' tenet.

The relapse of the mechanistic construal: Smart specialisation

In the mid-2000s a new turn in policy discourse emerged under the heading of 'smart specialisation' – an eclectic and inconsistent blend of old mechanistic ideas recast in a systemic setting, with doses of neoliberalism and dirigisme. As anticipated in CHORAFAKIS & PONTIKAKIS, 2011, this incoherent mix of ideas soon made headway in Brussels to become a pillar of the 'Innovation Union' flagship initiative, an objective of the 'Europe 2020' strategy, and also 'ex ante conditionality' for EU member-states and regions in the new EU cohesion policy [FORAY *et al.*, 2012].

Its popularity among certain circles of EU policy-makers in the current socio-political setting stems precisely from the fact that it embraces several aspects of the neoliberal discourse, and in particular the 'competitiveness' imperative and proposes a regressive redistribution of cognitive resources and funding in favour of the techno-industrially advanced regions, i.e. from the periphery to the core, as well as in the direction of the private appropriation of publicly funded technological knowledge, i.e. from the public to the private sphere, while it envisages centrally planned techno-economic trajectories for the regions under the command of Brussels. At the same time it purports to be systemic by mimicking the vocabulary of networks and regional innovation systems, while it employs the whole range of mechanistic 'common wisdoms', with which policy-makers in Brussels are particularly familiar.

In the next subsection I critically examine from a systemic perspective some of the mechanistic relics in knowledge governance discourse, and in particular those recently revived in the context of 'smart specialisation'.

Myths and realities in knowledge governance discourse

Myth 1: Duplication and emulation are detrimental to economic performance

The first myth goes that a major threat to the efficiency of any RTDI system, and indeed a persistent handicap of the European one, causing the dissipation of valuable and scarce financial and human resources and undermining the EU's ability to compete internationally, is the 'duplication' of R&D efforts [FORAY & VAN ARK, 2007]. This notion is given two distinct interpretations, both of which have negative connotations and prompt the necessity for policy intervention. The first interpretation is that duplication is the overlapping of national RTDI policy priorities among EU member states, which results in the same type of research being concurrently undertaken in several EU member-states. This duplication is allegedly the result of ill-conceived and inadequately coordinated national RTDI policies. It is also supposed to be a consequence of a sectorally and geographically unfocused EU RTDI policy [Ibid.]. The second interpretation is that duplication is, in a broader sense, the overlapping of the search paths of economic agents in a technological space implicitly perceived as measurable and bounded. This potentially entails the re-discovery of the same instances of technological knowledge that have already been discovered by others. The obvious policy recommendation in both cases is the inducement, through EU RTDI-related policy instruments, of a planned, 'rational' sectoral or geographical allocation of resources, which inevitably leads to their concentration and eventually specialisation.

In reality, exact duplication of research does not and cannot exist for a number of reasons: First, technological knowledge is an indivisible, infungible, and largely incommensurable asset, and in some of its forms, such as individual and organisational knowledge, a highly context-dependent one as well. Second, technological knowledge seen from the constructivist perspective, rather than being a static and immutable object is a dynamic phenomenon emerging through the systemic integration of individual knowledge, and more specifically, through an irreplicable process of co-adaptive interactions of cognitive agents, during which existing cognitive elements are recombined among the agents (a process resembling biological crossover) or radically transformed (a process resembling mutation). This process applied on the finite (but unbounded) set of existing cognitive elements has the potential to generate an infinity of knowledge outcomes, many of which are characterised by genuine novelty. This is evident in the unbounded nature of technological progress itself. The technological space where search takes place is, therefore, not finite; as a result, no two search processes will be identical, even if they have similar initial conditions. Moreover, in this non-finite space of unbounded technological opportunities each researcher or research group contribute their own unique cognitive assets to the search process. *Concurrent search processes* along parallel search paths give rise to innovation-based competition and to Red Queen-type technological dynamics, but also to potential collaboration leading to integration in knowledge networks with significant economies of complexity. *Sequential search processes,* on the other hand, whereby one research team emulates the search methods or even the search results of another, accelerates the adaptation of existing technological knowledge in new socio-economic contexts, the diffusion of scientific and technological advances and their productive adoption and utilisation. Both types of search process, therefore, reinforce the diversity and polymorphism of the knowledge plexus, which, as I argue elsewhere, contributes to its resilience and long-run dynamic efficiency.

Emulation in the 'sequential' type of search is a recurrent phenomenon in the technological history of the emerging, as well as of the advanced industrial economies, and as a matter of fact it is an imperative first step in the process of technological development [CHANG, 2002]. The development experience of technological latecomers like Germany in the 1850s, USA in the 1870s, Japan in the 1960s and the Southeast Asian NICs in the 1980s shows that long before attaining their positions as technological leaders they proved particularly good at appropriating foreign technological knowledge mainly through methodical emulation [MOKYR, 1992; LANDES, 2003]. Microeconomic studies of innovation confirm that a large part of the economic and social benefits of R&D stem from the adoption of technology invented elsewhere.[14] Even in an economy of the size and the technological capacities of the United States, foreign technological improvements account for roughly half of its productivity gains [EATON & KORTUM, 1995]. The relative importance of foreign technology is likely to be even greater at the level of the region [HOWELLS, 2005].

High performance in research is not an innate and immutable quality of cognitive agents, but the result of a dynamic co-evolutionary process, which involves perpetual adaptive learning through competition, collaboration, as well as emulation. In that sense, emulation, which from a static, global optimality perspective may appear obsolete, may be from a dynamic perspective the invaluable first step towards technological development. In the longer run, new entrants in the technological arms race, who in their early stages of technological development emulated the incumbents, start to challenge them, disrupt technological lock-ins and push the technological frontier forward, thus contributing to an overall more dynamically efficient techno-economic system.

Myth 2: Targeting 'excellence' can improve the effectiveness of RTDI funding

The second myth goes that RTDI policy instruments can lead to an improved allocation of resources by targeting revealed 'excellence' of research actors. As the argument more concretely goes, RTDI policy instruments should promote excellence by directing funding on the basis of the track record and past performance of research actors per se, from individual research-conducting organisations to regional and national RTDI systems.[15]

In reality, few notions in policy discourse are so value-laden and susceptible to confirmation bias as the term 'excellence', especially when used in the context of inter-individual comparisons of capabilities. In EU policy discourse, 'excellence' is increasingly replacing the more modest and economically meaningful notion of 'optimality' despite their substantial semantic differences: The latter implies the selection of the best among similar alternatives contingent on external constraints, while the former refers to absolute, innate superiority.

It can be argued that EU RTDI policy instruments already target optimality: The FP, for instance, have long-established, comprehensive and reputable evaluation and selection procedures for project proposals on the basis of their own merit, and this seems to have worked quite well so far.[16] The proponents of 'excellence', however, claim that the existing funding modalities of EU RTDI policy instruments do not sufficiently target revealed 'excellence', and this ostensibly entails a loss of performance and a dispersion of funds. By this they imply that funding should be more narrowly allocated to 'excellent' performers, instead of best proposals for research projects evaluated on an ad hoc basis.[17]

What at a first glance may seem to be a tenable argument, has a number of serious flaws: First, 'excellent' performers operate, by definition, on their optimality curves, and therefore any additional allocation of resources to them will be suboptimal. Social returns to investment in R&D will be higher when directed to promising but under-funded projects with a potential for good performance, rather than to research performers with a reputation for excellence, who already attain optimal results, and receive sufficient funding through other sources. Second, while assessing the quality of a research proposal is a straightforward and mostly incontestable process, assessing the quality of research groups, of research-conducting organisations, or even more so, of regional and national RTDI systems for the purpose of funding, will be highly controversial and widely contestable, and rightly so: In the case of research-conducting entities, this process will favour those who are able to attain high volumes of measurable R&D output (e.g. patent and publication counts), often because of their size or their privileged access to national funding. In the case of regional and national RTDI systems, conditioning the allocation of funding to individual researchers or groups on indicators of regional or national performance, instead of indicators of individual potential, is at best nonsensical, and at worst flagrantly discriminatory, and potentially reproducing national stereotypes.[18] Finally, conditioning research funding on performance history or *reputation for excellence*, instead of forward-looking criteria of performance potential, may reinforce existing patterns of path dependence and lock-ins of the techno-economic system and undermine the emergence of novelty.

Myth 3: Competitiveness should be the uttermost objective of RTDI policy

The third myth is probably the most pervasive and powerful of all: 'Competitiveness' has been proclaimed to be the cornerstone of a number of EU economic policies, from the most obvious, trade, to the least obvious, regional policy. It is also increasingly perceived as the principal objective of EU RTDI policy, especially in the context of the 'Innovation Union' initiative, while RTDI policy itself is seen as a pillar of EU competitiveness.[19] Competitiveness also figures prominently in practically all strategic agendas formulated by the EU since the mid-1990s, including the bitterly failed 'Lisbon strategy', which aspired to make the EU "the most competitive and dynamic knowledge-based economy in the world" by 2010 [EC, 2005].

In reality, the concept of competitiveness, a passe-partout term taken from business literature [e.g. PORTER, 1990], has surprisingly weak theoretical underpinnings and cannot be defined without making reference to proper economic terms such as productivity, growth, and efficiency. The term is applied indiscriminately to individuals, firms, organisations, institutions, policies, industrial sectors, as well as urban, regional, national, and supra-national economies. The macro-economic application of the term implicitly draws on the misleading analogy between a country and a corporation [KRUGMAN, 1994], and raises an even greater number of theoretical and empirical questions when considered in a regional context [KITSON *et al.*, 2004]. It is also an ambiguous term: In Porter's approach, competitiveness is essentially increased productivity caused by economies of scale – mainly of the

Marshallian type,[20] and various types of positive technological or soft informational externalities [PORTER, 1998]. The economy of the neoclassical competitive market is, therefore, not 'competitive' in the Porterian sense.

Competitiveness is generally assumed to yield significant benefits but it is rarely discussed to which segments of the economy and the society, i.e. its distributional implications. The concept is inextricably linked to the neoliberal rhetoric, as it is often considered to depend on trade and finance liberalisation,[21] market deregulation, the dismantling of redistributive mechanisms, the hollowing-out of the welfare state, the privatisation of public goods, etc. It has also evident Schumpeterian and Darwinian underpinnings, in that it is often associated on the one hand, with economies of scale and increasing returns, and hence with the concentration of market power, and on the other, with individual fitness and the evolutionary process of selection. Competitiveness is a chimerical creature with a neoclassical body, a Schumpeterian head, and a neoliberal tail.[22]

As a policy objective, competitiveness is persistently seen not as a means to an end but as an end in itself – an elusive end for that matter. In the particular context of RTDI policy, this has conveniently masked the neoliberal turn in EU policy discourse and its gradual displacement away from substantial socio-economic policy objectives, such as economic development at large, macroeconomic growth, industrial performance, employment, social welfare, socio-economic cohesion, and regional techno-economic convergence.

At the micro level of individual economic agents, where 'competitiveness' can have a meaningful economic interpretation, it is not the only rationale for (purposive) economic interaction, as it is usually depicted: from a co-evolutionary perspective, as we saw in Chapter 1, competition is just one form of symbiotic relationship; mutualism in the form of economic collaboration is an equally important type of rational and purposive economic interaction. This type of interaction is prominent in the production of technological knowledge and largely defines the evolutionary success of economic agents, but is systematically overlooked by the individualistic perspective of the neoliberal advocates of competitiveness.

Myth 4: Competiveness and cohesion are mutually exclusive RTDI policy objectives

The fourth myth goes that EU RTDI policies are faced with an inescapable cohesion-competitiveness trade-off.[23] As the argument goes, policies with a cohesion objective are by nature redistributive, and driven by distributional equity concerns, which serve predominantly political purposes, as opposed to policies aiming at enhancing competitiveness, which are motivated by economic optimality considerations. Cohesion-promoting policies, the argument goes further, inevitably lead to suboptimal allocation of resources and reduced overall policy effectiveness. Even if competitiveness-promoting policies work at the expense of cohesion and distributional equity, the choice between competitiveness and cohesion, the argument concludes, should be in favour of the former as the benefits of increased economic performance will spontaneously trickle down in the longer run.

In reality the perceived competitiveness-cohesion trade-off, which is based on a dichotomous perception of economic efficiency and distributional equity, is a typical neoclassical fallacy emerging from the narrow, reductionist perception of economic efficiency that the theory entails. In the systemic paradigm, cohesion is a quality of macro-systems intrinsically related to their internal stability, their resilience to exogenous shocks, as well as their dynamic efficiency. Policies promoting the cohesion of macro-systems also promote their dynamic efficiency, which in turn increases their long-run capacity to sustainably generate wealth. From the systemic perspective there is no inherent dichotomy between economic efficiency and cohesion, but complementarity. In this context, cohesion as a policy objective should be construed not as a call for interpersonal or interregional income redistribution but as a *basic capability equality* [SEN, 1980]. This translates into empowering regional economic systems to participate in the knowledge economy by reinforcing their knowledge generation and absorption capacities.

In the case of the EU, the core-periphery trickle-down argument is even less tenable than in the case of unitary or federal states, given that the EU redistributive mechanisms are weak and ad hoc, and inter-state labour mobility is low.[24] Specifically in the production of technological knowledge, the empirical analysis in the previous chapters indicates that even when peripheral regions are capable of generating technological knowledge of the universal type, they generally lack the capacity to economically appropriate this knowledge. In order for knowledge spillovers to diffuse to the techno-economic periphery in a way conducive to macroeconomic growth, therefore, considerable knowledge absorption capacities need to be built there, and this requires substantial cohesion policy measures.

Myth 5: Policy-induced specialisation will improve competitiveness

The fifth myth goes that the dispersion of scarce resources, in particular those used in the production of technological knowledge, over a multitude of industrial sectors, scientific fields, geographical localities and countries in the EU undermines the competitive edge of its economy. As a remedy to the perceived 'competitiveness deficit' and the related 'technology lag' of the EU economy (another myth in its own right), it is proposed that RTDI policy instruments be used to induce economies of scale in technological knowledge production by actively promoting the sectoral and regional concentration of cognitive resources in the direction of reinforcing the sectoral specialisation of EU regional (or national) economies according to their revealed comparative advantage [Foray & Van Ark, 2007; EC, 2007; Foray *et al.*, 2009; Barca, 2009]. This implicitly entails the concentration of RTDI investment within the leading industrial economies of the EU with the purpose of building capacities for competing with its perceived technological competitors, namely the US and Asian economies.

The argument here is complex, and consists of several layers of flawed theoretical conjectures and scant empirical evidence, all stacked together under the catchy banner of 'smart specialisation' (hereafter SS), which has recently become one of the pillars of the reoriented EU RTDI strategy.[25]

The first flawed conjecture of the 'SS myth' is that the policy-induced concentration of cognitive resources is able to increase productivity in technological knowledge production by inducing economies of scale. 'Concentration' here has two potential interpretations: it refers either to the concentrated allocation of RTDI funding to a restricted group of targeted beneficiaries or to the policy-induced concentration of knowledge production factors (through the coordination of RTDI with other policies, e.g. regional and industrial). Concentration has two facets, a sectoral, when it involves specific industries which are perceived as potentially more 'competitive', and a territorial, when it occurs in selected regions on the basis of their revealed comparative advantage. There are several arguments against this conjecture: If the preferential allocation of funding within a select group of beneficiaries follows sectoral criteria, the beneficiaries will most probably be large industrial leaders, who nevertheless already have the ability to optimise their levels of R&D investment and have specific interests in established technological trajectories. In this case funding will be an industrial subsidy in disguise.[26] This may lead to the encouragement of rent-seeking practices, the weakening of innovation-based competition, and the reinforcement of technological lock-ins, with distortionary effects for the long-run dynamic efficiency of the EU economy. If the allocation follows territorial criteria, it will entail a policy-induced redirection of investment, or even worse, the redistribution of knowledge production factors from the EU periphery to the core, which will dry up the cognitive resources of the 'laggards', reinforce existing cumulative causation tendencies, and aggravate the technology gap. The consequences of this type of policy on the dynamic efficiency of the EU economy will be even graver: The diversity and systemic complexity of the European knowledge plexus will be eroded, together with its resilience and stability. In both cases, therefore, the induced concentration of cognitive resources may have significant negative effects on the long-run dynamic efficiency of the knowledge plexus.

Moreover, 'traditional' internal economies of scale, typically induced by the sectoral concentration of production factors, are not relevant in the production of technological knowledge, or at least, their significance is offset by other types of increasing returns and externalities unrelated to concentration. The econometric analysis in

Chapter 4 clearly indicates that the effect of the regional concentration of cognitive resources on the efficiency of EU-funded research is insignificant (or even slightly negative), while the effect of connectivity is strongly significant. Even in the production of instrumental-type knowledge, connectivity has been found to play a central role comparable to that of agglomeration. External economies of scale may, therefore, have a certain effect on the productivity of some types of technological knowledge whose production is territorially dependent. However, inducing this type of economies requires much more than the collocation of economic agents involved in the knowledge production process or the increased selectivity of funding – it requires the integration of the economic agents in an external division of labour. Some types of localised externalities which are usually conducive to the establishment of this division of labour, e.g. Jacobs-type urbanisation economies, depend on related variety [Frenken *et al.*, 2007]. These are clearly not attainable through policy-induced concentration on the basis of comparative advantage – it can even be argued that this type of concentration is hostile to them. Finally, economies of complexity which are essential in the production of technological knowledge are not territorially specific, and do not depend on concentration but on connectivity and on diversity, which again concentration undermines. The conclusion here is that policy-induced concentration yields no proven productivity gains in technological knowledge production.

The second flawed conjecture of the SS myth is that 'specialisation' can be commanded by EU policy-makers, and should be based on existing patterns of regional, national or sectoral revealed comparative advantage. The main argument against this idea is that specialisation is generally desirable and yields undeniable efficiency gains when it occurs as a bottom-up, self-organised, co-adaptive integration of economic agents in a division of labour. The social planner has neither the cognitive capacities, for all the reasons explained before, nor the means to command in a top-down fashion the division of labour among economic agents in an efficient way, and this is especially true in the division of labour in technological knowledge production. Moreover, regional (or national) economies are not unitary economic agents but complex, heterarchical macro-systems consisting of a multiplicity of heterogeneous economic agents involved in various economic activities. Construing, therefore, the existence of some regional (or national) comparative advantage as an indication of 'specialisation' is simply a reductionist fallacy: regional (or national) economies cannot be said to 'specialise' – only unitary economic agents can.

The inducement of 'specialisation' on the EU scale would require the establishment of a comprehensive interregional division of labour, designed and coordinated by EU policy-makers – a perverse idea reminiscent of the centrally planned division of labour in command economies. Moreover, the proposed tools to inform EU policy-makers on the state of the regional economies (e.g. simplistic Balassa-type indices of revealed regional comparative advantage) are by any criterion of scientific adequacy substandard. But even if a more sophisticated way to reliably measure comparative advantage were proposed, there would still be no obvious reason for using it as a guide for induced specialisation. Following existing techno-economic trajectories reflected in the patterns of revealed comparative advantage simply reinforces path dependence. Besides, comparative advantage is not an immutable quality of a regional or national economy. Economic history again provides ample evidence of economies, which, in developing their national techno-industrial plans, strategically chose not to follow existing patterns of comparative advantage but to redefine it, and against all odds managed to develop and to prosper [CHANG, 2008].

A policy-induced re-concentration of research resources according to an ill-defined and ill-conceived regional specialisation plan on the basis of comparative advantage measured with substandard and blunt methods is doomed to fail and to cause damage. Policy interventions intended to eradicate diversity and polycentricism in technological knowledge production, and therefore also economies of complexity, à la dirigiste EU tradition, will simply undermine the dynamic efficiency of the European knowledge plexus. The overarching objective of dynamic efficiency can be supported not by greater concentration but, on the contrary, by promoting diversity and connectivity combined with enabling peripheral capacity building.

Myth 6: More R&D investment is always conducive to regional economic performance

The sixth myth goes that increasing the levels of R&D investment can only do good to a national or regional economy. The quantitative targets for national and regional R&D expenditure-to-GDP ratios set by the EU in the context of its various RTDI strategies (e.g. the 3% target set by the Lisbon agenda), are justified on the basis of this belief. As a matter of fact, increasing the levels of R&D expenditure is a typical EU policy prescription to the extent of becoming an objective per se, overshadowing more fundamental objectives of RTDI policy such as growth and employment.

Empirical evidence strongly supports the view that macroeconomic growth correlates with R&D investment.[27] However, correlation does not entail causation: Does R&D investment really *cause* economic growth or is it that economic growth causes a qualitative shift towards technology-intensive activities and hence a tendency to invest more in R&D? The empirical evidence does not show conclusively either the existence of such a causal relationship or the direction of a hypothetical causality, and from an econometric perspective this can be interpreted as a typical endogeneity issue. Even if the explanation that R&D investment *causes* economic growth is to be believed, it is still necessary to know the rates of return to R&D investment for different types of economies (i.e. advanced industrial, service-based or agricultural economies) and at different levels of economic aggregation (i.e. sub-national, national and supra-national), since there are clear indications that these are not the same in all cases [JONES & WILLIAMS, 1998; GRIFFITH *et al.*, 2004; CRESCENZI, 2005]. Before deciding in favour of increased levels of public R&D expenditure, it is also necessary to estimate the societal opportunity costs, i.e. to compare the social benefits of increased public R&D investment with those of alternative forms of public investment. This is of course not a straightforward procedure given the complexity of the technological knowledge production process, and the intangibility and inappropriability of technological knowledge.

In reality, the rate of return to public R&D expenditure is largely determined by the absorptive capacity of the economy, i.e. its ability to appropriate domestically or externally produced technological knowledge (where 'to appropriate' means to tap into, absorb and economically exploit). This capacity is determined by a plethora of contingent factors, among which the industrial structure of the economy and the strength of its industrial basis, the quality of its human capital, its institutional structure, historical experience with R&D activities, its position in the knowledge plexus, and its potential for social capital accumulation. Economies with weak industrial bases, human and social capital deficits and inadequate institutions are unable to reap the full range of benefits from increased R&D investment, unlike economies which already possess these characteristics and are close to the global technological frontier. For each type of economy there is, therefore, a threshold of public R&D expenditure, above which further increases are suboptimal given the existing opportunity costs. The exogenous imposition of blanket quantitative targets for R&D investment may, therefore, lead to inefficient resource allocation and deadweight losses. This is even more true in the case of EU regions, which exhibit a greater variation in the capacity to benefit from R&D investment compared to countries.

The above conclusions should not be construed, however, as a position against the aspirations of economies with low absorptive capacities to increase their technological intensity. It is only a reminder that increased R&D investment by itself cannot yield the expected macroeconomic effects, and that a comprehensive, long-term techno-industrial strategy for developing the capacity to appropriate technological knowledge, which combines industrial, trade, regional, education and technological policies, is needed in order for increased R&D expenditure in lagging economies to be efficient and effective. In the absence of such strategy, the technological knowledge produced as the result of public R&D investment will simply not generate the desired productivity and growth effects, and will most likely spill over to economies which are better positioned in the knowledge plexus and have the necessary absorptive capacities.

Myth 7: High-tech R&D investment is always conducive to regional development

The seventh myth goes that regional (or national) R&D investment directed to high-tech activities enhances the technological capacities of a region (or a country). This myth has prompted RTDI policy emphasis on technology- and research-intensive economic activities, and fed the aspirations of an increasing number of EU regions to develop high-tech capacities by committing large cognitive and financial resources to this endeavour.

In reality, developing high-tech capacities is neither a necessary nor a sufficient condition for wealth creation in regional economies. High-tech economic activity that expands the global technological frontier is concentrated in a very limited number of localities around the globe, among which the most celebrated is undoubtedly the Silicon Valley. It is probably the fascination exercised on economic geographers by the unprecedented techno-economic success of this unique case that inspired the proliferation of literature on high-tech clusters and the perception of high-tech-driven economic growth as panacea for regional development.

However, high-tech clusters, as empirical observation demonstrates, are 'outliers' rather than representatives of the knowledge-based economy, in the sense that they are too few and too exceptional to be considered as reproducible models of regional techno-economic development. It is not surprising therefore that no substantive causal link between 'frontier-expanding' R&D and regional growth has been shown to exist in econometric studies, despite the proven statistical correlation between R&D-intensity and economic growth.[28] Technological-frontier-expanding regions occupy a very sparsely populated niche in the interregional division of labour; on the contrary, the niches of 'knowledge brokers' and, even more so, of 'knowledge users' are significantly more populous. The last two types of regional economies most likely have only minor contributions, if at all, in the initial stage of the innovation process – the stage of radical innovation – but they play an essential role in the subsequent stages of diffusion of technological knowledge, its integration in productive activities, the standardisation of its use, and finally the establishment and consolidation of techno-economic paradigms. Interregional knowledge spillovers of all sorts, including spillovers through trade and labour mobility, which occur in the longer run, diffuse the benefits of new technological knowledge beyond the limited group of those that generate it to the larger group of those who can tap it and use it, especially in the maturation stage of a techno-economic paradigm. It is legitimate to conclude, therefore, that regional techno-economic development is more a result of technology diffusion and adoption than of radical innovation.

As in the case of the previous myth, the above conclusions do not question the legitimacy of regional (or national) aspirations to develop high-tech capacities in emerging technological fields. Technological leapfrogging is always possible when new windows of technological opportunity open following techno-economic paradigm shifts, while Red Queen-type technological competition in emerging fields constantly expands the global technological frontier and opens new windows of opportunity for all who are prepared to ride the wave. However, diverting funds to high-tech capacity-building along the beaten track, and often with the intention to replicate the success stories of outliers which are the results of unique historical conjunctures, is unlikely to be a successful regional (or national) techno-industrial strategy.

Myth 8: Improving human capital will enhance regional 'absorptive capacities'

The eighth myth goes that the root of the EU regional 'productivity gap', i.e. the observed differentials in labour productivity among the EU regions, which in turn is the main culprit for the EU core-periphery divide in terms of regional income, is the assumed 'knowledge gap', i.e. the interregional differentials in the quality of human capital. By bridging the 'knowledge gap', i.e. by improving the quality of human capital in the regions of the EU economic periphery, the myth goes further, their capacities to 'absorb' and utilise technological knowledge will be enhanced, the regional labour productivity gap will gradually close, and there will be economic convergence in the end. This line of reasoning is implicit in EU cohesion policy, which consistently prioritises the enhancement of human capital potential.

In reality, the empirical analysis in the previous two chapters gives no evidence for the existence of a core-periphery structure in the production of universal-type knowledge along geographical divides, and in particular along a North-South divide. In corroboration with this conclusion, the index of regional 'absorptive capacity' used in the knowledge production function in Chapter 4 (Equation 4.12), constructed as a location quotient of the levels of educational attainment, has proven to be statistically insignificant. On the contrary, there is evidence for a geographical core-periphery divide in the production of instrumental-type technological knowledge, reflected in the regional ability to locally retain and exploit technological knowledge in general. This is evident in the significant and systematic differences in the topological structures of the FP participation and the EPO patent co-inventor networks. A striking conclusion from this comparison is that while several regions in the European periphery – and in particular urban regions in the South – are able to produce technological knowledge of the 'pre-competitive', universal type on a large scale, the operationalisation and utilisation of the produced knowledge takes place in core regions with strong industrial bases. This is also supported by other types of statistical evidence: human development indices, various indices of educational attainment (including numbers of university graduates and PhD holders), counts of publications (with very high growth rates in the European periphery), etc., are in sharp contrast to indices related to technological capacities, namely ratios of employment in the high-tech sectors of the economy, levels of private sector R&D investment, patent counts, etc. Further to that, there exists a permanent pattern of technological dependence of the periphery on the core, which manifests itself in the intra-European trade balance in high value-added, and in particular high-technology, products, with a constant need for imported technology in the European periphery.

The conclusion is that while there is scant evidence for the existence of a regional knowledge gap along the lines of the regional income divide, there does exist a technology gap unrelated to the (insignificant) differentials in the quality of human capital, but highly related to the strength of the industrial bases of the regions. This technology gap cannot be addressed by increased investments in human capital or, for that matter, in R&D, in the absence of an industrial structure where human capital and technological knowledge output can be put in productive use. Another conclusion is that while generally the quality of human capital is a significant determinant of regional absorptive capacities, in the specific case of already rich in human capital EU countries the crucial determinant is the strength of their regional industrial bases.

Myth 9: Industrial policy is obsolete in the EU 'single market'

The ninth myth goes that inside a competitive 'single market' like the EU, industrial policy is obsolete, as it would pose a risk for EU national economies to regress to the state protectionism and 'techno-nationalism' of the Keynesian era. RTDI policy can be used in its place, the myth goes further, not only to address market failures related to the public-good nature of technological knowledge but also to provide support to innovative activities in the private sector, while regional and cohesion policies can compensate for any losses in regional 'competitiveness'.

In reality, while EU policy-makers have long considered industrial policy as a taboo, covert industrial support in a multiplicity of forms, ranging from direct subsidies to public procurement favouritism, and in a variety of industries, is endemic in EU member-states.[29] Besides, the EU itself provides institutionalised direct or indirect industrial subsidies through its regional and agricultural policy instruments, and in particular two of its largest, the Structural and the European Agricultural Guarantee Funds, which ironically tend to favour industrial leaders, large incumbents with asymmetric market power, and industrial interest groups with systemic political influence, mainly in the core economies. On the other hand, EU funds directed to (predominantly physical infrastructure in) the periphery as a counterbalance for the predictable dismantling of the industrial bases of peripheral member-states under the asymmetric competition from the industrialised core following the creation of the Single Market, created EU subsidy-dependent economies, fostered rent-seeking practices, clientelism and corruption, halted structural change, aggravated market distortions, reinforced dynamic inefficiencies, and had no (or even negative) impact on growth and productivity.[30] At the same time, the eventual dismantling of the industrial bases of peripheral member-states led to the deskilling of their economies and to the loss of their absorptive capacities, which accentuated technological dependence, perpetuated trade deficits, consolidated the core-periphery divide instead of bridging it, and kept peripheral economies trapped in the typical 'inferior attractor basin' of under-industrialisation.

By contrast, since the conception of the FP, RTDI policy maintained, as we saw, a certain 'distributional neutrality' through its competitive and meritocratic fund allocation modalities, which distinguished it from regional and cohesion policies, and which, counterintuitively, had positive effects on the knowledge economies of the EU periphery. Today, however, as the stakes in RTDI policy are becoming too large to be left to 'chance' (i.e. to non-politically controlled allocation mechanisms), RTDI policy gradually abandons its distributional neutrality and drifts towards industrial subsidisation under the guise of 'innovation support', most certainly to the (short-term) benefit of the industries of the core.

The industrial policy 'taboo' seems to be therefore only a pretext concealing a latent policy orientation consistent with the 'kicking-away-the-ladder' hypothesis [CHANG, 2002] in the following sense: While the industrially developed core through its systemic influence on EU governance has managed to incriminate industrial policy – to which ironically owes a good part of its economic prosperity – and to purge it from policy discourse, it prescribes policy interventions in the knowledge economy, which either are too 'soft' to have a substantial developmental effect on the periphery or, in the absence of sufficient absorptive capacities in the periphery, benefit asymmetrically the core, often functioning as covert subsidies to its industries. RTDI and knowledge-related regional policies are ineffective and imbalanced without a strategic industrial development policy aimed at closing the technology gap, designed specifically for technologically lagging regions, whose frail industrial tissue predominantly consists of SMEs unable to compete, grow, diversify, specialise, export, research and innovate.

Towards a systemic framework for knowledge governance

Spatio-temporal aspects of the innovation process and the policy mix

Innovation life cycle

The innovation process exhibits complex, inherently unpredictable dynamics, but also some qualitative spatial and temporal macro-regularities overlooked by the mechanistic construal, whose understanding is key to the design of effective and efficient knowledge-governance instruments.

One such macro-regularity is the innovation life cycle: At the *incubation* phase, just before the occurrence of a technological 'singularity' and long before the establishment of a new techno-economic paradigm,[31] the innovation process is fragmented, non-deterministic and involves 'duplication', emulation, dispersion, and, inevitably, 'waste' of resources, with externalities looming large. Then radical innovation emerges in a few specific locations, often in the periphery of established techno-economic systems, as economic history indicates, but its exact place, time and form cannot be predicted. As the new techno-economic paradigm is being established, the economic opportunities generated by the innovation process are sectorally and geographically concentrated. At the *maturation* phase, after the establishment of the new techno-economic paradigm, economies of scale and scope settle in, usually attracted to the core of established techno-economic systems. These economies are not related to innovation per se but to the industrial production of goods embodying the new technologies. This phase is characterised by incremental innovation, which is a more deterministic and path-dependent process, and which permits the gradual diffusion of the innovative activity, especially when combined with emulation. Economies of complexity are also present in the process of incremental innovation, in smaller innovation circles within the techno-economic paradigm. At the *saturation* phase, the intensification of competition leads to the exhaustion of economic opportunities, to the erosion of the technological rent reaped by economic agents located in the core of the techno-economic system, and to diseconomies of complexity. Here path dependence becomes a negative feature of the system. This is until a new big circle begins with the outbreak of the next radical innovation. All phases of this evolutionary cycle involve mutation and speciation, retention, selection, growth, domination, decline and extinction, very much like the process of biological evolution.

Technological knowledge types and policy mix

With regard to the typology of technological knowledge, scientific research leading to the production of universal knowledge is a geographically dispersed process as, among other things, it often involves less indivisibilities. Universal knowledge with its strong spillovers on general economic activity is socially beneficial, but non-excludable and limitedly appropriable. However, the spillovers of this type of knowledge are tapped by economic agents who possess the right type of organisational and individual knowledge, to be subsequently transformed into instrumental knowledge and eventually appropriated. These agents are usually located in core industrial regions with high absorptive capacities. In the process of its appropriation, technological knowledge is thus recombined, transformed and geographically 'concentrated', usually following a pattern of cumulative causation.

There are, therefore, significant complementarities among the four types of technological knowledge, universal, instrumental, organisational and individual, whose disruption or dysfunction may lead to a failure of the knowledge appropriation process. Each type of technological knowledge production is addressed by a different combination of policy instruments, a different 'policy mix': While the production of the universal type is mostly within the realm of research policy, that of the instrumental type is addressed by technological, innovation and industrial policies, of the organisational type mainly by industrial policy, and of the individual type by research and education policies. A systemic knowledge governance framework must recognise the complementarities of the four knowledge types and be able to specify the appropriate policy mix which ensures that all are present and properly combined in the production process. Any policy framework which fails to do so is doomed to be ineffective.

Developing policy synergies

EU RTDI policy is a 'soft' instrument with limited macroeconomic leverage compared to other policies in the current configuration of the EU budget – in particular regional and cohesion policies.[32] EU RTDI policy in isolation from other policies will find it impossible to achieve the goal of ensuring the dynamic efficiency of the EU knowledge plexus and the even more distant goal of putting the EU macro-economy in a techno-economic trajectory of sustained growth and high productivity. These targets can only be achieved if RTDI policy becomes part of a 'holistic' policy design which recognises the institutional complementarities of different policy domains, including industrial, regional, cohesion, (external) trade, intra-EU competition, and education policies, intelligently exploits the multiplier effects of their synergies, is able to identify their national and local specificities, and helps develop bottom-up techno-industrial strategies on the basis of these specificities.

This very generic recommendation can be, nevertheless, a double-edged sword, as synergies may well develop but in the wrong direction. Some synergies between RTDI and other policies are already being actively promoted in the EU, especially in the context of the 'Innovation Union', and in particular the coupling of RTDI with regional and cohesion policies with the commitment of significant pecuniary resources to regional RTDI through the European Regional Development Fund (ERDF), the European Social Fund (ESF) and the Cohesion Fund, at a scale almost matching that of the dedicated RTDI funding through the FP. However, this policy coupling takes place in the context of 'smart specialisation', whose flaws have already been discussed in previous paragraphs. The result is that while regional and cohesion policies were hitherto intended to serve the role of countering the cumulative causation propensity of the EU macro-economy, and therefore the purpose of a mild redistribution of resources from the core to the periphery (even though with little success), now they are turned to the opposite direction of reinforcing existing patterns of cumulative causation in the knowledge economy through the regional concentration of cognitive resources. In addition, the principal RTDI policy instrument, the FP for Research and Innovation (in its new phase as 'Horizon 2020'), while it retains many of the positive features of its predecessors, it becomes more 'directional' in an attempt to shift from funding 'pre-competitive' to 'competitive' research and industrial innovation.[33] This is in breach with the implicit logic of distributional neutrality in the allocation of funding based exclusively on meritocratic criteria followed until recently, and it also goes in the direction of reinforcing cumulative causation.

Strengthening the European knowledge plexus

A truly systemic framework for European knowledge governance would have two tiers of policy intervention, one defined by the macroscopic perspective of the European knowledge plexus as a system, and another defined by the microscopic perspective of its constituent elements, which in turn are organised in formations of various degrees of complexity, from individual firms and organisations to industrial districts. The policies required in each tier would be interrelated but have different modalities and specific objectives.

Integrating the disparate parts of the system

A fundamental macro-tier objective of systemic EU knowledge governance is to strengthen the European knowledge plexus by expanding and deepening the external division of labour in technological knowledge production. This entails either the establishment of new links among the micro-elements of the plexus or the deepening of existing ones. The efficiency gains from this type of intervention will come in the form of economies of complexity.

This task involves the creation of a supranational institutional structure which will allow the systemic integration and exploitation of the diversity of disparate and disconnected regional and national techno-economic systems, and requires new policies to complement existing ones, whose purpose will be twofold: The first would be to promote connectivity among isolated or loosely connected research communities, and hence among local techno-economic systems, instead of an artificial concentration of cognitive resources in select regions as suggested by the proponents of smart specialisation. Connectivity will reinforce mutualist and competitive co-adaptation, and therefore collaboration and competition respectively, both of which will accelerate – in an evolutionary analogy – technological 'variation' and 'selection'. The process of specialisation will only come through this spontaneous (i.e. self-organised and bottom-up as opposed to policy-induced and top-down) co-adaptation process, which is enabled, not commanded, by the social planner. The second would be to support the provision of universal technological knowledge of the international public good type, by funding large, pan-European scientific projects (mostly of basic, pre-competitive research) with strong spillovers and research infrastructures, which individual member-states are unable or unwilling to finance. These interventions fall par excellence within the realm of RTDI policy.

In historical perspective, a first step in this direction has been the conception of the European Research Area (ERA), envisaged as a complex multi-layered system that spans the EU territory and is built incrementally in the traditional 'functionalist' way of the European Communities. This may be an appropriate policy framework to address holistically the interventions needed for integrating and strengthening the European knowledge plexus. The ERA however has largely remained at the stage of rhetoric instead of materialising into a full-fledged functional system. And while EU RTDI policy in the context of the ERA has so far undeniably promoted the creation of international collaborative links, as well as inter-member-state researcher mobility, which helped connect hitherto disparate academic communities in the production of universal-type technological knowledge, the technological knowledge production systems of the EU member-states still remain distinctively national, at least with regard to the less 'mobile' types of technological knowledge, and the disparities in their absorptive capacities remain large and substantial. This means that the ERA has so far failed to bridge the technology gap.

Enabling the techno-industrial development of peripheral regions

Another fundamental objective of systemic EU knowledge governance would be the bridging of the intra-European technology gap, which is a permanent obstacle to EU cohesion, as it perpetuates technological dependence and under-industrialisation in the periphery.[34] As already discussed in previous paragraphs, this objective is dictated not only by distributional equity concerns in the narrow sense, but by concerns of dynamic efficiency and resilience of the European knowledge plexus, and, by extension, of long-run EU macro-economic performance. Nevertheless, bridging the technology gap is a macro-tier objective, which, as already implied in previous paragraphs, cannot be effectively implemented by means of policy interventions at the EU-level: Distributionally neutral EU policies, such as the current EU research policy, are generally too soft for this purpose [PAVITT, 1998], whereas 'directional' top-down EU policy instruments have been proven to generate considerable economic distortions, rent-seeking practices and subsidy dependence in the periphery, and to ultimately be beneficial only in the short-run and mostly to specific interest groups within the core economies. The macro-tier objective of bridging the technology gap, however, translates naturally into the micro-tier objective of enabling the technological development of peripheral regions by enhancing their absorptive capacities, which, in turn, translates into strengthening their industrial bases. This needs some further clarification.

We already saw a form of policy intervention consistent with the systemic framework, whose rationale goes well beyond the efficiency argument: the case in which a techno-economic system is caught in a 'low-level equilibrium trap', or more appropriately in dynamic terms, in an 'inferior attractor basin'. This situation is marked by persistent underdevelopment, despite the potentially efficient use of existing production factors, and is reproduced by a particular configuration of socio-economic forces consistent with circular and cumulative causation, as well as by established institutions and social norms whose origins are buried in history. In this case the social planner intervenes not just to improve the efficiency of the techno-economic system but to instigate its evolutionary leap from the inferior attractor basin to a superior one. This challenging objective may require the reform of the institutional structure which reproduces and sustains the inferior attractor trap, the provision of coordination and incentives to economic agents, or even the strategic mobilisation and control of production factors for the inducement of 'primary' accumulation.

In the particular case of the EU periphery, however, the source of techno-economic backwardness is not the level of human capital, the quality of the formal institutional structures, or even the level of investment in R&D, but the lack of an adequate industrial structure which would integrate existing cognitive resources in a knowledge-intensive production process. The evolutionary leap of peripheral economies to a higher techno-economic trajectory necessarily goes through their industrial restructuring and upgrading and entails a substantial shift in the form of their comparative advantage. This is in the opposite direction of the smart specialisation tenet, which envisages the reinforcement of existing patterns of comparative advantage. The leap requires a wide-ranging policy mix, whose main component will be a techno-industrial strategy conceived in the frame of a territorially specific, bottom-up, multi-dimensional, strategic development plan. During the incubation phase of the young industrial structure which will be born a certain level of protection against asymmetric competition, and a strategic mobilisation of resources through increased intervention of the social planner will be necessary. This requires an EU institutional framework which is more sympathetic to peripheral industrial development, and tolerates a certain level of necessary protection during the incubation phase.

The increase in the absorptive capacities of peripheral economic systems will empower them to participate in the knowledge economy, while in the longer run the industrial development of the European periphery will accelerate regional convergence, eliminate the need for permanent interregional and inter-member-state fiscal transfers, and dramatically improve the overall macro-economic performance of the EU.

Conclusion

A genuinely systemic EU knowledge governance would promote the cohesion and the dynamic efficiency of the knowledge plexus – two notions tightly interrelated in the systemic framework. These two generic policy priorities entail the following two specific objectives: (i) the extensification of the division of labour in the production of technological knowledge by reinforcing connectivity among isolated or loosely connected techno-economic systems in the EU, in a way that promotes both their mutualist and competitive co-adaptation; (ii) the bridging of the interregional technology gap by strengthening, reshaping and upgrading the industrial structures of peripheral economies, thus increasing their absorptive capacities and empowering them to drastically change the patterns of their comparative advantage. The first objective can be materialised through a policy mix dominated by a distributionally neutral RTDI policy aimed at integrating and developing complementarities instead of destroying diversity within the existing frame of the ERA. The second objective requires bottom-up, local techno-economic development strategies dominated by industrial policies aimed at offsetting cumulative causation.

Cohesion in the domain of science and technology will not only accelerate European unification but also stabilise the European economy as a whole, reinforce 'competitiveness' in today's European periphery, and, as a result, reduce the proneness of peripheral economies to lower factor productivity, trade deficits, and debt accumulation. In a converging EU knowledge economy, specialisation will emerge naturally, in a self-organised way. In the longer run, the systemic gains from the technological convergence of the periphery will be beneficial also to the core economies.

Unfortunately, EU knowledge governance is moving in the opposite direction: The pseudo-systemic tenet of 'smart specialisation' proposes a fundamentally regressive redistribution of cognitive resources in the direction of their sectoral and geographical concentration within a small group of existing industrial leaders (countries, localities and individual organisations) at the expense of perceived technological laggards, i.e. the largest part of the European economic periphery.

Beyond any 'fairness' consideration, the implementation of this agenda will not only jeopardise the uncertain paradigmatic shift of the EU RTDI policy to 'systemicity' and undermine EU cohesion as a whole, but most importantly, will deal the biggest blow to the long-run dynamic efficiency of the European knowledge plexus, as it may strengthen established monopolies, institutionalise technological lock-ins, perpetuate path-dependent inefficiencies, reinforce economic distortions and rent-seeking practices, deepen the internal technology gap of the EU, and eventually render the EU economy less, not more, globally 'competitive' in techno-economic terms. In the aftermath of the recent European sovereign-debt crisis and the onslaught of neoliberalism in European politics, the influence of the 'smart specialisation' tenet has only been accentuated. The foreseeable consequences of this policy for the RTDI systems of the European periphery in the new economic context may well be apocalyptic, as dire 'adjustment' policies of extreme fiscal austerity in EU debtor countries are counting among their first victims the knowledge sectors of their economies, namely research and education. In this post-crisis dystopia circular and cumulative causation is intensified by the immense outflows of unemployed scientists from the South to the North and the rapid brain drain of peripheral regions and countries, the obliteration of research budgets, the slashing of education budgets which leads to massive university closures, the impoverishment of academics and the discrediting of academia. In the longer run the annihilation of the remaining cognitive and technological capacities of the European periphery will have significant detrimental effects on the European knowledge plexus as a whole.

References

AGLIETTA, M. (1982): *Régulation et Crises du Capitalisme: L'Expérience des États-Unis.* Paris: Calmann-Lévy.

ALBIN, P. (1998): *Barriers and Bounds to Rationality. Essays on Economic Complexity and Dynamics in Interactive Systems.* Princeton, NJ: Princeton University Press.

ALTHUSSER, L. (1962): Contradiction et surdétermination. *La Pensée 106*: 3–22.

ARROW, K.J. (1962): Economic welfare and the allocation of resources for invention. In: *The Rate and Direction of Inventive Activity: Economic and Social Factors*, pp. 609–625. Princeton, NJ: Princeton University Press for NBER.

BARCA, F. (2009): An agenda for a reformed cohesion policy. A place-based approach to meeting European Union challenges and expectations. Independent Report prepared at the request of Danuta Hübner, Commissioner for Regional Policy.

BARDHAN, P. (1993): Economics of development and the development of economics. *Journal of Economic Perspectives 7* (2): 129–142.

BATOR, F.M. (1958): The anatomy of market failure. *Quarterly Journal of Economics 72* (3): 351–379.

BILBAO-OSORIO, B. & RODRÍGUEZ-POSE, A. (2004): From R&D to innovation and economic growth in the EU. *Growth and Change 35* (4): 434–455.

BOWLES, S. & GINTIS, H. (2000): Walrasian economics in retrospect. *Quarterly Journal of Economics 115* (4): 1411–1439.

BRACZYK, H.-J., P. COOKE, & M. HEIDENREICH, eds (1998): *Regional Innovation Systems. The Role of Governances in a Globalized World.* London: UCL Press.

BUSH, V. (1945): Science – The endless frontier. *Transactions of the Kansas Academy of Science 48* (3): 231–264.

CHANG, H.-J. (2008): *Bad Samaritans: The Myth of Free Trade and the Secret History of Capitalism.* New York, NY: Bloomsbury Press.

CHANG, H.-J. (2002): *Kicking Away the Ladder: Development Strategy in Historical Perspective.* London: Anthem Press.

CHORAFAKIS, G. & PONTIKAKIS, D. (2011): Theoretical underpinnings and future directions of European Union research policy: a paradigm shift? *Prometheus 29* (2): 131–161.

COE, D.T. & HELPMAN, E. (1995): International R&D spillovers. *European Economic Review 39* (5): 859–887.

COE, D.T., HELPMAN, E. & HOFFMAISTER, A. (1997): North-South R&D spillovers. *Economic Journal 107* (440): 134–149.

COHEN, W.M. & LEVINTHAL, D.A. (1989): Innovation and learning: the two faces of R&D. *Economic Journal 99* (397): 569–596.

COLANDER, D. & VAN EES, H. (2006): Post Walrasian macroeconomic policy. In: COLANDER, D. ed.: *Beyond Microfoundations. Post Walrasian Economics*, pp. 207–220. Cambridge: Cambridge University Press.

COOKE, P. (1992): Regional innovation systems: Competitive regulation in the new Europe. *Geoforum 23*: 365-382.

CRESCENZI, R. (2005): Innovation and regional growth in the enlarged Europe: The role of local innovative capabilities, peripherality, and education. *Growth and Change 36* (4): 471–507.

DOSI, G., FREEMAN, C., NELSON, R.R., SILVERBERG, G. & SOETE, L. (1988): *Technical Change and Economic Theory.* London: Pinter Publishers.

EATON, J. & KORTUM, S. (1995): Engines of growth: domestic and foreign sources of innovation. *Japan and the World Economy 9* (2): 235–259.

EC (2000): Towards a European research area. COM(2000) 6, Brussels: European Commission.

EC (2005): Common actions for growth and employment: The Community Lisbon programme. Brussels: European Commission.

EC (2010a): Europe 2020 Flagship Initiative Innovation Union. SEC(2010) 1161, Brussels: European Commission.

EC (2010b): Regional Policy contributing to smart growth in Europe 2020. SEC(2010) 1183, Brussels: European Commission.

EDGERTON, D. (2004): The 'linear model' did not exist: reflections on the history and historiography of science and research in industry in the twentieth century. In: GRANDIN, K., WORMBS, N. & WIDMALM, S., eds: *The Science-Industry Nexus. History, Policy, Implications.* Sagamore Beach: Science History Publications.

EDQUIST, C., ed. (1997): *Systems of Innovation. Technologies, Institutions and Organizations.* London: Pinter.

EICHENGREEN, B. (2008): *Globalizing Capital: A History of the International Monetary System.* Princeton, NJ: Princeton University Press.

ETZKOWITZ, H., & L. LEYDESDORFF, eds (1997): *Universities in the global knowledge economy: A triple helix of university-industry-government relations.* London: Cassell.

EXPERT GROUP ON FP6 EVALUATION (2009): Ex post Evaluation of the Sixth Framework Programmes for Research and Technological Development, 2002-2006. Brussels: European Commission.

FAGERBERG, J., VERSPAGEN, B. & CANIËLS, M. (1997): Technology, growth and unemployment across European regions. *Regional Studies 31* (5): 457–466.

FORAY, D. (2009): ERA: Entrepreneurial Regional Action. *Public Service Review 2*: 44–47.

FORAY, D. & VAN ARK, B. (2007): Smart specialisation in a truly integrated research area is the key to attracting more R&D to Europe. *Knowledge for Growth Expert Group Policy Briefs*, no. 1. Brussels: European Commission.

FORAY, D., GODDARD, J., GOENAGA BELDARRAIN, X., LANDABASO, M., MCCANN, P., *et al.* (2012): Guide to research and innovation strategies for smart specialisation (RIS 3). Brussels: European Commission.

FREEMAN, C. (1974): *The Economics of Industrial Innovation.* London: Penguin Books.

FREEMAN, C. (1996): The greening of technology and models of innovation. *Technological Forecasting and Social Change 53* (1): 27–39.

FRENKEN, K., VAN OORT, F. & VERBURG, T. (2007): Related variety, unrelated variety and regional economic growth. *Regional Studies 41* (5): 685–697.

FURMAN, J.L., PORTER, M.E. & STERN, S. (2002): The determinants of national innovative capacity. *Research Policy 31* (6): 899–933.

GRIFFITH, R., REDDING, S. & VAN REENEN, J. (2004): Mapping the two faces of R&D: Productivity growth in a panel of OECD industries. *Review of Economics and Statistics 86* (4): 13.

GRILICHES, Z. (1958): Research costs and social returns: Hybrid corn and related innovations. *Journal of Political Economy 66* (5): 419–431.

GUESNERIE, R. (2001): The government and market expectations. *Journal of Institutional and Theoretical Economics 157* (1): 116–126.

GUZZETTI, L. (1995): *A Brief History of European Union Research Policy.* Luxembourg: Office for Official Publications of the European Communities.

HAYEK, F.A. (1982): *Law, Legislation and Liberty: A New Statement of the Liberal Principles of Justice and Political Economy.* Abingdon: Routledge and Kegan Paul.

HOWELLS, J. (2005): Innovation and regional economic development: A matter of perspective? *Research Policy 34* (8): 1220–1234.

JESSOP, B. (2007): *State Power.* Cambridge: Polity Press.

JESSOP, B. (1990): *State Theory. Putting the Capitalist State in Its Place.* Cambridge: Polity Press.

JESSOP, B. (2002): *The Future of the Capitalist State.* Cambridge: Polity Press.

JONES, C.I. & WILLIAMS, J.C. (1998): Measuring the social return to R&D. *Quarterly Journal of Economics 113* (4): 1119–1135.

KATSAITIS, O. & DOULOS, D. (2009): The impact of EU structural funds on FDI. *Kyklos 62* (4): 563–578.

KITSON, M., MARTIN, R. & TYLER, P. (2004): Regional competitiveness: An elusive yet key concept? *Regional Studies 38* (9): 991–999.

KRUEGER, A.O. (1990): Economists' changing perceptions of government. *Weltwirtschaftliches Archiv 126* (3): 417–431.

KRUEGER, A.O. (1974): The political economy of the rent-seeking society. *American Economic Review 64* (3): 291–303.

KRUGMAN, P. (1994): Competitiveness: a dangerous obsession. *Foreign Affairs 73* (2): 28–44.

LANDES, D.S. (2003): *The Unbound Prometheus. Technological Change and Industrial Development in Western Europe from 1750 to the Present.* Cambridge: Cambridge University Press.

LUNDVALL, B.-Å., ed. (1992): *National Systems of Innovation. Towards a Theory of Innovation and Interactive Learning.* London: Pinter.

MACLAURIN, W.R. (1953): The sequence from invention to innovation and its relation to economic growth. *Quarterly Journal of Economics 67* (1): 91–111.

MALECKI, E.J. (1997): *Technology and Economic Development. The Dynamics of Local, Regional and National Competitiveness.* Harlow: Longman.

METCALFE, J.S. (1997): Technology systems and technology policy in an evolutionary framework. In: ARCHIBUGI, D. & MICHIE, J., eds: *Technology, Globalisation and Economic Performance*, pp. 268–296. Cambridge: Cambridge University Press.

METCALFE, J.S. & RAMLOGAN, R. (2005): Limits to the economy of knowledge and knowledge of the economy. *Futures 37* (7): 655–674.

MOKYR, J. (1992): *The Lever of Riches: Technological Creativity and Economic Progress.* New York, NY: Oxford University Press.

MOLAS-GALLART, J., & A. SALTER (2002): Diversity and Excellence: Considerations on Research Policy. *IPTS Report*, Vol. 66. Seville: Institute for Prospective Technological Studies.

NELSON, R.R. (1956): A theory of the low-level equilibrium trap in underdeveloped economies. *American Economic Review 46* (5): 894–908.

NELSON, R.R. (1959): The simple economics of basic scientific research. *Journal of Political Economy 67* (3): 297–306.

NELSON, R.R., ed. (1993): *National Innovation Systems: A Comparative Analysis*. Oxford: Oxford University Press.

NELSON, R.R. & WINTER, S.G. (1982): *An Evolutionary Theory of Economic Change*. Cambridge, MA: Belknap Press.

NISKANEN, W.A. (1971): *Bureaucracy and Representative Government*. Chicago, IL: Aldine Transaction.

OPEN EUROPE (2007): *Europe's dirty secret: Why the EU emissions trading scheme isn't working*. London: Open Europe (http://www.openeurope.org.uk).

PAVITT, K. (1998): The inevitable limits of EU R&D funding. *Research Policy 27* (6): 559–568.

PELLEGRIN, J. (2007): Regional innovation strategies in the EU or a regionalized EU innovation strategy? *Innovation: The European Journal of Social Science Research 20* (3): 203 – 221.

PEREZ, C. (2003): *Technological Revolutions and Financial Capital. The Dynamics of Bubbles and Golden Ages*. Cheltenham: Edward Elgar Publishing.

PETERSON, J. & SHARP, M. (1998): *Technology Policy in the European Union*. Basingstoke: Palgrave Macmillan.

PORTER, M.E. (1998): The Adam Smith address: Location, clusters, and the 'new' microeconomics of competition. *Business Economics 33* (1): 7–13.

PORTER, M.E. (1990): *The Competitive Advantage of Nations*. Basingstoke: Palgrave Macmillan.

PORTER, M.E. & STERN, S. (2000): Measuring the 'ideas' production function: evidence from international patent output. *NBER Working Papers*, no. 7891.

POULANTZAS, N. (1968): *Pouvoir politique et classes sociales.* Paris: Maspero.

RODRÍGUEZ-POSE, A. & FRATESI, U. (2004): Between development and social policies: The impact of European structural funds in objective 1 regions. *Regional Studies 38* (1): 97–113.

ROSENBERG, N. (1976): *Perspectives on Technology.* Cambridge: Cambridge University Press.

SCHUMPETER, J.A. (1942): *Capitalism, Socialism and Democracy.* London: Harper & Bros.

SEN, A.K. (1980): Equality of what? In: MCMURRIN S., ed.: *The Tanner Lectures on Human Values*, Vol. 1, pp. 195–220. Cambridge: Cambridge University Press.

SMITH, K. (2000): Innovation as a systemic phenomenon: Rethinking the role of policy. *Enterprise & Innovation Management Studies 1* (1): 73–102.

SOETE, L. (2005): Activating Knowledge. In: *The Hampton Court Agenda: A Social Model for Europe*, pp. 67-80. London: Policy Network.

STIGLER, G.J. (1971): The theory of economic regulation. *Bell Journal of Economics and Management Science 2* (1): 3–21.

TULLOCK, G., BRADY, G. & SELDON, A. (2002): *Government Failure: A Primer in Public Choice.* Washington, DC: Cato Institute.

VAN STAVEREN, I. (2012): An evolutionary efficiency alternative to the notion of Pareto efficiency. *Economic Thought 1* (1): 109–126.

VASCONCELOS VILAÇA, G. (2010): From Hayek's spontaneous orders to Luhmann's autopoietic systems. *Studies in Emergent Order 3*: 50–81.

ZACHARIADIS, M. (2004): R&D-induced growth in the OECD? *Review of Development Economics 8* (3): 423–439.

Notes

[1] European Strategic Programme for Information Technology.
[2] See BATOR, 1958, for a comprehensive review.
[3] The rationale for the provision of goods on the grounds of social or national interest or social equity is of a purely normative nature and unrelated to the conditions of Walrasian equilibrium and Pareto optimality.
[4] SCHUMPETER, 1942: 84, sketching the process of 'creative destruction' contends that: "the first thing to go is the traditional conception of the modus operandi of competition. [...] in capitalist reality as distinguished from its textbook picture, it is not that kind of competition which counts but the competition from the new commodity, the new technology, the new source of supply, the new type of organisation...competition which commands a decisive cost or quality advantage and which strikes not at the margins of the profits and the outputs of the existing firms but at their foundations and their very lives."
[5] HAYEK, 1982, defines *catallaxy* as "the order brought about by the mutual adjustment of many individual economies in a market", which emerges spontaneously from human interaction – a notion reminiscent of the Smithian 'invisible hand'. Hayek, one of the fathers of neoclassical liberalism, has also contributed significantly to systems theory, cybernetics and early complexity theory. Ironically, at the same time he is a staunch proponent of methodological individualism, who believes that individual economic agents make the most efficient use of information, and sees the economy as a complex, self-organised system impossible to fully know. These assertions are used as arguments *against* direct centralised (government) intervention in the market. Hayek distinguishes between *spontaneous order* and *organisation*, the latter being the result of purposive human action. He considers law as a set of rules resulting as spontaneous order, as opposed to 'command' – the set of rules issued by an authority [for a comprehensive critique see VASCONCELOS VILAÇA, 2010].
[6] In a macroeconomic context, GUESNERIE, 2001, considers these as 'knowledge failures' on the part of government, corresponding to individual agents' 'expectational market failures', i.e. failures of the market in coordinating (rational) expectations.
[7] This process, in simpler terms, is an equilibrium selection through the policy-induced coordination of agents' expectations [GUESNERIE, 2001].
[8] This view is summarised in Marx's famous aphorism that "the executive of the modern state is nothing but a committee for managing the common affairs of the whole bourgeoisie".
[9] Overdetermination is a (Freudian) term introduced in a structuralist Marxist context by ALTHUSSER, 1962, to refer to a type of multiple causality, in which the causal forces are structural, simultaneously present and possibly contradictory.
[10] FREEMAN, 1974; NELSON & WINTER, 1982; DOSI *et al.*, 1988; et al.
[11] LUNDVALL, 1992; NELSON, 1993; EDQUIST, 1997; et al.
[12] COOKE, 1992; BRACZYK *et al.*, 1998; et al.
[13] Among whom C. Freeman, L. Soete, C. Perez, G. Dosi, R. Nelson.
[14] See, among others, COHEN & LEVINTHAL, 1989; GRIFFITH *et al.*, 2004; ROSENBERG, 1976: 189.

[15] The excellence argument permeates EU RTDI policy discourse – see, for instance, MOLAS-GALLART & SALTER, 2002; SOETE, 2005.
[16] See, for instance, EXPERT GROUP ON FP6 EVALUATION, 2009.
[17] Funding on the basis of evaluations of research projects instead of evaluations of research performers is the current implementation modality of the EU Framework Programmes for RTD.
[18] See CHANG, 2008: 182-202, for a witty account of this type of stereotypes in economic history.
[19] This is clearly reflected, for instance, in the establishment of the EU Competitiveness Council in 2002 from the merger of three (inter-ministerial) EU Councils, namely the Internal Market, Consumer Affairs and Tourism Council, the Research Council, and the Industry Council.
[20] PORTER, 1998, downplays the role of traditional (internal) economies of scale in shaping regional 'competitive advantage'; however, some of the factors he identifies as sources of regional competitiveness are nothing but a recast of Marshallian external economies of scale.
[21] Economic history, however, amply demonstrates that today's most 'competitive' nations have climbed the ladder of economic development while being overtly protectionist [CHANG, 2002].
[22] Chimaera is a fire-breathing monster of the Hellenic mythology with the head of a lion, the body of a goat and the tail of a serpent.
[23] It should be clarified that this is a relatively recent way of reasoning, which constitutes a retrogression from the more 'systemic' neo-Schumpeterian views pervading EU policy discourse throughout the 1990s, in which competitiveness and cohesion were seen as complementary.
[24] For comparison, the federal budget of the USA represents an approximate 20% of the GDP, the sum of national budgets of the EU member-states is an estimated 45% of their aggregated GNI, while the EU budget represents a meagre 1% of the aggregated GNI. Interregional income disparities in the USA are much smaller than those in the EU, while the rate of interregional labour mobility in the USA is estimated to be about twice as high.
[25] See, for instance, EC, 2007.
[26] This type of policy prescription suspiciously resonates the blatantly failed 'national champions' policies in the IT industry of the early 1980s.
[27] For example, COE & HELPMAN, 1995, find a strong positive correlation between a country's total factor productivity and domestic R&D expenditure as well as R&D expenditure of its trade partners in a group of advanced economies, and estimate that the rates of return to R&D for this group are high. COE *et al.*, 1997, find that this result holds for a large group of developing countries too. In a study of 10 OECD countries for the period between 1971-1995, ZACHARIADIS, 2004, also finds that R&D intensity is positively correlated with the growth rates of productivity and output. PORTER & STERN, 2000, and FURMAN *et al.*, 2002, in their cross-country studies find a (weak) positive correlation between patent output and total factor productivity.
[28] See, inter alia, FAGERBERG *et al.*, 1997; BILBAO-OSORIO & RODRÍGUEZ-POSE, 2004; HOWELLS, 2005.
[29] A recent example is exposed in OPEN EUROPE, 2007.

[30] See RODRÍGUEZ-POSE & FRATESI, 2004; KATSAITIS & DOULOS, 2009.
[31] 'Techno-economic paradigm' is a term introduced by PEREZ, 2003.
[32] The FP7, the main RTDI policy instrument, represents 5.2% (€50.5 bn) of the EU budget compared to a 35.7% (€347 bn) of the budget dedicated to regional and cohesion policies for the period 2007-2013. The budget for Horizon 2020 (the 8th FP) is expected to be allocated around €80 bn for the period 2014-2020, a significant increase given that the EU budget for that period is proposed to be marginally smaller.
[33] Its reformulated priorities are to attain 'excellence in the science base', to strengthen 'industrial leadership' in a competitive framework, and to tackle 'societal challenges'. The policy re-orientation is also reflected in the recent addition of the word 'innovation' to the names of the FP and of the EC Directorate-General which manages it.
[34] As PAVITT, 1998: 562, observes, "while the technological differences between Europe's leading countries, USA and Japan are often small and difficult to interpret, those amongst the EU member-countries themselves – present and potential – are large and unambiguous".

Conclusion

Theoretical proposals

The systemic framework in economic geography

This book examined various theoretical, empirical and normative aspects of the economic geography of knowledge production under a 'systemic' theoretical prism. This term refers to a proposed (pre-paradigmatic in the Kuhnian sense) epistemological framework for economic science, and by extension for its subdiscipline, economic geography, which aspires to unify under a single roof various 'heterodox' strands of theory and to subsequently free the discipline from the neoclassical shackles of equilibrium, rational choice and methodological individualism. This is hoped to make the discipline less reductionist, more responsive to socio-economic reality, and more able to inspire realistic, and less insular and harmful economic policies. It is also hoped to bring economics and economic geography closer together, by enabling the former to acknowledge the importance of geographical space, and the latter to reinstate its relational dimension. Most elements of this systemic framework already exist. Indeed, some of them either belong to long-established academic traditions, e.g. evolutionism in economics, or are new but have attracted the attention of theorists and researchers from a multiplicity of academic backgrounds, e.g. complexity theory. Moreover, economic geography, which is by disposition more open to paradigmatic change, has long overcome the 'neoclassical shackles' and embraced even in its most mainstream strands various heterodox tendencies in economics. However, an overarching and unifying epistemological framework is still missing from the subdiscipline.

I have identified the premise of emergence and the theories of evolution and complexity as the three pillars on which this post-neoclassical paradigm should be built. Emergence provides a complete conceptual framework for understanding the articulation, dependence and causal influence of the different hierarchical levels of economic reality, and in particular micro-meso-macro articulation. Evolution provides a deep insight in population dynamics and symbiotic relationships, which govern not only biological but also socio-economic systems. Complexity describes and explains the macroscopic constitution of open, dissipative, self-organised and novelty-generating systems, also known as 'complex adaptive systems'. With respect to economic geography, the proposed framework addresses what can be termed as the 'physicalist' fallacy, i.e. the conception of the physical space of economic geography as an ontological category in itself with a priori properties beyond those conferred to it by socio-economic relationships. The approach of this book is that geographical space should be conceived as a *relational space* with a contingent physical dimension, which, contrary to the static physical space, is an anisotropic, dynamic spatio-temporal structure with a variable architecture and a non-trivial topology.

Mesoeconomic plexus and economies of complexity

Under the systemic prism, the isotropic and structureless neoclassical market, in which agents are assumed to interact impersonally through equilibrium price signals, can no longer be considered as the principal regulatory apparatus of the economy. Interpersonal interactions are structured, path-dependent, subject to cognitive limitations of the interacting agents, and often purposive or strategic. These interactions shape the relational space. The market mechanism itself emerges in this relational space.

The book postulates that the level of the economy where interpersonal interactions of economic agents occur, and hence the locus where the division of labour unfolds and many essential economic phenomena emerge, is the *meso domain.* This indispensable economic level lies between the micro and the macro, and articulates them in a nested hierarchy imbued by emergence. The 'mesoeconomic plexus' is defined as the fundamental ontology of this domain, which embodies a complete external division of labour in a specific production process. This entity can be perceived as a quasi-integrated formation (although much more extensive and less spatially-embedded than typical quasi-integrated organisational forms), as a heterarchical network, as a distributed system, or as a complex adaptive system. Besides its theoretical implications, the assumptions that the mesoeconomic plexus is a network and a complex adaptive system imply that its analysis requires the development of different methodological tools, among which network analysis, inferential statistical methods for relational variables, and agent-based simulation.

Quasi-integrated and network-like organisational forms, such as industrial districts, regional clusters, and various types of economic networks, typically exhibit an increased efficiency attributed to various types of technological and informational externalities, and agglomeration economies. These are treated as unintended 'by-products' of economic activity. The extensive division of labour, however, is a different source of increased collective efficiency, which I call *economies of complexity*. This important type of collective efficiency is based on relatively stable socio-economic relationships, and is purposive or even strategic, and in that sense, distinct from externalities. It is also different from traditional economies of scale and scope in that it results not from increases in the scale of the productive units but from increases in the number and intensity of links among them with the extension and deepening of the division of labour. These economies are prominent in distributed systems, especially in the knowledge-intensive segments of the economy, and a typical feature of the mesoeconomic plexus.

Knowledge as systemic phenomenon

Technological knowledge, i.e. knowledge with a potential impact on economic activity, has a dual (objectivist-constructivist) aspect, as an intangible, capital-like factor of production, here termed 'cognitive capital', and as the outcome of the systemic process of economic cognition. As cognitive capital it is the most important factor of production in modern knowledge-based industrial economies, and can be distinguished into 'individual' and 'relational'. The former is no other than human capital, while the latter is a specific form of social capital related to distributed knowledge. As a systemic process economic cognition is a process of symbiotic (mutualistic and competitive) co-adaptation of reflective (i.e. with own schemata) economic agents, subject to emergence and co-evolutionary dynamics. Co-adaptation aligns and systemises technological knowledge belonging to the 'intersubjective domain' of economic agents' schemata.

From both perspectives technological knowledge is produced and diffused in a specific type of mesoeconomic plexus, the *knowledge plexus*. This embodies the complete division of labour in technological knowledge production.

Empirical findings

In the above theoretical context, the book analyses empirically the topological structure of specific knowledge networks that constitute the knowledge plexus, and investigates their effects on knowledge production as sources of *distributed cognitive capital*, of structural and spatial dependence, and of *economies of complexity*.

More specifically, the book examines three interregional knowledge networks which are assumed to correspond to three distinct technological knowledge types, the *universal*, the *instrumental* and the *organisational*. The EU Framework Programmes for RTD (FP) fund 'pre-competitive' research of a public good nature and for this reason the network of FP-funded research collaboration is associated in this book with the creation and diffusion of universal technological knowledge. Patents embody knowledge of the instrumental type, and therefore the network of patent co-inventors is seen as a source and a diffusion medium for this type of technological knowledge. Finally, the network of joint ventures and strategic alliances in R&D (JVSA), which consists of relatively stable inter-firm collaborative ties, is considered to support (although not exclusively) the production and accumulation of technological knowledge of the organisational type.

Topology of the knowledge plexus

All three networks are found to have small-world and core-periphery structures, with truncated power-law distributions of vertex degrees. The small-world structure seems to be a global characteristic of knowledge networks, as it combines local clustering with shorter geodesic distances, which makes efficient the local production and global diffusion of knowledge. This structure reflects, therefore, the global-local duality of the knowledge economy itself. Moreover, the 'universal' and 'instrumental' knowledge networks are partially interdependent, and connected by a relatively large and diverse group of core regions but with a small number of stable multiplex ties. These two networks are large, dense and well-connected, contrary to the 'organisational' knowledge network, which is fragmented and sparse.

The FP participation network is more open, inclusive and geographically diffused with no indications of assortative mixing of any type. It is therefore a genuinely transnational network serving the European Research Area as designed. The core-periphery structure of the network neither coincides with the regional 'core-periphery divide', nor does it reproduce it in any evident way. Its core predominantly consists of urban regions which contain national or large regional capitals with large academic communities from both sides of the 'regional divide'. Academic institutions cohere this network and broker universal knowledge across longer distances. Industry participation is of a comparable magnitude and importance to that of academia, but much more fragmented and ad hoc. Academia-industry ties play an essential role in connecting the network, but are still relatively weak and unstable.

By contrast, the patent co-invention and the JVSA networks are more exclusive and clustered. They exhibit assortativity in terms of income, national and super-regional groupings, and their core-periphery structures reflect the North-South regional divide within the European economic space. The core of the former consists of regions with strong industrial bases, and is dominated by northern, and in particular German, regions. This network exhibits significant spatial dependence, consistent with the assumption that the production of technological knowledge of the instrumental type is more territorially embedded. However, it seems to evolve in the direction of becoming more inclusive and geographically diffused, which is another indication that 'open innovation' is becoming the dominant paradigm in knowledge production.

Productivity of the knowledge plexus

Econometric analysis confirms and extends the findings of network analysis. The production of universal technological knowledge is found to depend on relational proximity in the knowledge plexus rather than on physical distance in geographical space. It is also generally more dispersed in physical space and less attracted to localised economies of scale. Moreover, the agglomeration (i.e. territorial concentration) of cognitive resources seems to have a slightly negative or at least non-significant effect on the productivity of EU R&D investment in universal technological knowledge. This indicates that this type of investment is more productive when it is geographically diffused beyond highly-agglomerated regions.

Interestingly, the collaborative production of instrumental technological knowledge is also found to be conditioned by relational distance, although this type of knowledge production is also clearly affected by physical distance. Here the agglomeration of cognitive resources has a more significant, positive impact on the productivity of R&D investment. The regions' own cognitive resources (i.e. domestic cognitive capital stocks) also appear to have a stronger effect on knowledge output than relational cognitive capital – an indication that the production of instrumental technological knowledge is attracted by agglomeration economies.

Finally, there are indications that economies of complexity, especially in the production of universal-type technological knowledge, do exist but their exact magnitude is difficult to estimate due to the fact that their effect cannot be easily separated from that of 'economies of experience' and agglomeration economies within the KPF framework.

Normative implications

Motivated by the systemic theoretical framework developed here and in the light of the findings of the empirical analysis, the book identifies and refutes a number of myths which implicitly or explicitly dominate EU RTDI policy discourse, and proposes a normative framework for policy intervention aiming at the dynamic efficiency and cohesion of the knowledge plexus.

Policy myths and realities

Contrary to received wisdom the book argues that duplication and emulation can actually be conducive to techno-economic development. Explicitly targeting excellent research performers instead of best project proposals can be detrimental to the effectiveness of RTDI funding. 'Competitiveness' is a value-laden, elusive, and in most cases devoid of real economic meaning term often used as the back door to neoliberal ideologies and practices. There is no intrinsic cohesion-efficiency trade-off in RTDI policy but, on the contrary, cohesion is conducive to the dynamic efficiency of the European knowledge plexus. The concentration of cognitive resources will not improve the performance of the European macro-economy, but can only make it worse, especially when combined with top-down, policy-induced specialisation on the basis of existing regional comparative advantage. More R&D investment can be ineffective if the absorptive capacities of the recipient regional economies are not reinforced – and by absorptive capacities, in this specific context, I mean the capacities of their industrial bases. High-tech R&D investment rarely has detectable effects on regional development. Regional absorptive capacities in Europe are not constrained by the assumed 'knowledge gap', whose existence is anyway questionable within the EU, but by the technology gap, i.e. the gap in the ability to appropriate technological knowledge spillovers due to weak industrial bases. Finally, the book argues that developed industrial economies have a plethora of implicit or explicit industrial policies in place, which contributed to their development and prosperity in the historical past, but which today the EU denies as development tools for countries and regions in its economic periphery.

Systemic policy objectives

Under the systemic prism, the main targets of policy intervention in the context of EU knowledge governance are the *cohesion* and the *dynamic efficiency* of the knowledge plexus. These two generic policy objectives are intrinsically interrelated and can only be achieved jointly. On the one hand, they entail the integration of isolated or loosely connected techno-economic communities in the European knowledge plexus by encouraging their mutualist and competitive co-adaptation, which can only be achieved by reinforcing their connectivity. This requires a predominantly top-down systemic policy design, which is partially realised in existing EU RTDI policies aimed at funding the collaborative production of universal technological knowledge in the ERA context.

On the other hand, they entail the more complicated, challenging and sometimes contested target of promoting regional techno-economic convergence, and more concretely, the technological development of the EU periphery by enhancing regional 'absorptive capacities'. This translates into building peripheral industrial capacities, rather than merely supporting human capital development, since the latter is found to be already sufficiently developed even in the periphery. This target can only be served by bottom-up, local techno-economic development strategies based on solid industrial policies. Bridging the interregional technology gap is essential for achieving the dynamic efficiency of the entire knowledge plexus, and by extension of the EU macro-economy, as this will reduce the proneness of peripheral economies to lower factor productivity, current account imbalances, and debt accumulation. The long-run benefits from the technological convergence of the periphery will also positively affect the core economies.

Contributions and future directions

Theoretical and methodological novelties

The book introduces a number of theoretical and methodological novelties. It treats *emergence* in its philosophical context as a fundamental epistemological principle which connects the layered model of the economy, and in that light examines certain economic phenomena which could not be satisfactorily explained in the reductionist-positivist framework. It reinstates the *meso domain* in economic theory as the locus of interactions of economic agents, and therefore, as a *relational space.* It introduces the concept of *mesoeconomic plexus* as the fundamental ontology of the meso domain, which embodies a complete division of labour in a specific production process, and which is a heterarchical network and a distributed system. It introduces the concept of *economies of complexity* (or increasing returns to complexity) as a type of collective efficiency distinct from economies of scale or externalities, which emanates directly from the division of labour itself, and is the result of increased number and intensity of links among productive units rather than increased scale of production. It postulates that the *knowledge plexus,* which is a specific type of mesoeconomic plexus embodying the division of labour in the production of technological knowledge, behaves as a *complex adaptive system.* It further argues that technological knowledge is an emergent phenomenon in that system. It introduces the concept of *relational cognitive capital* as a type of social capital related to distributed technological knowledge. It proposes a constructivist approach to technological knowledge, whereby economic cognition is construed as a process of *mutualist* and *competitive co-adaptation* of economic agents. In general, it attempts to unify disparate theories in a single framework, which can serve as a component or just as a prefatory note for a future systemic theory in economic geography.

From the methodological perspective, the book combines and extends existing analytical methods in new directions, and proposes novel theoretical and statistical models. It introduces a novel, probabilistic way of imputing tie strengths (i.e. edge weights) in collaboration networks with multi-edges on the basis of interaction propensities. It integrates new relational variables in the traditional knowledge production function framework. It integrates in mixed-effects statistical models network metrics in interaction terms with traditional attributive variables. It develops new ways of measuring distributed technological knowledge and relational cognitive capital – the latter with the use of adjacency matrices of knowledge networks. It introduces in spatial panel models 'spatial weights matrices' based on inverse graph distances (i.e. relational proximity) in knowledge networks and structural dependence. It proposes a mixed-effects count data model with spatial lags and spatial error components introduced as grouping effects, which however is not empirically estimated here. It compares the relative influence of agglomeration and network complexity, and proposes a tentative way of measuring economies of complexity.

Finally, the study uses for the first time, to the author's knowledge, an integrated dataset of three consecutive Framework Programmes, which span a period of more than 12 years, and a dataset of joint ventures and strategic alliances in research. It focuses at the NUTS-3 level (when the vast majority of analyses in this topic are conducted at the NUTS-2 level) which eliminates the problem of inconsistent identification of organisations at the micro-level, and reduces scale issues common at the country level.

Future directions of research

Before the systemic framework, tentatively discussed in this book, becomes truly paradigmatic, a vast amount of additional theoretical and empirical work is needed. The notion of emergence and its applicability to the explanation of specific economic phenomena should be further theorised. Co-evolutionary dynamics in socio-economic systems, and in particular co-adaptation dynamics, are relatively underexplored, despite the fact that they are rich in economic insight and intuition, and also deserve more investigation from a modelling perspective as well as on a case-specific basis. The constructivist theory of technological knowledge sketched in this book needs further development and research.

The empirical mapping and analysis of the knowledge plexus presented here are by no means complete either. More work on theoretical modelling of the knowledge plexus is needed. Other types of knowledge networks, such as patent citation, co-publication and academic citation networks, should be analysed in the same methodological context, and compared, while more consistent, unbiased and complete datasets on joint ventures and strategic alliances should be produced. This study, on methodological grounds but also due to a number of practical limitations, examines only interregional knowledge networks. The dissection of the knowledge plexus cannot be complete, however, without analysing networks formed at the scale of individual organisations. Only this type of analysis can provide an insight in the dynamics of sub-regional formations, such as industrial districts and cities. These pose formidable data and computational difficulties when examined at the massive scale of the EU.

Finally, agent-based simulations are indispensable for modelling complex adaptive systems, such as the knowledge plexus, and also may prove to be the ultimate method for capturing multi-domain emergence. This is the natural future extension of the present book.

Index

D

E

F

G

H

I

J

K

L

M

N

O

P

Q

R

S

T

U

V

W

www.ingramcontent.com/pod-product-compliance
Lightning Source LLC
LaVergne TN
LVHW050805220926
848485LV00013B/1429/J
* 9 7 8 1 6 2 2 7 3 0 0 6 3 *